W9-DFO-482

THE ARCHAEOLOGY OF
NEW ENGLAND

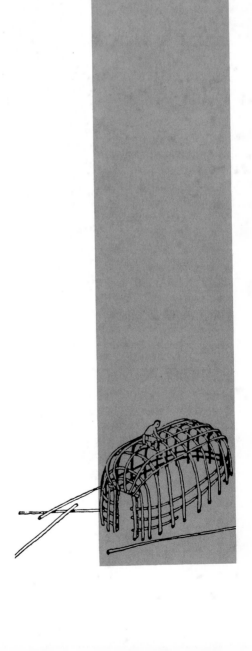

NEW WORLD ARCHAEOLOGICAL RECORD

Under the Editorship of

James Bennett Griffin

Museum of Anthropology
University of Michigan
Ann Arbor, Michigan

In preparation:

Ronald J. Mason, Great Lakes Archaeology

Published:

Dean R. Snow, The Archaeology of New England
Jerald T. Milanich and Charles H. Fairbanks, Florida Archaeology
George C. Frison, Prehistoric Hunters of the High Plains

THE ARCHAEOLOGY OF NEW ENGLAND

Dean R. Snow

Department of Anthropology
State University of New York at Albany
Albany, New York

ACADEMIC PRESS

A Subsidiary of Harcourt Brace Jovanovich, Publishers

New York London Toronto Sydney San Francisco

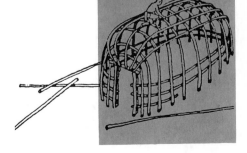

ACADEMIC PRESS, INC.
111 Fifth Avenue, New York, New York 10003

United Kingdom Edition published by
ACADEMIC PRESS, INC. (LONDON) LTD.
24/28 Oval Road, London NW1 7DX

Library of Congress Cataloging in Publication Data

Snow, Dean R.   Date
    The archaeology of New England.

    (New World archaeological record)
    Bibliography: p.
    Includes index.
    1. Indians of North America——New England——
Antiquities. 2. Indians of North America——New
England. 3. New England——Antiquities. 4.
Excavations (Archaeology)——New England.
I. Title. II. Series.
E78.N5S58   974   80–982
ISBN 0–12–653950–2

PRINTED IN THE UNITED STATES OF AMERICA

80 81 82 83   9 8 7 6 5 4 3 2 1

For Jan

CONTENTS

PREFACE

This is the first book-length attempt to synthesize New England prehistory since Willoughby's (1935) *Antiquities of the New England Indians.* Much has changed since then, and it is well past time for someone to attempt a new synthesis. The Indians of New England entered the seventeenth century nearly 200,000 strong, with 12,500 years of time behind them. The evidence of that prehistory has accumulated steadily in recent decades, chronologies have been built and refined, and archaeology itself has evolved from antiquarianism to true science. What I have written, therefore, is a generalized and somewhat idiosyncratic view of New England prehistory and of the discipline of archaeology as of A.D. 1980.

I have written this book for advanced undergraduate students, beginning graduate students, and educated laymen. There are over 370 sources, most of which are designed to lead the reader to other sources too numerous to cite separately. I have, in other words, been deliberately superficial—as one must be in a brief synthesis. Moreover, I have restricted coverage to the archaeology and to some extent the ethnohistory of the aboriginal inhabitants of New England. Historical archaeology and industrial archaeology are rich areas of interest in New England, but there is no room for them here.

The result of a synthesis is inevitably that other archaeologists will see what they regard as important issues glossed over or perhaps even ignored. I have deliberately left many minor arguments behind in an effort to define and discuss larger issues. I regard the larger issues as the proper ones to be discussed in a regional synthesis. The issue, for example, of whether a particular set of potsherds should be assigned to an existing type or defined as a new type has no place in a major synthesis. Moreover, resolution of such issues one way or the other often does not contribute to the solution of larger problems. In other words, much of the classification and other activities that have dominated Northeast archaeology for decades are not heuristic, in the sense that they do not contribute directly to the solution of larger problems that archaeologists now consider to be important. This point will be made clear by example in the chapters that follow.

Many readers will notice a subtle change in the way archaeology is conceived in this book as opposed to the way it has been traditionally conceived. Technical advances of the last quarter century, particularly in the area of radiocarbon dating, have forced fundamental changes in our thinking, changes that have not yet been fully assimilated by professional archaeologists. We have all clung to outmoded notions to some degree, and rightly so, for such conservatism is the only way that a discipline can maintain continuity over time. However, I have found myself forced to rethink the fundamental assumptions of archaeology, and it is only fair to make the results of that rethinking explicit at the outset. To colleagues who have provided me with valuable insights during this process, I extend my thanks.

It is a general rule of science, one that has been cleverly exploited by universities for centuries, that lines of investigation often lead to unexpected results. I originally designed the riverine model to lead to this book or one very much like it. What happened along the way was quite unexpected. The modern Indians of Maine brought suit against the federal government, claiming that the federal branch had not adequately defended them against state government as the Constitution required. The Indians won and the Department of Justice unexpectedly found itself going to court on behalf of the Indians against the state in what might be the biggest Indian land claim ever. My 1968 article on Penobscot territoriality, which had led to the riverine model, was eventually discovered, and I was brought in to help define the extent of the land claim. Although anthropology did not help create the problem, it may well help to resolve it. Yesterday's impractical academic frill may be tomorrow's growth industry, and politicians should take note.

ACKNOWLEDGMENTS

James Bennett Griffin, William Starna, Peter Thomas, and Neal Salisbury read all or parts of the manuscript and provided very useful criticisms. Robert Funk has assisted me in many intangible ways over the past decade, and in this project was particularly helpful in securing plates from the collection of the New York State Museum and Science Service. William Turnbaugh and Herbert Kraft each supplied plates at nominal cost, which were produced in the first instance for their own publications. Bruce Bourque assisted me by allowing me to examine the collections at the Maine State Museum over several years, and eventually supplying me with several of the plates used in this volume. Maurice Robbins allowed me to photograph artifacts in the collections of the Bronson Museum, and Margaret Belknap helped me with that chore in 1978. I was assisted by Kathy Flynn at the Peabody Museum of Salem, and Mark Sexton later printed several of the plates I have used here. Kathleen Bragdon helped me through the collections of the Haffenreffer Museum, Brown University, and found the space for me to take several of the photos included here. I was helped similarly by Richard S. MacNeish at the R.S. Peabody Foundation for Archaeology, a continuation of the kindness he first extended to me in Mexico in 1964. I have, with his permission, also reproduced a drawing by Douglas Byers, an archaeologist who made us feel at home when we first arrived in New England, but who died before this writing. I was assisted by Roger Moeller and Edmund Swigart at the American Indian Archaeological Institute, and I eventually used some of the photos I took there. Daniel Jones, Debbie Stein, and Lisa Kamisher helped me sort through the negative file at the Peabody Museum, Harvard University, and Sandra Bou-Assi supplied me with a few prints on behalf of the museum. Donald Grant, Unit Manager of Gillette Castle, gave me access to the collection of Shantok materials excavated by Bert Salwen and owned by the state of Connecticut. Richard Emerick, Robert MacKay, and David Sanger gave me, as always, all the help I could hope for in examining and photographing the collections of the University of Maine. That institution gave me my first academic appointment, gave me the time to develop many of the ideas in this book, and gave me these and other friends to cherish. William Sturtevant provided me with encouragement in general and the drawing of a typical wigwam in particular. Father Ronald Schultz provided the drawing of Caughnawaga, the only New York Iroquois site that still preserves a full-scale village plan. Louise Basa furnished me with photos and unpublished information on the Boucher site. Ronald Wyatt and Dan Kaplan helped me when I visited Garvies Point Museum, and some of the resulting photos are published here. I thank all of these people, for without their help I could not have finished this project.

I also thank colleagues such as Gary Wright, Dena Dincauze, William Ritchie, Elisabeth Tooker, Bruce Trigger, James Wright, William Engelbrecht, Donald Grayson, Jacob Gruber, and many of the others already mentioned who have helped me shape my vision of prehistory in ways difficult to define. At greater distance in time and space are Don Dumond and Albert Spaulding, who influenced my thinking during and after my graduate study. Most importantly, I thank my wife, Janet Snow, and our children, Katherine, Barbara, and Joshua, whose unfailing patience and assistance with my academic obsessions have allowed me to complete this and other tasks. Jan and Joann Somich were also responsible for all of the manuscript typing, no small task and one not easily done with such speed and skill. Finally, I thank James Bennett Griffin, series editor, and the staff of Academic Press for their trust, encouragement, and practical assistance. I leave it to the reviewers to comment upon their wisdom.

THE ARCHAEOLOGY OF
NEW ENGLAND

INTRODUCTION

Few regions of North America have the distinctiveness and age of New England. Others have changed shape, and their names have come and gone, but New England has kept much of its original shape and meaning since John Smith explored and named it in 1614. For a while it had been known as North Virginia, part of a stretch of coastline extending from the 34th to the 45th degree of north latitude opened for colonization by James I of England in 1606. Smith's glowing *Description of New England* (Arber & Bradley 1910) was published in 1616, just about the time that the first hideous wave of European diseases that would clear much of the region for colonization swept through its Indian communities. By 1620 there was a new royal charter that defined New England as lying between the 40th and 48th degrees of north latitude, a stretch of coastline running from central New Jersey northward to include all of what is now New England and the Maritime provinces of Canada. French colonization of the Maritimes and Dutch colonization of the Hudson River and Long Island soon put a narrower definition on New England, however, and it assumed more or less the shape it now has.

Yet, despite the antiquity of New England, it remains a recent phenomenon, carved by the events of colonial history from the geography of northeastern North America. This is a book on the prehistory of New England, but the political boundaries of the six states that constitute the region had no meaning for the people who lived there for 12,000 years before the first European sails came over the horizon. For that reason I have redefined New England and its subdivisions, broadening the region somewhat and giving its parts different shapes. "A good argument can be made for the view that the careful regional summary is the most generally valuable form of publication in prehistoric archaeology. It is often true that the region de-

1

scribed is a modern political unit . . . rather than a natural area defined by ecological criteria, but this theoretical defect is more than offset by the fact that modern political units are natural regions for the operations of archaeologists [Spaulding 1966:677]."

Figure 1.1 shows aboriginal New England superimposed on a map of its modern political boundaries. It is defined by the river drainages that were often the geographic containers of prehistoric communities. European colonists were interested in land and what land could produce. They settled in bounded and permanent tracts whose definitions were critically important. Much of the land was wilderness and accurate surveys were difficult, so it is no surprise that they often used rivers and major tributary streams as land boundaries. As we shall see, Indian communities, even horticultural ones, did not have the same highly developed sense of territoriality. Moreover, rivers were arteries of communication that flowed through the centers of aboriginal territories and not along their margins (Snow 1968a). To the Indians, the high country that separated drainages was remote boundary land that might be pierced by portages, but more often served as a buffer zone between population concentrations. Though we may for convenience refer to drainage boundaries as crisp lines separating clearly bounded territories, the reality was that high country was used less often and for special purposes such as hunting. It served as the *zwischenraum* that human and many other animal populations seem to need to space themselves, the buffer we use to ensure our identities and often our survival.

As we shall see, the notion of how large communities could be and how much space had to be maintained between them changed over time in aboriginal New England. Populations were nearly stable for thousands of years at levels far below the carrying capacity of the land, in the warm months at least. The control appears to have been the carrying capacity during the leanest part of the annual cycle. Over time, new storage techniques and horticultural production allowed this ceiling to rise. Population density rose with it, and standards of community size and spacing evolved accordingly. The appearance of village stockades and other evidence of warfare in the Late Prehistoric period (Table 1.1) indicate that there was not universal agreement on the new standards.

In fact, the river drainage subdivision of prehistoric New England had begun to break down in the last six centuries before European colonization. Just as important, the first colonists preserved much of it because they, too, needed the rivers for transportation and communication. Thus, early Massachusetts and Rhode Island were defined by their bays, whereas Connecticut and New Netherlands were defined by their river valleys. Only later did rivers such as the Piscataqua, St. Croix, and Connecticut assume importance as political boundaries. At the same time, however, surveyors began to run their straight neat lines through the woods of the Northeast. The states of New England assumed their present shapes by the middle of the nineteenth century. Despite the fact that these shapes have little to do with the distribu-

FIGURE 1.1. Modern political New England and prehistoric New England as defined by its constituent river drainages.

TABLE 1.1
Prehistoric Periods and Their Ages[a]

Periods	Years B.P.	Years B.C., A.D.
Paleo-Indian	12,500–10,000	(10,500–8,000 B.C.)
Early Archaic	10,000–8,000	(8,000–6,000 B.C.)
Middle Archaic	8,000–6,000	(6,000–4,000 B.C.)
Late Archaic	(6,000–3,700)	4,000–1,700 B.C.
Terminal Archaic	(3,700–2,700)	1,700–700 B.C.
Early Horticultural	(2,700–1,000)	700 B.C.–A.D. 1,000
Late Prehistoric	(1,000–400)	A.D. 1,000–1,600

[a] Figures in parentheses are not used in this volume. The standard A.D. 1950 references for B.P. (before present) have been rounded to 2000.

tions of prehistoric cultures, for decades archaeologists have tended to use them as organizational units.

To the confusion caused by the use of modern state boundaries we can add the confusion inherent in the written sources relating to the historic Indian communities of the region. A specific Indian group referred to in a colonial document may be an ethnic unit, a village name, a river name, a personal name, a kin unit, a cluster of refugees, a complete fabrication, or a slip of the pen. One cannot understand the prehistory of New England, particularly late prehistory, without also understanding the historic end point of that prehistory. Furthermore, one cannot hope to understand the historic Indians without taking some steps to organize and evaluate the confusion surrounding them. It was with this in mind that I developed a river drainage model for the reconstruction of the prehistory of all Eastern Algonquian-speaking Indian communities (Snow 1973). This includes most of the Indians living in coastal drainages from Nova Scotia to North Carolina in A.D. 1600. Figure 1.1 shows the part of that larger area set aside for discussion in this volume.

I have included the St. John drainage because its prehistory and its historic Indian inhabitants were closely linked to those of Maine. Indeed, much of the St. John drainage lies in northern Maine and is therefore politically part of New England.

I have also included the drainage of the Hudson, including the important tributary drainage of the Mohawk River. The prehistory and aboriginal history of the Hudson are both closely linked to New England, closer in some ways than they are to those of central New York. The Hudson valley was occupied in early historic times by the Mahican, Algonquian speakers with close ties in New England communities. The Mohawk valley was occupied by the easternmost of the five Iroquois nations of New York. The Iroquois were quite different from the Algonquians both linguistically and in terms of their cultural system, and the cultural frontier between the two was a very important one. The presence of that frontier cutting through the western part of the Hudson drainage, severing the Mohawk drainage from it, provides us with both a logical western boundary for this volume and an area in which to examine the dynamics of cultural exchange (or lack of it) across a major ethnic boundary. As we shall see, the frontier was in place for perhaps more than 3000 years.

Both the southern part of the Hudson drainage and Long Island form a logical part of prehistoric New England. In late prehistoric times part of the Algonquian-speaking Delaware Indians moved from the Delaware drainage eastward into the lower Hudson and the western end of Long Island. This, too, gives us an opportunity to examine unusual cultural dynamics.

I have included the Champlain drainage at various points partly as a concession to modern political boundaries, partly because it was occupied by historic Algonquian speakers, and partly because with the Hudson it was an important corridor of prehistoric communication. New England, the Maritimes, and southeastern Quebec form a large peninsula with the Atlantic on one side and the St. Lawrence estuary on the other. The Hudson–Champlain corridor is clearly the most important prehistoric route across the base of that peninsula. Apart from the Champlain tributary drainage, the St. Lawrence River was occupied largely by Iroquoian speakers in A.D. 1600, and its prehistory is the proper subject of a separate volume.

Thus, prehistoric New England as defined in Figure 1.1 is a meaningful region for study. The river drainages into which I have subdivided the region are also archaeologically significant units. The only significant difficulty with the model is that small coastal drainages are not easily accommodated. For example, in Maine the major Kennebec and Penobscot drainages are in fact separated along the coast by minor drainages such as the Sheepscot, Damariscotta, and St. Georges. As with all drainage areas, the boundaries of the Kennebec drainage converge at the point where the river reaches the sea. The boundaries of the Penobscot drainage do the same, and the roughly triangular territory left between them is drained by the smaller coastal drainages just mentioned. I have normally split triangular areas like this one, putting part in each major drainage. In this I have often depended on sources that give the territorial boundaries of historic Indian communities. Large island and peninsular areas such as Long Island and Cape Cod have been left to stand by themselves. Medium-sized drainages have been left to stand alone in some cases (Thames) and have been combined with larger drainages in others (Housatonic), depending again on their significance in historic ethnic divisions. The reader will find that even the larger drainages are lumped together in discussions of early periods, because the complex subdivision of Figure 1.1 is one that developed slowly over time. It should be no surprise that prehistory (or at least our understanding of it) involves greater uniformity over larger areas the further back into it one explores.

Physiographically, New England is usually treated almost entirely as a single province (Hunt 1967:167). Only Long Island, Nantucket, Martha's Vineyard, and Cape Cod qualify as northern fragments of the Coastal Plain that is so broad farther south. Also physiographically, the Hudson and Champlain valleys are a north–south boundary area that separates the New England province from the Adirondack Province of northern New York and the Appalachian Plateau that begins in southern New York and stretches southwestward to Alabama. Southeast of New England there are two additional physiographic provinces sandwiched between the Appalachian Plateau and the Coastal Plain. Both the Valley and Ridge Province and the Piedmont Province lie outside our area, but were the settings of important external contacts for New England at various points in prehistory.

All of New England was glaciated prior to the Paleo-Indian period, and its soils reflect that prolonged process. The soils of Long Island, Cape Cod, and the islands between them are predominantly deep, strongly acid soils that have developed in unconsolidated sand and clay. The Hudson drainage, Connecticut, Rhode Island, Massachusetts, southern New Hampshire, and southwestern Maine have soils that are predominantly stony or sandy loams that are low in silt or clay. Much of this area has glacial till overlying a variety of bedrock types, and the soils tend to be well or moderately well drained. The mountainous areas of Vermont, northern New Hampshire, and most of Maine have predominantly shallow and very stony or sandy loams. These soils tend to be very well drained. The Champlain valley is part of the St. Lawrence plain and has predominantly poorly drained silty clay loam soils interspersed with a few moderately well drained areas (Lull 1968:14).

Variations in physiography, soils, and climate have produced a succession of forests in New England over the past 12,500 years. The modern forest, to the extent that it has survived, is dominated by yellow pine and hardwoods on Long Island and Cape Cod. The southern Hudson drainage, Connecticut, and Rhode Island forests are dominated by oak and yellow poplar. The rest of southern New England, southern New Hampshire, southwestern Maine, and the Champlain valley are dominated by white pine, hemlock, and various hardwoods. Most of the Hudson–Mohawk drainage, Vermont, and northern New Hampshire are dominated by beech–birch–maple forests. The highlands of northern New York, Vermont, New Hampshire, and most of Maine are covered by spruce–fir forests (Lull 1968:7). The prehistoric Indians of the region adapted to these and predecessor environments in ways that we are still trying to understand.

GOALS OF ARCHAEOLOGY　Modern scientific archaeology has been in the throes of rapid change since the early 1960s. There have always been and probably always will be a few extraordinary scholars ahead of their times who are understandably annoyed by the pretensions of scientific revolutionaries. Just the same, it cannot be denied that the discipline as a whole has undergone a dramatic change in the past two decades. Archaeology as an amateur sport is long since dead, having been recognized by most as a form of vandalism. Archaeology as natural history or art history lives on, although it is no longer the mainstream of research and writing. What has replaced them both is a discipline of explicitly scientific archaeology, something that has been quietly practiced by a few archaeologists all along but which has only recently come to dominate the field. The careful excavation, measurement, and preservation of archaeological data are only the first steps of scientific archaeology. Radiocarbon dating, trace element analysis, and magnetómeter survey are techniques borrowed from other sciences. Archaeology as a modern science begins where these leave off and goes far beyond the establishment of accurate chronologies and distributions. This is a book on prehistory, not archaeological theory and method, so I am not about to use this or later sections to discuss the science of archaeology. However, we will encounter some examples of it along the way, and the reader should be aware in advance of the problems and interests that propel archaeologists working in New England today.

There is another quite different theme in modern archaeological research. Legislation by federal and state governments in recent years has done much to force the preservation or salvage of archaeological remains faced with destruction. This is sometimes called "public" archaeology. In many places all major construction that is not carried out with exclusively private funds must be preceded by archaeological survey and, if necessary, project redesign or salvage. Much of the emphasis has been placed on preservation, with excavation often being an option of last resort. Even so, salvage excavation has increased dramatically. One of the most important features of this new trend in archaeology is that sites that might have been regarded as inferior and not worth excavating a few decades ago are now being excavated. No site is unimportant when faced with destruction. The result of this trend has been a broadening of our understanding of prehistory, for it has helped to break down our bias favoring large sites with heavy artifact concentrations.

Thus, on the public side we have important new research trends directed toward the practical matters of preservation and salvage. On the academic side we have the continuing development of explicitly scientific (as opposed to historic) approaches. Both have already done much to enrich a general summary of prehistory such as this one, and both will certainly continue their exciting rapid developments for some time to come.

The goal of this book is not to document the civic achievements of public archaeology, nor is it to provide a series of elegant scientific solutions to archaeological problems. My goal is to provide an outline of regional prehistory and touch on the other issues only incidentally. This is perhaps a rather old-fashioned approach, but one that remains attractive. My own interests in anthropology seem to center on time's arrow and the consequences of its flight for humanity. This interest led me into archaeology and has more recently led me into ethnohistory. New England offers an almost unrivaled setting for such explorations because it provides not only a rich 12,000-year prehistory, but a deep and well-documented arena for the ethnohistorian. The surviving New England Indians stand at the end of histories that are documented back to before A.D. 1600, the longest histories of any surviving Indian cultures north of Mexico.

Chapter 2, "The Historic Baseline," deals with the historic tribes of New England as we know them for the years around A.D. 1600. I have made little effort to detail their histories subsequent to that date except to show how they connect with living tribes, because their ethnohistories are centuries long and could in almost every case fill a separate volume. Anyone interested in historical sketches of these groups should go first to the new Northeast volume (Volume 15) of the *Handbook of North American Indians* published by the Smithsonian Institution. I have put the historic tribes in the second chapter rather than at the end of the volume for three reasons. First, many readers will pick up this volume of prehistory thinking quite incorrectly that they already know what historic Indians generally and New England Indians in particular were all about. Since one's understanding of any historic culture colors one's view of its prehistory, it is essential that misconceptions be eliminated at the beginning rather than the end of the volume. Second, hindsight is the province of the archaeologist, and it is useful to know well the A.D. 1600 baseline toward which prehistory was moving for over 12,000 years. This is not to say that prehistory or its actors knew where time was leading them, only that knowing the end of the story is something we should take advantage of. For the most part, archaeologists swim against the stream of time. We take what we know of the present and the historic past and use it to understand the scraps and traces of prehistory. Historical linguists do this explicitly, but all too often archaeologists pretend to start at the beginning when in fact they could not do so if they did not already know the ending. This is not a mystery story, and I see no point in saving the denouement until the end. Third, I want the reader to derive a feel for the humanity of both the subject matter and the archaeologists studying it. The waters of Chapter 3, "Paleo-Indians: The First Arrivals," are cold indeed, and quick plunges can be hard on the heart. This is above all an introduction to and a synthesis of the prehistory of native New England, not a compendium of it. We are well beyond the descriptive stage in archaeology, for no single mind can absorb all that is presently available if it is presented in that form. Funk (1976) has written a tightly packed, 300-page summary description of the prehistoric archaeology of just the Hudson valley. A similarly descriptive approach to the prehistory of aboriginal New England would be impossible to either write or read. I have skipped over many details and have avoided clogging the text with the exhaustive citations required in technical writing. Instead I have cited a relatively small number of usually recent sources that contain more extensive bibliographies. I expect the reader to use these as bridges to more detailed treatments. Despite the emphasis on synthesis, I have tried not to avoid controversy. There are many unresolved problems in Northeast prehistory and, although I doubt that I could conceal my own preferences, I have tried to present alternative hypotheses where appropriate. I hope that at least a few students will be stimulated to formulate research strategies that will facilitate choosing between such alternatives, and lead us toward a resolution of these outstanding problems.

The business of synthesis also forces one to come to conclusions with regard to issues that archaeologists often like to leave open for the time being. Inevitably this means that I have reached conclusions that some of my colleagues will regard as erroneous, and I am prepared to accept responsibility for the (I hope) small number of instances where future research will show me to have been in error. However, I do not apologize for risking error when the only safe alternative is silence or uninformative equivocation, for there is no progress without risk. Neither do I apologize for pointing out the errors of others when I find them, although I have discovered that making this kind of archaeological omelet is not at all popular with the people who laid the eggs.

I urge the reader to remember that this is a secondary source. It is not desirable or even possible for such a book to cover exhaustively all the issues touched on. Chapter 2 is a very brief overview of ethnohistory around A.D. 1600, something that has occupied the attentions of dozens of scholars and thousands of printed pages. Many historical points are still debated, and the reader should regard the chapter as an introduction to that debate, not a resolution of it. Similarly, the chapters on prehistory that follow Chapter 2 barely summarize the current status of the field as I perceive it. Others perceive it somewhat differently and all of our perceptions are bound to evolve with time and advances in the field. I have tried to present opposing viewpoints where appropriate and give some indication where future research is apt to lead us, but again my intent is only to introduce readers to an exciting field of investigation, not to imprison them in a definitive work.

It has become clear over the past decade that single-minded empiricism has failed. It would probably fail even if archaeological data were not too scanty and the samples not too small and not usually obtained in an unsystematic way. But archaeological data are typically characterized by all of those traits, and we have had to abandon hope that they will ever speak for themselves. Ritchie's (1969a) summary of New York prehistory was written before this was generally appreciated.

> Despite Ritchie's best efforts, detailed explanation of the sequences in technological–environmental terms is not possible. We lack anthropologically satisfying explanations for such phenomena as the domination of the Lamoka [Mast Forest] people by the Laurentian [Lake Forest] invaders and the slow progress of the pottery-using people during the 2000-year period between 1000 B.C. and A.D. 1000. This unsatisfactory situation is surely not the fault of Ritchie; it is a general condition, and it can be improved only by the development of more adequate anthropological theory [Spaulding 1966:677].

I hope that Spaulding will find my treatment of these two problems in Chapters 5 and 7 to be somewhat more satisfying, and as his former student I absolve him of any blame if they are not.

I have inserted other theoretical and methodological arguments in places where they are relevant, but I have tried to keep those arguments from interfering with the flow of the prehistoric narrative. For example, Chapter 4, with its data on Early and Middle Archaic projectile point styles, is an appropriate place to discuss the issues of typology, horizons, and recent paradigmatic changes in archaeology. Chapter 5, which contains data relating to possible population surges in the Late Archaic, provides a platform for the discussion of prehistoric demography.

In the past, archaeologists not only have tended to operate at a purely inductive level but have sometimes compounded difficulties by treating evidence as if it were the end product of unique events rather than spin-off from patterned behavior. If, after excavation, one discovers that the lithic contents of the site are 30% exotic cherts, this probably says something about regular interaction with the region(s) that produced it. It is very unlikely that this is evidence of a community moving from one area (where the exotic chert originated) to a new one. The chances that we would find evidence of such a unique event, an event that would happen only once in the course of centuries, are almost nil. Moreover, we know that, for most of prehistory at least, that is not the way in which populations expanded or contracted their ranges. Furthermore, there has for years been a regrettable tendency among archaeologists to offer interpretations of evidence that are often merely educated guesses presented without any consideration of possible alternatives. Thus, an archaeologist might blandly assert that a prehistoric village was abandoned after an unusually brief occupation because the community overtaxed the carrying capacity of the surrounding land. The hypothesis is advanced uncritically and left untested, a serious failing in light of a current reaction against studies that have made altogether too much of imaginary carrying capacities (Cowgill 1975). Alternative explanations are not even mentioned. We are asked to believe in the writer's implicit expertise and accept his interpretations on faith. Some archaeologists raise this dubious practice to mystical levels by prefacing their observations with clauses such as "it is my personal belief" or "having worked in this area longer than anyone else, I conclude." Such statements are not at all scientific and clearly invite our distrust. I have tried to avoid such pitfalls here. However, I have also had to avoid a turgid formal presentation of data and hypotheses that would discourage most readers. The results are, I hope, scientifically rigorous within the limits imposed by my primary objective: to present a rational and readable summary of prehistory in the Northeast.

I have, as I describe in later chapters, also been frustrated by the unsophisticated use of environmental arguments by archaeologists. Too often archaeologists have treated environments as if they were near steady states in the short run that changed gradually over time in response to long-term climatic shifts. Yet we know that the forests of the Northeast have always been subject to catastrophic changes that interrupted their slow developments to climax states. For example, the forest of northern Minnesota, which is a northern hardwood forest in many ways equivalent to that of most of the Northeast, had a natural fire rotation of 100 years before European settlement began. That is, an area equivalent to the whole was burned every 100 years (Bormann and Likens 1979:662). Any cultural system adapting to such a continuously changing environment would have had to make many adjustments, and the net effect of all those small adjustments would necessarily be a continuously evolving cultural system. Thus, long-term plateaus of adaptation can have been real only in a general sense.

The need for new directions is recognized by many archaeologists.

> The need for elaborated detail on site-specific and seasonal-specific activities in all periods of Northeastern prehistory is obvious. Research programs should be planned to meet that need—by selecting sites where such data can be gathered and by adopting appropriate wide-exposure excavation techniques. Simple stratigraphic excavations for sequence data are no longer high priority needs in southern New England and can scarcely be justified any more [Dincauze 1976:137].

The roots of many of the problems I discuss in the pages that follow are epistemological. Specifically, they have to do with the complex relationships among what we can observe, what we can assume, and what we can conclude as a result. More than any other single development I can think of, the emergence of radiocarbon dating in the early 1950s drastically changed those relationships. It was a slow change that depended on the slow emergence of a large inventory of dates, and being slow it has not been detected by some and not incorporated in the thinking of many. As a discipline we have still not adjusted our thinking to that new development, for many of our terms and categories are implicitly based on an old pre-radiocarbon paradigm (Snow 1978c). The old McKern Midwestern Taxonomic System was developed as a means to make up for a lack of independent chronological control. McKern found that he could not control the three independent variables—time, space, and form—so his system explicitly dealt with the second two while ignoring the first. In fact, assumptions about time were implicit in the system, for two components that were close in space but formally distinct were assumed to be temporally distinct as well, and two components that were widely separated in space but formally quite similar were assumed to be coeval. This set of implicit relationships was central to such important archaeological operations as cross dating, horizon style definition, tradition definition, and seriation, all of which were initially designed at least in part to make up for our lack of independent chronological control. Willey and Phillips (1958) revamped and updated the old paradigm, but they did not really revolutionize the old pattern of thinking; radiocarbon dating and other independent dating techniques were still too new for that in the 1950s. Stoltman's (1978) new temporal model for the Eastern Woodlands attempts a partial solution for the general problem, but the fact is that most of us have adopted and perpetuated the older organizational system, and in doing so have perpetuated the pattern of thinking that underlies it. We are now too often assuming what we should be trying to discover, taking as given assumptions that can and ought to be tested as hypotheses. Interspersed throughout the following chapters are examples of this general malaise.

I have also concluded that we need temporal and spatial "containers" if we are to compare and contrast sets of components. Radiocarbon provides us with temporal containers of a sort. We can define a time span using statistical techniques and clusters of radiocarbon dates and come up with time-unit frameworks like that proposed by Stoltman (1978). The definition of spatial containers is another matter, and not one that many archaeologists have addressed forcefully. How widely separated in space can sites of similar content and similar age be and still be considered sites of the same phase or archaeological culture? I have seen statements in print that seem to say that there was such a thing as Point Peninsula Culture and that it existed as a system in an area larger than (though not including) Texas. As a means of avoiding this trap of overextension, I have explicitly adopted river drainages as spatial units. These can be subdivided by tributary drainages as necessary to accommodate cases like the Mohawk, or they can be defined together as larger units as might be appropriate in Maine. But the riverine model is just that—a model—and I hope that the ways in which I use it will not encourage anyone to conclude that I believe in it more than I do. To be useful, any model must be assumed to be valid, then allowed to be distorted by reality. If distorted too much it will collapse, and the modeler in that case is advised to construct a new one. But a little distortion does not invalidate a model. In fact, the ways in which reality impinges on a model very often elucidate matters more than either the model or reality could do alone. So we will see that the Mohawk Indians pressed beyond the constraints of their natural riverine boundary, and we will find the reasons why they did so to be enlightening. We will see that the Munsee Indians occupied the upstream portion of one drainage and the downstream portion of another, and we will find good reasons for that, too.

There are dangers inherent in defining a priori territorial containers for comparative analysis. There is, for example, a historical case in western Canada where the same area was the northern part of one tribal territory and the southern part of another tribal territory, one tribe using it in the summer, the other in the winter. Yet, even with similar problems, the approach is preferable to the lack of spatial control that permeates much of the older literature. Not least important is that it helps to fix the burden of proof. One can assume, for example, that a given drainage area was a single phase area until that assumption is proven false. There is always the hazard that the investigator will shirk repeated testing of a favored hypothesis, but we must have some faith in scientific integrity. Even with their difficulties, such assumptions are preferable to the freewheeling practice of letting the data speak for themselves. I have had my ear to the ground for over 20 years and have yet to hear archaeological data say so much as one word.

The use of radiocarbon and other independent dating techniques to define temporal containers and the use of river drainages to define spatial containers are exactly opposite to the procedure dictated by the old paradigm. The old paradigm tells us to allow interassemblage similarities to define the spatial extent of phases, and I am sure that I can find archaeologists willing to tell me that I am putting the cart before the horse by defining a priori spatial units. Yet we have seen that, despite claims to the contrary, phases have more often than not been defined as sets of assemblages that appear to be linked by a single artifact class or even a single artifact type. In short, the definition of phases on the basis of formal analysis and the assumption that the resulting unit has temporal and spatial discreteness have not often worked well and are no longer a viable approach to archaeological data. We must more explicitly impose some prior temporal and spatial constraints on our data if we really hope to make some sense of them. Only then will we see an end to the cavalier discarding of "bad" radiocarbon dates that interfere with the assumptions of cross dating, and the too frequent resort to migration as an explanation for the appearance of artifacts away from their areas of presumed origin.

Most of the dates referred to in Chapters 3–8 are in radiocarbon years and are reported as years B.P. (before present). By convention, "present" means A.D. 1950. Beginning with Chapter 5, I give dates in years B.C. or A.D., but even here the dates are obtained by simply subtracting 1950 from relevant radiocarbon dates. Recent research has shown that this simple arithmetic does not yield an accurate Christian calendar date because the amount of available ^{14}C has varied over the centuries. However, no reliable system for correcting radiocarbon dates to calendar years yet exists. Others may wish to correct the dates as reported, but since no other dating system other than radiocarbon is being used extensively for the prehistoric periods, such an exercise will be relatively uninformative. That is, virtually all dates for prehistoric periods are radiocarbon dates and, as such, are consistent with each other even though they may not be consistent with some other calendrical system. Just the same, the reader should bear in mind that a conventional radiocarbon date that converts to 3000 B.C. might have a true age of around 3600 B.C. As new dating techniques become available in the Northeast, we will have to work toward reliable conversion techniques that will allow us to convert radiocarbon dates to accurate dates in the Christian calendar (Ogden 1977b).

Another problem has to do with the differential ratios at which various plant and animal species acquire the three isotopes of carbon—^{12}C, ^{13}C, and ^{14}C. Since radiocarbon dating is based on the proportion of ^{14}C remaining in a sample, its proportion to the other isotopes while the sample was part of a living organism can, to the degree that it deviates from a standard norm, distort the age determination. Table 1.2 shows dates that a radiocarbon laboratory might provide for samples that are all of precisely the same age. All of the samples are similarly distorted by a difference between relative

TABLE 1.2
Hypothetical Laboratory Results on Six
Radiocarbon Samples Each Having a True Age of
7160 B.P. (5210 B.C.)[a]

Sample	Results
Pine	6560 ± 100
Seal blubber	6730 ± 100
Fish flesh	6510 ± 100
Deer antler	6390 ± 100
Mammoth ivory	6310 ± 100
Maize	6440 ± 100

[a] All are uniformly distorted 600 years by changed isotope ratios. All but pine have been further distorted by metabolically based variations in isotope preferences.

isotope availability at the time they were living and modern ratios. They are further distorted by their own specific isotope preferences. Finally, the plus-or-minus factor reported with the date is approximately 1 standard deviation from a statistical mean; this means that, even after one corrects for other distortions, there is one chance in three that the true date does not fall within the 200-year range indicated by the laboratory. Thus, there are good reasons not to take radiocarbon dates at face value, but failure of a date to fit well with a particular archaeologist's expectations is not, all by itself, one of them. As we shall see, radiocarbon dates in the Northeast have been discarded frequently for this single spurious reason, but rarely for valid statistical or technical reasons. Stuckenrath (1977) provides an up-to-date set of rules for the proper use of radiocarbon dates.

Another vestige of the old paradigm that confuses contemporary issues is the stage concept. In applying this concept, or terms that imply it, we must accept certain assumptions regarding cultural evolution and the sequence of archaeological remains that such an evolution leaves behind. I find many of these assumptions to be rather naïve in light of more recent advances in anthropology. For example, some of the assertions I have read about Ohio Hopewell culture (such as the existence of a priesthood) make no sense to me at all in terms of later ethnohistory and what we know about how human beings behave generally. Such assumptions, however wrongheaded, were once widely used in generating archaeological sequences in the absence of radiocarbon dating. The problem is that, although the need for them has disappeared, the stages linger on, serving as built-in conclusions that should be sought, not assumed. The best regional example of this difficulty is the use of the term *Transitional* (see Chapter 6), a term that I think should be abandoned. The periods that I have used to organize the chapters that follow do not carry any of the outdated connotations of stages.

Table 1.3 contains the terms I have adopted as a means to describe prehistoric and historic cultures in a rigorous and consistent way while at the same time avoiding swamps of wearisome descriptions. The table lists seven

TABLE 1.3
Seven Primary Types of Community Patterning[a]

Supranuclear integrated
Advanced nuclear centered
Simple nuclear centered
Semipermanent sedentary
Central-based wandering
Restricted wandering
Free wandering

Focal ←——————————————→ Diffuse

[a] Economic adaptations ranging from extreme focal to extreme diffuse are possible within each type of patterning (Beardsley *et al.* 1956; Cleland 1976).

major types of community patterning derived from Beardsley *et al.* (1956). Other categories could be proposed, and a few of the seven are not entirely satisfactory for our region, but they are useful standard units for describing settlement systems and the patterns they produce. To them I have added Cleland's (1976) concept of focal–diffuse economic adaptation, which is useful in scaling particular subsistence systems in terms of a range from extreme specialization to extreme diversification. All of these terms will be defined with greater precision as necessary, but not repeatedly, in the chapters that follow. The distinctions drawn by Beardsley *et al.* are not nearly fine enough. Many of the specific cases from the Northeast lie on a continuum between the types central-based wandering and semipermanent sedentary. Clearly a system will have to be devised that will allow the description of important differences along that continuum, but for now I deal with them only in relative terms, as in Chapter 7 where settlement in the Hudson drainage is described as being closer to central-based wandering while settlement of the same period in central New York was nearer semipermanent sedentary.

Fine distinctions are not an issue with Cleland's focal–diffuse continuum, because it assumes a continuous scaling between extremes. We will see that through prehistory high quantities of resources relative to the population exploiting them tended to select for focal adaptations. Increased variety of resources tended to select for diffuse adaptations. The cycles of high availability and low availability that focally adapted cultures tended to experience were dampened by high mobility, as in the case of Paleo-Indians, or sophisticated storage techniques, as in the case of Late Prehistoric horticulturalists. These general principles were further modified by varying perceptions of what was or was not food, the quality of information regarding possible uses and availability of specific resources, and the secondary effects of decision making. A community might choose to exploit a specific resource and thereby find itself out of position to exploit others available at the same time. The community might also decide that the cost of moving or sending special task groups to locations where they might exploit a resource was higher than the possible benefits could justify. All of these complications contribute to the specific features of every economic system. They help explain why "obvious" resources seem not to be exploited at certain times or places and why human populations generally live so far below theoretical carrying capacities. I describe several specific cases through the course of this volume.

Three levels of sociopolitical organization are so important to the chapters that follow that I must define them carefully at the onset. I use *band* to mean a set of nuclear families that regularly live and travel together. They are typically patrilocal: The adult male members are related by blood and the adult female members are largely in-marrying women from other bands. Bands therefore often amount to patrilineal extended families. However, room must be left for cases in which young married couples and established nuclear families can choose or change band affiliation according to practical demands apart from kinship. It is likely that bands came together from time to time to form larger composite bands. In any case, leadership resided in adult men who gained it by virtue of personal strength, wisdom, and charisma. It was in most respects an egalitarian society in which roles were assigned on the basis of age, sex, and ability. Bands were often linked to other bands such that they formed overlapping *connubia*, the consequences of which I explore in Chapter 3 (see Williams 1974 with references).

I use *tribe* to mean a set of extended families or lineages that regularly reside together for at least part of the year. Social organization is still based on kinship, but there is often a formal council of leaders from the member extended families or lineages. Leaders are still chosen for their personal qualities but often come from ranking families or lineages. Tribes were sometimes lineal, sometimes cognatic, a distinction that I make clear through example in Chapter 2. They have defined territories but are not necessarily dependent on horticulture. Clans are sometimes present, but as noted in Chapter 7 they should not be assumed to have had great sociopolitical significance. Tribes sometimes resided in two or more separate communities that were linked in a relatively loose way by language and mutual interest. In such cases leadership might be exercised by the leaders of a ranking community. It is important to distinguish between connubia of bands that have overlapping membership and tribal societies, which were mutually exclusive.

A *chiefdom* implies "not just greater chiefs but a *system* of chieftainship, a hierarchy of major and minor authorities holding forth over major and minor subdivisions of the tribe: a chain of command linking paramount to middle-range and local level leaders [Sahlins 1968:26]." Archaeologically the evidence for such an organization is usually in the form of sets of communities in which one is clearly dominant and the others satellite. In terms of ethnohistory the evidence is usually that same physical dominance and clear indications of a regularized system for succession in leadership, a deference on the part of local leaders to a paramount leader, and some control of the legitimate use of force by the central leadership. Here again territoriality is well defined, but with the advantages of centralization and stability in political and military matters. The chiefdom was rare in aboriginal New England, but made an appearance near the end of prehistory.

A traditional difficulty has been in the area of comparing archaeological cultures across time and space. Part of the difficulty is in the nature of the data themselves. Archaeology allows the direct recovery of only a small portion of the material culture of an extinct community and none of its nonmaterial culture. The solution for many years has been to resort to ethnographic analogy, a procedure that emphasizes a comparison of archaeological assemblages with those of historically known groups, followed by the inference of traits that did not survive from similarities seen with those that did. This too has been difficult because the results are often incomplete and unstructured, so that two archaeological cultures that have been fleshed out by ethnographic analogy might still be difficult or impossible to compare. One result has been that archaeologists repeatedly fall back on a comparison of only those material traits that have survived in assemblages. Consequently, there are cases of a single prehistoric culture being viewed as two or more because evidence has been drawn from sites where different activities were carried out and contrasting assemblages were left behind. Conversely, two or more quite different cultures have been classed as one because they shared one or two artifact types that preserved well or are easily recognized. We can avoid such pitfalls if we think of archaeological cultures as complete cultural systems and devise ways to describe them more broadly and consistently on the basis of the available evidence. David Clarke (1968:101–128) has devised a way to do just that by suggesting we describe extinct cultural systems in terms of abstracted subsystems and their characteristics.

I have defined cultural systems in terms of four subsystems, with each subsystem described in terms of two or four categories (Table 1.4). It is important to realize that these are not mutually exclusive categories but rather abstractions that overlap in many ways. In some cases these categories are directly observable in the archaeological record, for example, the category of food resources and seasonality. In other cases, as in the case of settlement unit, categories must be inferred from our general knowledge of ethnology. The categories cannot and should not be weighted equally in any analysis, but they at least provide us with 14 specific points on which to compare any two cultural systems. One of the nicest features of this approach is that it allows direct comparison of historic and prehistoric cultures and thereby enables us to trace the ancestry of historic tribes backward into prehistory with greater accuracy. As we shall see, it allows us to follow the evolutions of whole cultures through their successive phases, long developments that are usually called *traditions*. Traditions have always been considered whole cultural phenomena unless specifically defined otherwise. Unfortunately, up to now it has been more often the practice to define traditions in terms of one or two stone artifact types or a series of related pottery types.

TABLE 1.4
Four Subsystems Abstracted from the Larger
Cultural System[a]

I. Economic subsystem
    1. Site types and distribution within the area
    2. House types and distribution within settlements
    3. Food resources and seasonality
    4. Seasonal movements

II. Social subsystem
    5. Household unit
    6. Settlement unit
    7. Other inferred institutions
    8. Inferred community activities

III. Technological subsystem
    9. Artifact types
    10. Trade goods
    11. Raw materials
    12. Specific activities

IV. Ideological subsystem
    13. Mortuary site types
    14. Burial programs

[a] These four subsystems are not mutually exclusive. The specific categories listed under each subsystem are in some cases directly observable, in other cases inferable. They should not necessarily be weighted equally in analysis.

Application of the 14 categories in Table 1.3 has shown that in some cases these artifact traditions do not stand for whole cultural traditions at all.

I have taken a systems perspective in this volume, but do not pretend that it amounts to more than that. There is as yet no unified systems theory to embrace and test through application in a regional prehistory. "At base, systems theory is a general perspective, a way of looking at the relationships among variables that has much in common with traditional anthropological holism [Rodin *et al.* 1978:748]." Flannery (1973) has noted that archaeologists interested in process as well as prehistory have tended to divide into two camps. One camp of the "new archaeologists" is occupied by those who take a relatively narrow positivist view and seek to explain process through the discovery of lawlike generalizations. Flannery calls these the "law-and-order archaeologists." The other camp is occupied by those who prefer a systems approach, whom Flannery calls the "Serutan" archaeologists. The cultural materialist stance that often characterizes law-and-order archaeology is not without serious hazards. I have pointed this out elsewhere (Snow 1974) in connection with the interpretation of shell middens, and Potter and Waselkov (1976) have done the same for eastern archaeology generally. The issue must permeate any discussion of coastal adaptation in general and shellfish exploitation in particular in prehistoric New England; it appears more than once in this volume.

On the other hand, Spaulding (1973) points out that some Serutan archaeologists have adopted an almost mystical commitment to something called general systems theory. Such a commitment would be dangerously dogmatic if a general systems theory actually existed, but as it does not the commitment is merely ludicrous. Much the same sort of thing can be said regarding the archaeological application of mathematical systems theory, which at least has the advantage of existing. However, even this theory offers the archaeologist little more than stimulation by analogy (Salmon 1978). I agree with Spaulding, Salmon, and with Cowgill (1975:129) that many systems concepts are useful, and I allow that perspective to dominate from time to time in the following chapters. But I make no pretense that my systems perspective is anything more than that.

I am at pains in Chapter 2 to generate population estimates for local New England cultures for the period preceding the onset of epidemics. I use the resulting figures in a variety of ways later in the volume, but never as an explanatory device. Cowgill (1975) has summarized the problems that surface when one attempts to use population pressure as an explanation of prehistoric change. Very simply stated, he sees the sort of approach taken by Esther Boserup, in which population pressure is seen as pushing society toward more efficient forms of subsistence (particularly food production), as fallacious. A fairly extreme version of this approach has been briefly stated by Cohen (1975), who assumes that such pressure exists and goes on to itemize 14 kinds of archaeological evidence indicative of it. Of course, if the assumption is incorrect as Cowgill concludes it is, then each of the 14 kinds of archaeological evidence cited by Cohen is indicative of something else. In other words, Cohen's 14 points are not in themselves evidence of a causative relationship from population pressure to unidirectional change in the subsistence system, only logical consequences that will follow if the assumption is correct. At the other extreme in this theoretical debate is the Malthusian view that advances in subsistence efficiency are the cause (not the effect) of population expansion. Clearly there is no advantage to a dogmatic adherence to this extreme point of view either. I am struck by the fact that no primate species (humans included) ever seems to live near the limits of the carrying capacity of its environment. I am also struck by the general observation that sooner or later any community can come up against a temporary shortage, a short-term reduction in carrying capacity. That the shortage is temporary is more than balanced by the fact that it can be lethal for all or part of the group. Thus, population and subsistence efficiency are clearly related, but in a complex way that sees the balance tipped first one way and then the other by such things as advances in storage techniques, crop failures, the introduction of new cultigens, and long-term climatic deterioration. If it does nothing else, a systems perspective at least rescues us from our temptation to choose between the extremes of Boserup and Malthus. This book takes the middle road advocated by Dumond (1972), among others, in that the emphasis is on individual cases, unique evidence, and special hypotheses rather than theoretical ax grinding.

A few special usages need definition. Archaeological sites contain one or more *components*, each containing evidence of a separate occupation by a distinct prehistoric culture. It may be that a two-component site contains evidence of two different periods in the evolution of the same culture or the replacement of one culture by another, unrelated one. The total inventory of archaeological material from a single component is its *assemblage*. A *phase* is a set of components that appear to be closely related in time and space on the basis of dating, proximity, and similarities in their assemblages. A phase is therefore roughly the archaeologist's equivalent of the ethnologist's "culture." Sites are typically named, as are diagnostic artifact types. Components and assemblages are typically not named. Sets of diagnostic artifacts that often appear together in assemblages are sometimes described as named *complexes*. Thus, it is not unusual to speak of burial complexes. *Tool kits* are special kinds of complexes that often occur as overlapping sets of tools found within assemblages. Thus, prehistoric butchering tools, woodworking tools, fishing implements, hunting tools, and so on are usually not mutually exclusive sets of tools.

MYTHS OF NEW ENGLAND'S PAST

Another archaeologist has said it better than I can:

In this presentation of the prehistory of Eastern North America there are no vanished races, no mysterious Mound Builders; no wandering Welshmen, Lost Tribes of Israel, Irish Monks, German ironmongers, Scandinavian intruders . . . , Phoenicians around Lebanon, Pennsylvania, or angels and golden tablets in New York. These concepts of the 18th and 19th centuries, with unfortunate hangovers up to the present, were a product of the ignorance of that period [Griffin 1967].

Unfortunately they still sell books.

New England has been producing both serious and silly studies of prehistory for over a century, longer than most regions of North America. George Peabody endowed the museum that bears his name at Harvard in 1866, and the following year its first curator set off on a research expedition. Jeffries Wyman went off to Maine to explore the coastal shell heaps there. It was by no means the first such investigation; H. P. Chadbourne had established to his own satisfaction that the shell heaps were of human rather than natural origin by 1859 (Snow 1968b). New England's Indians had long since ceased to be enemies and had fought with the Americans in the Revolution, so there was no embarrassment involved in crediting them with responsibility for prehistoric remains. Farther west, where the remains were grander and the bitterest Indian wars still to come, there was less willingness to credit them, and the elaborate Mound Builder myths were the result (Silverberg 1968). However, balancing rationalism in New England was the region's proximity to the North Atlantic, which put it in a position to receive any number of imaginary pre-Columbian visitors. Thus, while New England is rich in sober archaeological research, it is also dubiously rich in nonsense.

New England's myths of prehistory come in three basic guises. First, there are the pseudolinguistic studies. One author published a seven-volume work at his own expense in order to advance the thesis that Eastern Algonquian languages derive from Old Norse. Another has attempted to show connections between Eastern Algonquian and Portuguese. Such studies are always unsystematic and fail to mention that by using the same approach one can show connections between any two of the world's languages chosen at random. Using systematic comparative techniques, competent linguists have in many cases been able to reconstruct partial vocabularies and grammatical structures of the extinct languages from which groups of related living languages descend. For example, much of proto-Indo-European, from which English and most other European languages descend, has been extensively reconstructed. Proto-Algonquian, the ancestral language of all but the Mohawk Indians in our region as well as such far-flung groups as the Shawnee and the Blackfoot, was being spoken in North America 4000 years ago (Snow 1976a). Proto-Northern-Iroquoian and ancestral Cherokee split 3500–3800 years ago (Lounsbury 1961). Thus, all the languages of aboriginal New England have deep roots that go back long before Norse and Portuguese, perhaps even before their own Germanic and Latin ancestors.

The second guise of New England's myths comes in the form of ethnographic comparisons. I once received a letter from a man eager to prove that the Iroquois were related to the Scots on grounds that both wore kilts. Such arguments are usually much more elaborate, and some seem superficially scholarly, but they remain myths nonetheless. A curious feature of these and most other myths is that they generally involve people coming from the Old World to show the benighted Indians how to pile rocks or engage in some other activity characteristic of higher civilization. The spate of imaginary visits from outer space generated by the space program in recent years at least avoids racism by presuming that no human culture could have achieved much without cosmic assistance.

The third class of myths is composed of notions based mainly on archaeological evidence that is either fabricated or misinterpreted. These often also have linguistic or ethnographic components. The most stunning example of this kind of myth in New England is the megalithic site at North Salem, New Hampshire. Notwithstanding sober published interpretations to the contrary (Hencken 1939, 1940), the stone structures on the site were once promoted as a pre-Viking Irish monastery (Goodwin 1946). The only report on the site by a professional archaeologist that I have seen concludes that it was built by a nineteenth-century farmer with bizarre architectural tastes (Vescelius n.d.). The site is often linked to the stone "beehives" found around New England, which are trapping cubbies built between the 1880s and the 1930s (Hall and Woodman 1973). These, too, are thought by some to have been built by pre-Columbian Irish or Vikings. Enthusiasts even found a nineteenth-century lime kiln in northern Maine and called it the "tomb of the lost Red Paint prince" (born of another myth discussed in Chapter 5). The kiln became "caves used by the Red Paint People" on a map published by the National Geographic Society in 1955. The Celtic connection has been recently revived, and books on the subject are enjoying great popularity. The inevitable upshot of the rediscovery of Goodwin's monks was the 1977 variation on a theme by Thor Heyerdahl in which five men sailed from Ireland to Newfoundland in a leather boat. The voyage proved beyond any doubt that five twentieth-century men could sail from Ireland to Newfoundland in a leather boat (Severin 1977).

The most famous New England archaeological myth may be only partly so. Carl Rafn introduced the general public to the Vinland sagas in 1837. In the course of preparing his work for publication, he wrote to every historical society in the eastern United States asking for evidence of Viking visitors. His requests touched off a frenzied search for artifacts, inscriptions, and architecture, and as usually happens in such cases the evidence came pouring in. A stone mill in Newport, Rhode Island, became a Viking tower. An Indian burial with copper ornaments became a Viking in full armor, and any boulder ever scratched by an iron plow became a candidate for fame as a rune stone (Morison 1971:37). I was born near the place in Minnesota where the fraudulent Kensington Rune Stone was carved, and I admit its importance in interesting me as a boy in archaeology. In my three years on the faculty of the University of Maine I saw several more candidates, but not one could pass even the easiest test of authenticity. The discovery and dramatic publication of Yale's Vinland Map by Skelton, Marston, and Painter on Columbus Day 1965 raised the hackles of Italian-Americans and the hopes of most others. Nine years later it too was declared a probable fake, having flunked a test of its ink dye. We are left with the site at L'Anse aux Meadows on the northern tip of Newfoundland as the only reasonably possible evidence for a Viking presence in North America (Ingstad 1977). Even this site has not convinced everyone, however. Even assuming its authenticity it still lies 1500 km from the New England coast. The only scrap of evidence for Norse contact to come from within aboriginal New England is a Norse coin from a coastal Maine site, described in Chapter 8.

The revived interest in Vikings has touched off a new round of imaginative runology and creative linguistics. Plow-scarred boulders, old survey markers, and gravestones have been examined all over again. Suspicious stones have been plucked from garden walls and foundations, and creative pranksters have added to the inventory of hoaxes. All of these have been "read" by self-taught runologists despite assurances from trained professionals that they amount to nothing more than gibberish (Thompson 1975). An example is the set of small boulders with runic inscriptions that turned up at the Spirit Pond site in coastal Maine in 1971. There were arguments about ownership and authenticity, all reported in the popular press, followed by at least one payment of a large sum of money and surrender of the stones to the Maine State Museum. Einar Haugen (1972) subsequently examined the inscriptions and declared them to be fakes on linguistic grounds. O. G. Landsverk (1973), an amateur runologist, subsequently claimed that the runes were authentic, but written in cipher, which he then attempted to decipher and translate. Haugen (1973) then demolished Landsverk's imaginative interpretation in a terse rejoinder that must convince any scientifically competent third party. Subsequent excavations at Spirit Pond have supported Haugen's findings by turning up typical prehistoric and historic remains, none of them Norse (Lenik 1975, 1977). The example is an important one because it shows that fraud and foolishness are still with us. Self-taught amateur archaeology is no more trustworthy than self-taught amateur surgery, although it seems to be less dangerous to the public health.

It has become traditional among professional archaeologists simply to avoid mention of myths like the ones just discussed except as playful exercises away from more serious writing. It is probably true for most regions that the problem will go away if simply ignored. However, the roots of archaeological mythology are deep in New England and the myths are numerous. I have broken tradition in order to comment on a few of them and make plain what otherwise might not be assumed by the reader. As a final note on the subject, I should say that I have left many more unmentioned in their specifics. My readers should not conclude that this is evidence of either approval or ignorance on my part.

HISTORIC
BASELINE

I have already defined aboriginal New England and its subdivisions in terms of river drainages (see Figure 1.1) and sketched some of the reasons for that format. Various complications will become apparent in subsequent chapters, some of them as major developmental themes, but this organizational structure will remain essentially intact. Boat transportation, which reinforced the territorial significance of drainages, was important throughout much of the prehistoric sequence. In northern New England the pattern was especially reinforced by the development of the birchbark canoe. Dugout canoes remained important in southern New England where suitable birch trees were not available, and the riverine pattern was breaking down there in A.D. 1600 due to the increasing importance of horticulture and large semipermanent villages. By that time, the Indians of southern New England were following the lead of communities to the west and south, using overland trails more frequently and canoe travel less frequently. There was also increasing differentiation between upstream and downstream communities in drainages such as the Hudson and Connecticut because the climate was suitable for agriculture in downstream areas but not in upstream areas. Thus, in southern New England generally there was a tendency for the old riverine pattern to break down in late prehistoric times. Nevertheless, enough of the old pattern remained intact in A.D. 1600 for us to rely on it as an organizational structure.

Figure 2.1 shows the river drainages of Figure 1.1, this time with the drainage names replaced by the native cultures of the seventeenth century. I avoid the term *tribe* at this point because it has come to have very specific social and legal connotations that I do not mean to imply, but the reader is free to think of them as tribes in a nontechnical sense. For the most part, each local culture was also a single speech community, its members speaking

CHAPTER 2

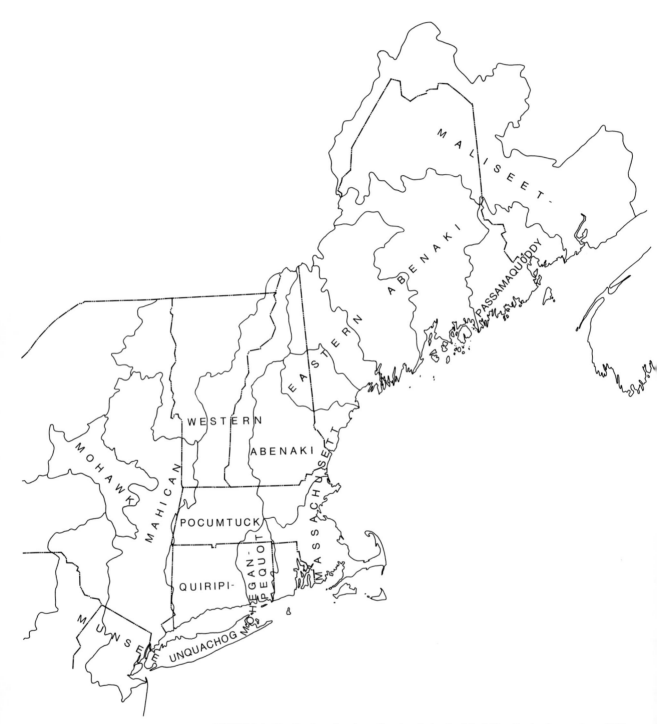

FIGURE 2.1. Distribution of major cultural units in aboriginal New England around A.D. 1600. Each corresponds to a major language. Subdivisions and names that came into use in later times are not shown.

a unique language or a dialect of a language shared with one or more neighboring cultures. Unfortunately, the linguistic evidence for this early period is so spotty that we cannot demonstrate clear correspondences between all the cultures I have listed and known languages and dialects. What little we do know has been summarized by Goddard (1978a).

With the exception of the Mohawk, all of the people of the coastal drainages from Nova Scotia to North Carolina spoke Algonquian languages. The languages of this coastal region are more similar to each other than any of them are to the other Algonquian languages of North America, and they are therefore classified together as the Eastern Algonquian bloc. The Eastern Algonquian languages were geographically separated from the other Algonquian languages by Iroquoian and other languages to the interior. The Northern Iroquoian languages, including the Mohawk, were particularly important insulators that formed a bloc through central Pennsylvania and New York, and then down the St. Lawrence valley to the Gulf of St. Lawrence. The distribution of Iroquoian languages suggests that they intruded into the region at some time in the past, cutting the Eastern Algonquian speakers off from their linguistic relatives to the west and north. One of the most interesting aspects of the prehistory of New England is the exploration of how and why this occurred.

Various linguistic estimates are available for the timing of the presumed Iroquoian intrusion into the Northeast and the consequent isolation of Eastern Algonquian. Lounsbury (1961:11) estimates that the Northern Iroquoians split from the Cherokee about 3500–3800 years ago. Siebert (1967:39) once estimated that the Algonquians were a single speech community as recently as 3200 years ago but has since disowned that date as being too recent. An age closer to 4000 years for that speech community, which linguists call proto-Algonquian, would be more consistent with Lounsbury's estimate for Northern Iroquoian. As we shall see in Chapter 6, it is also more consistent with archaeological evidence. Goddard (1978a:70) estimates that Eastern Algonquian languages have been diverging from their common origin for about 2000 years. Thus, taken by itself, the linguistic evidence suggests an intrusion of Northern Iroquoians around 3500–3800 B.P., which was followed by the isolation of Eastern Algonquians from the main body of the Algonquian family and the beginnings of internal divergence by 2000 B.P. Although protolanguages such as proto-Algonquian and the later proto-Eastern-Algonquian are often discussed as if they were relatively small homogeneous speech communities, it seems more likely that a protolanguage is a normative construct that stands for speakers of related dialects scattered over a relatively wide area (Snow 1976a:344). It is important to realize that a protolanguage is a linguistic reconstruction based on a set of related historic languages, and that it does not necessarily represent a single small real language of prehistory. Our perspective is often biased by our familiarity with modern standardized languages. Modern languages are artificial in the sense that they deliberately suppress diversity and enforce that standardization through systems of writing. Such languages have no prehistoric equivalents. Thus, while we might date our proto-Eastern-Algonquian to around 2000 B.P., we need not necessarily presume that the distribution of this protolanguage was substantially less than the region occupied by Eastern Algonquian languages in historic times. The point is an important one, for it does away with any need to seek archaeological evidence for a precise local homeland for proto-Eastern-Algonquian speakers, or for the speakers of any other protolanguage for that matter. Indeed, the archaeological record is much more consistent with this generalized and normative view of protolanguages than it is with a narrow particularistic view of them. The farther back one goes in the archaeological record the more widespread and generalized prehistoric cultures seem to be. The reconstructions of historical linguistics should be expected to apply to similarly generalized communities, and all the more so the farther back one probes. Therefore, when Haas (1958:258) suggests that all Algonquian as well as all Gulf (generally southeastern) languages descend from a common protolanguage base that split 5000–6000 years ago, we should have no difficulty imagining a single widespread community of related dialects in the Eastern Woodlands prior to that date. As we shall see, the archaeological evidence for that remote period is similarly widespread and generalized.

An alternative accommodation is favored by some historical linguists to regard protolanguages as if they were real languages rather than normative reconstructions. If this view is adopted, then one must treat such reconstructed languages as very small speech communities in both time and space, each a tiny subset of a much larger set of related dialects. Implicit in such a view is that the protolanguage later gives rise to all descendant languages while other variants spoken at the time of the protolanguage become extinct. This view is at odds with the treatment of human prehistory as the prehistory of populations and cannot be made to fit with archaeological sequences. For this reason, I do not subscribe to this conception of protolanguages in the chapters that follow.

Maliseet–Passamaquoddy is a single language having two dialects that are still spoken in the St. John and St. Croix drainages, respectively. Goddard (1978a:70–71) discusses a language he calls "Etchemin" that may have existed in this area around A.D. 1600, but the evidence is limited to a list of ten numbers copied down by Marc Lescarbot. At the time the list was made, Etchemin was being used to refer to the Indians of New Brunswick and Maine in a very broad way (Snow 1978a), and I regard the linguistic evidence as too slight to be taken very seriously. It is conceivable that such a language could have been spoken in the St. Croix drainage. Goddard indicates that it resembles Eastern Abenaki, which was spoken in the adjacent Penobscot drainage. No more than a few hundred people would have lived in the St. Croix drainage in A.D. 1600, and the epidemics, which caused mortality rates to reach approximately 70%, could have reduced the population so much that survivors joined other communities and lost their linguistic distinctiveness. A later reoccupation of the St. Croix by Maliseet–Passamaquoddy speakers would explain why we get no clear reference to the Passamaquoddy as a separate tribe until 1727 (Gyles 1853) and why the Passamaquoddy dialect is so similar to Maliseet. However, this is all conjecture, for we cannot be sure that a distinct Etchemin language ever existed at all.

Eastern Abenaki was spoken throughout western and central Maine. The Penobscot dialect, which apparently had upstream and downstream subdialects, survived into modern times, becoming a language in its own right by default as the other Eastern Abenaki dialects became extinct. There was a distinct Caniba dialect in the Kennebec drainage, and probably at least two additional dialects in the Androscoggin and Presumpscot drainages, respectively. The latter survived only as recombined fragments in the historic Abenaki refuge communities at St. Francis and Becancour, Quebec.

Western Abenaki was spoken by the people of the upper Merrimack drainage. It may well also have been spoken by the Sokoki of the upper Connecticut drainage, and these people in turn may have occupied what is now Vermont as far as the shores of Lake Champlain. Apart from that possibility we are not at all sure who was living in the Champlain drainage in 1600. The St. Lawrence Iroquois dominated the valley with the same name at the beginning and the Mohawk and other New York Iroquois nations dominated the Champlain valley from the later 1600s on. The Western Abenaki language survives at St. Francis (Odanak), Quebec, but its history and original distribution are very poorly known.

Southeastern New England was occupied by Indians who spoke a number of dialects that were similar enough to be considered a single language. The shattered communities and dialects of this area are known to us by a series of confusing local names that I have chosen to lump under the heading "Massachusett." It is not clear that the Rhode Island Narragansett were distinct as a language or culture in 1600, and I have accordingly lumped them with the Massachusett. The larger term therefore also subsumes such local groups as the Pawtucket, Pokanoket, Wampanoag, Nantucket, and Nauset. Although the Massachusett were for the most part a solid bloc of southeastern New England groups, some were living in the lower Merrimack drainage and into the coastal areas of New Hampshire and southernmost Maine. This distribution appears to have resulted from a northward spread of Massachusett communities in late prehistoric times and is taken up again in Chapter 8.

The middle portion of the Connecticut drainage was occupied by people usually called the Pocumtuck. Pocumtuck is a village name. There never was a Pocumtuck confederacy, and we should probably not extend the village name to apply to a whole culture, but there seems to be no other label available. I use *Pocumtuck* with the understanding that, like *Penobscot*, it is a term that has come to mean something quite different to us than to the people who coined it. They appear to have spoken a language identified as "Loup A" by Goddard (1978a:71). They probably shared this language with people called the Nipmuck, who lived in settlements just outside the Connecticut drainage in eastern Massachusetts in the seventeenth century. The southern portion of the Connecticut drainage as well as the central portion of Long Island were occupied by speakers of closely related dialects that Goddard has called the Quiripi–Unquachog language. I have adopted this linguistic designation as a means to lump these people into two cultural units, the Quiripi of the lower Connecticut and Housatonic drainages, and the Unquochog of central Long Island. There are many local names in the literature that refer to parts of this larger entity, but their recitation here would only be confusing. One point that is very clear is that there was no early historic culture in this area that was bounded on the east by the Connecticut River and on the west by the Hudson. Many older sources insist that such a "Wappinger" entity existed as either a culture or a political confederacy, but that conclusion was based on faulty linguistic analysis combined with the European habit of using rivers as boundaries (Goddard 1971; see also p. 96). The Connecticut drainage was occupied by speakers of three distinct languages, each of which appears to have been spoken in at least one adjacent drainage area. If the Connecticut drainage had ever been the home of one and only one distinct language, that rather neat adherence to the riverine model had clearly begun to break down by A.D. 1600. Yet the situation in 1600 was still far from the complete reversal of cultural geography that a Wappinger Confederacy with mountains at its core and rivers as boundaries would imply.

The Thames drainage, which lies between the Connecticut drainage and southeastern New England, was the home of a related set of dialects that also extended to the eastern tip of Long Island. The language is Mohegan–Pequot, sometimes called Mohegan–Pequot–Montauk to ensure inclusion of the Long Island branch. Mohegan–Pequot is a convenient term to use to refer to either the language or the culture of the people that spoke it. The Western Niantic and the Eastern Niantic, small communities that lived along this section of coast in the seventeenth century, might have spoken some form of Mohegan–Pequot or Massachusett. We know so little about either Niantic group that we are not even sure they were linguistically closer to each other than to their other neighbors.

The Mahican lived in the middle and upper Hudson drainage and spoke the language of the same name. It should not be assumed that they were closely related to the Mohegan simply because of the similarity in their names, nor should it be assumed that either of them has anything to do with James Fenimore Cooper's imaginary Mohicans. In fact, the Indians of the Massachusetts, Connecticut, and Rhode Island drainages form a bloc with many common features, and as a set they contrast with Mahican and Munsee on the west as well as the languages of northern New England.

Munsee was spoken in the southern Hudson drainage, in the northern

Delaware drainage, and on the western end of Long Island. Again we have a language made up of many minor dialects that are often recorded under different names in the literature. Munsee was very similar to Unami, which was spoken in the southern Delaware drainage. Unami is often called Delaware, and it is likely that Munsee and Unami were once simply the upstream and downstream speech communities of the Delaware drainage. Late in prehistory the speakers of Munsee appear to have expanded eastward out of the Delaware drainage and into the Hudson. This expansion is documented by archaeological evidence as well and is discussed in Chapter 8.

There are some relatively deep splits within the family of Eastern Algonquian languages generally, but none of these deep divisions falls within aboriginal New England. Micmac, located in Nova Scotia and that part of New Brunswick lying outside the St. John drainage, has undergone a grammatical evolution that distinguishes it from the Eastern Algonquian languages to the south and west. Mahican, Western Abenaki, and Eastern Abenaki seem to hang together as a set of northern languages, while the languages of southern New England form a separate nucleus. Munsee clearly forms a separate nucleus with Unami. Archaeological clues to the significance of these broad distinctions are discussed in the chapters that follow. Clearly a major archaeological parallel is found in the contrast between settlement and subsistence in the south with those same systems in the north. Unfortunately, key words and other features of language do not provide us with consistent patterns of distribution. One can create a migration hypothesis to explain one linguistic pattern only to find it contradicted by another. This is perhaps just as well, because migration should be used only as an explanation of last resort in any case. The mechanisms by which languages can change and influence one another are many and complex, just as they are for cultures generally. As we shall see in the chapters that follow, migration is not often an appropriate explanation for archaeology either, there being many mechanisms to account for the evidence of change in prehistory. The differences among the languages reflected in Figure 2.1 are perhaps roughly equivalent to those that exist among modern Romance languages. While Spanish and Italian are not mutually intelligible, I know from experience that a good knowledge of one makes the other rather easy to learn. The same can be said of most pairs of native languages in New England. The sole exception to this generalization is Mohawk, which as we have seen belongs to the Iroquoian language family and has its primary prehistoric connections outside aboriginal New England. The time and circumstances of its prehistoric intrusion are discussed in Chapter 6.

The coastal Algonquians were in sporadic contact with Europeans through much of the sixteenth century. Casual readers often assume otherwise and are surprised to discover that upon landing at Plymouth Rock the Pilgrims were greeted in English by an Indian named Samoset who said, "Welcome,

ABORIGINAL POPULATION

Englishmen." We may search through earlier documents in our attempt to
find evidence of first contact until we come up against Gosnold's 1602 voyage.
There we encounter Indians in European clothes rowing about in a Basque
shallop, and others said to be capable of tossing off English phrases such as
"How now are you so saucie with my Tabacco?" (Archer 1843).

Unfortunately, we have only a few written sources from this twilight
period; most of our more extensive early descriptions of these Indians come
from the first part of the seventeenth century. By then some changes were
already taking effect. The worst was to begin around 1615, when the first
waves of European diseases began to sweep over the native populations of
New England. The epidemics wiped out whole towns and permanently
altered the cultures of the survivors (Cook 1973a, 1973b).

It is possible that there were serious epidemics throughout the 1500s and
that the native population was larger by some substantial but unknown
degree in 1500 than it was in 1600 (Brasser 1978a:78). However, it seems
more likely to me that European disease did not have a significant impact on
the Indians of New England prior to the documented epidemics that began
around 1615. Although the evidence comes largely from maps rather than
written records, it is now generally accepted that Basque, Portuguese, English, Breton, and Norman fishermen frequented the northeast coasts of
North America through the sixteenth century. However, the earliest of these
fishermen often carried salt for packing their fish and did not have to contact
Indians or even land before returning home. Only after 1560, when beaver
furs were in heavy demand for felting, were there compelling reasons for
fishermen to seek out contacts with Indians in New England and elsewhere
in the Northeast (Snow 1976c:5). Even then, contacts were apt to be frequent
only with northern Europeans, who were experiencing shortages of both
beaver fur and salt. These fishermen had to establish fish drying stations on
land, and, while there, they had good economic reasons to trade for furs.
Thus, contacts between fishermen and Indians were at best sporadic for at
least two-thirds of the century. In addition, it is important to note that the
fishing vessels and their crews were small, and the passage long. Even the
large expeditions of the period were small compared to later ones. Columbus's *Niña* had a crew of only 22 men, and Cabot's *Mathew*, which sailed
in the same decade, carried only 18. These small companies were at sea for
long periods; in the case of Verrazzano's 1524 crossing it was a month and a
half. Therefore, the early voyages may well have involved crews too small to
provide reservoirs for European diseases through the quarantine period
imposed by long voyages.

After A.D. 1600, expeditions were larger and crossings shorter. Champlain
was accompanied by more than 100 men in 1604, and their crossing took less
than a month (Grant 1907:25–26). The incubation period for smallpox is
8–10 days, and the disease reservoir is always someone ill with or convalesc-
ing from the disease. The incubation period for measles is 8–21 days, and the
reservoir consists solely of active cases of the disease. Both diseases are

transmitted directly from one human to another, and it is not likely that either could survive a quarantine of a month and a half in a reservoir made up of a half-dozen fishermen. The odds increased dramatically that either or both diseases would survive the Atlantic crossing with the large and relatively fast-moving expeditions that came out of Europe in the first decade of the seventeenth century. It seems likely that only then did the awful contamination of European disease leak across the ocean to New England. The cycles of epidemics and mass deaths that began in 1615 were therefore a new phenomenon, for any occurrence before that date would have been just as devastating. There is no convincing evidence that anything like the epidemics of the seventeenth century took place in the previous century. Therefore, we can probably conclude that population levels in 1600 were not substantially different from those of 1500.

Because of some extraordinarily complete data for pre-epidemic and post-epidemic population levels among the Eastern Abenaki, I have been able to generate fairly convincing population figures for aboriginal New England around A.D. 1600 (Table 2.1). My figures are for the most part much higher than those proposed by Mooney (1928) and others who have dealt with the

TABLE 2.1
Drainage Divisions of Aboriginal New England, A.D. 1600: Areas, Cultures, and Enumeration

Drainage	Area (km^2)	Culture	Estimated population		Population density per 100 km^2
St. John	59,000	Maliseet	7,200	} 7,600	12
St. Croix	3,000	Passamaquoddy	400		12
Penobscot	26,000	Eastern Abenaki	3,200		12
Kennebec	18,000	Eastern Abenaki	5,300	} 11,900	29
Androscoggin	10,000	Eastern Abenaki	2,600		26
Presumpscot	6,000	Eastern Abenaki	800		13
Upper Merrimack	9,000	Western Abenaki	2,000		22
Upper Connecticut	17,000	Western Abenaki	3,800	} 10,000	22
Champlain	19,000	Western Abenaki	4,200		22
Lower Merrimack	8,000	Massachusett	15,500		193
Southeastern				} 36,700	
New England	11,000	Massachusett [a]	21,200		193
Thames and eastern					
Long Island	5,000	Mohegan–Pequot	13,300		266
Middle Connecticut	8,000	Pocumtuck	15,200		190
Lower Connecticut and					
central Long Island	13,000	Quiripi–Unquachog	24,700		190
Middle and upper Hudson	17,000	Mahican	5,300		31
Mohawk	10,000	Mohawk	9,000–11,300		90–113
Lower Hudson	17,000	Munsee	15,300–32,300	} 24,300–51,300	90–190
Upper Delaware	10,000	Munsee	9,000–19,000		90–190
Totals	266,000		158,000–187,300		

[a] Includes Narragansett.

problem. They are, however, justifiable. Dobyns (1966) has argued forcefully that there is a standard ratio of 20 to 1 between populations at initial contact with Europeans and those same populations at their subsequent low ebb. This is a much higher epidemic mortality than almost any of those implied by published estimates. Where Kroeber (1939), following Mooney, proposes that there were 5500 people within the five Iroquois nations, Dobyns argues that the actual population in A.D. 1600 was perhaps 10 times that size (Dobyns 1966:402). Trigger (1966) agrees that Kroeber's figure is too low, but is unwilling to readjust upward to the degree suggested by Dobyns. My own calculations for one of the five nations, the Mohawk, indicate that an upward revision by a factor of from 3 to 5.5 would be appropriate.

Some readers will probably regard my A.D. 1600 population projections as inflated. Driver and Massey (1957:186) indicate 2–5 people per 100 km^2 in aboriginal Maine, whereas my calculations lead to 12–29 people per 100 km^2 for the same area. Similarly, they suggest a level of 30–75 people per 100 km^2 for southeastern New England, whereas my figures indicate that it was about 193. However, none of my upward revisions is as extreme as Dobyns recommends for the hemisphere generally, and they are within the bounds considered reasonable by Ubelaker (1976). We have all been conditioned to think of native American societies in terms of their sizes when they were first encountered by Europeans, and not after the wave of pestilence that followed contact almost everywhere in the hemisphere.

A major difficulty inherent in projecting A.D. 1600 population levels is that we are dealing with such extreme mortality rates that even when we have accurate census data small rate differences yield very different results (Table 2.2). For example, a population of 10,000 people suffering a 50–55% mortality rate in an epidemic will end up with a post-epidemic population of

TABLE 2.2
Aboriginal Cultures of New England[a]

Culture	Pre-epidemic population	Post-epidemic population	Mortality[b]
Maliseet–Passamaquoddy	7,600	2,500	67
Eastern Abenaki	11,900	3,000	75
Western Abenaki	10,000	250	98
Massachusett[c]	36,700	5,300	86
Mohegan–Pequot	13,300	3,000	77
Pocumtuck	15,200	800	95
Quiripi–Unquachog	24,700	1,200	95
Mahican	5,300	500	91
Mohawk	9,000–11,300	4,100–5,100	55
Munsee	24,300–51,300	4,500	81–91

[a] Pre-epidemic population estimates apply to the sixteenth century, whereas post-epidemic levels are those reached by the middle of the seventeenth century.
[b] In percentages.
[c] Includes Narragansett.

4500–5000 people. However, the same population suffering a 90–95% mortality rate will be reduced to 500–1000 people. In this case a 5% variation in mortality leads to a 100% range (from 500 to twice that number) in the survivor population. The New England epidemics of the early seventeenth century were of this latter type, and ethnohistorians are often faced with the need to project pre-epidemic populations from post-epidemic data. Thus, if there is a survivor population of 350 people, it makes a very big difference for the projection if the mortality rate was 90% or 95% because the figures that result are 3500 and 7000, respectively. In a few specific cases I have not had even post-epidemic figures to work from and have had to estimate A.D. 1600 population levels on the basis of presumed population densities in areas of known sizes. It is essential, therefore, that none of the figures that follow be taken seriously except as very general comparative population baselines. Where the evidence has been weakest I have given population ranges based on the extremes of known variation in population density and epidemic mortality in New England.

S. F. Cook (1976) has dealt with the problem of aboriginal population levels in New England at much greater length, particularly for the area between the Hudson and Saco rivers. Unfortunately, the issue of pre-epidemic levels is confused in his work by the inclusion of many post-epidemic data. Moreover, the ethnic units he uses are in some cases late seventeenth-century units and in other cases divisions that we now know never really existed at all. His spatial units resemble mine only very generally. Nonetheless, there is remarkable similarity between his figures and my own independently generated figures for some comparable areas. He estimates that there were 12,000 "Pennacook" a unit that includes my Western Abenaki (which I estimate to have numbered about 10,000) and some Massachusett communities. Cook estimates that there were 5000 Mahican, compared to my estimate of 5300 for the same group. We begin to diverge in southern New England. There he estimates that there were only 25,400 people in the unit I have called Massachusett (including Narragansett), whereas I estimate a total of 36,700. The gap widens for other parts of southern New England, where I think that Cook depends too much on low post-epidemic figures. Where I see 13,300 Mohegan–Pequot in A.D. 1600 he sees only 3500. The result is that for the area between the Hudson and the Saco rivers Cook estimates a total of 71,900 people, whereas I estimate 105,200. Nevertheless, those numbers are very close together considering the quality of the available data. Indeed, they are closer to each other than either is to Mooney's very low estimates or the very high one Dobyns would prefer. Moreover, they bracket the independent estimate of 72,000–90,000 for the same area made by Peter Thomas (1977, 1979:28).

In order to put pre-epidemic population levels in the St. John drainage into proper perspective, we must start with their Micmac neighbors to the east. According to Biard (Thwaites 1959:Volume 3, 111), there were 3000–3500 Micmacs in 1616 after the first epidemics had already gone through their country. If the mortality rate during the epidemics was equivalent to that of the Eastern Abenaki, we can presume a pre-epidemic population of 11,900–13,883 for the Micmac. Looked at another way, the Micmac country consisted of 97,000 km^2 if one includes all of Nova Scotia, Prince Edward Island, and that part of New Brunswick not within the St. John and St. Croix drainages as I have defined it. If the population density of the Micmac in their country was proportional to that of the Penobscot (12.3 per 100 km^2), the population would have been about 12,000 for the Micmac. This is comfortably within the range predicted on the basis of projected mortality rates during the epidemics, and I accept it as a reasonable figure for the A.D. 1600 Micmac population. This is quite different from Miller's (1976:125) essentially unsupported guess of 35,000, but substantially more than the post-epidemic figures that are usually used. For example, Hoffman (1955:230) puts his estimate at 6000, whereas Bock (1978:117) uses Biard's lower figure of 3000 for A.D. 1600 and guesses that there were only about 4500 Micmacs in A.D. 1500.

The situation is different for the Maliseet–Passamaquoddy area. Here Biard reports a post-epidemic population of 2500 (Thwaites 1959:Volume 3, 111). If mortality were the same here as in the adjacent Eastern Abenaki drainage, a pre-epidemic population of 9917 would be indicated for the St. John and St. Croix drainages taken together. Together the two drainages contain 62,000 km^2. A population density equivalent to that of the pre-epidemic Penobscot drainage would indicate a population of 7631. As I have shown, a population density for the Micmac that was roughly equivalent to that of the Penobscot is supported by independent calculations based on estimated mortality. Based on this and other considerations, I consider it more likely that epidemic mortality varied from drainage to drainage more than pre-epidemic density did in this nonagricultural northern region. Among the other considerations is the fact that mortality was considerably more severe in Massachusetts than it was in Maine. Thus, it could have been even less severe in New Brunswick. In short, it seems likely that the epidemic mortality was relatively lower for the Maliseet–Passamaquoddy and that the pre-epidemic population was about 7600. This means that, in contrast to the 75% mortality among the Eastern Abenaki (from 11,900 to 3000), the Maliseet–Passamaquoddy probably experienced a mortality rate of about 67% (from 7600 to 2500). The portion of that population in the St. John drainage probably would have been about 7200, whereas the St. Croix share was probably only about 400.

There are several sources relating to Eastern Abenaki ethnohistory before 1620, but one extraordinary source stands out among them. The origins of this source stem from the George Waymouth expedition to the Maine coast in 1605. Waymouth kidnapped five Indians, one of whom eventually made his way into the household of Ferdinando Gorges in England. This man and others were apparently interviewed by James Rosier, and Purchas (1625) subsequently published a very detailed accounting of the villages of the

Eastern Abenaki. Each village is identified in terms of the river on which it was located, and in many cases it is possible to rediscover the exact locations of these villages (Snow 1976d) (Table 2.3). Purchas lists 21 villages and 23 leaders called *sagamores*. In the case of one village no sagamore is listed. However, three other villages are listed as having dual leadership. Best of all, Purchas lists both the number of adult men and the number of houses per village in most cases. He indicates a total of 2930 men. In the eighteenth century, adult men made up about 30% of the total population, a ratio that I

TABLE 2.3
Population Data Derived from Purchas (1625)[a]

Rivers		Villages		Men	Houses	Sagamores
Purchas	Modern	Purchas	Modern			
Penobscot						
Quibiquesson	Union	Precante	Ellsworth	150	50	Asticou
						Abermot
*Pemaquid	Penobscot	Upsegon	Bangor	250	60	†Bashabes
		Caiocama	Indian Island	(130)		Maiesquis
		Shasheokeing	Old Town	(130)		Bowant
Ramassoc	Orland	*Panobscot	Orland	80	50	Sibatahood
Apanawapeske	Bagaduce	*Mescombe	Camden	80	50	Aramasoga
		Chebegnadose	Castine	90	30	Skanke
Kennebec						
Apanmensek	St. Georges	*(Nusconcus)	Muscongus	(130)		†(Cabahis)
Apponick	Damariscotta	Appisham	?	(130)		Abochigishic
		Mesaqueegamic	?	80	70	Amniquin
		Matammisconte	?	90	80	Narracommiqua
Aponeg	Sheepscot	Nebamocago	?	300	160	†Mentaurmet
		Asshamo	?	70	80	Hamerhaw
		Neredoshan	?	100	120	Sabenaw
*Sagadohoc	Kennebec	*Kenebeke	Augusta	100	80	Apombamen
		Ketangheanycko	Waterville	330	90	Octoworthe
		Naragooc	Norridgewock	150	50	Cocockohamas
*Sagadohoc	Eastern	Massakiga	Dresden	40	8	
Arosaguntacook						
*Sagadohoc	Androscoggin	*Amereangan	Lisbon Falls	260	90	Sasnoa
						Scawes
		Namercante	Livermore	120	40	Octoworokin
		Buccawganecants	?	400	60	Baccatusshe
Pequawket						
Ashamabaga	Presumpscot	Agnagebcoc	?	240	70	†Maurmet
						Casherokenit
Massachusett[b]						
*Shawakotoc	Saco		?			†(Onemechin)

[a] Names preceded by an asterisk (*) are found in Arber and Bradley (1910:192–193). Names preceded by a dagger (†) are found in Grant (1907:44–77). Names in parentheses are found in one of those sources but are missing from Purchas (1625). Numbers in parentheses are my estimates for villages for which Purchas provides no numbers. The table is divided into major ethnic subdivisions (see text and Snow 1976d).

[b] Northernmost villages of Massachusett only.

use throughout this chapter. I have estimated the number of adult men for those four Eastern Abenaki villages lacking census data by providing an average number (130) for nearby drainages. The result is a projected total population of at least 10,000 and probably 11,900 for 1605. Purchas's total of 1238 houses gives us a figure of just under 8 people per house, a reasonable figure in light of other data on the sizes and shapes of Abenaki houses.

Purchas's data are supplemented by those supplied by Grant (1907:44–77) and Arber and Bradley (1910:192–193). Of the six sagamores mentioned by Champlain in his account of explorations in 1605, four are clearly included on the Purchas list and the remaining two appear to fill two important gaps on the list. John Smith gives us nine place-names, of which seven can be found on Purchas's list. The remaining two either are alternate names or were missed by Purchas (Snow 1976d:304). Altogether the data are so complete that we can calculate pre-epidemic populations for each of the four main branches of the Eastern Abenaki and calculate population densities for each of them as well. The densities range from 12 to 29 per 100 km^2, a range that even at its lower end is far above the 2 to 5 people per 100 km^2 suggested by Driver and Massey (1957:186). Driver and Massey's range is clearly too low by a factor of 6, not as far off as Dobyns's analysis might suggest, but significantly so nonetheless.

The first waves of European disease killed thousands of Eastern Abenaki. Biard estimates the total Eastern Abenaki population at only 3000 in 1616, a decline of 75% (Thwaites 1959:Volume 3, 111). Levett (1905) provides some independent confirmation by mentioning only 7 sagamores in the year 1623, less than a third the number we know existed 20 years earlier. All of these numbers are useful, for they provide us with a standard of reference for northern New England. We can be quite sure of pre- and post-epidemic populations, densities, and mortality rates for the Eastern Abenaki. Extension of those statistics to neighboring drainages, where necessary, helps fill gaps in a credible way.

Population levels for the upper Merrimack and Connecticut River drainages together with the Champlain drainage are difficult to estimate. Day (1978:153) concludes that this entire area was probably occupied by Western Abenaki and that a reasonable guess for their pre-epidemic population would be around 5000. My own conclusion is that his figure is too low by half. Daniel Gookin (1970:10) estimated that there was a pre-epidemic population of 3000 men for this area, a figure that suggests a total population of about 10,000. Smith's 1614 estimate of over 20 habitations (which becomes at least 30 in another place) stretching from the Merrimack to Lake Champlain is consistent with such a population level (Arber and Bradley 1910:204, 707, quoted on p. 69 in this chapter). If the villages were similar to those of the Kennebec and Androscoggin, an average of 100–150 adult men per village would not be excessive, and such an average would produce a total population of about 10,000. Indeed, figures from the Kennebec and Androscoggin would suggest somewhat larger numbers, as many as 200 men per village, which in turn would lead to a projected total population of 13,000–20,000. I am inclined to regard Gookin's lower figure as the more trustworthy, especially since Smith appears to have been rather careless with his estimates and might have included some Massachusett villages in his 20–30 figure. Together the upper Merrimack, upper Connecticut, and Champlain drainages contain about 45,000 km². A population of 10,000 in that area yields a density of about 22 per 100 km², a reasonable figure compared to densities elsewhere in northern New England. It is likely that the population was not evenly distributed through the three partial drainage areas, but we have no grounds for adjusting the proportional breakdown in Table 2.1. It is interesting that Gookin (1970:12) estimates the post-epidemic population to have been about 250, a disastrous reduction that yields a mortality rate of 98%. We probably need look no further for reasons why Western Abenaki culture is so poorly represented in seventeenth-century writings.

Gookin (1970:7–8) says that the Mohegan–Pequot could field 4000 men before the epidemics but only 300 afterward. These numbers indicate a pre-epidemic population of 13,300 and a post-epidemic population of 1000, for a mortality rate of 93%. These people occupied a territory of only 5000 km², so the pre-epidemic population would have been distributed at a density of 266 people per 100 km², an even higher figure than that generated for the Massachusett. The 93% decline includes the effects of the Pequot War, however, which was fought between 1634 and 1635. There may well have been 3000 Mohegan–Pequot people before the war, for about 600 adult men appear to have been lost in the fighting (Mooney 1928:230; Cook 1973b:7–8). A decline to an immediate post-epidemic population of 3000 would indicate a mortality rate during the epidemics of only 77% for the Mohegan–Pequot. When one considers the latter figures, a pre-epidemic population of 13,300 does not seem at all unreasonable. Indeed, despite the high population density this total implies, it seems doubtful that the Mohegan–Pequot could have had a significantly smaller pre-epidemic population than that which I have proposed.

Daniel Gookin also provides us with the best available basis on which to estimate the pre-epidemic population of the Massachusett. Gookin (1970:10) indicates that the Massachusett proper could field about 3000 men, a figure that apparently includes those Massachusett living in the lower Merrimack drainage. For the Pokanoket (later called the Wampanoag) he indicates an additional 3000 men (1970:9). The Narragansett, whom I have included with the Massachusett for present purposes, appear to have had at least 5000 adult men (Gookin 1970:8). Therefore, the area I have delineated as southeastern New England and the lower Merrimack (including the lower Saco) drainage appears to have held 11,000 adult men. Again assuming that adult men comprised about 30% of the population, we get a total population of about 36,700 for this area in A.D. 1600. This in turn would indicate a relatively high density of 193 people per 100 km². Gookin (1970:8–10) further indicates that after the epidemics there were only 1000 Massachusett (300 men) and about 3300 Narragansett (1000 men). Such figures indicate a mortality rate of 80–90% for the area. Although Gookin gives no post-epidemic figures for the Pokanoket, he implies that mortality within that group was at least as high as for the Massachusett (90%). We can therefore project a pre-epidemic population of 10,000 for the Pokanoket and a post-epidemic population of 1000. Thus, the total pre-epidemic population for the area would have been about 36,700 and the total post-epidemic population about 5300, for an overall mortality rate of 86%.The Narragansett branch suffered least, having started out with the largest share of the population and suffering the lowest mortality rate. This may help explain why the Narragansett emerged as a separate and strong political force in historic times.

I have divided the total Massachusett population of 36,700 into two parts that are proportional to the sizes of the lower Merrimack drainage and southeastern New England (Table 2.1). This was done in order to provide a population baseline for both areas at the level of about 193 people per 100 km^2. This is an extraordinarily high figure when compared to the densities calculated for drainages farther to the northeast. Both the total population and the density it indicates are much higher than Mooney's (1928) estimates, which I have been largely ignoring throughout this analysis. Brasser (1978a:78) says that "the available data suggest a population density of about 45 persons in each 100 square kilometers for the horticultural area," a figure that he might have derived from Mooney's estimates. Both Mooney's population estimates and Brasser's suggested density of 45 per 100 km^2 strike me as more appropriate for the period following the epidemics than for A.D. 1600. Ellis and Morris (1906:56) conclude that the Narragansett were able to field 1000 men in King Philip's War (1675), a number they could not have achieved at that time if they had a population of only 4000 in A.D. 1600, as Mooney (1928:2–4) suggests they had. A total of 1000 adult men suggests a total population of 3300 in 1675, which in turn would imply that the Narragansett were almost unaffected by the epidemics. We know otherwise, and we must conclude that in order to end up with the population levels that existed in the later seventeenth century, the Indians of southeastern New England and the lower Merrimack drainage must have started out that century at about the 36,700 level I have generated from Gookin's data. Even at that high pre-epidemic level, the figures indicate that the Massachusett suffered a lower mortality rate than their Western Abenaki neighbors, 86% as compared to 98%.

There are almost no data on which to base a population estimate for the middle and lower Connecticut and central Long Island drainages. The main river valleys within the area are within the zone having at least 150 frost-free days per year, and migratory fish resources were available as well. Thus, the area is similar to southeastern New England and we can probably assume that population density was roughly equivalent to that of the Massachusett, or about 190 per 100 km^2. Taking that as a guide we get 15,200 people for the middle Connecticut drainage and 24,700 for the lower Connecticut drainage and central Long Island in A.D. 1600. These would be the Pocumtuck and Quiripi–Unquachog, respectively. Bradford (1908:312) notes that there was a 95% mortality rate during a 1634 epidemic in the Connecticut drainage. If this is any indication of the general severity of the epidemics in this area we see that the two populations could easily have been reduced from 15,200 and 24,700 to under 800 and 1300. These small numbers are consistent with the low tallies cited by Salwen (1978:169), the general scarcity of references to these people in early documents, and their consolidation into refugee communities during the seventeenth century. These numbers are also consistent with Mooney's (1928:4) low population estimates for the area, whose estimates I have already pointed out tend to be much closer to post- than pre-epidemic levels elsewhere in New England.

Peter Thomas's (1979) more recent and more thorough research in the middle Connecticut drainage has yielded figures that indicate "a 1663 population estimate for communities between Springfield and Squakheag . . . between 1764 and 2200 individuals [p. 308]." This post-epidemic population may well include remnants from both the middle and lower Connecticut as well as refugees from elsewhere in southern New England.

Brasser (1974:9) cites unpublished Dutch sources that indicate that there were more than 1600 adult Mahican men in 1610. Although he regards the figure as inflated, I do not. The number suggests a total population of at least 5300. Given that the middle and upper Hudson drainage area contains 1700 km^2, a population density of 31 people per 100 km^2 is suggested. This is quite consistent with densities through the northern drainage areas, so there would seem to be little reason to discard the 5300 figure. Certainly it is well above Mooney's estimate of 3000, but most of his estimates are much too low. Due to disease and warfare the tribal population collapsed to about 500 by A.D. 1700. It is not possible at this writing to determine what proportion of that loss was suffered early on as a direct result of disease or what portion of the remaining 500 were in fact non-Mahican refugees from southern New England. Assuming for the present that 500 is also appropriate as the number of Mahicans surviving in 1620, a mortality rate of 91% is indicated. This is consistent with other mortality rates.

Fenton (1940:205) has calculated that the population of the Mohawk was about 2700 in A.D. 1634. He bases this figure on data drawn from a narrative of a journey into Mohawk and Oneida country that is now attributed to van den Bogaert (Jameson 1909:139–162). Working with a new translation of van den Bogaert and a somewhat more sophisticated analysis, Starna (1979) has estimated that the figure should actually be in the range 4100–5100. Starna has worked from van den Bogaert's house counts, estimating house sizes, family sizes, numbers of hearths, storage area, and other factors closely on the basis of data drawn from all over Iroquoia. If we assume a relatively low mortality rate of 70%, a pre-epidemic population of 13,700–17,000 is projected. Starna thinks that the rate may have been lower, perhaps around 55%, the death rate apparently experienced by the Huron in Ontario. This lower rate produces a pre-epidemic range of 9000–11,300 Mohawk. Even this lower number is equal to some estimates of the total for all Five Nations Iroquois, but I do not think it too high. Recent estimates put the pre-epidemic Huron population at more than 20,000, and it seems unlikely to me that they could have approached the combined Five Nations in size. Starna's lower estimates are acceptable, and perhaps even conservative. They lead to an A.D. 1600 population density of 90–113 per 100 km^2 in the Mohawk drainage, more than that of the less horticultural Mahican, but less than that of the Massachusett and other agricultural groups in southern New England. A higher mortality rate would yield a much larger pre-epidemic population size and density. If we eventually revise these estimates, they will almost certainly increase, not decrease.

The aboriginal Munsee population is also difficult to estimate. Feest (1978a:242) estimates that there were at least 12,000 Nanticoke and other groups living around Chesapeake Bay just to the southeast of Munsee and Unami country in A.D. 1600. Strachey's census suggests that there were almost that many people in Powhatan villages in tidewater Virginia around the same time (Feest 1978b:257). These numbers for relatively small drainage areas taken together with figures from southeastern New England make Goddard's (1978b:214) estimate of 4500 Munsee in A.D. 1600 seem much too low. He cites a more certain figure of 1200 Munsee for A.D. 1779, which if correct would imply a population decline of only 73% in 180 years. We have already seen that mortality soared to over 90% in many areas for the first two decades of that period alone. Goddard cites Mooney as an authority in this matter, and once again we appear to have an immediate post-epidemic population level, not a pre-epidemic level. If we apply the 190 person per 100 km^2 factor here as we have in the lower Connecticut drainage, we get a Munsee population of 51,300 in A.D. 1600. A post-epidemic decline to 4500 would represent an epidemic mortality rate of 91%, almost exactly what Feest (1978a:242) suggests for the Nanticoke and about what we have seen for much of New England generally. Certainly the Munsee population density must have been at least equal to the lower figure cited for the Mohawk (90 per 100 km^2), a figure that gives us a minimum possible population of 24,300 and a rather modest epidemic mortality of 81% (95% as of A.D. 1779).

ETHNOGRAPHIC SKETCHES

In this chapter I have attempted brief reconstructions of New England cultures for the years just before the disastrous epidemics. The reader will probably note with mixed feelings of gratitude and disappointment that I have avoided most of the confusing babble of names by which New England Indians were known in later times. The colonial and modern histories of these cultures are rich and complex, and proper subjects for at least two separate volumes. Where appropriate I have simply noted the primary modern descendants of the seventeenth-century cultures I describe.

Each of these cultures is discussed according to the drainage(s) it occupied and in terms of the four major cultural subsystems and 14-point outline discussed in Chapter 1 (Table 1.4, p. 18). This is an important point even though it may not be obvious in the narrative. The same 14-point outline is used repeatedly in subsequent chapters so that all the cultural systems discussed, both historic and prehistoric, can be compared in the same terms. I have deliberately left some cultural sketches incomplete in cases where I am discussing intermediate groups that share traits with others already discussed in detail, or where information is missing from the historic record. In all cases, readers interested in pursuing ethnological or ethnohistorical topics are referred to other sources, most notably the excellent summaries provided in Volume 15 of the Smithsonian Institution's new *Handbook of North American Indians*.

St. John Drainage

Four leagues farther on is a fine bay running up into the main land, at the extremity of which there are three islands and a rock, two of which are a league from the cape towards the west, and the other is at the mouth of the largest and deepest river we had yet seen, which we named the river St. John, because it was on this saint's day that we arrived there. By the savages it is called Ouygoudy. This river is dangerous, if one does not observe carefully certain points and rocks on the two sides. . . . We did not explore it farther up. But Ralleau, secretary of Sieur de Monts, went there some time after to see a savage named Secondon, chief of this river, who reported that it was beautiful, large, and extensive, with many meadows and fine trees, as oaks, beeches, walnut-trees, and also wild grape-vines. The inhabitants of the country go by this river to Tadoussac, on the great river St. Lawrence, making but a short portage on the journey [Samuel de Champlain 1604, cited in Grant 1907:38–39].

They have no beards, the men no more than the women, except some of the more robust and virile. They have often told me that at first we seemed to them very ugly with hair both upon our mouths and heads; but gradually they have become accustomed to it, and now we are beginning to look less deformed. You could not distinguish the young men from the girls, except in their way of wearing their belts. For the women are girdled both above and below the stomach, and are less nude than the men; also they are usually more ornamented with matachias, that is, with chains, gewgaws, and such finery after their fashion; by which you may know that such is the nature of the sex everywhere, fond of adornment. . . . Their food is whatever they can get from the chase and from fishing; for they do not till the soil at all. . . . In the month of February and until the middle of March, is the great hunt for beavers, otters, moose, bears (which are very good), and for the caribou, an animal half ass and half deer. If the weather then is favorable, they live in great abundance, and are as haughty as Princes and Kings; but if it is against them, they are greatly to be pitied, and often die of starvation. . . . In the middle of March, fish begin to spawn, and to come up from the sea into certain streams, often so abundantly that everything swarms with them. . . . From the month of May up to the middle of September, they are free from all anxiety about their food; for the cod are upon the coast, and all kinds of fish and shellfish. . . . In the middle of September [they] withdraw from the sea, beyond the reach of the tide, to the little rivers, where the eels spawn, of which they lay in a supply; they are good and fat. In October and November comes the second hunt for elks [moose] and beavers . . . [Pierre Biard 1616, cited in Thwaites 1959:Volume 3, 72–83].

Champlain and other French writers of the early years of the seventeenth century provide us with our earliest reliable accounts of the Indians of the St. John drainage. However, fragments of information from a variety of sources suggest that European fishermen had been in sporadic contact with these and other Indians of New England for almost a century prior to that time. Maps of the period show that the Portuguese were increasingly familiar with the Newfoundland coast and the Grand Banks in the early sixteenth century, and they may have engaged in some incidental trading with the Indians. However, codfishing was the primary enterprise, and the Portuguese, Spanish, and French all had plenty of cheap salt in which to pack their fish for the voyage home. They rarely established drying stations on land, and, unless they ran low on provisions, they had no good reason to land at all. The English were officially indifferent to the codfishing industry and Newfoundland during the first half of the sixteenth century, and English fishermen appear to have been not much more interested. However, by the last quarter of the century English fishermen were dominating the harbors of Newfoundland. The English and other northern Europeans did not have easy access to cheap salt, and consequently they established land stations for the purpose of drying their catches before returning home. Thus, the opportunity for trade with the Indians was at hand (Snow 1976c).

It seems likely that by the time Champlain and the other chroniclers of the early seventeenth century described them, the Indians of the St. John and other drainages had already had their lives altered by decades of sporadic contacts with Europeans. The primary commodity in this early trade relationship was the beaver pelt. The European fur market had changed dramatically through the middle decades of the sixteenth century. In 1532 an English yeoman might wear gray rabbit fur, but such a common pelt was unthinkable for a gentleman. However, as rare pelts became even rarer over the following 40 years, prices rose and gentlemanly standards declined. In the midst of this period, furriers found themselves increasingly occupied with the felting of sheared fur rather than the preparation of elegant bits of fur trim. Beaver was the preferred fur for felting, and beaver pelts were used almost exclusively for the manufacture of felt hats, which became the fashion rage in the court of Elizabeth I around 1560. By that time, the European beaver survived only in a few places in southern Europe. It was scarce everywhere on the continent by the end of the century. Therefore, the Portuguese, with adequate supplies of both salt and beaver, would not have been much interested in North American land bases for either fish drying or trading, whereas the English, having neither cheap salt nor home grown pelts, would have found both bases and trading attractive.

Thus, although the quotes from Champlain and Biard describe the Indians of the St. John drainage from the period before the horrible epidemics of the second decade of the seventeenth century, there is some reason to believe that Indian culture there had already been altered somewhat by contacts with northern Europeans. Indeed, Bruce Bourque (1973) has argued that data from late prehistoric coastal sites in northern New England indicate seasonal scheduling and settlement patterns different from those suggested by the early written sources. He sees this as a shift that is best explained by the emergence of a pattern of summer coastal trade with European vessels in the sixteenth century. Specifically, he sees archaeological evidence for late winter and early spring residence on the coast, contrasting with historical evidence for summer residence there. However, Bourque's hypothesis rests heavily on negative evidence, both archaeological and historical. The archaeological evidence indicates that the Indians were taking migratory fish and waterfowl on the coast in the spring, but the data do not rule out summer residence as well. Conversely, the historical sources indicate that the Indians were on the coast in the summer receiving European visitors, but Indian coastal encampments in the springtime cannot be ruled out simply because European sailors were smart enough not to sail there at that dangerous time of the year. The historical sources also indicate that most permanent Indian villages were located on salt water, usually protected locations along estuaries. The most likely settlement pattern is one that involved the dispersal of small bands from the villages into the upstream forests in the winter and to coastal encampments in the late spring and summer (Figure 2.2). In all cases, travel along the major streams in birchbark canoes was easy, and movement to temporary camps either upstream or downstream could not have been arduous. Bourque's suggestion remains an interesting unproven hypothesis. Unfortunately, although he is able to add to the archaeological data as a means to test it further, the historical sources remain few and incomplete, and it is unlikely that he will ever be able to test the hypothesis as fully as he would like. However, sectioning techniques for determining the season of death for mammal teeth found in archaeological sites may eventually clarify the seasonality of coastal residence (Bourque *et al.* 1978).

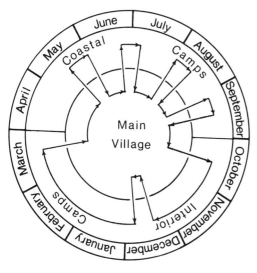

FIGURE 2.2. Hypothetical seasonal movements of a Maliseet family. The inner core represents the main village, the lower half of the outer ring is a representation of winter hunting camps in the interior, and the upper half of the outer ring indicates summer camps on the coast.

For now, we must conclude that the settlement system, and the pattern it generated at the time Biard observed it in 1616, was substantially the same as that which had prevailed just before the arrival of the first European fishing boats. The sixteenth century fur trade probably intensified the hunt for beaver during the winter months, when the Indians would have been in the forests carrying on subsistence hunting anyway. It probably also led to the introduction of copper kettles and other European trade items, but left the basic economic subsystem unaltered. Only after 1600 did the fur trade become large enough and regular enough to be made a central part of the Indians' adaptive strategy. Thus, community patterning in the St. John drainage throughout the sixteenth century was probably semipermanent sedentary, which is defined by Beardsley et al. (1956) as consisting of communities that can be identified as villages, which in turn establish themselves in successive locations, occupying each for a period of years. Most ethnographic examples of this kind of community patterning have economy subsystems that center on agriculture. Consequently, by focusing on horticulture, most tend to lie toward the focal end of Cleland's (1976) focal–diffuse continuum (see Table 1.3, p. 15). Compared to these, the Indians of the St. John drainage had a relatively diffuse adaptation that took them to winter hunting camps in the interior and summer fishing camps on the coast. The addition of the fur trade as a regular activity after 1600 made their adaptation more diffuse for a short time, but this gradually evolved into a focal adaptation with the fur trade at its center. There is some evidence that the ancestors of the Maliseet and the Micmac to the northeast had tried horticulture but found it unproductive this far north. Brasser (1978a:83) suggests that what little incentive there was to take up horticulture disappeared with the advent of the fur trade. His point may well apply for the Maliseet even though he makes it in connection with Maine Indians. I argue in the section on the Penobscot that in the case of Maine the fur trade actually lowered the risks inherent in horticulture there and in the long run encouraged its development.

Caribou, the animal that struck Biard as being half ass and half deer, was still an important game animal in 1600. Although they persist on the Gaspe Peninsula of Quebec, they disappeared in Nova Scotia and New Brunswick early in the twentieth century (Banfield 1974:388). It seems likely that they were still numerous in the upper St. John drainage in 1600 and that the Indians exploited them. Caribou are more gregarious than the solitary moose and often run in bands of 10–50 individuals, a difference that required different hunting tactics. While a few winter hunters might pursue a single moose through deep snow and make a kill when the animal bogged down, caribou could be ambushed in groups on known trails by larger hunting bands. We can infer that winter hunting bands were at least sometimes larger than would have been the case if moose were the only large game available (deer were probably not numerous).

Curiously, the early historic Indian settlements on the St. John and its tributaries may well have been more permanent than those of southern New England, even though they were probably abandoned for longer periods during the year while people moved off in family bands to interior or coastal camps. The horticulturalists of the Northeast practiced extensive rather than intensive farming techniques. There were no large domesticated animals and therefore no manure fertilizer, no plows, and no wagons to haul produce. Because they lacked the first two they had to seek land that could be tilled with simple hand tools, and they had to be prepared to move every decade or so when it became depleted. Lacking draft animals and wheeled transportation they could not make widespread use of fish as fertilizer, for the labor cost of getting it to the fields was simply too high in most areas. Thus, the only viable option for horticulturalists was a semipermanent settlement pattern: year-round occupation of a particular site for several years and then abandonment of the village and surrounding farmlands. Typically the village was moved only a few kilometers and stayed well within traditional drainage boundaries. This settlement pattern had serious consequences for the Indians of southern New England, who later had to compete with intensive farmers and permanent villages imported from Europe (Thomas 1976). The Indians of the St. John, however, could not afford to take a chance on horticulture, a focal adaptation that because of the shortness of the growing season entails considerable risk this far north. Not having any commitment to horticulture they had less need to move every few years, and their villages were probably more permanent than most semipermanent sedentary communities in southern New England. This may well help explain why they were later more successful in holding on to their traditional sites than were many of the communities of southern New England; with regard to village permanence they were clearly more like their European competitors.

Data from a variety of sources indicate that the permanent villages in northern New England ranged in size from a half-dozen houses up to 160 or more. The houses were typically bark-covered wigwams constructed on frames made of saplings bent to a dome shape. Figures from one early source indicate an average of eight people per house, which in the case of a large village could mean a total population easily exceeding 1000 (Snow 1978b). There is no mention of palisaded villages until later in the colonial period. Sites of this major type are distributed along main streams, often at protected locations on tidal estuaries. In addition to this site type there were the smaller winter camps in the interior and summer camps on the coast. Winter camps probably featured one or two houses. Summer camps may have been of about the same size, but because of the fair weather the houses would not have needed to have been as substantial, and may have been little more than windbreaks. Winter campsites can be found scattered along the shores of most ponds, lakes, and tributaries of the St. John; the summer campsites occur as shell middens along the coast. In both cases locations that catch the morning sun and are protected from prevailing winds were preferred.

The quote taken from Pierre Biard sums up most of the important food resources, their seasonality, and the seasonal movements of the Indians. Together with the information just presented on settlement and house types, they define the economic subsystem in the narrow sense that I am using it here. The social subsystem appears to have included small extended families that typically contained a monogamous nuclear family and perhaps a grand-parent or two. Certain men were powerful in what we (but not they) would regard as the separate areas of politics, personality, and sexual potency. Such men often had two or more wives, and the character of their household units was accordingly different from the norm.

Socially the settlement unit can be best described as tribal, a set of bands in which one or two bands and therefore their male leaders were preemi-nent. As Champlain observed, one village leader was generally recognized as spokesman for all the Indians of the drainage. Typically such a man would emerge from a village and family that were traditionally prominent to play the role of sagamore for life. There would have been formalities of ratifica-tion but no democratic election in the modern sense. The strength of the man's personality and his family power base would have been sufficient to command the respect of other leading men in the drainage, but not sufficient to allow him to impose unpopular measures on them. Thus, the powers of sagamores, village chiefs, and even family band leaders were not so much inherent in their offices as in their personal charisma. Dissatisfied people could and did change band affiliation and village residence, or even leave the drainage altogether.

The evidence indicates that the Indians of the St. John had a somewhat more elaborate social organization than that of the northern Algonquians, which Steward (1955) describes as being based on composite bands. Such a loose organization was the result of a dependence on migration and low population density. With their nearly permanent villages, regular seasonal scheduling, and relatively dense population, the Indians of the St. John could afford something more elaborate. Here, a technical use of tribe is appropri-ate. It is not clear from the sources whether the tribal society they did have was *lineal* or *cognatic* in the terms used by Service (1912:120–139). Lineal tribes are those that have basic rules of unilocal residence and reckon descent through lineal groups such as lineages. Cognatic tribes are those in which membership is based on family connections through either the father's or the mother's side, or perhaps even through one's spouse. As we shall see, the Mohawk and other Iroquois nations of New York were quite clearly a confederation of lineal tribes. Mohawk descent and residence were reckoned strictly along female lines with the resulting villages of long houses, each house containing closely related females and their spouses. The Indians of the St. John did not reside in long houses, and the size of the typical household unit suggests that there was no strong lineal principle. This, plus the apparent ability of disaffected people to shift family band residence, suggests that in 1600 the St. John drainage contained a multi-village cognate tribe.

I have argued elsewhere that the tendency for the Indians of northern New England to have family totems and traditional family hunting territories in the interior during the colonial period might well indicate that clans were beginning to develop (Snow 1968a). However, the issue is badly confused by the depopulation brought on by colonial wars and epidemics and the advent of the fur trade. There is simply no strong evidence to indicate that clans or anything like them functioned importantly in residence or descent determination. As we shall see, the archaeological evidence from Iroquois country suggests that there was a considerable amount of village nucleation in late prehistoric times there, with the result that previously separate villages joined to form larger communities, and clans emerged as social units within them. There is no evidence for such village nucleation before 1615 in northern New England, which was outside the zone of widespread warfare and long-distance trading that appears to have affected the Iroquois so deeply.

The technological subsystem involved the use of a wide range of artifact types, only a few of which would have been preserved archaeologically. Stone artifact types included projectile points, knives, scrapers, and ground-stone adzes. The points were of the small triangular Madison type, which was popular throughout New England and many other parts of the Eastern Woodlands at the time of first European contact. Adzes were smaller and less numerous than they had been in earlier prehistoric periods, probably because of the dominance of the birchbark (or occasionally moose-hide) canoe in later centuries throughout northern New England. Ceramic vessels with conical bases and various forms of plastic decoration were used in the sixteenth century as they had been for many centuries previously, but they were quickly replaced by copper trade kettles. Lumps of native copper had long been popular for the production of breastplates and other adornments, and there are a few examples of its use in finished prehistoric tools. The introduction of copper kettles vastly increased the supply of this preferred metal, and worn-out pots became the raw material for points, knives, breastplates, and other things of native manufacture in the colonial period. Traditional raw materials included local cherts and other stone for the lithic artifacts, while ceramic vessels were made from a blue marine clay, the origin of which is mentioned in the next chapter.

Late spring and summer residence on the coast involved the utilization of shellfish, and the resulting middens still lie like overgrown snowbanks around productive tidal flats. Most of the shellfish remains are the valves of the common clam (*Mya arenaria*). When compared to the bones of game animals, clam shells are bulky relative to the amount of meat they represent and preserve unusually well. This has led some investigators to overestimate the importance of shellfish in the aboriginal diet (Newman 1974; Snow 1974). Bourque (1973) has shown that summer subsistence on the Maine coast was quite diffuse, as it would have to have been given the limited nutritional and caloric values of even the most productive clam flats. The real importance of clam gathering to the archaeologist is not its role in early historic subsistence, but rather its central role in preserving artifacts that would have otherwise perished. Shell middens neutralize the normal soil acidity that destroys bone, antler, fiber, and wood, with the result that many otherwise unknown artifact types are preserved archaeologically. Thus, we know that the Indians used nets, bone hooks, points, harpoons and leisters of bone, wood, and fiber; beavertooth cutting tools with bone or antler handles; and combs, bodkins, and awls made from a variety of these materials. Better yet, we know this from both archaeological and written sources.

Pierre Biard offers us an unusually detailed account of mortuary practices in 1616:

They swathe the body and tie it up in skins; not lengthwise, but with the knees against the stomach and the head on the knees, as we are in our mother's womb. Afterwards they put it in the grave which has been made very deep, not upon the back or lying down as we do, but sitting. . . . When the body is placed, as it does not come up even with the ground on account of the depth of the grave, they arch the grave over with sticks, so that the earth will not fall back into it, and thus they cover up the tomb. . . . If it is a man, they place there as a sign and emblem, his bow, arrows, and shield; if a woman, spoons, *matachias* or jewels, ornaments, etc. I have nearly forgotten the most beautiful part of all; it is that they bury with the dead man all that he owns, such as his bag, his arrows, his skins, and all his other articles and baggage, even his dogs if they have not been eaten. Moreover, the survivors add to these a number of other such offerings, as tokens of friendship [cited in Thwaites 1959:Volume 3, 128–131].

Burial programs like this one would produce single burials or cemetery clusters archaeologically. The burials would be flexed, usually seated, and would be accompanied by grave goods. Analysis of grave goods by burial lot would probably show significant differences on the basis of age and sex, and probably some differences according to the individual's status in the community. A sagamore would probably have had more elegant personal possessions than others, and tokens of friendship would have been both more numerous and more elegant than most grave offerings.

In the preceding paragraphs I have covered all of the 14 specific categories I previously designated to describe economic, social, technological, and religious subsystems. The result has been a very brief ethnographic sketch of the St. John drainage for the archaeologist, one that admittedly leaves out many points ethnologists and ethnohistorians might like to see included. The purpose, however, has been to provide a historic baseline that is directly comparable to prehistoric cultures that are known only archaeologically. Persons wishing to have a fuller view of early ethnohistory in the St. John drainage and a clearer understanding of how the Indians of 1600 gradually became the modern Maliseet should see Erikson (1978) in Volume 15 of the new *Handbook of North American Indians*.

St. Croix Drainage   We proceeded to a river on the main land called the river of the Etechemins [Passamaquoddy], a tribe of savages so called in their country. We passed by so many islands that we could not ascertain their number, which were very fine.

. . . There are many good places capable of containing any number of vessels, and abounding in fish in the season, such as codfish, salmon, bass, herring, halibut, and other kinds of great numbers. . . . In May and June, so great a number of herring and bass are caught there that vessels could be loaded with them. The soil is of the finest sort, and there are fifteen or twenty acres of cleared land, where Sieur de Monts had some wheat sown, which flourished finely. The savages come here sometimes five or six weeks during the fishing season. All the rest of the country consists of very dense forests. If the land were cleared up, grain would flourish excellently [Samuel de Champlain 1604, cited in Grant 1907:39–41].

Or so it seemed at the time. At 45° north latitude the mouth of the St. Croix is no farther north than Bordeaux, France, and Champlain expected a long summer and a mild winter. He got neither. Except on the narrowest fringe of coastline there are fewer than 150 freeze-free days per year here, and the winters are both cold and long. The Indians of this drainage were closely related to the people of the St. John. Near the end of the colonial period the residents of the drainage, by this time called Passamaquoddy, sided with the colonists and the other Indians of Maine. The political split with the Maliseet reinforced the presumed ethnic distinctiveness of the two, but they continue to share a language and we can presume that they were culturally quite similar in 1600.

If we were to examine each of the 14 descriptive categories for the culture of the St. Croix in 1600, we would find few significant differences between them and those already discussed for the St. John (Figure 2.3). Perhaps the most important point of contrast would be the somewhat greater reliance on marine resources by the Indians of the St. Croix. As can be seen in Figure 2.1, these Indians did not have the easy access to the vast interior enjoyed by the Indians of the St. John and Penobscot rivers. Consequently there is some evidence that they shared a greater dependence on the sea with the Micmac of Nova Scotia. In the last century and a half, the Passamaquoddy have built and used sea-going birchbark canoes for fishing and even for sea hunting. Porpoise, which can be hunted with a harpoon, is still a favored meat among the Passamaquoddy. This is not to say that the Indians of the St. Croix did not find it necessary to hunt in small bands during the winter. Champlain states clearly that they did. There were portage connections linking the St. Croix with both the St. John and the Penobscot Indians, and we can assume that connections with their kin on the St. John would have facilitated some trade as well. Thus, although we lack clear evidence, it is possible that the ancestral Maliseet with their vast inland resources and the early Passamaquoddy with their marine resources may have found it mutually advantageous to exchange food products.

Penobscot Drainage

The Pentegoet [Penobscot] is a very beautiful river, and may be compared to the Garonne in France. . . . When we had advanced three leagues or more into the current of the river we encountered another beautiful river called Chiboctous [Bagaduce], which comes from the northeast to discharge its waters into the great Pentegoet. At the confluence of these two rivers there was the finest assemblage of Savages that I have yet seen. There were 80 canoes and a boat, 18 wigwams and

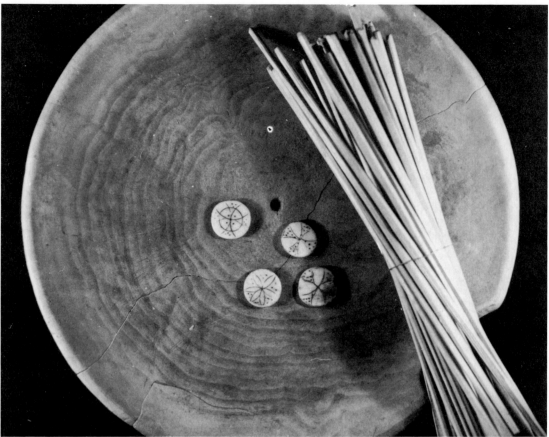

FIGURE 2.3. Top, a Passamaquoddy game consisting of a wooden bowl, bone disks decorated on one side only, and stick counters (on loan to the University of Maine Anthropology Museum from the Peabody Museum of Archaeology and Ethnology, Cambridge, Mass.). Bottom, prehistoric gaming stones, 59 and 68 cm in diameter (Bronson Museum, Attleboro, Mass.).

about 300 people. The most prominent Sagamore was called Betsabes [Bashabes], a man of great discretion and prudence; and I confess we often see in these Savages natural and graceful qualities which will make anyone but a shameless person blush, when they compare them to the greater part of the French who come over here [Pierre Biard 1616, cited in Thwaites 1959:Volume 2, 46–49].

I directed our interpreter to say to our savages that they should cause Bessabez [Bashabes], Cabahis, and their companions to understand that Sieur de Monts had sent me to them to see them, and also their country, and that he desired to preserve friendship with them and to reconcile them with their enemies, the Souriquois [Micmac] and Canadians, and moreover that he desired to inhabit their country and show them how to cultivate it, in order that they might not continue to lead so miserable a life as they were doing, and some other words on the same subject. This our savages interpreted to them, at which they signified their great satisfaction, saying that no greater good could come to them than to have our friendship, and that they desired to live in peace with their enemies, and that we should dwell in their land, in order that they might in future more than ever before engage in hunting beavers, and give us a part of them in return for our providing them with things which they wanted [Samuel de Champlain 1604, cited in Grant 1907: 49–50].

Farther east Champlain had adopted a word the Indians used for themselves and called them "Etechemin." He later extended the term to include most of the Indians of Maine as well, but this seems to have been only a convenience, for he lumped all of the Indians of New England and the Maritimes under three broad headings: Almouchiquois, Etechemin, and Souriquois. The first included all the Indians of southeastern New England and the last all those of what is now Nova Scotia. In the twentieth century "Etchimin" (spelled variously) has sometimes been used as a label for the Maliseet and Passamaquoddy, the modern Indians of the St. John and St. Croix drainages, respectively. This has led to some confusion, most notably the conclusion by some that ancestors of the Maliseet–Passamaquoddy inhabited most of the drainages of both Maine and New Brunswick when Champlain explored their coastlines in 1604. This, of course, would require a major emigration of Etchimin from Maine in the first decades of the seventeenth century, and a major immigration of the ancestors of modern Maine Indians shortly thereafter. There is no evidence for such a major population replacement in Maine except for the remarks of Champlain and the few authors that followed his lead, and we must conclude that he was simply generalizing in his use of the term "Etechemin" (Snow 1976d).

Giovanni da Verrazzano sailed eastward along the Maine coast in 1524, and for us the real significance of his voyage is that a map that resulted identifies the Penobscot River as "Oranbega." This term, which is clearly a native word identifying the lower portion of the Penobscot River, is the only native name on the map. The inclusion of this single native term is especially strange in light of the fact that it was here where Verrazzano had greatest difficulty contacting the Indians. In fact, he probably never spoke to them at all. Samuel Morison (1971:489) and other historians think that Verrazzano or his cartographer brother might have had access to Portuguese sources before the map was complete in 1529. In this way, the native name could have found its way onto the map through Fagundes or some other Portuguese explorer.

Whatever the specific source of the place name, the Verrazzano map gave rise to the myth of Norumbega. The existence of a country and even a city by that name was spread through Europe by imaginative explorers and their advocates. Reports and descriptions of the day were often heavily embroidered with fantasy, but the art reached a high point with the narrative of David Ingram. Ingram was put ashore on the Mexican Gulf coast in 1568. He eventually made his way on foot through Maine and was finally picked up at the mouth of the St. John River in New Brunswick by a French ship. Or at least so he said. While it is true that the disastrous Hawkins expedition marooned about 100 men on the Gulf coast, Hawkins would have us believe that he then walked at least 5500 km. It is more likely that he was picked up by the French ship much farther south than he claimed, but he found that his stories were a source of profit for him in England. Hakluyt took him seriously at first, but eventually like many others dismissed him as a liar (Hakluyt 1965:557–562; Quinn and Dunbabin 1966). Ingram talked of Norumbega and invented stories of great cities of gold, whose inhabitants were festooned with riches. There are shreds of truth in what Ingram said, such as his quaint description of a moose, but most of his story was fantasy.

There is a later source that is full of information on the Indians of several Maine river drainages. The source is extraordinary, for the information contained within it is unusually detailed and apparently trustworthy. To understand the source and its origins, we return to the movements of European explorers in the first decade of the seventeenth century. After losing nearly half of their party of 79 during the winter, Champlain and De Monts explored the coast westward again in 1605. They went almost directly to the Kennebec River, stopping at what is now Wiscasset Harbor to meet with the leader of the Sheepscot. They attempted to meet with other local sagamores as well, not always successfully, but Champlain was able to collect a list of names of local leaders. They met some of these on the way back eastward to Port Royal. At one of their stops they were told of another ship in the vicinity, an English one commanded by a man named Waymouth. The Indians were bitter because five of their men had been taken and presumably killed by the English. The French avoided the English ship, but stopped at St. Croix Island to salvage what they could before heading for Port Royal.

The Waymouth expedition had been organized to meet the challenge of French exploration in North America and establish an English presence there. Waymouth set sail from the Thames in March and was off the coast of southern New England by the middle of May. He sailed eastward, and his first contact with Indians occurred somewhere around the mouth of St.

George's River, just west of Penobscot Bay. He was initially asked to leave, but the mood quickly changed when he produced metal knives, combs, and mirrors. Suspicion continued on both sides, however, and Waymouth eventually decided that a proposed trading convention was in fact a trap. Waymouth's mind became set against them, and, although canoeloads of Indians still came to the ship as before, he no longer felt the need to treat them civilly. Instead, his thoughts turned to how best to capture a few to take back to England. Because they had no reason to expect it, five were captured without much difficulty. Together with their two canoes and personal belongings, the five were stowed on board the ship for the return voyage (Rosier 1905).

Taking the Abenaki view, I suppose that Waymouth's five captives could be credited with the discovery of England. The highest ranking of the five, Nahanada, returned to Maine with Martin Pring the following year. Skidwarres returned with Gilbert and Popham 2 years later, by which time Nahanada had become a local sagamore. Two others, Assacomoit and Manida, were with Chalons on their way back to Maine in 1606, but were captured by the Spanish and held as slaves. Later, Assacomoit was rescued by the English, and eventually he made his way into the household of Ferdinando Gorges.

The five captives, probably Assacomoit in particular, appear to have been the source for the most important document on the Abenaki for the period. In 1625, Samuel Purchas published a description of what he called the country of "Mawooshen." Gorges (1890:76) calls the same place "Moasham." Both references are to the area later clearly identified as belonging to the Eastern Abenaki. The Purchas list in particular is quite explicit. He defines the area in terms of a series of river drainages extending from Mount Desert Island on the east to the upper portion of the Saco River on the west.

Purchas gives us 10 terms that lead us to the modern names of 11 rivers (Table 2.3). These include the Union, Penobscot, Orland, Bagaduce, St. Georges (?), Damariscotta, Sheepscot, Kennebec, Androscoggin, Presumpscot, and Saco (Snow 1976d).

Purchas's tenth and last river is given as the "Shawakotoc." It is the westernmost in his list. The term is clearly cognate with other early names for the now-shortened Saco River (Eckstorm 1941:172–173). This leaves the ninth in Purchas's list, the "Ashamabaga," lying between the Saco and the Androscoggin. The Ashamabaga is therefore almost certainly the modern Presumpscot River. The Saco was probably not a regular part of Eastern Abenaki territory despite its inclusion on Purchas's list. Purchas provides figures that suggest a population of about 10,000 for 17 villages and a projected total of 11,900 for all 21. Purchas's total of 1238 houses gives us a figure of just under 8 persons per house.

John Smith (Arber and Bradley 1910:192–193) gives us nine place-names for 1614, of which seven can be found on Purchas's list. Champlain (Grant 1907:44–77) mentions five sagamores, two of which fill blanks in Purchas's list. One of those on both lists is Bashabes, who appears to have been first among about two dozen Eastern Abenaki leaders. This appears to have been a case of a strong man assuming leadership of a confederacy of Eastern Abenaki groups, not an example of a more highly structured chiefdom. Purchas's brief description lists Bashabes as "chiefe Lord," whereas other leaders are listed simply as "Sagamo" or "Lord." Some of the latter are specifically noted as being subjects of Bashabes. Rosier (1905:124) says that the Indians "often would (by pointing to one part of the maine Eastward) signe unto us, that their Bashabes (that is, their King) had great plenty of Furres, and much Tabacco."

As we shall see, there was a west-to-east transition from horticultural communities on the Merrimack, through communities on the Androscoggin and Kennebec where there was a tentative commitment to horticulture, to the nonhorticultural communities of the Penobscot. This transition was also marked by house forms, which tended to be larger communal structures to the west and single family dwellings to the east, and by the social units that occupied them. The primary constraint on the spread of horticulture appears to have been the shorter growing season in the eastern drainages. Later in the seventeenth century reduction of the native population coupled with the development of a regular fur trade allowed the Indians of the Penobscot to adopt horticulture even with all its risks of failure. The fur trade provided them with access to food from southern New England and the means to pay for it. Therefore, the fur trade became not just a means for the Indians to enter a larger economic system and acquire imported manufactured goods, but was also a hedge against crop failure. In 1600 they did not yet have that reliable hedge and could not risk adopting horticulture as some of their relatives to the west had done (Snow 1976d). As quoted at the beginning of this section, in 1604 Champlain noted that the Indians "desired to live in peace with their enemies, and that we should dwell in their land, in order that they might in future more than ever before engage in hunting beavers, and give us a part of them in return for our providing them with things which they wanted [Grant 1907:49–50]." The Indians understood their predicament and knew what had to be done to change it.

There are additional sources and additional complexities to confuse the early history of Maine Indians, and I have discussed them at greater length elsewhere (Snow 1978b). What is important here is that Purchas and the other early sources combine to give us demographic data that are simply not available for other parts of our region. Indeed, such data are rare for any part of North America during the decades prior to American independence. There were at least 8 permanent towns in the Penobscot drainage and adjacent coastal drainages in 1605. Purchas's figures indicate an average town size of 48 houses and an average adult male population of 130. Assuming that adult men accounted for 30% of the population, the average town population would have been 433, or about 9 to a house. The largest town, which was located on the present site of Bangor and appears to have been a seat of regional leadership, had 60 houses and 250 adult men, for a projected total population of 833. The actual figure might have been a bit smaller, but it remains clear that the Indians of the Penobscot enjoyed life in relatively large villages. The settlement pattern was therefore similar to that on the St. John, semipermanent sedentary with winter camps in the interior and summer camps on the coast. These villages were similarly nonhorticultural in 1605 and were probably therefore also somewhat more permanent than those of southern New England.

House types, food resources, and seasonal movements were also very similar to those we have seen for the St. John. Later houses in the Penobscot drainage combined European log walls with bark roofs, and later villages were palisaded, but there is little to suggest that the houses of 1605 were anything other than large bark wigwams (Figure 2.4). Either conical or domed bark shelters may have been used at temporary camps.

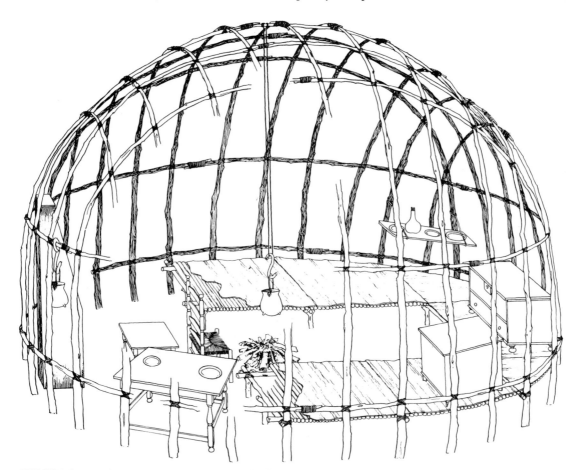

FIGURE 2.4. A graphic reconstruction of a New England wigwam based on early drawings and other archaeological and documentary evidence (Sturtevant 1975:439).

Purchas's figures indicate an average household unit of about 9 people. This in turn suggests a small extended family, the actual makeup of which varied from house to house. One household might have contained a senior man, his wife, and their children. Another might have contained two brothers, their wives and small children, and a grandparent or two. The village was made up of a few dozen such units, one per house, and it seems likely that village leaders were drawn from a traditionally strong family. Some villages had two leaders, perhaps for specific historical reasons we shall never know, and in the case of one village the local leader was held as first among equals for the entire drainage. In fact the leadership of Bashabes extended from his village at modern Bangor to Mount Desert Island on the east to the Saco drainage on the west. As in the St. John drainage, the evidence suggests that the Penobscot drainage contained a multi-village cognate tribe and that it was loosely confederated with related cognate tribes in the river drainages of western Maine in 1605. This confederation lasted until the death of Bashabes at the hands of the Micmac in 1615 and the epidemics that struck at about the same time. Thousands died in the first waves of disease. Biard estimates the total population for the Penobscot, Kennebec, Androscoggin, and intervening drainages at only 3000 in 1616 (Thwaites 1959:Volume 3, 111). This and some other evidence suggests a 70% mortality rate between 1615 and 1618.

The technological subsystem of the Penobscot was similar to that of the Indians on the St. John. Hooks, leisters, purse nets, and wiers were used to take migratory fish such as alewife, salmon, shad, eel, and smelt (Figure 8.13, p. 338). Salmon and eel were taken both as they swam upstream and as they returned to the sea. Some fish, especially sturgeon, were taken with harpoons. Most such equipment was made of wood, bone, and fiber. Simple digging sticks served to harvest the ground nut (*Apios apios*) and were also used in tentative experiments with horticulture (Figure 2.5).

Winter required the use of snowshoes and toboggans. Hunters usually carried bows and arrows, long lances, and knives. Skin bags were used to carry game and fire-making kits of iron pyrite and chert nodules. Their canoes, which were made of the bark of the white (not gray) birch, were usually large enough to hold families of five or six, plus dogs and belongings. Bark was used to make containers as well. Containers, spoons, and trays were also made of leather, rush, and wood burls; sandals were sometimes made of rush (Figure 2.6). Widemouthed pottery vessels with thick walls, shell tempering, and cord impressed decoration were also made, but were soon replaced by European pots of metal. The ash splint basketry for which the Penobscot and others are well known today was introduced later in the colonial period by Swedes on the Delaware River and was therefore not part of the A.D. 1600 inventory (Brasser 1974). Smoking pipes were made of both clay and stone.

Like most other Algonquian speakers living in northern areas, the Penobscot carried "crooked knives." This tool may have originally been a beaver

FIGURE 2.5. Penobscot cornhusk dolls from the University of Maine Anthropology Museum. Such dolls must postdate the introduction of horticulture into the Penobscot drainage.

incisor hafted into a bone, antler, or wooden handle. Alternatively, it may have been introduced by the Europeans. In either case it had a metal blade by A.D. 1610, a curved blade similar to that of a farrier's knife.

The most striking native raw material is a distinctive rock of volcanic origin called Kineo felsite. Artifacts made from this material are found all over Maine. Major quarry sources occur in the vicinity of Moosehead Lake in the upper Kennebec drainage, an area that connects to a major stream in the Penobscot drainage by way of an easy mile-long portage. Kineo felsite was a popular raw material even though it is difficult to work, and its distribution outside of Maine could be used to define the extent of prehistoric trade connections. The Indians of the Penobscot also used various cherts, including a distinctive red chert from somewhere in the upper reaches of the Penobscot

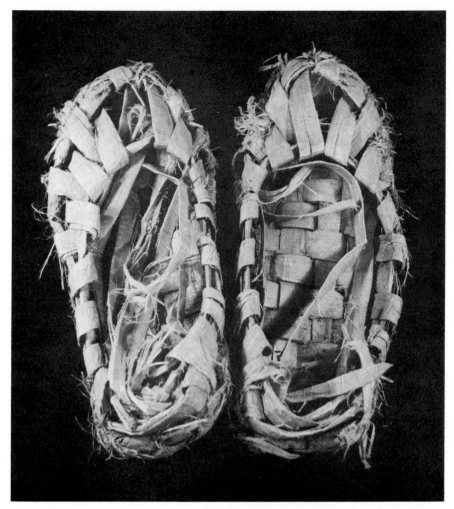

FIGURE 2.6. Woven rush sandals found in the Alton Bog north of Old Town, Maine. Each measures 29 cm long. (University of Maine Anthropology Museum.)

drainage. Cherts, however, are less easily identified as to their origin than Kineo felsite. Like quartz and quartzite, they will probably continue to frustrate our efforts to pin down quarry sources. The situation is made even more difficult by the fact that any of these raw lithic materials can occur as boulders in glacial deposits far from their bedrock sources.

Mortuary site types and burial programs were closely similar to those already described for the St. John drainage. A dying man might distribute some of his belongings to relatives, but the bulk of his possessions were buried with him. Readers wishing to examine the ethnology of the Penobscot and the Indians of western Maine should consult the Eastern Abenaki chapter in Volume 15 of the *Handbook of North American Indians* (Snow 1978b).

We found a high country full of very dense forests, composed of pines, cypresses, and similar trees which grow in cold regions. The people were quite different from the others, for while the previous ones had been courteous in manner, these were full of crudity and vices, and were so barbarous that we could never make any communication with them, however many signs we made to them. They were clothed in skins of bear, lynx, sea-wolf and other animals. As far as we could judge from several visits to their houses, we think they live on game, fish, and several fruits which are a species of root which the earth produces itself [groundnut]. They have no pulse, and we saw no sign of cultivation, nor would the land be suitable for producing any fruit or grain on account of its sterility. If we wanted to trade with them for some of their things, they would come to the seashore on some rocks where the breakers were most violent, while we remained in the little boat, and they sent us what they wanted to give on a rope, continually shouting to us not to approach the land; they gave us the barter quickly, and would take in exchange only knives, hooks for fishing, and sharp metal. We found no courtesy in them, and when we had nothing more to exchange and left them, the men made all the signs of scorn and shame that any brute creature would make. Against their wishes, we penetrated two or three leagues inland with 25 armed men, and when we disembarked on the shore, they shot at us with their bows and uttered loud cries before fleeing into the woods. We did not find anything of great value in this land, except for the vast forests and some hills which could contain some metal: for we saw many natives with "paternostri" beads of copper in their ears [Giovanni da Verrazzano 1524, cited in Wroth 1970:140–141].

Vp this Riuer [at Sagadahock], where was the Westerne plantation, are *Aumuckcawgen*, *Kinnebeck*, and diuers others; where there is planted some corne fields. Along this Riuer 40 to 50 miles, I saw nothing but great high cliffes of barren Rocks, ouergrowne with wood: but where the Saluages dwelt, there the ground is exceeding fat and fertill [John Smith 1614, cited in Arber and Bradley 1910:203].

There are a great many small oaks, and very little arable land. Fish abound here, as in the other rivers which I have mentioned. The people live like those in the neighborhood of our settlement [St. Croix Island]; and they told us that the savages, who plant the Indian corn, dwelt very far in the interior, and that they had given up planting it on the coasts on account of the war they had with others, who came and took it away [Samuel de Champlain 1605, cited in Grant 1907:60].

The Indians of the Androscoggin River are known best to history as the Arosaguntacook. The river started out with the same name, but its name was later changed in honor of the colonial governor Edmund Andros (1637–1714). The Indians of the Kennebec are best thought of under that name even though the later importance of the village of Norridgewock led to the more frequent use of that name in late colonial documents. Wawenoc Indians, who appear in many later documents, were simply residents of the coastal drainages between the Kennebec and Penobscot that I have chosen to lump with the Kennebec.

The first clear account of these people was written by Verrazzano in 1524, but there is little in it that we could not otherwise guess. Verrazzano received a warm welcome in southern New England, but his reception on the coast of Maine was much less gratifying. Perhaps because they had some prior experience with Europeans, the Indians refused to meet directly with him.

From the shore they shouted what must have been derisive comments, laughed, and made obscene gestures. They could be induced to trade only by means of a rope raised and lowered from a cliff to a waiting boat. Verrazzano peevishly called the place the "land of bad people" (Wroth 1970:140–141). No one is sure where Verrazzano landed, but Morison (1971:308) suggests that it was Bald Head near the mouth of the Kennebec.

Shamanism was an important institution here and is presumed to have been as important elsewhere in northern New England. In this part of our area at least shamanistic power was probably seen as just another dimension of the personal charisma and sexual potency that characterized Maliseet and other northern sagamores. A petroglyph site on the shore of the Kennebec River near the village of Solon is an archaeological expression of this form of shamanism. Petroglyph sites are rare in New England, and this is one of only a few at which the glyphs are numerous and well preserved. The glyphs (Figure 2.7) fall into a small number of categories. There are houses, canoes containing human figures, birds, phallic males, squatting females, phalli, and vulvas scattered among less obvious glyphs. A similar but much larger set of petroglyphs near Peterborough, Ontario, has been described by Joan and Romas Vastokas (1973). Their interpretation is very similar to my own (Snow 1976b). In both instances we appear to have the symbols of shamanistic power. The easy translation between political power, sexual potency, and social status and these technological expressions may defy categorization by a Western mind, but fits well with the local ideological subsystem as we currently understand it to have been.

The Indians of these two drainages were by 1605 part of the confederacy we call Eastern Abenaki. The leader of the confederacy was Bashabes, who lived in a principal village on the Penobscot. According to Purchas (1625), there were 7 villages on the Androscoggin and Kennebec and 6 more on the coastal Damariscotta and Sheepscot rivers just to the east. The 13 villages averaged 77 houses each, with an average adult male population of 170. Both figures are higher than those from the Penobscot drainage. Moreover, there is a tendency for Purchas's figures from western Maine to suggest a larger number of people per house than was the case for the Penobscot. One village on the Androscoggin had a population of 1333 based on Purchas's figure of 400 adult men, yet the same village had only 60 houses. This yields an average of 22 people per house, a figure that suggests that elongated wigwams resembling Iroquois longhouses may have spread from southern New England into western Maine by 1605. As we shall see, the Iroquois and those heavily influenced by them had lineal tribal societies in which residence and descent were determined by lineal groups such as lineages and clans. It may be that, unlike their relatives to the east, at least one community of Indians on the Androscoggin had adopted some of these principles. In this case, each elongated house would have contained one to as many as four or five nuclear families bound together by kin ties. Like the Western Abenaki and groups in southern New England, these would probably have been patrilineal kin groups if they existed at all.

Thus, the economic subsystem on the Kennebec and Androscoggin was probably quite similar to that of the Penobscot. Settlement units were somewhat larger and household units may well have been both larger and more elaborately developed along patrilineal lines. While we can guess that such relatively elaborate social institutions would have produced other more elaborate institutions and activities within these communities, we have no basis upon which to infer what they might have been.

Both the technological and the religious subsystems were quite similar to those we have already seen in the Penobscot drainage. This is complicated somewhat by the possibility that horticulture had made an appearance here, but it had been abandoned again by 1605. This part of New England is agriculturally marginal even today. The risks are high and it seems likely that experimentation with horticulture here would have been tentative at best and easily abandoned in favor of tried and true hunting and gathering practices when times got hard.

Both the Champlain and Smith quotes seem to provide clear evidence that horticulture was being practiced along the upper course of the Androscoggin and Kennebec Rivers. Smith mentions two specific villages, Aumuckcawgen and Kennebec. These would appear to be Amereangan and Kenebeke on the Purchas list, places that I identify with modern Lisbon Falls and Augusta (Snow 1976d). People living in these and other villages away from the coast had direct access to their Western Abenaki relatives in the Merrimack drainage via interior water routes and portages. The Western Abenaki communities to the west were certainly horticultural, and the Eastern Abenaki communities in the Penobscot drainage were not. Thus, the Androscoggin and Kennebec drainages were a zone of transition in both time and space, where horticulture and its social consequences were making tentative inroads during the first two decades of the seventeenth century.

Champlain mentions raids by other Indians (probably Micmac) that discouraged horticulture along the coast. It is doubtful that such raids would have had such an effect in southern New England where the commitment to and the productivity of horticulture were greater. Conversely, it is doubtful that horticulture would have been risked at this time in the Penobscot drainage even if the pressure of Micmac raiding were absent.

All of the Indians of these two drainages and the adjacent Penobscot and Presumpscot drainages are usually lumped for convenience under the heading Eastern Abenaki (Snow 1978b). Those of the upper Saco and Merrimack drainages are usually called Western Abenaki (Day 1978). In fact we know little of the languages of this period, and it may well be that Eastern Abenaki and Western Abenaki were not real speech communities in 1600. Indeed it seems plausible that each river drainage contained its own speech community, and that each was most similar to its neighbor(s). I would hypothesize that there was considerable mutual intelligibility overall with the greatest

FIGURE 2.7. Petroglyphs near Solon, Maine. The sexual content of many of the glyphs probably represents the close linkage of personal power, charisma, status, and shamanism in the ideological subsystem of the Eastern Abenaki.

difference being between the speech community in the Merrimack drainage and that of the Penobscot. The dialect(s) of the Androscoggin and Kennebec were therefore intermediate. Thus, the convenient distinction between Eastern and Western Abenaki rests not so much on linguistic, cultural, or economic principles as on the evidence from Purchas (1625). The Eastern Abenaki consisted of those communities that were within the confederacy headed by Bashabes in 1605. The Western Abenaki were simply those Abenaki that were not part of that confederacy.

As a final note on the continuum of change from west to east through this area, there is the matter of upstream–downstream contrasts within river drainages. By 1600 such contrasts were well developed in the southern New England drainages, largely because lower (and also more southerly) portions of those drainages would support horticulture, whereas upper reaches would not. The contrast was heightened by a tendency for Indians of one drainage to shift eastward into the lower portion of the adjacent drainage when the opportunity presented itself. As we shall see, this happened on the lower

Hudson as well as on the lower Merrimack and Saco. In all three cases we have evidence of migration from adjacent drainages to the west by people carrying horticultural technology and the knowledge needed to apply it. To the east the upstream–downstream dichotomy was more subtle. In the Androscoggin–Kennebec area it emerged with the differential adoption and retention of horticulture. On the Penobscot it was not visible at all except for the social and subdialect division between a moiety of upstream families and another composed of downstream families, a division that shows up in nineteenth-century documents.

Presumpscot Drainage

The waters are most pure, proceeding from the intrailes of rocky Mountaines. The Herbs and Fruits are of many sorts and kinds, as Alkermes, Currans, Mulberies, Vines, Respises, Gooseberies, Plums, Wall-nuts, Chesse-nuts, Small-nuts, Pumpions, Gourds, Strawberies, Beanes, Pease, and Maize; a kinde or two of Flax, wherewith they make Nets, Lines, and Ropes, both small and great, very strong for their quantities. Oake is the chiefe wood, of which there is great difference, in regard of the soyle where it groweth, Firre, Pine, Wall-nut, Chesse-nut, Birtch, Ash, Elme, Cipris, Cedar, Mulbery, Plum tree, Hazell, Saxefras, and many other sorts. Eagles, Grips, diuers sorts of Hawkes, Craines, Geese, Brants, Cormorants, Ducks, Cranes, Swannes, Sheldrakes, Teale, Meawes, Gulls, Turkies, Diue-doppers, and many other sorts whose names I know not. Whales, Grompus, Porkpisces, Turbut, Sturgion, Cod, Hake, Haddocke, Cole, Cuske or small Ling, Sharke, Mackarell, Herring, Mullit, Base, Pinnacks, Cunners, Pearch, Eeles, Crabs, Lobsters, Mustels, Wilks, Oisters, Clamps, Periwinkels, and diuers others, etc. Moos, a beast bigger than a Stag, Deare red and fallow, Beuers, Wolues, Foxes both blacke and other, Aroughcunds, wilde Cats, Beares, Otters, Martins, Fitches, Musquassus, and diuers other sorts of Vermin whose names I know not [John Smith 1614, cited in Arber and Bradley 1910:721].

Purchas (1625) gives us only one village for this relatively small drainage in 1605. The village had 2 sagamores, 70 houses, and 240 adult men. Those figures yield a projected total population of 800, fewer than 12 people per house. The quote from John Smith's writings makes it clear that these people still practiced extensive hunting and gathering, but had also adopted horticulture from their relatives to the west. With fewer than a dozen people per house, it appears that the village on the Presumpscot had not adopted the elongated lineage dwellings that at least one village on the Androscoggin had by this time.

It seems likely that in all respects the Indians of the Presumpscot were similar to their neighbors in the upper drainages of the Androscoggin and Merrimack, and that they spoke a language that was dialectically intermediate between the two. The Indians of this drainage are known to history as the Pequawket, or alternatively the Pigwacket. The primary reason for calling attention to this westernmost component of the Eastern Abenaki confederacy is the Smith quote. He gives us a relatively complete inventory of food plants and animals (Tables 2.4 and 2.5) when compared to most other early sources. Given the intermediate position of the Presumpscot, we can safely assume that these resources were also exploited by other Eastern and Western Abenaki.

TABLE 2.4
Plants Mentioned by John Smith in 1614 with Modern Common Names and Scientific Names

Fruits	Woods	Modern common name	Scientific name
Alkermes		Dwarf oak (?)	*Quercus prinoides*
Currans		American black currant	*Ribes americanum*
Mulberies	Mulbery	Red mulberry	*Morus rubra*
Vines		Fox grape	*Vitis labrusca*
Respises		Raspberry	*Rubus idaeus*
Gooseberies		Smooth gooseberry	*Ribes hirtellum*
Plums	Plum tree	American plum	*Prunus americana*
Wall-nuts	Wall-nut	Black walnut	*Juglans nigra*
Chesse-nuts	Chesse-nut	Chestnut	*Castanea dentata*
Small-nut		Butternut (?)	*Juglans cinerea*
Pumpions		Pumpkin	*Cucurbita pepo*
Gourds		Gourd	*Lagenaria siceraria*
Strawberies		Common strawberry	*Fragaria virginiana*
Beanes		Bean	*Phaseolus vulgaris*
Pease		Bean	*Phaseolus vulgaris*
Maize		Corn	*Zea mays*
Flax		Yellow flax (?)	*Linum virginianum*
	Oake	White oak (?)	*Quercus alba*
	Firre	Eastern hemlock (?)	*Tsuga canadensis*
	Pine	White pine (?)	*Pinus strobus*
	Birtch	American white birch (?)	*Betula papyrifera*
	Ash	White ash	*Fraxinus americana*
	Elme	American elm	*Ulmus americana*
	Cipris	Tamarack (?)	*Larix laricina*
	Cedar	Atlantic white cedar	*Chamaecyparis thyoides*
	Hazell	American hazelnut	*Corylus americana*
	Saxefras	Sassafras	*Sassafras albidum*

TABLE 2.5
Birds, Mammals, and Fish Mentioned by John Smith in 1614 with Modern Common Names and Scientific Names

Wildlife	Modern common name	Scientific name
Eagles	Bald eagle	*Haliaeetus leucocephalus*
Grips	Turkey vulture (?)	*Cathartes aura*
Hawkes	Hawk (3)	*Accipitrinae*
Craines	Great blue heron (?)	*Ardea herodias*
Geese	Canada goose	*Branta canadensis*
Brants	Brant	*Branta bernicla*
Cormorants	Double-crested cormorant	*Phalacrocorax auritus*
Ducks	Sea duck (12)	*Aythyinae*
Cranes	Great blue heron (?)	*Ardea herodias*
Swannes	Whistling swan	*Cygnus columbianus*
Sheldrakes	Merganser (3)	*Merginae*
Teale	Marsh duck (± 5)	*Anatinae*
Meawes	Mew gull	*Larus canus*

(continued)

TABLE 2.5 (continued)

Wildlife	Modern common name	Scientific name
Gulls	Gull (10)	*Larinae*
Turkies	Turkey	*Meleagris gallopavo*
Diue-doppers	Loon (2) and/or Grebe (2)	*Gaviidae* and/or *Colymbidae*
Mammals		
Whales	Whale	Various *Cetacea*
Grompus	Risso's dolphin	*Gramphidelphis griseus*
Porkpisces	Common porpoise	*Phocaena phocaena*
Moos	Moose	*Alces alces*
Deare red	Wapiti or elk	*Cervus canadensis*
Deare fallow	White-tailed deer	*Odocoileus virginianus*
Beuers	Beaver	*Castor canadensis*
Wolues	Wolf	*Canis lupus*
Foxes black	Gray fox	*Urocyon cinereoargenteus*
Foxes (other)	Red fox	*Vulpes fulva*
Aroughcunds	Raccoon	*Procyon lotor*
Wilde Cats	Bobcat	*Lynx rufus*
Beares	Black bear	*Ursus americanus*
Otters	River otter	*Lutra canadensis*
Martins	Marten	*Martes americana*
Fitches	Striped skunk	*Mephitis mephitis*
Musquassus	Muskrat	*Ondatra zibethicus*
Fish		
Turbut	Flounder	*Pleuronectidae*
Sturgion	Sturgeon	*Acipenser sturio*
Cod	Cod or tomcod	*Gadus morrhua* or *Microgadus tomcod*
Hake	Silver hake	*Merluccius bilinearis*
Haddocke	Haddock	*Melanogrammus aeglefinus*
Cole	?	?
Cuske (small ling)	Cusk	*Brosmius brosme*
Sharke	Shark	Various
Mackarell	Mackerel	*Scomben scombrus*
Herring	Herring	*Clupea harengus*
Mullit	Mullet	*Mugil cephalus*
Base	Sea bass	*Centropristes striatus*
Pinnacks	?	?
Cunners	Cunner	*Tautogolabrus adspersus*
Pearch	Perch	Various
Eeles	Eel	*Anguilla rostrata*
Crabs	Crab	Various
Lobsters	Lobster	*Homarus americanus*
Mustels	Blue mussel	*Mytilus edulis*
Wilks	Whelk	*Buccinum undatum*
Oisters	Oyster	*Ostrea virginica*
Clamps	Clam or quahog	*Mya arenaria* or *Venus mercenaria*
Periwinkels	Periwinkle	*Littorina littorea*

These savages shave off the hair far up on the head, and wear what remains very long, which they comb and twist behind in various ways very neatly, intertwined with feathers which they attach to the head. They paint their faces black and red, like the other savages which we have seen. They are an agile people, with well-formed bodies. Their weapons are pikes, clubs, bows and arrows, at the end of which some attach the tail of a fish called the signoc, others bones, while the arrows of others are entirely of wood. They till and cultivate the soil, something which we have not hitherto observed. In the place of ploghs, they use an instrument of very hard wood, shaped like a spade. . . . We saw their Indian corn, which they raise in gardens. Planting three or four kernels in one place, they then heap up about it a quantity of earth with shells of the signoc before mentioned. Then three feet distant they plant as much more, and thus in succession. With this corn they put in each hill three or four Brazilian beans, which are of different colors. When they grow up, they interlace with the corn, which reaches to the height of from five to six feet; and they keep the ground very free from weeds. We saw there many squashes, and pumpkins, and tobacco, which they likewise cultivate. . . . The forests in the interior are very thin, although abounding in oaks, beaches, ashes, and elms; in wet places there are many willows. The savages dwell permanently in this place, and have a large cabin surrounded by palisades made of rather large trees placed by the side of each other, in which they take refuge when their enemies make war upon them. They cover their cabins with oak bark. This place is very pleasant, and as agreeable as any to be seen. The river is very abundant in fish, and is bordered by meadows [Samuel de Champlain 1605, cited in Grant 1907:61–63].

From thence doth stretch into the Sea, the faire headland *Tragabigzanda* [Cape Ann], fronted with three Iles called the three *Turks heads:* to the North of this, doth enter a great Bay, where wee founde some habitations and corne fields. They report a great Riuer, and at least thirtie habitations, doe possesse this Countrie. But because the *French* had got their Trade, I had no leasure to discouer it. . . . For their Trade and Merchandize, to each of their principall families or habitations, they haue diuers Townes and people belonging, and by their relations and descriptions, more then twentie seuerall habitations and riuers that stretch themselues farre into the Countrey, euen to the Borders of diuers great Lakes, were they kill and take most of their (Beuers and) Otters [John Smith 1614, cited in Arber and Bradley 1910:204, 707].

We know less about the upper reaches of these drainages for the early seventeenth century than these quotes might suggest. Gordon Day has puzzled more than most over the lack of good data from the upper Androscoggin, Saco, Merrimack, and Connecticut drainages and the rivers that flow westward into Lake Champlain. "Ethnographically, it has been a virtual *terra incognita*. There does not seem to be, either in print or in manuscript, a single account of any group settled within the entire area prior to King Philip's War [Day 1962:28]."

I have already suggested a pre-epidemic population of about 10,000. This appears to have collapsed to only 250, for a mortality rate of 98%. The Indians were generally friendly to the English and some stayed in the drainage until well into the eighteenth century. Yet we have almost nothing describing them. We are not even sure of their linguistic affiliation apart from the fact that they spoke some form of Eastern Algonquian. The absence of linguistic data has not prevented the fabrication of the "Pennacook" language from sources that really related to the Abenaki and the Massachusett. Two nineteenth-century writers went on at great length on the subject of this imaginative creation, with the result that even today many sources can be found incorrectly claiming that a Pennacook language existed and is known to historical linguists (Day 1962:29). Unless and until more documentary sources are uncovered in dusty archives, our best guess must be that there was a language that we can refer to as Western Abenaki in the Merrimack drainage. It probably extended across the upper Connecticut to the eastern shore of Lake Champlain, a distribution that violates our riverine model but that is consistent with our understanding of late prehistory in southern New England. As the communities in the lower drainages of the rivers flowing southward through that part of our region became horticultural, the people of the upper parts of the same drainages could have found more in common with each other than with their erstwhile relatives downstream. Thus, a single language across much of what are now Vermont and New Hampshire is not impossible and can be regarded as a reasonable consequence of the political and social readjustments of late prehistory. During the colonial period bands of Indians from all over New England gathered in refugee communities where their related languages gradually became molded into new hybrid languages. It may be that this process had a prehistoric precedent in Western Abenaki.

It was at the Saco River that Champlain first encountered the Indians he later lumped under the heading "Almouchiquois." He used the term to label all the people of southeastern Massachusetts. On the basis of that and some other early evidence, there is a good possibility that the people living at or near the mouths of both the Saco and the Merrimack rivers in 1600 were actually Massachusett people who had carried horticulture into this productive coastal area from the south. Horticulture was not as productive farther upstream, and it seems likely that Western Abenaki speakers remained there, perhaps cut off from summer coastal resources. One thing seems certain, neither the Massachusett Indians at the mouth of the Saco River nor the Western Abenaki in the interior Saco drainage can be identified as Sokoki. This error was concocted and perpetuated by nineteenth-century writers. The Sokoki were a separate local group living in the upper Connecticut drainage (Day 1978).

The boundary between Massachusett Indians on the lower Merrimack and Western Abenaki in the interior part of the drainage is very unclear. Communities around modern Concord and northward were probably Western Abenaki, but we are unsure of the affiliations of those near modern Manchester and Lowell. These communities, which were under the general leadership of a man named Passaconaway in the seventeenth century, may have spoken either language. The situation is even more confusing because this is a part of New England where historical documents refer to Indians and their communities by a large number of poorly defined terms including *Amoskeag, Pawtuckett,* and *Nashaway.*

The earliest known Western Abenaki villages were all palisaded for defense. They were typically located on bluffs overlooking major streams or lakes. Water, fish, and canoe routes were therefore close at hand. Bluff locations provided an added measure of security while not keeping the Indians too far from the flat alluvial plains below on which they grew their corn, beans, and squash. As was the case among the Eastern Abenaki, the villages were semipermanent sedentary communities. However, depletion of horticultural lands and firewood supplies probably forced the Western Abenaki to move every decade or so. Each move would probably have been only a few kilometers from the abandoned site and well within the drainage area, but strictly speaking the Western Abenaki villages were less permanent than those of their neighbors in Maine and New Brunswick. It seems likely to me that there were at least some winter camps in the interior. The presence of Massachusett villages on the coast would have discouraged the use of summer hunting and gathering camps there by the Western Abenaki. However, the adoption of horticulture would have made travel by family bands to coastal summer camps away from the main villages less critical. Figure 2.8 shows hypothetical relationships between village permanence and degree of sedentism for local communities on a line extending from southeastern Massachusetts to New Brunswick. Here sedentism is measured in terms of the amount of time spent by people in main villages as opposed to temporary camps either on the coast or in the interior. Permanence relates simply to the frequency with which main villages were moved to new locations.

Houses were rectangular structures with arched roofs and covered with bark. They therefore tended to resemble the Iroquois longhouse at least as much as the northern New England wigwam. This is not unexpected given horticulture and their patterns of sedentism and permanence. These were multifamily homes with separate smoke holes for multiple fires. Only the round dome-shaped sweat lodges retained the wigwam shape.

The seasonal round was a compromise between the hunting and gathering patterns of northern New England and the more exclusively horticultural

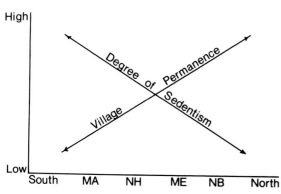

FIGURE 2.8. The historic Indians of southeastern Massachusetts had a focal economy based largely on horticulture with a consequent high degree of sedentism and a low degree of village permanence. Those of northern New England had more diffuse economies and therefore reversed the relationship of sedentism to permanence.

practices farther south. Maple and birch syrup was made in the spring from sap boiled in native ceramic vessels or copper trade kettles. Fish runs and passenger pigeon flocks were harvested for immediate use and for smoking and storage. Fish were taken by means of weirs, traps, spears, hooks, and nets. Groundnuts were gathered here as they were to the north, along with other spring greens. In May, however, attention turned to the planting of maize, beans, squash, and tobacco, and much of the summer was spent tending these crops. There were fishing trips separated by returns to main villages to weed the fields, but the trips typically took them to large interior lakes rather than the seashore. In the fall passenger pigeons were again taken during their southward migration. At that time waterfowl, eels, butternuts, and chestnuts also became available. Much of this was stored for the winter. During the winter men hunted bear, deer, and moose, and trapped fur bearers. They followed the northern pattern of stalking deer rather than driving or snaring them as was done in southern New England. Although the northern hunting techniques were retained, it seems likely that the Western Abenaki depended heavily on stored food and made comparatively brief trips into interior hunting grounds. It is important to note that they also retained the birchbark canoe, a boat much better adapted to quick travel and deep penetration of small streams than the southern New England dugout. Nevertheless, by 1600 they had also adopted the use of overland foot trails, which along with their palisaded villages indicates that the spread of intertribal warfare had reached this part of New England.

The household unit consisted of one to several nuclear families living together in a single house. Although the unit appears similar to the Iroquois longhouse, it is important that the basic social unit was a patrilineage, not a matrilineage as was the case among the Iroquois. Thus, the residents of a single house were related through the male line, and married women within each house tended to be from other houses or even other villages. There were totems, but it is not clear whether there were ever strong clans or if so whether they were ever major social units of settlements. It seems safest for now to stipulate that villages were made up of patrilineages and that it is likely that leaders tended to come from dominant patrilineages. Of course such a rule can fulfill itself even when it seems to be violated, because a rising strong man can turn his patrilineage from a subordinate one to a dominant one as he rises. There was a tendency for there to be both a civil sagamore and a war chief. The sagamore usually held office for life, and it seems likely that among related villages there would have been one sagamore that dominated the others. Given so much flexibility within the system it would appear to be intermediate between cognate and lineal tribal organizations. The wampum complex appears to have reached the Western Abenaki in the seventeenth century, about the time it also reached the Indians of the upper Hudson and Mohawk. This, however, was a historical, not a prehistoric, development.

We know of certain public ceremonies such as weddings, funerals, war declarations, and the first corn harvest. Most of these fit the New England pattern. Of them perhaps the most significant is the first corn ceremony, for this community activity would have been frequent in the horticultural south and nonexistent in the north.

There have been no major excavations of Western Abenaki sites, and documentary sources are too vague on the subject of artifact types to allow us to compare the historic tool inventory with prehistorical archaeological remains. The Western Abenaki made pottery and the usual range of late prehistoric stone tools found in New England. By 1600 these had been replaced by trade copper analogues. Nets were used to take both fish and passenger pigeons, and the range of additional items used to take fish has already been recited. The birchbark canoe and snowshoes were also important artifacts. Clay pipes were used to smoke tobacco. The bow, arrow, knife, and spear were basic hunting weapons, to which for warfare was added a war club with a ball head made from the root crown of some small hardwood tree. The stubs of the projecting roots were sharpened. The man's tool kit retained the crooked knife of northern New England and the woman's kit included the wood or stone mortar and pestle that came with horticulture.

Trade goods included the copper kettles already mentioned as well as some later iron kettles. Glass beads, flint-and-steel fire-making kits, and other common trade items were probably also part of their general tool inventory by 1600 (Figure 2.9). We know little of the raw materials used in the manufacture of native artifacts beyond the general categories of chert, clay, leather, wood, and so on.

At least in later historic times the Western Abenaki buried their dead in extended burials, the bodies wrapped in rolls of bark. Those that died in the winter were kept on scaffolds for spring burial whenever possible. The graves were covered with tent-shaped structures of poles and bark. Weapons and utensils that the deceased would need in the next world were buried with the person, but it is not clear how many of the grave goods were personal and how many were funerary gifts. Graves typically faced east, and those of sagamores were often ringed with planted tree seedlings. Children were especially mourned, an attitude that might have led to the inclusion of grave goods in unusual quantities or of unusual quality, making them archaeologically verifiable.

These people are the most beautiful and have the most civil customs that we have found on this voyage. They are taller than we are; they are a bronze color, some tending more toward whiteness, others to a tawny color; the face is clear-cut; the hair is long and black, and they take great pains to decorate it; the eyes are black and alert, and their manner is sweet and gentle, very like the manner of the ancients. . . . Their women are just as shapely and beautiful; very gracious, of attractive manner and pleasant appearance; their customs and behavior follow womanly custom as far as befits human nature; they go nude except for a stag skin embroidered like the men's, and some wear rich lynx skins on their arms; their bare heads are decorated with various ornaments made of braids of their own hair

Lower Saco and Merrimack Drainages and Southeastern New England

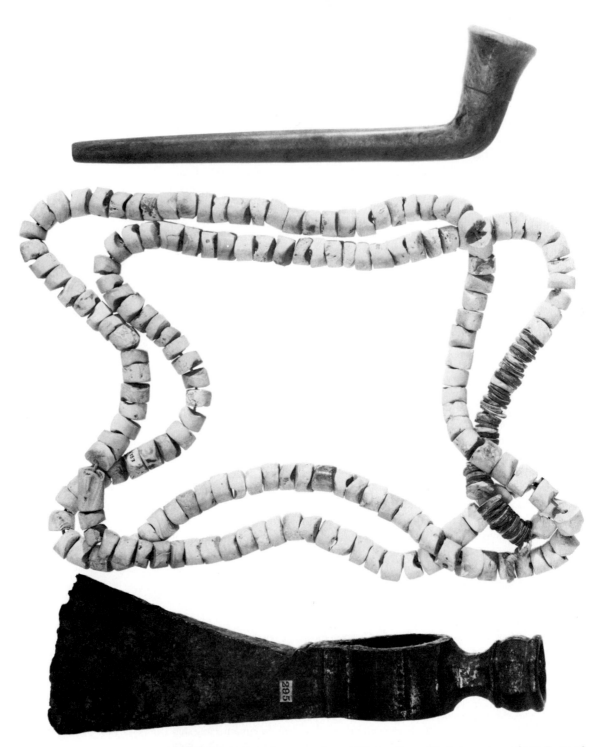

FIGURE 2.9. Artifacts from around A.D. 1600. A native polished stone pipe and two forms of traditional shell disk beads from burials at Revere Beach, Mass. Bottom, a trade tomahawk-pipe from Union Springs, N.Y. Shown at three-quarters actual size. (Courtesy of Peabody Museum, Salem, Mass.)

which hang down over their breasts on either side. . . . They had many sheets of worked copper which they prize more than gold. They do not value gold because of its color; they think it the most worthless of all, and rate blue and red above all other colors. The things we gave them that they prized the most were little bells, blue crystals, and other trinkets to put in the ear or around the neck. They did not appreciate cloth of silk and gold, nor even of any other kind, nor did they care to have them; the same was true for metals like steel and iron, for many times when we showed them some of our arms, they did not admire them, nor ask for them, but merely examined the workmanship. They did the same with mirrors; they would look at them quickly, and then refuse them, laughing. They are very generous and give away all they have. . . . We frequently went five to six leagues into the interior, and found it as pleasant as I can possibly describe, and suitable for every kind of cultivation—grain, wine, or oil. . . . There is an enormous number of animals—stags, deer, lynx, and other species; these people, like the others, capture them with snares and bows, which are their principal weapons. Their arrows are worked with great beauty, and they tip them not with iron but with emery, jasper, hard marble, and other sharp stones. They use the same kind of stone instead of iron for cutting trees, and make their little boats with a single log of wood, hollowed out with admirable skill; there is ample room in them for fourteen to fifteen men; they operate a short oar, broad at the end, with only the strength of their arms, and they go to sea without any danger, and as swiftly as they please. When we went farther inland we saw their houses, which are circular in shape, about fourteen to fifteen paces across, made of bent saplings; they are arranged without any architectural pattern, and are covered with cleverly worked mats of straw which protect them from wind and rain [Giovanni da Verrazzano 1524, cited in Wroth 1970:138–139].

Verrazzano might have been describing early Narragansett or Wampanoag people, either of whom would fit the more general heading of Massachusett as I am using it here. There were minor local differences, but all of the Massachusett of this corner of New England shared a common economic adaptation and settlement system. The total population probably came close to my estimate of 36,700. The area contained only about 19,000 km², so the population density must have been around 193 per 100 km², 9 times the density of the Western Abenaki and 16 times that of people living in northeasternmost New England. Main villages were semipermanent sedentary communities built away from the coast. They were most fully occupied during winter seasons and were apparently moved every dozen years or so when local firewood supplies and agricultural lands became depleted. Ceci (1975) has argued convincingly that the use of fish as fertilizer in southeastern New England is a historic American myth. While it is true that Squanto showed the neophyte pilgrims how to use fish as fertilizer, it is also the case that he had lived for a short time in Europe, returning to his homeland by way of Newfoundland. Squanto learned English and much more while away, and it is likely that he was simply teaching the pilgrims a European technique that he knew would be compatible with their use of draft animals and permanent settlements. Crop fertilization was a labor-intensive technique that required the use of wagons and draft animals. Tons of fish or animal manure would have been required annually, and Indian farmers simply did not have the capacity to acquire and move that much fertilizer. Their practice of moving their fields every few years was therefore a very reasonable strategy.

In fact, the local depletion of firewood may have been the more compelling factor in the periodic relocation of main villages. During the warm months families dispersed to individual farmsteads of single houses surrounded by horticultural fields. The farmsteads would have been more subject to periodic relocation because of soil depletion. There was also a third site type, special purpose camps at which individual families or perhaps special task groups harvested seasonal resources. These included fishing stations, marsh camps for taking migratory waterfowl, camps at plant collecting localities, shellfish collecting camps on the coast, and deer-hunting camps in the interior. With the population density at 193 per 100 km^2, main villages and their satellite farmsteads and camps were probably structured spatially less along drainage principles and more in terms of nearest neighbor principles than was the case farther to the northeast. In other words, main villages were probably spaced more relative to each other than relative to major waterways. Canoe transportation was still important, but travel by overland trails was easier and much more frequent here than in northern New England.

Only the northernmost Massachusett villages appear to have been stockaded in A.D. 1600 (Salwen 1978:165–166). This may well have been the consequence of their location on the frontier separating the Massachusett from Abenaki groups, an area into which the Massachusett may well have only recently intruded. Stockaded villages later became much more frequent throughout the area. However, the Massachusett suffered an 86% mortality rate during the epidemics, and as Thomas (1976) has pointed out the Indian villages were in any case at a competitive disadvantage against European colonization. Stockades made the Massachusett villages more easily defended against attacks, but did not make them as permanent as European settlements. As long as the villages were required to move periodically the Indian land base was subject to piecemeal alienation, and the few surviving Indians found it difficult to retain a territorial foothold.

Houses in main villages were up to 30 m long and 9 m wide. These dwellings were covered with bark and apparently used primarily during the winter, as were the main villages generally. Each could hold 40 or 50 people, probably patrilineages. Village sizes and plans are unknown, but villages of 10 or 20 such houses probably existed. Residence with the man's family after marriage may have been a strong principle, but there is evidence that residence was optional or perhaps even tending toward residence with the woman's family in some places in A.D. 1600. The latter pattern, matrilocality, was the rule among the Mohawk and many other sedentary horticulturalists to the west and south.

Farmsteads were apparently occupied by nuclear families or small extended families. Farmstead houses were large round wigwams 4–5 m in diameter. They were covered with mats that were taken along when the families moved off to temporary camps or main villages. Whether or not they built any shelters at all at their temporary camps probably depended on the season (Figure 2.10). Some shelter would have been required at winter hunting camps but was not necessary at summer shellfishing camps on the coast.

Early writers report a wide range of wild game animal resources, but Salwen's (1970:6) research suggests that deer provided close to 90% of the whole. Deer were stalked, snared, and caught in communal drives, primarily in the winter. Beached whales were used when available. The Indians ensured variety by harvesting seasonal fish runs, gathering shellfish during the summer, shooting and netting migratory fowl, and stalking seals along the coast. The full range of wild New England plant resources was gathered as they became available through the warm months. However, the staples were corn, beans, squash, and Jerusalem artichoke (a tuberous sunflower). Tobacco was also grown, apparently by men, but the cultivation of other crops was usually the work of women. Dried maize was stored underground in baskets for the winter months. This storage strategy combined with reliable harvests made survival through the winter much less problematic than was the case in northern New England. While the Eastern Abenaki and others of the north were forced to disperse to winter hunting camps, the Massachusett did so only as their desire for fresh meat required (Figure 2.11).

The basic household unit would appear to have been a small extended family or nuclear family during the farming season, and a lineage unit during most of the cold months. Although patrilineality appears to have been the general rule, the trend may have been toward bilateral kin groups in some areas and perhaps even matrilineal groups in a few. The settlement unit appears to have been a lineal tribe in Service's (1962:120–139) terms. Town leaders were generally from high-ranking lineages, such that, while there was not necessarily strict patrilineal inheritance of leadership, there was a strong tendency for successive leaders to be related patrilineally. Again there is evidence to indicate that this was evolving (or had already evolved) into a bilateral or matrilineal system in some localities. Towns were clearly united in alliances like that already described for the Eastern Abenaki. Indeed, Champlain (Grant 1907:44–52, 61) used the term *Almouchiquois* to refer to all of the people of this drainage area, a term that might imply some political unity. Epidemics and political factionalism in the seventeenth century have badly confused the picture by presenting the ethnohistorical with a bewildering array of ephemeral sociopolitical units. Gookin (1970: 7–12) indicates that there were basically three main units (Massachusett proper, Pokanoket, and Narragansett) at some point during that period. Perhaps the best strategy is to assume that there was considerable fluidity in political structure above the village or town level around A.D. 1600.

The technological subsystem was fundamentally the same as that for groups already discussed. To the basic inventory were added tools made necessary by the broader range of subsistence and other activities in southern New England. In addition to ceramic vessels these people made large

FIGURE 2.10. Top, a full-scale reconstruction of a Massachusett summer camp. Wigwams of northern New England would have been covered with birchbark; this one is covered with rush thatching. Bottom, the permanent houses and enclosed fields of European settlements had a clear advantage over semipermanent Indian settlements in the territorial struggles of the seventeenth century. Both reconstructions are at Plimouth Plantation, Mass.

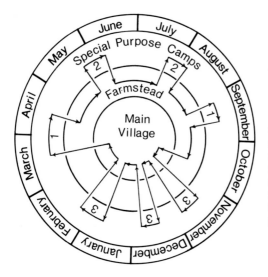

FIGURE 2.11. Hypothetical seasonal movements of a Massachusett family. The inner core represents the main village, the inner ring farmstead residence, and the outer ring temporary camps. Trips to fishing and fowling camps (1) and to shellfishing and plant gathering camps (2) were made from the farmstead, whereas trips to winter hunting camps (3) were made from the main village.

wooden mortars for reducing corn to flour. Similarly, in addition to bark canoes, these people made large dugouts.

One of the most distinctive material goods from the Northeast had its origins and subsequent center of manufacture in southern New England. Wampum was made in limited amounts prior to A.D. 1600 in coastal areas. The cylindrical beads were made from whelk (*Busycon*) in the case of white examples and quahog (*Venus mercenaria*) in the case of blue or black ones (Figure 2.12). The production of these beads and the strings and belts made from them increased sharply after the introduction of iron drills, eventually becoming a true medium of exchange. Even before then, however, wampum was used to pay bride price to prospective fathers-in-law and to pay tribute, blood money, and ransoms. Its discovery in archaeological contexts therefore can have significant social implications.

There is some evidence that formal trade was going on prior to A.D. 1600, particularly trade carried out as gift exchange. This appears to have been frequent in frontier areas where nonagricultural groups could exchange furs for produce. Ceramic pots, maple bowls, and chestnuts were also traded (Figure 2.13), and there was little difficulty involved in incorporating European trade goods (Figure 2.14) into the system during and after the sixteenth century.

The production of elbow pipes, sometimes with effigy figures, continued into historic times despite the availability of European kaolin pipes. Two unfinished examples were recovered from a historic Narragansett grave complete with the European iron file the dead man presumably needed to finish them (Figure 2.15). Both were made of a dense greenish-gray siltstone (Turnbaugh 1976).

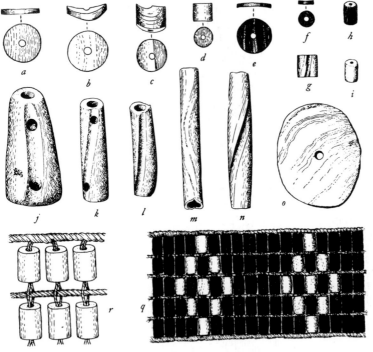

FIGURE 2.12. Shell beads. All except h, i, q, and r are from graves. Beads labeled a and b are from Waterville, Maine; others are from eastern Massachusetts. Artifacts labeled h, i, r, and q show individual historic wampum beads and belt construction. All others are before contact with Europeans. Shown at actual size. (After Willoughby 1935:267.)

FIGURE 2.13. Native seventeenth-century pottery. Left, Guida Incised vessel from Titicut, Mass.; 38 cm tall. Right, vessel No. 25 from Fort Shantok, Conn.; 30 cm tall. (Collections of the Haffenreffer Museum, Brown University, and the state of Connecticut.)

FIGURE 2.14. Top, iron strike-a-lights (74 and 58 mm long). These trade items replaced pyrite nodules used with chert nodules in fire-making kits. Bottom, metal trade spoons (17 and 15 cm long). The shorter specimen is a silver-plated spoon found with an Indian burial in the Burrs Hill burial ground site, R.I. (Haffenreffer Museum, Brown University.)

FIGURE 2.15. Native artifacts showing European influence. Top, unfinished stone pipes and an iron file recovered from a Narragansett grave (Turnbaugh 1976). Bottom left, a steatite goblet (97 mm high); bottom right, a spoon (17 cm) made from trade metal (both at the Haffenreffer Museum, Brown University). Bottom center, a mortuary pot having European rim motif (on loan to Bronson Museum, Attleboro, Mass.). All Massachusett.

Some early historic cemeteries are reported by Willoughby (1935:231–241), and there are several other more recent sources. Taken together, the data indicate that the Massachusett buried their dead either singly or in small groups. The burials were generally flexed and lying on one side, usually aligned toward the southwest. Grave goods were often but not always included, usually sheets of trade copper, rolled tubular copper beads, glass beads, knives, spoons, pottery, and European trade items (Figure 2.16). The grave goods tend to be personal items suitable to the age and sex of the owner. Children were buried with toys, sometimes miniature examples of adult items, if they were buried with anything at all. Men were buried with things such as weapons and wampum, while women were more often buried with hoes, spoons, clay pots, and metal kettles. Perhaps the best documented historic Indian cemetery is Cautantowwit's House on an island in Narragansett Bay (Simmons 1970). The patterns just described can be observed in considerable detail in the site report. Of 42 flexed burials, 32 were on their right sides, only 10 on their left, the distinction apparently having nothing to do with sex or the presence or absence of grave goods. In a total of 59 graves, virtually all individuals were aligned toward the southwest, conforming with the Narragansett belief that paradise laid in that direction. Early sources indicate that the dead were sewed into mats before burial, but the material has not survived in most archaeological contexts.

Thames Drainage

We find on the main a small stream to which our people gave the name of the Frisian River [Thames], where some trade is carried on with the natives, who are called Morhicans [Mohegan–Pequot] [Johan de Laet 1614, cited in Jameson 1909:43].

Their houses, or wigwams, are built with small poles fixed in the ground, bent and fastened together with barks of trees oval or arbour-wise on the top. These houses they make of several sizes, according to their activity and ability; some twenty, some forty feet long and broad. Some I have seen of sixty or a hundred feet long, and thirty feet broad. Their food is generally boiled maize, or Indian corn, mixed with kidney-beans, or sometimes without. Also they frequently boil in this pottage fish and flesh of all sorts, either new taken or dried, as shads, eels, alewives or a kind of herring, or any other sort of fish. Also they mix with the said pottage several sorts of roots; as Jerusalem artichokes, and ground nuts, and other roots, and pompions, and squashes, and also several sorts of nuts or masts, as oak-acorns, chestnuts, walnuts; these husked and dried, and powdered, they thicken their pottage therewith. The pots they seeth their food in, which were heretofore, and yet are, in use among some of them, are made of clay or earth, almost in the form of an eff, the top taken off, but now they generally get kettles of brass, copper, or iron. Their dishes, and spoons, and ladles, are made of wood, very smooth and artificial, and of a sort of wood not subject to split. The wompompeague [wampum] is made artificially of a part of the wilk's shell. The black is of double value to the white. With this wompompeague they pay tribute, redeem captives, satisfy for murders and other wrongs, purchase peace with their potent neighbours, as occasion requires; in a word, it answers all occasions with them, as gold and silver doth with us. For their water passage, travels, and fishing, they make boats, or canoes, either of great trees, pine or chesnut, made hollow and artificially; which they do by burning them; and after with tools, scraping, smoothing, shaping them. Of these they make greater or lesser. Some I have seen will carry twenty persons,

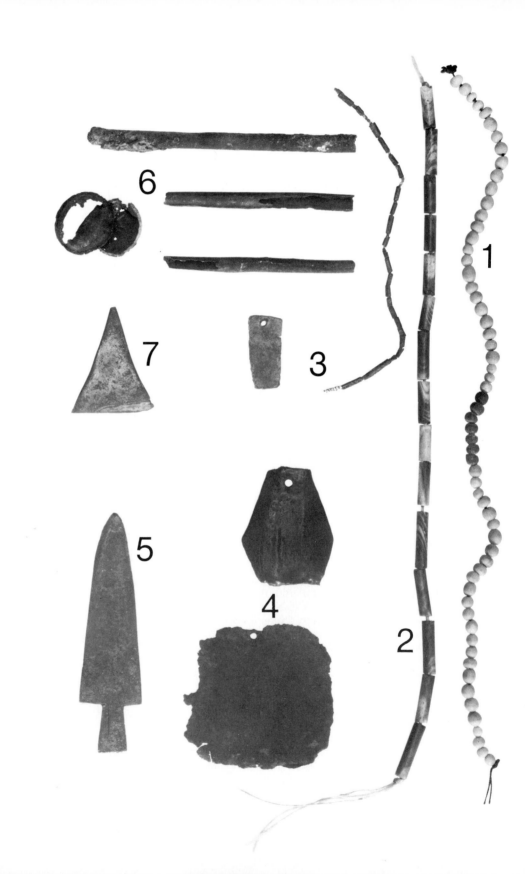

being forty or fifty feet in length, and as broad as the tree will bear [Daniel Gookin 1674, cited in Gookin 1970:14–18].

The Mohegan–Pequot were much like the Massachusett in terms of the 14 categories I am using to define economic, social, technological, and religious subsystems. They diverge from the other cultures of southern New England in having a very high population density, apparently around 266 per 100 km². Although their total population, an estimated 13,300, was not high, their 5000-km² territory was relatively small. It may be that there was some compacting of aboriginal population in southern New England that went along with the late prehistoric movement of Munsee speakers into the lower Hudson drainage and western Long Island.

The quote from Daniel Gookin regarding boats is interesting for a number of reasons. For one thing he indicates that dugouts varied up to 50 feet (15 m) in length. While he reports that some carried 20 people, other sources indicate twice that number. He goes on to explain that dugouts were not as easily capsized as bark canoes, which these people also made and used. The implications of this and other descriptions are that bark canoes were used for travel on interior streams, particularly those requiring portaging. The dugouts were used on larger rivers and at sea. In Chapter 5 I offer evidence that dugouts were used much more extensively in northern New England during the Late Archaic period for reasons of stability, strength, crew size, and seaworthiness. Gookin's observations therefore have significance far beyond the present chapter.

Smith (1950:110–116) has investigated the Mohegan–Pequot archaeologically. His Shantok aspect was defined on the basis of excavations at three seventeenth century Mohegan–Pequot sites: Fort Shantok, Pantigo, and Fort Corchaug. The last two are located on the eastern end of Long Island, which shows that the Mogehan–Pequot had expanded to that area by at least historic times. Salwen (1970) has more recently undertaken the analysis of faunal remains from Fort Shantok and two other related sites in order to show changing subsistence patterns through the seventeenth century (Figure 2.17). However, all of these investigations relate to developments that postdate A.D. 1600 and cannot be detailed here.

A few hundred people of Mohegan–Pequot descent still survive. Readers interested in this culture and the others of southern New England should see Salwen (1978), Simmons (1978), and Conkey et al. (1978), all in Volume 15 of the *Handbook of North American Indians*.

FIGURE 2.16. Seventeenth-century artifacts. 1, Venetian glass beads from a burial at Revere Beach, Mass.; 2, tubular wampum of European manufacture; 3, small rolled copper beads on a twisted fiber cord and a copper pendant from a burial at Ipswich Beach, Mass.; 4, sheet copper pendants from Ipswich; 5, iron point from Newburyport, Mass.; 6, rolled copper tubes (shortest 6 cm long) from Marblehead, Mass.; and a copper bell; 7, copper point from grave at Revere Beach. Shown at three-quarters actual size. (1–6 and photo courtesy of Peabody Museum, Salem; 7 courtesy of Peabody Museum of Archaeology and Ethnology, Cambridge, Mass.)

FIGURE 2.17. Top, trade ax, 16 cm long (Bronson Museum, Attleboro, Mass.). Bottom, iron trade hoe, 13 × 23 cm, Fort Shantok (collection of the state of Connecticut).

Next, on the same south coast, succeeds a river named by our countrymen Fresh River [Connecticut], which is shallow at its mouth. . . . There are few inhabitants near the mouth of the river, but at the distance of fifteen leagues above they become numerous; their nation is called Sequins. . . . The natives there plant maize, and in the year 1614 they had a village resembling a fort for protection against the attacks of their enemies. . . . They are called Nawaas, and their sagamore was then named Morahieck. They term the bread made of maize, in their language, *leganick*. This place is situated in latitude 41°48′. The river is not navigable with yachts for more than two leagues farther, as it is very shallow and has a rocky bottom. Within the land dwells another nation of savages, who are called Horikans; they descent the river in canoes made of bark [Johan de Laet 1614, cited in Jameson 1909:43].

The Horikans appear to have been Indians living in several communities of the middle Connecticut drainage. They would have been speakers of the language called Loup A by Goddard (1978a:71). Documentary sources later refer to them by several different names including Podunk, Agawam, Nipmuck, and Pocumtuck. The Pocumtuck emerged as leaders after the epidemic of 1635, but it is not certain that they were dominant before that time. I use their name to refer to the whole as a matter of convenience only.

As I indicated nearer the beginning of this chapter, the people of the middle Connecticut may well have had a population density approaching that of the Massachusett. Such a density in an area containing 8000 km^2 would suggest an aboriginal population of about 15,200. Only 800 survived the epidemics, a number that indicates a severe but not unusual mortality rate of 95%. If that rate were less, a smaller pre-epidemic population would be suggested. However, a growing season of at least 150 days extends well up the Connecticut through this area, and there is no good reason to presume that its population density was significantly lower than that of the rest of southern New England.

The southern Connecticut drainage, the Housatonic drainage, and central Long Island were all occupied by a speech community called Quiripi–Unquachog (Goddard 1978a). The eastern tip of Long Island was occupied by Montauk speakers who were probably closely related to the Mohegan–Pequot, while the western tip of the island was occupied by Munsee speakers. Johan de Laet refers to them as Nawaas, but we have not consistently applied cultural names for the various small communities in this area that survived the epidemics. The diseases and wars of the seventeenth century forced them into refugee communities at very early dates, and we have few trustworthy descriptions of them in their pre-epidemic state.

What little we do know of the Indians of these drainages as of A.D. 1600 conforms to my earlier sketch of the Massachusett. There are some archaeological indications that they or some of them were displaced from previously occupied territories to the west by the Munsee. This evidence is discussed in Chapter 8.

Upper Hudson Drainage   I sailed to the shore in one of their canoes, with an old man, who was the chief of a tribe consisting of forty men and seventeen women. These I saw there in a house well constructed of oak [really of elm] bark, and circular in shape, so that it had the appearance of being well built, with an arched roof. It contained a great quantity of maize, beans of the last year's growth, and there lay near the house for the purpose of drying, enough to load three ships, besides what was growing in the fields. On our coming into the house, two mats were spread out to sit upon, and immediately some food was served in well made red wooden bowls. Two men were also despatched at once with bows and arrows in quest of game, who soon after brought in a pair of pigeons which they had shot. They likewise killed a fat dog, and skinned it in great haste, with shells which they had got out of the water. They supposed that I would remain with them for the night, but I returned after a short time on board ship. The land is the finest for cultivation that I even in my life set foot upon, and it also abounds in trees of every description. The natives are a very good people, for when they saw that I would not remain, they supposed that I was afraid of their bows, and taking the arrows, they broke them in pieces, and threw them into the fire [Henry Hudson 1609, cited in Asher 1860:161–162].

The main villages of the Mahican were usually stockaded communities on protected hilltops. Each such village contained 3–16 elongated wigwam longhouses. These averaged 3 hearths each, indicating an equivalent number of nuclear families, which in turn suggests village populations ranging from 45 to 240. I have already suggested a total Mahican population of 5300 for an overall density of 31 per 100 km^2. This rather thin density is consistent with what we have already seen for other parts of northern New England. When at fishing or hunting stations the Mahican probably lived in single-family wigwams.

The Mahican were separated from coastal lands and their resources by the Munsee of the lower Hudson. In this they were similar to the Western Abenaki and it is no surprise that linguistic evidence suggests links from the Mahican across northern New England (Goddard 1978a:76). However, Mahican territory stretched far enough south to include Catskill Creek and tributary drainages from that latitude northward on both sides of the Hudson, excepting only the Mohawk. In A.D. 1600 the Hudson was teeming with fish, being an unusually broad and deep river all the way to the mouth of the Mohawk. The Mahican, therefore, were horticulturalists and fishermen. The first runs began in March, at which time the people dispersed to fishing stations (Figure 2.18). They probably returned to main villages with dried and smoked fish after the first runs were finished. Women remained there through the growing season to plant and tend the standard aboriginal crops while men returned to fishing and mussel gathering. All returned in late August to harvest crops and take part in Green Corn ceremonies. In the fall they dispersed once again to harvest the fall fish runs. There were also deer drives at this time, apparently followed by Deer Sacrifice ceremonies. As in many other places in New England there were two main winter hunts separated by a midwinter ceremony at the main village in December. These hunts were made on snowshoes, and everyone attempted to return to the

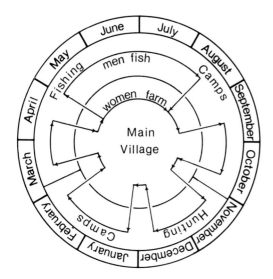

FIGURE 2.18. Hypothetical seasonal movements of a Mahican family. The inner core represents the main village, the lower third of the outer ring winter encampments, and the upper two-thirds of the outer ring fishing stations. Women remained behind to farm during the growing season.

main villages before the snow and ice melted. There was a lean period until the maple sap and fish began to run, and the passenger pigeons moved north once again.

The single family wigwam probably contained a single nuclear or small extended family. The larger and more permanent longhouses probably contained lineages or lineage segments. Brasser (1978b) suggests that these were matrilineal family units. It is not clear that the Mahican had clans, but some have suggested that the three-clan system that they are known to have had later on already existed in A.D. 1600. These divisions, called Bear, Wolf, and Turtle, respectively, appear to be a direct borrowing from their Mohawk neighbors. There again appear to have been high-ranking lineages that produced most village leaders. As was also the case with at least the Eastern Abenaki, leading men generally had more than one wife. This suggests that political power, sexual prowess, charisma, and shamanistic power were all dimensions of the same quality. As with most other groups, there appears to have been a loose alliance of villages, and perhaps a single village leader to whom all others deferred to as long as it was convenient to do so.

Little can be said of the technological subsystem as of A.D. 1600 except for its presumed general similarity to those we have already examined. The Mahican probably preferred bark to dugout canoes like their cultural analogues elsewhere in northern New England. They had and used wampum at least in later times. Some of their pottery resembles Mohawk and other Iroquois pottery quite closely, leading materialist scholars to conclude that they were culturally not much more than impoverished Iroquois. Fishing gear was relatively elaborate as we should expect. Nets and weirs were used to take fish, as were lines equipped with either simple or compound barbed hooks. Barbed bone points were used on leisters.

Funk (1976:301) reports flexed burials without grave goods for the late prehistoric Hudson drainage. There is, in fact, little to go on regarding the burial practices of the historic Mahican. We can assume that the archaeological evidence of single flexed burials and the ethnographic evidence for the same thing for the historic Algonquian peoples of neighboring drainages are sufficient evidence that this was the rule for the historic Mahican. However, details regarding grave goods and orientations are not yet known.

The Mahican eventually became refugees in their own land and joined others in the Stockbridge community. What little is known of the early Mahican and their subsequent ethnohistory has been summarized by Brasser (1974, 1978b).

Mohawk Drainage

Farther inland, and beyond the Armouchiquois [of southeastern New England], are the Iroquois tribes, also stationary, because they till the soil, whence they gather maize . . . , beans, edible roots, and in short all that we have mentioned in describing the Armouchiquois, even more, for from necessity they draw their sustenance from the earth, as they are far from the sea [Marc Lescarbot 1610, cited in Thwaites 1959:Volume 1, 84–87].

In the morning we went together to the castle over the ice that during the night had frozen on the kill [stream], and, after going half a league, we arrived in their first castle, which is built on a high hill. There stood but 36 houses, in rows like streets, so that we could pass nicely. The houses are made and covered with bark of trees, and mostly are flat at the top. Some are 100, 90, or 80 paces long and 22 and 23 feet high. There were some inside doors of hewn boards, furnished with iron hinges. In some houses we saw different kinds of iron work, iron chains, harrow irons, iron hoops, nails—which they steal when they go forth from here. Most of the people were out hunting deer and bear. The houses were full of corn that they call *onersti*, and we saw maize; yes, in some of the houses more than 300 bushels. They make canoes and barrels of the bark of trees, and sew with bark as well. We had a good many pumpkins cooked and baked that they called *anansira* [Harmen Meyndertsz van den Bogaert 1634, cited in Jameson 1937:140–141].

The Mohawk were the easternmost of the five Iroquois nations, the only group treated in this chapter that did not speak an Algonquian language. I have estimated that there were at least 9000 of them in A.D. 1600, perhaps as many as 11,300. They were distributed through as many as 9 villages, 3 of which were principal "castles" by the middle of the seventeenth century. By that time they were reduced by epidemics to 4100–5100 people, over a thousand of which were living in a single castle. It may well be that all Mohawk villages were this size or larger before the epidemics.

As the term *castle* implies, Mohawk villages were stockaded communities located on protected bluffs overlooking the Mohawk River (Figure 2.19). The villages were few in number but individually large by northeast standards. The houses within the stockades were the well-known Iroquois longhouses, some of which van den Bogaert describes as being 100 paces long. Such a house could accommodate as many as 40 nuclear families, each in a compartment on one side or the other of a central aisleway. Villages contained as

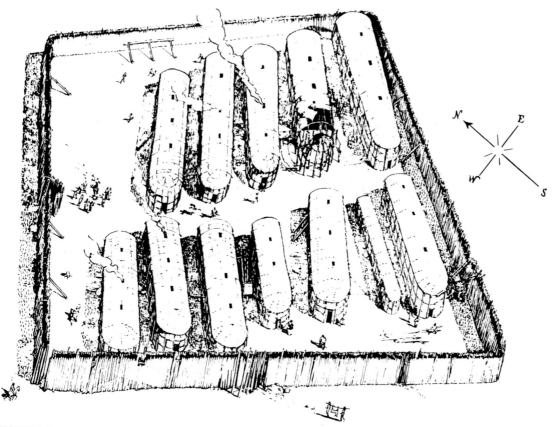

FIGURE 2.19. The historic Mohawk village of Caughnawaga, inhabited A.D. 1666–1693. (Courtesy of the Tekakwitha Shrine, Mohawk–Caughnawaga Museum, Fonda, N.Y.)

few as 4 or 5 houses to as many as 55. Rare single-family houses were 6 × 4.5 m in size, while two-family houses were up to twice that size. The communal longhouses probably ranged from 15 to 94 m in length, with the average around 36 m. All houses were bark-covered, arbor-roofed structures about 5.5 m high. They were packed closely together within their protective stockades, which in turn were built of from 1 to 4 lines of vertical logs set in the ground. There were occasionally earthen ramparts, ditches, and battlements atop walls that might be as much as 9 m high. Because their castles were strong and because they spent much of the year at home within them, the Mohawk were defensively stronger than the other groups I have sketched. Thus, while they were able to attack others with relative ease, counterattacks were not a serious threat. This military advantage, backed up by a strong alliance with other Iroquois nations, was a major factor in warfare involving the Mohawk and other Indians during the seventeenth century and probably earlier as well.

There were no individual farmsteads, but task groups made seasonal trips to fishing stations and hunting grounds (Figure 2.20), where they built small bark tepees. Such structures would therefore have been found at special-purpose sites with some evidence of specialized activity. Nuclear families may have occupied temporary houses at special-purpose sites, but most indications are that many women remained in main villages for most of the year.

Main villages were often surrounded by separate smaller hamlets. This had been interpreted by some scholars as evidence of dissident families moving away from the social and spatial confines of the larger settlement. While this might be true in part, the interpretation masks some possible political significance to the settlement pattern. Small hamlets in the vicinity of larger stockaded villages were probably tied politically and socially to the main village. If so, the pattern implies at least some of the characteristics of a chiefdom.

The retreat of the Mahican into refugee communities and the political expansion of the Mohawk and other Iroquois during the seventeenth century led to a significant enlargement of Mohawk territory. Many maps prepared on the basis of seventeenth-century data show Mohawk territory to include much of the upper Hudson and Champlain drainages. However, this appears to be a post-1600 distortion of Mohawk territoriality. The riverine model predicts that the home range of the Mohawk Indians was confined to the Mohawk River drainage in and before A.D. 1600, and there are no convincing archaeological data to dispute that prediction. Moreover, despite an apparent reference to Iroquois on Lake Champlain by Champlain himself, Day (1971) concludes that at least the eastern side of the lake was inhabited by Abenaki

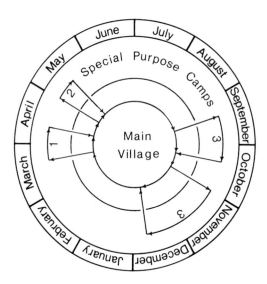

FIGURE 2.20. Hypothetical seasonal movements of a Mohawk family. Women tended to stay at the main village. Men moved out in task groups for (1) trapping and fishing, (2) fowling, and (3) hunting and raiding. Male subsistence activities tended not to occur during the warm months.

in the early seventeenth century. The western shore of the lake, which is a comparatively narrow strip with its back to the Adirondack Mountains, may not have been occupied by any permanent villages at all.

During the spring men fished and harvested passenger pigeons. Because of the steep falls near its mouth, the lowermost stretch of the Mohawk River was not navigable by either canoes or migratory fish. Therefore, the riverine environment was much different for the Mohawk than it was for the Mahican along the mainstream of the Hudson. Spring fishing for the Mohawk did not involve concentrated and highly productive efforts at key stations. Instead, the Mohawk often used nets and traps to take resident fish, sometimes driving them into the traps. While the men fished, women planted the crops standard for aboriginal farmers in the Northeast. Fields were cleared near villages, usually on river floodplains. Exhaustion of the land required periodic movement of the villages, as was the case elsewhere in New England.

Men spent much of the summer in military, political, and social activities while women tended the crops. The crop harvest was followed by a Green Corn ceremony, after which families dispersed to hunting camps for the fall hunt. They returned at midwinter for ceremonies in the main village. They dispersed once again in early spring to collect maple sap, fish, and hunt pigeons. Overall they appear to have spent more time in their main villages than did many other Indians of New England, crop productivity and storage techniques being adequate for that much sedentism. Thus, the Mohawk, although still dependent on deer and other animals for meat protein, had a more strongly focal adaptation to horticulture than the others. Their settlement system was semipermanent sedentary as was the case elsewhere, but, although Mohawk villages were no more permanent than those of the Massachusett, the degree of sedentism was apparently greater when measured as the number of months per year of residence.

Together the nuclear families of a longhouse formed a matrilineage. All female residents of the longhouse were members of the same clan and adult men were in-marrying husbands from other clans. Temporary camps, particularly those used in spring and fall, were often occupied by individual nuclear families. It seems likely that many hunting camps, particularly those used in winter, were occupied by male task groups rather than complete nuclear families. The village appears to have been composed of several lineages, each with its own longhouse. The lineages were grouped into three clans: Turtle, Bear, and Wolf. Some writers have concluded that these three kin divisions corresponded to the three main villages of the Mohawk in the middle seventeenth century. However, there are good reasons to conclude that every clan must have been represented in most villages, and that no village had fewer than two clans (Fenton and Tooker 1978:467).

Because women resided with their clan sisters all their lives and because women were the potters, one should expect to find that individual longhouses formed de facto pottery guilds. That is, pottery decorations from within a single longhouse should resemble each other more closely than they resemble those from other longhouses even within the same village. A test of this hypothesis is a test for an archaeological confirmation of matrilocal residence. Tests of this basic hypothesis have been attempted on the Great Plains and in the Southwest. Preliminary tests on ceramics from Mohawk sites indicate that the hypothesis is valid here, too.

Various institutionalized ceremonies were keyed to the seasonal round. The Green Corn ceremony followed the harvest and the midwinter New Year ceremony usually came in early February. There was a Maple ceremony when the sap began to flow, a Planting ceremony, and a Strawberry ceremony when the berries became ripe. A Harvest ceremony separate from the Green Corn ceremony was a thanksgiving for all crops. Some archaeological evidence of ritual activity might be discoverable because the Iroquois were known to occasionally practice dog sacrifice. However, the dogs were typically burned rather than buried after being strangled, and archaeological evidence is apt to be slim.

The False Face Society was another important institution, and one that might leave archaeological evidence behind. The false faces were grotesque wooden masks, preferably carved from living basswood. Corn husk masks were also made, and some models of both in more durable materials are known from archaeological contexts (see Chapter 8).

The most important institution above the community level was the League of the Iroquois. The Mohawk were the easternmost member of this originally five-nation confederacy. It is not clear when the league was formed, but most scholars agree that it was in existence by my baseline date of A.D. 1600. Engelbrecht (1972) has attempted to find archaeological evidence for the age of the league, a topic that is discussed in Chapter 8. The settlement pattern of smaller hamlets clustered around larger stockaded villages suggests that the Mohawk had at least some of the characteristics of a chiefdom. The existence of the league adds a third layer to this political hierarchy, such that we can conceive of the Iroquois in A.D. 1600 as being composed of a set of chiefdoms confederated or at least allied in a larger political organization. Chiefdom, as opposed to tribal, organization implies a more rigid political structure, one in which leaders were not simply leaders because it was convenient for others to let them lead. Indeed, the Mohawk had appointed sachems, three for each of their three clans, who represented them to the league. They were appointed for life and were apparently powerful leaders in their home communities. Their appointments were made formally by the senior women of the ranking lineage, a degree of structure and continuity not seen for the Algonquian-speaking tribes of New England.

Each village had a headman and a council of elders, an institution much more like leadership as we have seen it for Algonquian groups to the east. Although these two were apparently appointive positions, appointments of this sort were in a sense after the fact. Men who had not shown the leadership qualities valued in all New England cultures were simply not appointed, so that achievement was the rule and ascription only its formal recognition. The English and French who dealt with these people in the seventeenth century may well have wished that they themselves had a comparable system for keeping incompetents from positions of power.

The Mohawk used mace-like clubs of ironwood in combat, and it may be that they did not use a weapon like the tomahawk until metal tomahawks were made available as trade items by Europeans. It is interesting to note that as late as 1634 they still had not obtained guns in significant numbers, although van den Bogaert noted that they were hanging doors on iron hinges in the European fashion.

The Mohawk, like all Iroquois, favored wood, bark, bone, antler, and pottery over stone. Work in chipped chert was particularly limited although points of the Madison type were made. Ground stone adzes and celts were also made. Mohawk pottery was usually made with a globular base, with cylindrical, castellated, and incised collars above constricted necks. This familiar style was copied by potters in many Eastern Algonquian communities, but remains an Iroquois trademark nonetheless. Mohawk men made clay elbow smoking pipes, often with effigy decorations, for tobacco smoking. Items such as awls, points, fishhooks, beads, spearpoints, and combs were usually made of bone or in some cases antler. Wampum became important among the Mohawk as it did among other aboriginal New England groups, particularly in the seventeenth century. Wampum belts took on strong public ceremonial significance in most areas, but perhaps most of all among the Iroquois. Here the belts came to have a central ritual role in the activities of the League of the Iroquois.

Bark canoes were made and used, but they were of elm not birchbark and were clumsy craft that no sane person would use on any but calm waters. Because of this and the pressures of endemic warfare, the Mohawk preferred overland travel on networks of trails, much as was the case in southern New England.

In early historic times the Mohawk probably buried their dead in flexed seated positions, facing east, in cemeteries near villages. There is no evidence of exposure on scaffolds with subsequent burial of bone bundles around A.D. 1600. Grave goods included personal belongings, in the case of a man typically his bow and arrows, his pipe, and some food. The Mohawk tortured prisoners, mutilating and dismembering them prior to killing them. The body of a tortured person was often cooked and eaten, more for ritual purposes than food value. Under these circumstances human body parts were apt to be scattered around the village site or tossed into trash pits. Archaeologically, therefore, some burials would show up as food refuse outside cemetery contexts. There is little from the ethnohistoric record to suggest that we should expect to find similar evidence of cannibalism from sites outside the Mohawk drainage in aboriginal New England.

For further information on the Mohawk, readers should start with Fenton (1978), Fenton and Tooker (1978), and Oswalt (1966:396–461).

Lower Hudson Drainage

This day the people of the countrey came aboord of us, seeming very glad of our comming, and brought greene tobacco, and gave us of it for knives and beads. They goe in deere skins loose, well dressed. They have yellow copper. They desire cloathes, and are very civill. They have great store of maize or Indian wheate, whereof they make good bread. The countrey is full of great and tall oakes. . . . Some women also came to us with hempe. They had red copper tabacco pipes, and other things of copper they did weare about their neckes. At night they went on land againe, so wee roade very quiet, but durst not trust them [Robert Juet 1609, cited in Asher 1860:79].

Goddard (1978b:214) estimates that there were only 4500 Munsee in A.D. 1600. I have argued that this number was probably only a fifth and possibly only an eleventh of the total Munsee population at that time. Even if there were only 24,300 Munsee in 1600, that number would indicate an unusually modest population density of 90 per 100 km^2 and an equally modest epidemic mortality rate of 81%. A population density and epidemic mortality rate more in line with what we know for the rest of New England would indicate that there were about 51,300 Munsee at the beginning of the seventeenth century.

Goddard (1978a) concludes that there were two Delaware languages around A.D. 1600. Munsee was spoken in the upper Delaware and lower Hudson drainages. The people of the lower Delaware drainage, below the Delaware Water Gap, spoke Unami, close but not identical to Munsee. We will see that archaeologically the Munsee had strong traditional links with the Iroquois and others north and east of them. Unami connections were largely with the Delmarva Peninsula and elsewhere to the south.

I have assigned the Munsee to the upper Delaware and the lower Hudson drainages. They appear to have occupied the entire 17,000-km^2 lower Hudson despite claims in some of the older literature that they lived only on the west side of the river, the river forming a boundary between them and a "Wappinger Confederacy" to the east. If true this would be a clear violation of the riverine model and a unique exception to aboriginal custom. Fortunately, Goddard's (1971) review of the linguistic evidence has corrected the traditional error. It happens that "Wappinger" means "opossum" in Munsee, and that there is evidence that it was applied in later times to people of Munsee descent on both sides of the Hudson River. "Wappanoo" or "Wampanos" carries the meaning "Easterner" in Munsee, and could presumably be applied to virtually anyone living east of the speaker. Confusion of the words by Europeans and assumption that they were really a single word caused the creation of the Wappinger Confederacy in much older literature. The confederacy, which older sources and those following them place between the Hudson and Connecticut rivers, never really existed.

Munsee longhouses were covered with chestnut bark as opposed to the elm bark used by the Mohawk (Figure 2.21). Interior arrangements were also somewhat different. There is archaeological evidence for aisles running down the side rather than the center of the longhouse. Each family may have

FIGURE 2.21. Munsee longhouses, based on archaeological evidence from the Miller Field sites (Kraft 1975b:83). Note rounded ends, interior partitions, and storage pits.

had its own fire rather than sharing it as the Mohawk did, and each family may also have had a somewhat more private partitioned compartment than was the case among the Mohawk. Overall the Munsee longhouse has the flavor of having been somewhat less communal than the Mohawk longhouse. Houses in which leaders lived were apparently decorated with carved wooden faces and may have been used for public ceremonies.

Site types and their distributions appear to have been similar to those of the Massachusett. Like the Massachusett they had farmsteads surrounded by fields and may have lacked nucleated villages altogether. We have yet to find evidence of either large villages or stockades despite some published claims for both (Kraft 1970b). Thus, residence was in distinctive longhouses either dispersed singly as isolated farmsteads or clustered in small hamlets. They probably dispersed for winter hunting, spring fishing, and fowling in small task groups. They had access to coastal resources as well and spent part of the summer gathering shellfish and other resources at the shore. Moreover, they were better able than the Mohawk to exploit migratory fish runs and we can presume that their harvesting of this resource paralleled that of the Mahican in a general way.

Farmstead houses were covered with mats rather than bark as were the small temporary shelters erected at special-purpose campsites. The Munsee also constructed sweathouses in the same manner. Sweathouses were used by men and were always located near running water in order to facilitate the obligatory plunge at the end of the sweat bath. Although specific mention in early records is hard to find, sweating of this sort was probably practiced throughout aboriginal New England.

It seems likely that all of the Delaware were at one time distributed within the drainage of the same name. Eventually an upstream–downstream division developed, much as it did in other major river drainages of the Northeast. The upstream Munsee subsequently moved into the lower Hudson drainage such that by A.D. 1600 they occupied the headwaters of one drainage and the tidewater of another. The lower portion of the Delaware drainage was therefore left to the Unami branch of the Delaware culture. Thus, the seasonal movements of the Munsee probably involved frequent crossing of the drainage boundary between the upper Delaware and the lower Hudson. The Munsee did not make heavy use of bark canoes, and it seems likely that movements between drainages were most often by overland trails.

The longhouse social unit was probably a matrilineage. At least in later times the Munsee had three major clans (Turtle, Turkey, and Wolf) to which lineages belonged. The settlement unit of the main village was a collection of lineages apparently led by a man from a high-ranking lineage. There were various council mechanisms to help the leader achieve consensus when necessary. Clearly effective leadership depended much on the leader's personal charisma, a pattern resembling that of other Algonquian groups much more than the more highly structured Mohawk system.

Artifact types were similar to those of their neighbors. Like the Mohawk the Munsee carried ironwood clubs for use in combat. In addition, they appear to have used wooden helmets and rectangular wooden or moose-hide shields in 1600. Munsee women made both the more traditional Algonquian conical-bottomed clay pots and the globular and collared pots in the Iroquois style. They shared the wampum complex with the other cultures of southern New England, and like the Massachusett made use of large dugout canoes as well as lighter bark canoes.

Burials were flexed and in a sitting position. Some graves were clustered in cemeteries while others were isolated. Personal items were buried with the deceased along with food and wampum. Wood or boughs were put around the body and the grave was capped with earth or stones. In the case of a man, a post with pictorial representations of his history or personal characteristics was erected over the grave. Afterward, the grave was tended and kept free of grass by mourners. Archaeological research has shown that the Munsee of the upper Delaware and lower Hudson drainages generally buried their dead with heads oriented to the west or southwest, a practice still observed by the descendant Munsee Delaware living in Canada. In contrast, the Unami-speaking people of the southern Delaware drainage buried their dead with heads to the east, and this practice has been continued by the descendant Oklahoma Delaware Indians (Kraft 1975b:90). What little is known of the seventeenth-century Munsee is summarized by Goddard (1978b).

PALEO-INDIANS: THE FIRST ARRIVALS

We now reach back to the beginning of the long cultural trajectory through time that ended with the historic Indians of New England. The Paleo-Indians of North America were first recognized for what they were and named in the 1930s. Most of the sites discovered early on were in the western half of the continent. A curious feature of the early discoveries and excavations was that most of the western sites appeared to be kill sites while most of the few known in the East appeared to be camp sites. New discoveries and reanalyses of old discoveries have made this dichotomy less pronounced, but it has not disappeared. Kill sites with masses of animal skeletons, particularly those of extinct Pleistocene species, remain for the most part a western phenomenon. The diagnostic artifact type of Paleo-Indians is the fluted point. I describe variants of this type for the Northeast at a later point in this chapter. For decades the most popular generalization regarding the cultural system was that they were specialists in the hunting of big game. Given the apparent coincidence of the demise of the Paleo-Indian cultural systems and the extinction of many Pleistocene game animals, the possible cause and effect relationship between the two has been one of the most debated subjects of modern archaeological research. I will touch on this and other broad issues only as appropriate to a regional volume on the prehistory of New England.

In our region the Paleo-Indian period lasted from 12,500 to 10,000 years ago. We may yet find clear evidence of an earlier starting date, but the presence of Pleistocene glaciers over all of the region now above water will probably preclude the discovery of anything more than 2000 years older.

Over the past 20 years I have been fortunate to have been able to learn much from colleagues in glacial and Pleistocene geology, paleobotany, and paleozoology. It is clear that without such associations no archaeologist would be able to understand the setting in which the drama of the Paleo-

CHAPTER 3

Indian period was played out. To be sure, scholars in these other disciplines still have many problems to work out, and I would not want to suggest that my summaries of their work to date are either fully comprehensive or likely to stand without further revision. However, it is probable that currently accepted summaries are correct in their broad outlines. Certainly we must start somewhere, and we have no hope of beginning to understand the evidence of Paleo-Indians without some attempt to set the stage of their physical environments.

LATE GLACIAL HISTORY

The Wisconsin was the last great episode of the North American Pleistocene. It began tens of thousands of years ago, and during its course mankind completed its long evolution to biological modernity and spread into areas of the world that humans had not previously occupied. Biologically modern people emerged only about 40,000 years ago, and it was not until about 30,000 years ago that technological developments enabled them to penetrate the cold hunting regions of the world. For reasons that I have argued at greater length elsewhere (Snow 1976e:18–21), there is good reason to conclude that the earliest arrivals in North America did not drift across the exposed Bering Strait land bridge until sometime after 28,000 years ago at the earliest. Arguments for and against clear evidence of human hunting bands on the continent after that date are numerous and complex. However, we are saved from a lengthy discussion of them by the late glacial history of the Northeast, for all of the area covered by this volume was scoured and reshaped by ice advances that did not begin to melt back until after 18,000 years ago. The slate on which the human prehistory of the Northeast has been written was wiped clean, and we are left with only what time has written on it since then.

Pleistocene geology is the study of a relatively small band of geologists interested in the events of the Quaternary, the last geological period. Strictly speaking it includes today, and although we do not know how much longer it will continue it will remain the shortest period for some time to come. As in all of historical geology, reconstruction of the events of the Pleistocene depends on a thorough understanding of geological processes as they can be observed happening today. The study of modern glaciers has enabled Pleistocene geologists to identify and to describe events of thousands of years ago on the basis of the characteristic remains they left behind. Some charming anachronisms remain to remind us that there is such a thing as the history of geology, which is quite different from geological history. One such anachronism is the type of deposit known as *drift*. A century or more ago such deposits were thought to have been left behind as the result of gravels falling out of icebergs adrift on a biblical flood. This quaint interpretation of their origin has disappeared, but drift lives on in modern geology. *Till* is the unsorted kind of drift laid down like a carpet under moving ice. *Stratified drift* includes a number of well-sorted deposits washed into position by glacial meltwater. That which is built up beyond the glacier itself is called *outwash*, and outwash deposits can be marked by a number of special features, each of which has a name of its own.

There are many more terms in the special vocabulary of Pleistocene geologists, only a few of which need to be defined at this point. A *moraine* is the huge deposit left along the margins of a glacier that is in balance, its melting roughly equaling its slow advance. The debris carried along by the ice therefore gets deposited under the ice as till or dumped along the margin as moraine. *Kames* are piles of gravel left behind when the ice around pockets of gravel within glaciers stagnates and melts away without significant forward movement. *Drumlins* are hills that look like teardrops from the air due to shaping by glacial ice that once passed over them. I have defined additional terms as needed in the pages that follow. Anyone interested in a more complete understanding of the subject and its vocabulary should consult Richard Flint's (1971) text.

The advance of late Wisconsin ice was not uniform all along its southern margin. As a result, there was no single time when coverage was simultaneously at its maximum throughout our region. However, we can be fairly sure that maximum ice advance was reached at various places in the Northeast between 18,000 and 16,000 years ago. Thereafter the general trend was for the ice to retreat as its slow grinding advance out of Canada no longer exceeded or even kept up with melting. From time to time lobes of ice would readvance with relative suddenness, but the overall picture was one of retreat (Ogden 1977a:23). By 15,300 B.P. the ice front stood on what are now Long Island, Martha's Vineyard, and Nantucket. Ice advance and melting remained in balance for a time, and the glacial ice acted like a conveyor belt dumping glacial gravel along its steadily melting margin. This huge gravel formation is called the Ronkonkoma Moraine, and it forms much of the southern side of Long Island and virtually all of Martha's Vineyard and Nantucket (Figure 3.1). Within a few centuries the ice had retreated northward and paused once again, this time forming the Harbor Hill Moraine on what is now the north side of Long Island, Fisher's Island, coastal Rhode Island, and the south shore of Cape Cod. Over the next millennium and a half the ice front retreated to the 13,500 B.P. position shown in Figure 3.1. The main edge of the ice crossed what is now the middle Hudson Valley, ran along the northern boundaries of Connecticut and Rhode Island, and then veered north across southeastern Massachusetts to run along the northern New England coastline. Stagnating caps of ice probably remained behind in places, and huge blocks were left insulated under blankets of gravel in others. These gradually melted too, and in the case of the buried blocks left large pits called *kettles*. These often became basins holding small ponds, and with the accumulation of sediments many later evolved into bogs.

Thus, by at least 13,500 B.P., the southernmost edge of our region was open for the reestablishment of plant and animal communities. The earliest vegetation to reoccupy the area was composed of tundra flora. Once estab-

FIGURE 3.1. Excavated Paleo-Indian period sites and published fluted point finds. Dashed line shows maximum exposure of continental shelf. Mastodon and mammoth finds are shown for subsequently submerged areas only. Broad dotted lines show ice front positions at 15,300 and 13,500 B.P.

lished, this in turn supported grazing game animals, including species such as the caribou, which no longer live in the Northeast, and mastodons, which are extinct everywhere. Once these game animals were reestablished, bands of Paleo-Indians would have been able to drift into the region as well.

It is important to have some basic understanding of the complex interrelation of ice retreat and sea level changes during this period. At the height of the Wisconsin glaciation, much of the world's water was locked up as ice in the continental ice sheets. About 15,000 years ago the sea level was therefore about 130 m below its present level, a worldwide phenomenon that along the coast of the Northeast resulted in the exposure of huge tracts of continental shelf (Edwards and Emery 1977). By 13,500 B.P. the exposed area had been somewhat reduced as ice melted and the sea level rose, but the area shown in Figure 3.1 still remained (Borns 1971). Dry land extended eastward from southern New England to what we now call Georges Bank. South of Long Island the band of exposed continental shelf was more than 100 km wide (Emery and Edwards 1966). The peninsula of Nova Scotia was much enlarged and, as can be seen in Figure 3.1, was separated from the exposed extension of southern New England by the relatively narrow Northeast Channel. The large number of mastodon and mammoth teeth that have been pulled off the continental shelf by fishing boats are clear evidence that the exposed area was inhabitable (Figure 3.1). However, we have yet to recover any of the comparatively small traces of human occupation that might have been left behind. The previously exposed portions of the continental shelf has been regarded as a potentially rich archaeological zone by scholars such as Emery and Edwards (1966) (Figure 3.2), but our increasing understanding of the ways in which coastlines are affected by rising seas has dampened much of that enthusiasm (J. Kraft 1977). We cannot be sure that Paleo-Indians followed game onto the continental shelf. Even if they did, it seems unlikely that more than a few of their sites would have survived the erosion and reworking that would have attended inundation. Finally, the possibilities are remote that any surviving remains could be located using even the most sophisticated (and expensive) underwater equipment now available.

On land, the ice of 13,500 B.P. was as much as 2 km thick. The colossal weight of the ice mass depressed the land under it to as much as 1000 m below present sea level. The fringe of coastal Maine was free of ice, but was still so depressed that it was nevertheless submerged by the lowered ocean. Large rivers of meltwater formed on and in the melting ice sheet, building gravel riverbeds that were later deposited in long snakelike ridges called *eskers*. One of these runs southeastward across Maine, ending in a delta in the town of Cherryfield. The delta, once below reduced sea level, now lies high and dry overlooking the Gulf of Maine, lifted out of the rising sea by the even faster rebounding land. Indeed, geological research has shown that the depressed land rebounded so fast that most of the rebound could have taken place within a few centuries of final glacial retreat (Borns 1971).

Much happened during the thousand years that followed 13,500 B.P. From Cape Cod to the Hudson valley the land rebounded as the ice retreated

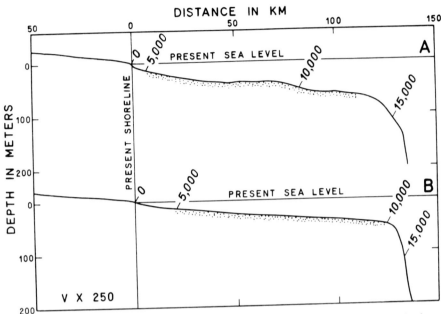

FIGURE 3.2. Cross sections of continental shelf off New Jersey (A) and Georgia (B). Slanted numbers represent the positions of the shoreline during the past 15,000 years. Dotted areas show areas of relict sediments. (From Emery and Edwards 1966.)

northward. The coastal zone reacted first, while interior parts of the region, which had undergone greater depression and lost their ice cover later, got a later start and had farther to rebound. The result was that drainages such as the Hudson and the Connecticut became long shallow basins holding glacial lakes. There were several lake basins, and geologists have given the lakes they contained different names for their different levels. We will examine only a few of the better known cases here.

Bedrock and glacial gravels in the lower Hudson Valley formed a broad sill that held back the waters of glacial Lake Albany. The Hudson ice block still stood in the northern part of the drainage with its southern margin in the lake, while water from the exposed portions of the basins that now hold Lakes Michigan, Huron, and Erie flowed down what is now the Mohawk valley into the lake from the west (Hough 1963; LaFleur 1976). By 13,200 B.P. the upper Hudson Valley had rebounded enough to partially decant Lake Albany and force the ancestral Mohawk River to divert northward at Schenectady such that it emptied into Lake Albany in the present basin of Saratoga Lake. The ice had by this time retreated into the Champlain valley so that there was a continuous lake from the middle Hudson valley to the middle Champlain valley. This huge but short-lived lake has been rather arbitrarily divided into two units, Lake Albany and Lake Vermont. At this level the latter is sometimes called Lake Quaker Springs. The basin of modern Lake George like that of modern Lake Champlain was dammed by ice at its northern end, with the result that glacial Lake Bolton occupied it and drained southeastward into Lake Vermont.

By 13,000 B.P., Lake Albany was lower and narrower due to continued rebound of the land and perhaps some downcutting through the gravel sill at its southern end. Lake Vermont had also fallen to a lower level, a change that some geologists think requires it to take on a new name, Lake Coveville. The lower course of the ancestral Mohawk River had been forced to relocate again, this time to a channel south of the one just abandoned but still north of its present channel. While it had been flowing through the trough that now holds Ballston Lake and Saratoga Lake, by this time it was veering from Ballston Lake into the Round Lake trough and entering Lake Albany where Mechanicville now stands. It took only a century longer for crustal rebound to reduce Lake Vermont to an even lower level, sometimes called Lake Fort Ann. Lake Albany had by this time fallen and narrowed to become the Hudson River. Lake Bolton had lost its glacial dam and become Lake George, its outlet now on its northern end at Ticonderoga. The lower course of the ancestral Mohawk had fallen or was about to fall into its present channel. However, as long as ice still stood in the St. Lawrence valley, Lake Vermont (i.e., Lake Fort Ann) was forced to drain southward into the Hudson River (Connally and Sirkin 1971).

To the east, a similar but less understood episode of lake formation took place in the Connecticut valley. Lake Hitchcock paralleled Lake Albany both developmentally and physically. Here, however, there were not the complications of an extension of the St. Lawrence lowlands paralleling the Champlain basin or the massive flow of water from the Great Lakes basin. As in the Hudson drainage, lakes formed in the depressed basin of the Connecticut behind a broad gravel sill near the coast. As ice retreated from the valley, Lake Hitchcock formed against it, held back by a sill in the vicinity of Middletown, Connecticut. When the retreating ice and the lake that lapped against it reached the vicinity of Lyme, New Hampshire, crustal rebound and erosion of the sill in Middletown combined to drain the lake. South of Claremont, New Hampshire, the lake basin became the valley of the new Connecticut River. North of Claremont the lake remained at a lower level and resumed its expansion northward as the ice continued to retreat. This northern lower lake, Lake Upham, gradually expanded as far as St. Johnsbury, Vermont, before it, too, drained and gave birth to the upper Connecticut River.

There is still some controversy regarding the dating of events relating to Lakes Hitchcock and Upham, more so than in the case of Lakes Albany and Vermont (Figure 3.3). The accuracy and interpretation of different dating techniques are still debated. Despite these difficulties, it seems likely that Lake Hitchcock began to form at about the same time as Lake Albany, around 13,500 B.P. Lake Hitchcock probably drained at about the same time as Lake Albany, around 12,900 B.P. This would make Lake Upham roughly contemporary with Lake Fort Ann (Curran and Dincauze 1977).

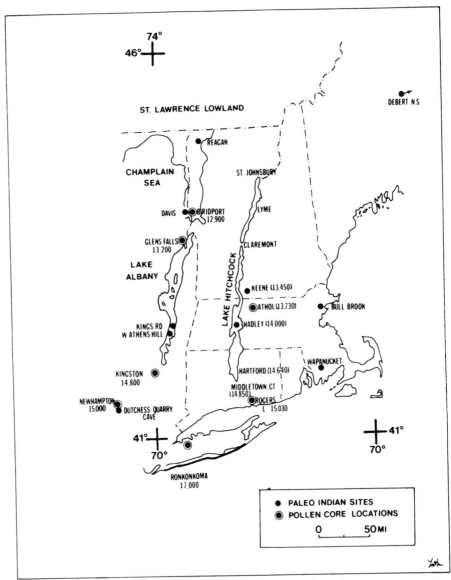

FIGURE 3.3. Paleo-Indian and pollen core sites showing deglaciation dates where known. Pollen core dates are based on radiocarbon dates and sedimentation rates. Lake and sea shorelines shown were not contemporaneous. (From Curran and Dincauze 1977:335.)

Events of the period were quite different but no less dramatic in Maine. Here the rebound of the land did not keep up with rising sea level. Instead of seeing the development of interior glacial lakes, this part of our region was inundated by seawater from the Gulf of Maine. The ocean penetrated up what are now the Kennebec River and Penobscot River valleys and submerged much of the low coastal land between them. Coastal inundation was less pronounced in New Brunswick, and nonexistent in Massachusetts, where much of the continental shelf still laid exposed. Nova Scotia, still fringed by exposed shelf along most of its coastline, was nevertheless insulated from New Brunswick by the temporary inundation. By 12,500 B.P. the salt water had reached the present sites of East Millinocket in the Penobscot valley and Bingham in the Kennebec valley (Borns 1971). By this time, too, glacial ice had retreated northward out of the St. Lawrence valley, allowing the Great Lakes to drain that way instead of down the Mohawk valley, and allowing Lake Vermont to abandon its drainage into the Hudson River. However, the St. Lawrence valley was still depressed from its recent load of ice, and the consequent entry of seawater converted Lake Vermont into the Champlain Sea. Figure 3.4 shows the consequence of all these events as of 12,500 B.P. Although dry by that time, the basins of Lake Albany, Lake Hitchcock, and other large glacial lakes had become only slightly less forbidding expanses of sand dunes.

The Sea of Champlain may have formed as early as 12,800 B.P., giving Lake Fort Ann (the last stage of Lake Vermont) a life of only a century. The sea may also have persisted until 10,000 years ago. Although it would have shrunk in size over this period, 2800 years would have been a very long life compared to the ephemeral lakes I have been discussing thus far (Kirkland and Coates 1977). We do not yet know the degree to which plant communities were able to establish themselves around the lakes and seas of the late Pleistocene, or the degree to which freshwater and marine animal populations were able to move into them. It seems likely that many lakes were too cold, too brief, and too loaded with glacial sediments to have supported much animal life. However, the Sea of Champlain attracted fish, seals, and other animal populations during its relatively long existence. Whether these in turn attracted human populations is a matter for speculation later in this chapter.

Complex as it may seem, this has been only the barest outline of the late glacial history of our region. The geography of New England would have been difficult for the modern observer to recognize at any of the stages I have described, and an understanding of how it got to be that way even more difficult. However, a review of these events is essential for an understanding of Paleo-Indian prehistory, and a prehistory of the Indians who followed them. The strange geography of Figure 3.4 was very real to the first Paleo-Indians who encountered it, and they had to deal with it on its own terms. They and those who came after them all had to adapt to a topography shaped by the violent events of the late Ice Age. Whether it was a man portaging along a natural highway in the abandoned channel that once drained Lake Vermont into the Hudson or a woman digging for the fine blue marine clay left behind in central Maine by the sea, all of the prehistoric people of New England had their lives shaped by Pleistocene events that human eyes may never have seen.

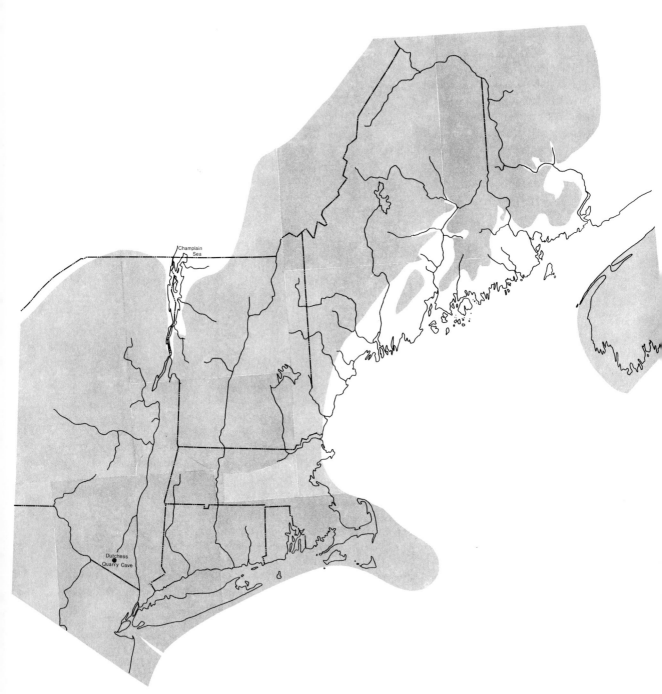

FIGURE 3.4. New England at the beginning of the Paleo-Indian period (12,500 B.P.). Vast areas of continental shelf were still exposed while some northern areas now above sea level were submerged. Glacial lakes (not shown) came and went in some interior basins while the ice caps still persisted in some mountainous areas.

Early Paleo-Indians and later cultures had to adapt to New England's plant environments too. Some species are capable of rapid migration, and it seems likely that a few were quick to become established on the cold barren sands and gravels of southernmost New England by 13,500 years ago. The mammoths and mastodons whose teeth have been dredged from the continental shelf must have been living on things that herbivores would regard as edible. Archaeologists have looked to paleobotany for reconstructions of early environments that permit them to hypothesize the subsistence strategies and other adaptations of early animal and human populations. The primary tool used has been palynology, the study of pollen grains. The kettles that dot the New England terrain formed soon after glacial retreat, as we have seen. In many cases these have held water since their formation. Many have bottom deposits 1–10 m thick, which contain organic material that has settled there under quiet subsurface conditions. Among the organic remains are billions of pollen grains that have been carried by the wind from flowering plants to pond surfaces. The tough little grains settle on the bottom in proportion to their presence in the air, and they can survive there with relative ease for thousands of years. Because the trained eye can distinguish plants at the genus (and sometimes at the species) level on the basis of pollen alone, it is possible to get some idea of the proportions of plant species in a given forest on the basis of its pollen deposits in a nearby pond. Cores of pond deposit are extracted and sliced stratigraphically like pieces of salami. Some samples are set aside for radiocarbon dating and others are cleaned and refined so that their pollen contents can be examined. Complete and undisturbed cores can contain evidence of local vegetational history from the end of the Pleistocene to the present. Pollen samples of selected slices of the core are examined under a special microscope and the grains are individually identified and counted. This tedious and time-consuming chore eventually results in inventories of the local forest environment at intervals in its postglacial history. However, there are problems with the technique that go far beyond eye strain and boredom.

Some plant species, pines for example, are very heavy pollen producers. Anyone who has been in a pine forest during pollenation can testify to clouds of pollen that fill the air and cover the ground as a thick layer of yellow dust. In contrast to this, many grasses and sedges are very low pollen producers and are therefore underrepresented in pollen cores. The problem is that pollen counts are usually expressed in terms of the percentage of each type within the total sample, so minor and perhaps insignificant fluctuations in major pollen producers can cause apparently (but only apparently) significant fluctuations among low pollen producers. Another problem is that variations in deposition rates and the tendency for the lower portions of pollen cores to have been compressed by the weight of later deposits mean that a segment of core taken from near the bottom represents more time than a segment of the same length taken from near the top. As we shall see, there are now techniques for overcoming both of these problems. However,

VEGETATIONAL HISTORY

paleobotanists have yet to devise foolproof techniques to avert the misuse of their data by archaeologists.

Archaeologists have always depended heavily on scientists in other fields whenever attention has become focused upon prehistoric environments. That dependence has sometimes been attended by more than a little naïveté on the part of the archaeologists. A good example of this dates from the late 1950s, when there was a rush to explain postglacial North American prehistory in terms of a climate cycle proposed by Ernst Antevs (1955). Antevs's cycle was explicitly designed to explain evidence from the West, and even its use there has been sharply criticized. Unfortunately, this has not prevented some archaeologists in the East from using Antevs's scheme as a causal explanation for changes they have observed in the archaeological record. As we shall see, palynology is itself a blunt instrument for the reconstruction of past environments. The past climates that in part produced those environments are even harder to reconstruct and even further removed from the human adaptations to which we hope to link them. James B. Griffin (1961a) warned against the misuse of paleoclimatic data long ago and made an effort to steer research in a direction that would ultimately produce valid results. Fortunately, we now have the work of researchers such as Wendland and Bryson (1974), who used masses of archaeological and climatological data to convincingly show broad connections between prehistoric cultural developments and climate. They have gone on to tackle the more difficult task of linking specific climatic episodes to variations in such things as pollen cores and tree ring sequences. Only after all these complicated links are understood will we really begin to understand the effects of climatic change on prehistoric cultures.

Generally speaking, the effects of relatively small fluctuations in climate are more pronounced in regions such as the Arctic and the American Southwest than they are in regions such as New England. The persistence of plant and animal populations in the Arctic or the Southwest is relatively precarious, and small changes in local climate can lead to extensive changes in their distributions. This is why dendrochronology (tree ring dating) works well in these areas. Annual variations in tree rings, which result from minor climatic variations, are both widespread and uniform. Human adaptation in these can also be precarious, and the impact of climate change on human populations can be similarly uniform and widespread. Thus, demographic and other cultural fluctuations that show up in the archaeological record there can often be related directly to fluctuations in climate.

In contrast, there are many more intervening variables in the forests of the Northeast. The specific makeup of these forests depends on such things as drainage, relief, mineral nutrients, soil development, and radiation, all of which tend to mask the more generalized influences of climate. In a temperate forest, specific composition can be expected to change strikingly within a matter of a kilometer or two. Two trees of the same species can exhibit contrasting patterns of ring growth even though they may be only a few meters apart. Thus, temperate forest habitats can be expected to absorb without noticeable effect small variations in climate that have far-reaching consequences in desert regions and in higher latitudes. We can expect to find evidence of environmental and human response only to relatively pronounced long-term fluctuations in climate in New England.

It follows from this that it will probably not be possible for prehistorians in areas like New England to key local sequences to climatic histories with the success of Southwestern and Arctic archaeologists. Instead, it seems likely that the effects of climate on human prehistory in our area have been both subtle and gradual, often masked by human demographic and technological factors.

Through palynology, paleontology, and related disciplines, we have almost direct access to prehistoric environments. It makes little sense to reconstruct environments on the basis of meteorological guesswork, when palynologists can now do the same thing with more compelling accuracy. We need to make no direct reference to climate, which is only one of several factors that have influenced prehistoric environment in New England. The midwestern drought of the 1930s had little significant effect in the Northeast, and it is quite possible that "the trend toward warmer, drier climate 8000 years ago in the Midwest may have been accompanied by little significant changes in the Northeast [Wright 1971:459]." The primitive level of our understanding of air mass patterning is documented daily by our local weather forecasters. We have no reason to believe that we can do any better with the traces of extinct weather patterns, generated at a time when average temperatures, ice distributions, and ocean levels that influenced air masses were quite different from the modern case. This, of course, leads to the observation that in some cases the ecological contexts of prehistoric cultures might have no modern analogues. Proglacial tundra, for example, probably differed significantly from modern tundra if for no other reason than the fact that it existed in latitudes where there are no extreme seasonal variations in solar radiation. Such differences have important consequences for tundra fauna, not to mention palynologists, geologists, and archaeologists.

We must also avoid relying on outdated ecological literature. Such sources usually emphasize the largely intuitive concept of climax forests that either are supposed to have once existed in a pristine state or could be expected to develop if left undisturbed (Davis 1965:381). Advances in our knowledge of such subjects as soil evolution, erosion, cycles of forest fire, and climatic instability have long since modified this ethereal concept. Any archaeologist who has struggled with the culture area concept knows enough to be wary of its biological analogue, the biotic province. Both ideas were designed as means to classify and to generalize regionally, primarily for the beginning student who needed a simplified introduction to a complex subject matter. Culture areas lump historically known Indian cultures into regional units that mask their individual identities for the sake of common denominators. The lines that separate the regional units therefore typically exaggerate both the sharpness and the amount of difference between the neighboring cultures they separate. Biotic provinces similarly gloss over internal microenvironmental variations for the sake of characterizing broad regions, and similarly create a false impression of sharp lines between regional units. Clearly neither of these classificatory schemes was ever intended to provide scientifically useful analytical units. Thus, it is improper for archaeologists to insert prehistoric human populations into biotic provinces as a means to find an easy explanation for their regional distributions and ecological adjustments.

With those cautions in mind, I now turn to the techniques by which the vegetational history of New England has been reconstructed in a way useful to the archaeologist. One of the best understood pollen sequences in the region has resulted from Margaret Davis's work in Connecticut (Davis 1967, 1969). There, tundra followed deglaciation that occurred about 14,000 B.P. (Table 3.1). Initial evidence for tundra depended on high frequencies of

TABLE 3.1
Palynological Chronologies[a]

	Upper Hudson	Connecticut	Central Maine	
1,000 B.P.	C3 Spruce rise, pine–birch–	C3 Oak–chestnut		A.D. 1,000
2,000	hemlock			0
3,000	C2 Beech–pine– hemlock–oak–	C2 Oak–hickory	III Hardwood–conifer	1,000 B.C.
4,000	birch			2,000
5,000				3,000
6,000	C1 Hemlock–birch– pine–oak	C1 Oak–hemlock	IIb Conifer–hardwood	4,000
7,000	B2 Pine–oak			5,000
8,000	B1 Pine–birch	B2 Pine–oak		6,000
			IIa Conifer–hardwood	
9,000				7,000
	A4 Spruce–alder–pine	B1 Pine–birch–alder		
10,000	A3 Pine–spruce	A4 Spruce–fir		8,000
	A2 Spruce–fir		Id	
11,000		A3 Pine–spruce		9,000
	A1 Spruce–pine	A2 Birch–spruce	Ic	
12,000		A1 Spruce		10,000
			Ib Tundra	
13,000	T Tundra	T Tundra	Ia	11,000
14,000				12,000
15,000 B.P.	Glaciated	Glaciated	Glaciated	13,000 B.C.

[a] For the upper Hudson drainage (Connally and Sirkin 1971), the lower Connecticut drainage (Davis 1969), and central Maine (Davis *et al.* 1975). Zones defined for Maine reflect Davis *et al.*'s reluctance to characterize complex forest compositions with simple labels.

nonarboreal pollen (NAP) in this zone. The situation has been further clarified by the development of techniques for the estimation of absolute pollen influx (API), expressed as the number of pollen grains per square centimeter of pond surface per year. As mentioned earlier, nonarboreal plants are generally low pollen producers, and the pollen deposition rate in a tundra environment is therefore similarly low. Spruce trees in distant forests provided as much as 30% of the pollen deposited in the tundra zone through long-distance transport. API work has shown this to be partly a function of heavy pollen production by spruce and partly a function of differential deposition rates over time. One important feature of the API technique is the precise measurement of the amount of sediment from which the pollen is extracted. Another is the use of radiocarbon dating to date a core at several points so that variations in sedimentation rates can be measured.

Unfortunately, we are still not entirely sure whether the postglacial nonarboreal pollen zone actually represents tundra or something that is more closely paralleled by modern northern prairies. The fossil pollen percentages do not resemble modern pollen percentages from the Labrador tundra, and it is possible that a modern analogue will never be found. Just the same, it is probable that the fossil pollen represent an optimal environment with a high carrying capacity for hunter–gatherers. Modern high-latitude tundras receive less solar radiation and are subject to greater seasonal extremes in that radiation than were the tundras of Ice Age New England (Butzer 1971).

Deglaciation and subsequent tundra environment came and went somewhat earlier on Martha's Vineyard and Long Island, and somewhat later in northern New England. Tundra persisted until about 10,500 B.P. on Cape Breton Island. Despite time differences, there is presently no reason not to equate these middle-latitude tundra habitats in terms of carrying capacity. The biomass probably supported a hunter–gatherer population equivalent to modern middle-latitude grasslands, or about 5–12 persons per 100 km².

Tundra is followed by a spruce zone (period) in the Connecticut pollen sequence. Terasmae and Mott (1965) describe the environment at that time as "open park-like woodlands of black spruce, with an associated ground-cover of lichens [396]." Wright (1971:439) adds that the forest appears to have contained pine and some warmth-loving deciduous species, most notably oak and hornbeam. The rise of oak pollen at the base of the spruce zone probably represents an advance of oak trees toward the spruce–pine forest as the climate warmed. API data indicate that the subsequent decrease in oak pollen percentage resulted not from a decrease in absolute oak pollen influx, but from a surge in the absolute influx of pine pollen. Thus, there was apparently no absolute decrease in the frequency of oak pollen and therefore probably no climatic reversal.

The spruce zone lasted from about 12,000 to 9500 B.P. in Connecticut. The upper boundary is very sharp, particularly now that API analysis has shown the dramatic speed with which the pine–birch forest developed after 9500 B.P. Both the onset and the end of this zone date later in northern New

England (see Table 3.1). An important feature of the spruce zone is that the pine pollen in it was mostly from jack pine and red pine trees. The species that expanded so rapidly after 9500 B.P. was white pine. Pine probably took refuge in the Appalachians during glacial maxima, expanding into the Great Lakes drainage as well as the Northeast after glacial retreat. Wright (1971:446–448) suggests a relatively slow migration rate for white pine to explain its relatively late arrival in Connecticut.

Davis's analysis of surface pollen samples has shown that there is no modern analogue of the spruce zone in eastern Canada, as some palynologists have supposed. Surface samples from the spruce–oak woodland of southern Manitoba do resemble the zone, however. Native hunter–gatherer groups populated that area about as densely (5–12 per 100 km^2) as the grasslands to the south, and therefore about as densely as Paleo-Indians probably populated southern New England during the period of the tundra zone. In short, there is no ecological reason to suppose that there was a significant decline in human population density in southern New England between 12,000 and 9500 B.P.

By the time white pine began to dominate the forests of southernmost New England, the climate had warmed to a point that also favored various deciduous species. Thus, through both the spruce and pine zones of the pollen sequence, a closed boreal forest never developed in that area except perhaps on a rather local basis. Instead, the Connecticut forest seems to have evolved directly from something similar to the Canadian forest tundra to a mixed deciduous–coniferous forest.

This seems not to have been the case in northern New England and the upland areas of southern New England and New York. In those areas, the B zone in local pollen sequences is dominated by pine, indicating a boreal forest. Therefore, except for southernmost New England and New York, much of the region probably came to be dominated by a forest environment having a somewhat reduced carrying capacity after 9500 B.P. There is little herbaceous vegetation and therefore relatively few gregarious herbivores in such an environment. Indians historically inhabited the boreal forests of Canada at a density of fewer than two persons per 100 km^2 (Driver and Massey 1957:186). I conclude that human occupation of most of the region was reduced for the duration of the pine maximum, and this is why we will see relatively little evidence there for human population immediately after the waning of the Paleo-Indians. The data on the pine maximum vary according to location, but, because of steadily warming climate, it did not last long in the southern sections of the Northeast. The transition to an oak–hemlock forest began by about 7500 B.P. in southern New England. A similar transition toward a more temperate forest type took place in northern New England a few centuries later.

The vegetational history of New England for the centuries during and just after the Paleo-Indian period is clearly complex. The earliest traces we know about thus far were in the lower Hudson valley about 12,500 years ago, after the drainage of Lake Albany but during the time when the region was still dominated by tundra. To be sure, it was a lush middle-latitude tundra, not an environment that duplicated any we might find nearer the Arctic Circle today. The tundra lasted until about 12,000 B.P. in the southern part of the region, but persisted until 9700 B.P. in the north and probably longer in mountainous areas. The sequence and migration rates of tree species that established themselves in the region after that vary from place to place. I have argued that generalized concepts of biotic zones and forest types have little utility for the study of human ecology in modern forests, and it should be clear that the boundaries of zones defined for modern forests cannot be projected into the past. There is some evidence that pine was coming to dominate in many parts of the region around the end of the Paleo-Indian period, and we shall see that the rise of what is sometimes called a boreal forest could have forced a readjustment on the Indians and an abandonment of their Paleo-Indian cultural system.

People became biologically modern rather late in the Pleistocene. Prior to that time they were largely confined to tropical and temperate parts of the Old World. Cultural and biological factors were woven together in a complex fabric in the course of this evolutionary development, and part of the cultural side of it had to do with growing sophistication in the areas of cooperative hunting, shelter, food preparation, and clothing. All of that adds up to an ability to penetrate cold areas of Eurasia. When people eventually learned to build and use boats, previously unapproached islands became available to them as well. People did not migrate suddenly or blindly into these virgin territories, but were attracted there by huge populations of game animals, many of which subsequently became extinct. Lowered sea level left Siberia connected to Alaska in a broad area now submerged, and some species lived in unbroken distributions that covered parts of both continents. Late Pleistocene extinctions were so massive (perhaps two-thirds of the mammalian herbivore species of North America disappeared) that no modern zoo can assemble more than a few survivors. However, Paul Martin and John Guilday (1967) have compiled a recreated bestiary for Pleistocene biologists. I have drawn on this extraordinary array of strange creatures for a description of those now extinct species that roamed the Northeast for a few thousand years after the beginning of the last glacial retreat. They do not include the 5-m-tall giant ground sloth (about the size of the largest living giraffe) or the woolly rhinoceros, but they would shock modern eyes just the same.

Perhaps the best known Pleistocene animals are the mammoth species. These were rather closely related to the living elephants, but generally adapted to more northerly grassland environments. In order of increasing size the North American species were the dwarf mammoths, the woolly mammoth, Jefferson's mammoth, the Columbian mammoth, and the imperial mammoth. Standing 4 m tall at the shoulder, the imperial mammoth

GAME ANIMALS OF THE LATE PLEISTOCENE

was considerably larger than the largest African elephant (3.52 m). However, even the imperial mammoth was dwarfed by the Mosbach elephant of Eurasia, which has been estimated to have been 4.5 m tall. Dwarf mammoths (2 m) evolved when they were isolated by rising sea levels on islands such as Santa Rosa Island off the California coast. Mammoths have molars similar to those of living elephants, washboard-like teeth designed to grind tough grasses. The mammoth was clearly a grazing animal, and it is not surprising that its remains are much more frequent on the Great Plains than they are in the East. A few have been found in direct association with Paleo-Indian remains in the American West, but none of the mammoth remains of the Northeast have been associated with Paleo-Indians thus far. It is estimated that 117,000 mammoths have been discovered in Russia in the past 250 years, some of them almost perfectly preserved in the permafrost (Martin and Guilday 1967:38–39).

Mastodons are much more frequently found in the Northeast than mammoths. Although similar, these creatures do not belong to the elephant family, but represent an older separate line of proboscideans. The most telling difference between them and the elephants (including mammoths) is that their molars are cusped and therefore adapted to browsing rather than grazing. They were adapted to forest rather than grassland environments. Adults stood 2–3 m tall at the shoulder. The remains of at least a thousand mastodons have been found in North America, primarily in the East. Figure 3.1 shows the locations of finds on that part of the once-exposed continental shelf I have already discussed. Their occurrence in proportion to mammoth finds seems appropriate. Mammoths probably moved into the area with the tundra shortly after deglaciation (Figure 3.5) and were replaced by mastodons as the tundra gave way to a forest environment. Radiocarbon dates on mastodon bones run as young as 6000–8000 B.P., but even without these

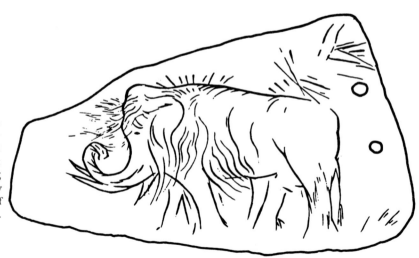

FIGURE 3.5. The Holly Oak Pendant (Smithsonian Institution Cat. No. 148313). The whelk shell is holed twice and engraved with a sketch of a woolly mammoth. Although a few archaeologists accept it as evidence of the contemporaneity of Paleo-Indians and mammoths on the East Coast, most consider it a fake. The engraving appears to have been copied directly from published illustrations of the European Upper Paleolithic. (After J. Kraft 1977.)

questionable recent dates it seems likely that mastodons were in our region longer than mammoths (Martin and Guilday 1967:36–37). There have been many more mammoth and mastodon finds on dry land in the Northeast, but information on them has not been assembled uniformly for each state. I have therefore not attempted to show them on Figure 3.1. The best single review of Pleistocene game animals for a northeastern state is Fisher's (1955) summary for New York, reproduced by Ritchie (1969a:10–11).

Horse bones are less common in North American Pleistocene deposits, and a few have been found in the Northeast. Although they are sometimes stratigraphically associated with Paleo-Indians, we have yet to find obvious evidence of horse kills similar to those known in Europe. Just the same, North American horses survived into the Paleo-Indian period as we have defined it for the Northeast, and we can predict that some direct evidence of horse kills will eventually turn up. It is interesting that, although Pleistocene horses became extinct, domesticated Spanish horses multiplied phenomenally after their introduction in the sixteenth and seventeenth centuries. The difference may have hinged on two factors. First, there are about eight living species, and there were undoubtedly several more distinct species during the Pleistocene. A small subset of one of these, the tarpan of Europe and Asia, provided the initial strain from which all domesticated horses descend. Many of the others, most zebras for example, are simply unsuitable for domestication. It is likely that the North American Pleistocene horses were valuable only as game animals. Once again, even a low level of hunting pressure on these herds might have been sufficient to unbalance their birth/death rate ratio and push them slowly toward extinction.

The second factor is attitudinal. Paleo-Indians had no reason to think of horses as anything but game animals. In contrast, the first Spanish were trained and equipped for riding. The whole set of attitudes and habits that went with the use of horses for transportation was picked up quickly by Indians. The spread of the horses themselves barely kept up with the spread of this exciting new idea. Thus, the phenomenal spread of the horse through colonial America was promoted by the Indians. Herds were propagated, protected, and used with a care that stood in stark contrast to the parasitic relationship between Paleo-Indians and Pleistocene horses. Horses did not survive the Paleo-Indian period in the Northeast, and it is fair to assume that hunting helped to bring about their disappearance (Martin and Guilday 1967:41–42).

The remains of other Pleistocene animals that are now extinct have been found in small numbers in the Northeast. There were bears that were comparable in size to the surviving Kodiak bear, a subspecies of the Alaskan brown bear. They may have had the relatively gentle disposition of Kodiaks, or they might have been more similar to that tough survivor of the Pleistocene, the grizzly bear. There were also giant beavers, 2 m long from nose to tail, that survived into the Paleo-Indian period. Only their smaller relative survives today (Martin and Guilday 1967:25, 30–31).

Finally, there were other Pleistocene game animals that survived into or through the Paleo-Indian period in the Northeast, but that are no longer found here. These include bison (the modern, not the larger extinct forms), elk, caribou, and musk ox. The musk ox retreated out of the region very early and managed to survive the Pleistocene by moving into Arctic refuges that humans did not penetrate until the arrival of the Eskimo within the last 4000 years. These animals have a defense strategy that involves backing into a circle and waiting out the attacker, something that works against any predator except man. The others, bison, elk, and caribou, have flight strategies that are better adapted to survival in the face of human hunters, and all of them might well have survived into the colonial period in the Northeast. Readers should be wary of early sources reporting their presence, however. Early English used the word *elk* to describe what we now call *moose*. Our elk (wapiti) would have been a stag, hart, or red deer to an early Englishman, and our caribou would have been a reindeer.

Many other smaller animals became extinct as well, or at least left the Northeast. Many of them must have been lost in the general disruption of the ecological balance to which Paleo-Indians contributed. Some species both large and small managed to survive only by retreating to remote refuge areas, but others appear to have had nowhere to go. The precise role of human hunters in this complex systemic imbalance is still debated. Two decades ago the debate was still focused on a simplistic choice between whether or not people were the single significant cause of Pleistocene extinctions. Certainly our recent record when confronted with formerly isolated and almost defenseless oddities such as great auks, dodo birds, and Galapagos tortoises suggests that we have an easy capacity for overkill. However, these are not giant bison and mastodons, and many investigators seek alternative or at least additional factors. Still our thinking returns repeatedly to the key role of human hunters.

Paul S. Martin (1973) has elaborated this general picture into a scenario of dramatic expansion and overkill. He sees the expansion of Paleo-Indians as keyed directly to the extinction of Pleistocene game species. His model proposes that there was a single expanding front of Paleo-Indians that advanced in a broad arc out of northwestern Canada, exterminating game animals as it swept over North America. In this model, the wave front would have been about 160 km thick, within which the human population would have been 40 individuals per 100 km². The front would have advanced radially at a rate of 16 km per year, leaving behind a residual population of 4 individuals per 100 km² to mop up what large game animals might have survived the initial shock wave. Among its other assumptions, the model calls for a human population growth rate amounting to a doubling every 20 years. Martin concludes that Paleo-Indians would have wiped out the two-thirds of all herbivore species that became extinct around the end of the Pleistocene in a matter of only 1000 years. The high drama of this scenario alone arouses skepticism in the minds of many archaeologists.

Still, Martin has noted elsewhere that the entry of human bands into territories where they were never previously present has always preceded wholesale extinctions of animal populations (Martin 1967). Thus, we must not exclude the very real possibility of a direct connection between the arrival of Paleo-Indians and the extinction of Pleistocene herbivores. However, I see this as I see most prehistoric relationships—as a systemic connection, not as a simple cause and effect. Large game animals became extinct in wholesale lots over a relatively short time span, but so did many smaller bird and animal species whose passing is much more difficult to attribute directly to human overkill. It seems likely on the basis of what we presently know that hunting by bands of Paleo-Indians was just one of several pressures that operated on North American animal populations at the close of the Pleistocene. In many cases it must have been negligible, but in others it may well have been the last straw. Herd animals may already have been reduced by steadily shrinking ranges. Gestation periods may have failed to adjust to postglacial changes in seasonal patterns, with the result that many young were born too early in the spring. Unknown diseases and parasites may have weakened whole species. Into this period of readjustment came skilled human hunters, either as a wave of newcomers or as a development out of a thin population that had already been in residence for thousands of years. It is entirely likely that many species were caught without adequate instinctive defenses against the new human predator, and that there was too little time for such defenses to evolve given the pressures already existing.

Although Martin's model might seem attractive for its dramatic simplicity, this is its very weakness. Although there is evidence to suggest that early human bands reached the New World by 27,000 B.P. (Irving and Harington 1973) and expanded as far as Peru by 20,000 B.P. (MacNeish et al. 1970), we know that glacial ice gave them no access to the Northeast until after 15,000 B.P. Haynes (1964, 1969, 1977) has asserted for years that there is little convincing evidence for the presence of Paleo-Indians in North America much before 12,000 B.P. and that most sites cluster between 11,000 and 11,500 B.P. If we concede that some bands of humans might have been in North America as early as 27,000 B.P. and attribute massive extinctions to advanced hunters spreading into the continent with weapons tipped with fluted points, then Haynes's arguments appear to support Martin's model. As it happens, however, the northeastern sites I have just summarized have yielded the oldest (12,530 ± 370 B.P.) as well as some of the youngest radiocarbon dates for fluted point sites in North America, and there is little or no evidence internal to the Northeast to suggest that an exterminating wave of Paleo-Indian bands ever swept over the region. Everything we have seen thus far suggests that Paleo-Indians maintained a stable cultural system in the Northeast for over two millennia. Thus, Martin's argument suffers from proposing not only a single cause for Pleistocene extinctions but a catastrophic one as well.

Human hunters had never come as such a shock to the large game species of the Old World, where for the most part human cultural advances evolved slowly enough to allow time for other animal populations to adjust biologically. Thus, bands of human predators were probably one of several ingredients in the extinctions that followed the North American Pleistocene, in some cases crucial but in others insignificant. A few species escaped by adapting quickly enough (American bison), retreating to inaccessible mountain areas (wild sheep and goats), or retreating to the far north (musk oxen). The musk ox is the prime example of a Pleistocene anachronism, for the defense mechanism of a herd of these beasts is to back into a circle and glower. This may be an adequate defense against marauding wolves, but it is an irresistible invitation to human hunters.

PALEO-INDIAN ARTIFACTS The Indians who drifted into the new postglacial environment of New England carried tool kits designed for efficiency and portability. The most easily recognized artifact class, which is also the most diagnostic Paleo-Indian trait in sites east of the Rocky Mountains, is the fluted point. The two most widely known types, Clovis and Folsom, were first defined by archaeologists working in New Mexico, and, although analogous types can be found in New England, it would be stretching definitions to say that either type has ever been found here. Instead, we have about seven distinctive type styles, two of which can be regarded as similar but not identical to Clovis and Folsom. Our most serious problem at present is that this handful of styles has been found scattered through an equivalently small handful of excavated Paleo-Indian sites. Dozens of specimens have also been found as isolated surface finds, but these usually lack most of the context we need for analysis. Even more troublesome is the general lack of radiocarbon dates for excavated Paleo-Indian remains. Only one of the sites discussed here, Debert, Nova Scotia, has been accurately dated, and strictly speaking this site lies outside the regional scope of this volume. Other sites have been dated, but as will be seen later either the dates themselves are suspect or their associations with Paleo-Indian remains have not been established beyond doubt. Thus, we are faced with the task of interpreting a 2500-year-long period on the basis of only about a dozen excavated components, few of which have been convincingly dated. I must resort to including some information from the Plenge and two other sites in New Jersey, the Shoop site in Pennsylvania, and the Debert site in order to provide even a rough outline of Paleo-Indian culture. Even so, we are still far from knowing which of the stylistic variables we can observe in Paleo-Indian remains are temporally significant, and which (if any) are spatially significant. For the moment I can offer only a few possible conclusions with respect to stylistic variation.

Most fluted points in our area fall between 25 and 100 mm in length. By definition their common characteristic is a flute on each face, produced when long channel flakes were struck from their bases. Paleo-Indian knappers typically began with a leaf-shaped preform with defined central ridges on

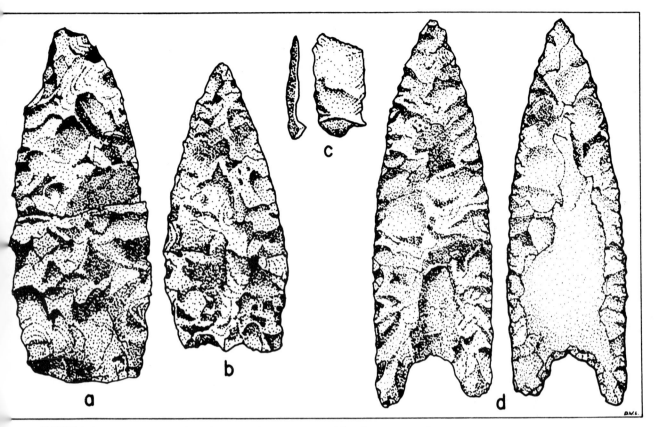

FIGURE 3.6. Specimens from the Debert site showing stages of fluted point manufacture. Beginning with a preform (a), the knapper prepared the base (b) for removal of a channel flake (c) in order to produce a finished piece (d). Finished points range in length from 32 mm to the 109-mm specimen shown here. Shown at actual size. (From MacDonald 1968:71–74.)

both sides (Figure 3.6). Central ridges were essential to guide the fractures of the channel flakes as they detached from the preform, clearly the most difficult single step in the production of fluted points. Sometimes pairs of guide flakes were struck parallel to and on either side of each central ridge to provide additional control over the removal of the channel flake (Witthoft 1952:474). This and other preparations of the point base left a nipple at the center, which, when ground to provide a tiny flat area for the punch, became the striking platform by which the channel flake was struck off. In some instances the punch, which was struck with a hammerstone to remove the flake by indirect percussion, was held almost on the axis of the point. The result was that remains of both the nipple and the guide flakes can sometimes be seen. In other cases, particularly at the Debert site, the punch was tipped so that the entire nipple as well as the guide flake scars were all detached with the channel flake (MacDonald 1968:75). In these cases a second nipple had to be prepared from scratch for the removal of the second channel flake. When it, too, was detached, the point was left with an unusually deep basal concavity. Multiple flutes are sometimes noticed on points, but it is not always clear whether these are channel flake scars with traces of guide flake scars or repeated attempts to produce an adequately thinned point. Occasionally a channel flake thinned a point so drastically that the knapper was unable to remove a channel flake from the reverse side. It was rare that a preform was already so thin that no channel flakes could be removed at all and it was simply finished by means of pressure retouch flaking and grinding of basal edges. All fluted points that were carried to completion have secondary pressure retouch and basal grinding, the latter probably meant to prevent the point from cutting its lashing.

Notwithstanding that some of the details have been questioned in recent years (Cox 1972), I have emphasized specific steps in the manufacture of fluted points because the skill and care they represent were only rarely equaled in other times and other places in the prehistoric world. If Paleo-Indians had other arts that they took as seriously as this one, we have yet to find evidence of them. Their high standards are reflected in the large percentage of points that were broken or rejected during manufacture. Fewer than half of the points uncovered on the Debert site were completed and used (MacDonald 1968:75). Breakage prior to completion was also the result of failed attempts to remove a channel flake properly. Sometimes the channel flake fractured through the point; sometimes it broke out short of its intended length. At other times unintended flakes were spalled off from the point tip backward because the point had been improperly braced before the channel flake blow was struck. This kind of accidental bipolar flaking has to be expected whenever a blow of such necessarily high force is applied to a small chert artifact.

There has been much speculation regarding the function of flutes on Paleo-Indian points. Suggestions that they were intended to promote bleeding when used on large animals, that they were designed to make detachable "bullets" of the points that would stay in the animal after hitting home, or that they were purely aesthetic features have all been considered and rejected. The best explanation is that they were designed to facilitate hafting the point in a spear or lance. The presence of basal grinding to protect lashing and the absence of barbs or even pronounced shoulders on the points further indicate that the weapon was designed to penetrate deeply and retract easily. Such a weapon would be well suited to the Paleo-Indian hunter, who was compelled to travel light. He could not afford to carry more than a few such weapons, nor would he have relished seeing one of them disappear over the hill stuck in the flank of a superficially wounded animal.

Some of the points were probably used as tips of lances that were used at close quarters. Others were probably mounted on light throwing spears, and it is likely that these were used in conjunction with spear-throwers like those that could still be found in parts of the New World in historic times. The bow and arrow were introduced later in prehistory, but Mexican armies still used the spear-thrower (or "atlatl" as they called it) in mass attacks. Simply put, the purpose of the spear-thrower was to artificially lengthen the hunter's arm, allowing him to deliver the spear with greater speed and thereby with greater impact than would otherwise have been the case. The hunter held a shaft about half a meter in length at one end (see Brennan 1975:30–33 for illustrations). The other end was equipped with a hook if it was of the "male" type or alternatively a trough with a nipple at the far end if it was of the "female" type. A small socket at the base of the spear was designed to receive either the hook or the nipple. The hunter could begin this throw with the spear-thrower held by the last three fingers of his hand, the thumb and forefinger holding the spear near its midpoint. The base of the spear and the spear-thrower were articulated, and as the hunter began his throw he released his light grip on the spear so that he could whip it forward, his only contact with it now being indirect through the end of the spear-thrower. Thus, the Paleo-Indian hunter delivered his spear with greater speed than he could have done with his arm alone for the same reason that a jai-alai player can throw with greater speed than a baseball pitcher can. Impact and penetrating power depend on sharpness, streamlining, velocity, and weight. By maximizing the first three, the Paleo-Indians were free to reduce the last, giving them the well-armed mobility they needed.

Having made a strong case for the fluted point as an art form and key element in a sophisticated and specialized weapon system, I am afraid I must now deflate that image a bit. Analysis of wear on fluted points suggests that some of them were used as knives. Moreover, many of them show evidence of resharpening and multiple use. In fact, it is quite possible that some of the stylistic variations we observe in assemblages of fluted points are the result of resharpening of dull or broken points. But none of this really takes away from the technical qualities of fluted points. The idea of multiple uses and reuse of points is clearly consistent with Paleo-Indian requirements of portability and versatility.

The Paleo-Indian tool kit also included leaf-shaped and ovate bifacial knives, some of them as long as 150 mm. Microscopic examination of edge wear on these artifacts has revealed polishing and long striations that experiments have shown to be the result of meat cutting. At least some of the knives must have had handles since only this would account for some of the observed wear patterns. Some of the knives that have been uncovered appear to have been simple waste flakes that were hastily retouched, used, and discarded. Others, especially those that show evidence of hafting, were made from carefully prepared preforms, thinned by the removal of broad flakes with a soft hammer, and edged by pressure retouching that was as careful as that applied to fluted points. The soft hammer was probably a heavy baton or antler, while pressure flaking tools and fluting punches were probably made from bone or antler tines.

End scrapers are found on most Paleo-Indian sites, as well as most sites belonging to later prehistoric periods. The difference is that most Paleo-Indian scrapers in our area are equipped with graving spurs. End scrapers are unifacial and are usually made from single chert flakes that bear the scars of previously removed flakes on their dorsal or upper surfaces, a single scar constituting the ventral or lower surface. Secondary pressure flaking on the dorsal surface only, away from the bulb of percussion on the ventral surface, produced the characteristic scraper edge. Wear studies have shown that scrapers were probably hafted and used to scrape hides and to plane harder materials by being drawn toward the user with the ventral surface leading. Graving spurs were typically left like horns at either end of the scraper edge. Since scraping wear is heaviest near the center of the scraping edge (as would be expected if the scraper were hafted), the spurs did not interfere with scraping. The spurs could have been used to slot bone and other perforating and engraving tasks. Clearly scrapers with graving spurs are an example of efficient tool combination by Paleo-Indians. Other unifacial tools are variously described as side scrapers, flake knives, and retouched flakes. All seem to have been used as scrapers and are therefore probably hastily made tools that were discarded after brief use.

Tools called *pieces esquillees*, a term that we have borrowed from the European Upper Paleolithic, are found at some sites (Figure 3.7). They appear to begin as thick flakes or core fragments. Heavily rippled bipolar flakes indicate that they were struck by unusually heavy direct percussion

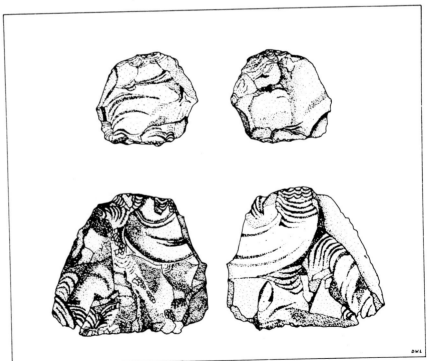

FIGURE 3.7. *Pieces esquillees* from the Debert site. Lengths of specimens in this highly variable artifact class range from 16 to 56 mm. Shown at actual size. (After MacDonald 1968:86.)

blows such that flakes detached not only at the striking point but at the opposite (working) end of the tool as well. Most of these tools are 20–30 cm long and curious because they appear never to have been finished tools. They began as nondescript flakes or core fragments and ended as battered discards. Experiment and Old World analogies suggest that the *pieces esquillees* were used to split bone, wood, antler, and ivory, driven like wedges or chisels by repeated hammer blows. Gravers may also have been used to cut through the hard outer layer of antler so that slivers could be pried away and made into awls, points, and other tools. All of these materials could have been used in a variety of ways once reduced to splinters of useful size (MacDonald 1968:85–90). However, we have yet to find any of these nonlithic materials preserved in a Paleo-Indian site in our area.

Various perforators, drills, and awls of chert have been found associated with other Paleo-Indian tools. Twist drills particularly show evidence of use in their microscopic wear patterns. Striations spiral around their tips and tiny flakes were repeatedly spalled from the trailing edges as the users simultaneously pushed and twisted the implements through some softer material. Awls were used with a thrusting motion only and lack signs of twisting. Like drills, they might have been hafted. Perforators were used much like awls but were more simply made, usually from a discarded flake, and appear not to have been hafted. All of these tools show up primarily on larger sites that were probably band camps. They are generally absent from small hunting camps and other special-purpose sites, suggesting that they were used primarily in the manufacture of other tools and clothing, probably by women rather than men.

Gravers that exist as separate tools rather than as parts of end scrapers are diagnostic Paleo-Indian tools. Quite often a flake 20–40 mm across was retouched and equipped with one to six sharp points around its edge. Some of the spurs might even have smaller subsidiary spurs. In the large sample from the Debert site, the spurs averaged only 2.5 mm in length, too small to have been used for heavy-duty work on bone or antler (MacDonald 1968). Thus, it seems likely that they were used for lighter tasks such as cutting eyes in bone needles.

Apart from miscellaneous chipped stone tools such as spokeshaves, we are left with rough stone tools such as hammerstones, abraders, and anvils. The abraders are often grooved and may have been used to polish awls and other tools made of softer materials. Tools such as these and the *pieces esquillees* offer tantalizing implications about what must have been a rich and efficient Paleo-Indian industry in nonlithic tools. For the present we can only hope for the discovery of a site in which some of them have been preserved.

PALEO-INDIAN SITES

Figure 3.1 shows the locations of major excavated sites in New England. The Plenge site in New Jersey lies just outside the Hudson drainage, but has been included as a means to fill out what is still a very sketchy picture. I have also included the Shoop site (Pennsylvania) and the Debert site (Nova Scotia) for the same reason.

Also scattered across the map are dozens of isolated fluted point finds. At this scale each point shown is 8 km long, a necessary exaggeration that might make our data seem more extensive than they really are. New England is an enormous haystack within which Figure 3.1 shows us only a thin scattering of fluted needles.

The Shoop site lies on what is now a remote hilltop in the Susquehanna drainage near Harrisburg, Pennsylvania. It is well outside our area, but I include it because it provides us with some useful lessons before we move through the series of excavated Paleo-Indian components to the Northeast. The Shoop assemblage was analyzed by John Witthoft (1952, 1954) in a pioneering effort at a time when radiocarbon dating was still in its infancy and few Paleo-Indian components were known for the East. At the time, he was puzzled by the location of the site in high and rugged country where few remains of later prehistoric cultures have ever been found. However, the pattern was repeated by components discovered more recently, and it now seems clear that there was a general Paleo-Indian preference for hilltop locations. Such sites might seem remote to us now, but during the Paleo-Indian period the environment was primarily tundra grassland near the glacial ice front and only very thinly forested for some distance south of it. Thus, far from being the remote deep forest location it later was, the Shoop site would have been a superb hilltop lookout station with a commanding view of much of the Susquehanna Valley. At that location, Paleo-Indians could have kept track of the movements of caribou and other game and planned their exploitation of them accordingly. It seems likely that hundreds of such hilltop hunting stations lie still undiscovered in remote parts of the Northeast forests.

The conclusion that the Shoop site was a hunting camp is also supported by the artifact classes found there. Knives, drills, hammerstones, and spokeshaves are among those items missing from the assemblage, indicating that food preparation and tool manufacture were not important activities there. What knapping was done there appears to have been limited mostly to resharpening and the finishing of preforms roughed out elsewhere, because the ratio of chip debitage to artifacts is only 2.5:1. Despite the fact that the site had been disrupted by recent plowing, Witthoft (1952:486) was able to observe 11 artifact concentrations, each about 10 m in diameter and on separate hilltop elevations about 100 m apart. He concluded that they were either individual camps used at different times or individual family hearth locations within a larger single encampment. Given the site's status as a temporary hunting camp and the settlement patterns we have observed in more recent years on other sites, the first interpretation seems by far the more likely. Thus, the Shoop site appears to have been repeatedly used, probably by small hunting bands moving in a seasonal round up and down the Susquehanna Valley. They headed for the same hilltop site again and again, but varied the exact location of their hearth within a set of at least 11 favorite spots. Such a pattern of repeated site use is not consistent with free wandering, which has often been attributed to Paleo-Indians and which implies frequent movement without restriction or direction (Beardsley *et al.* 1956:135). Instead, it conforms best to what Beardsley *et al.* define as restricted wandering, wherein communities "wander about within a territory that they define as theirs and defend against trespass, or on which they have exclusive rights to food resources of certain kinds. Movement within the territory may be erratic or may follow a seasonal round [1956:136]." This observation is important, for it reinforces the view that at the Shoop site, as at other Paleo-Indian sites, we are looking at samples of patterned behavior, not the unique remains of unrepeated single events. Indeed, archaeological remains of the latter type must be exceedingly rare, and few modern archaeologists would claim to have found them.

A last striking feature of the Shoop site that could not be properly interpreted in 1952 is that the vast majority of artifacts and waste flakes found there were of Onondaga chert, the nearest quarry source for which would have been up the Susquehanna Valley over 300 km to the north. Witthoft (1952:493–494) initially interpreted this as evidence of recent Paleo-Indian immigration from New York to the Shoop site, the last leg in a concerted migration that started in Alaska. I have already pointed out that such an interpretation is not consistent with the probable repeated long-term use of the Shoop site as a hunting camp in a restricted wandering settlement pattern. Therefore, we must conclude that both the use of the site and the use of Onondaga chert were regular components in an ongoing cultural system. It is not unlikely that a band of Paleo-Indians repeatedly visited both the Shoop site and a source of Onondaga chert in its seasonal round. Such long-distance travel over the course of a year can be documented for several similar hunter–gatherers that have been studied by ethnologists. Fitting *et al.* (1966) cite the Barren Ground Eskimo in their analysis of the Holcombe site in Michigan. MacDonald (1968:129) uses the analogy of the historic Montaignai–Naskapi in his analysis of the Debert case, and Funk (1976:226–227) refers to the Nunamiut Eskimo in his analysis of Paleo-Indians in the Hudson valley. All of them support the conclusion that the Shoop site was a temporary camp site, quite possibly used by small groups of males for brief periods. We must look elsewhere to find the remains of larger camps that these Paleo-Indians must have occasionally used. Our understanding of the ethnographic record indicates that there must have been periodic encampments of 50 or perhaps even 100 people of both sexes and all ages. Fortunately our small sample does include at least one such site.

The fluted points found at the Shoop site are generally similar to the Clovis points of western North America. According to Witthoft (1954), most show evidence of the removal of two marginal guide flakes before the removal of each channel flake, although Cox (1972) expresses a somewhat different opinion regarding the technique. This, plus careful grinding and pressure flaking, indicates that these knappers were as serious about their craft as any other Paleo-Indians. Given that, it is not difficult to understand why they were willing to go to the trouble of quarrying an especially high-quality chert at one end of their range and carrying the preforms with them on their seasonal round. Unfortunately, there are no radiocarbon dates from this site, and little chance that any will be obtained in the future, so we have no independent means to estimate the age of these Clovis-like points.

The next drainage east of the Susquehanna is the Delaware, still outside our area but nevertheless important because of its proximity. The most important Paleo-Indian site in this drainage is the Plenge site, which lies on a gently sloping terrace about 60 m from the Musconetcong River in northwestern New Jersey (Kraft 1973, 1977a). The site is spread across about 10 hectares (23 acres) of the terrace. Unfortunately, the Paleo-Indian remains are thoroughly mixed with remains from later periods in the site's plow zone. Herbert Kraft and his assistants have had to separate the remains on the basis of what they already know about the differences between Paleo-Indian and later materials, and they have given up any hope of stratigraphic separation or radiocarbon dating. Plowing has also destroyed the internal settlement pattern of the site, so we must depend on the artifact inventory to tell us whether this was a relatively large band camp or a smaller hunting or other special-purpose camp. As it happens, the knives, drills, spokeshaves, and hammerstones that were all so conspicuously absent from the Shoop site are all found here. The site was therefore probably a large seasonally used habitation site at which a relatively large range of activities was carried out. Such activities would have included food preparation, tool and clothing manufacture, and the range of social activities that such a gathering would allow but for which there can be no direct archaeological evidence. We can even speculate that separate bands that did not ordinarily travel together might have camped together on such a site on an occasional basis. Ethnographically known bands of this sort are always exogamous except under the most severely restrictive circumstances. That is, band members always look to other bands for mates. Moreover, among hunting cultures like the Paleo-Indians, newly married couples probably normally resided with the man's band. This patrilocal residence rule ensured that men stayed within the hunting ranges and with the hunting partners with which they were most familiar. At the same time, bands maintained good relations with adjacent bands by virtue of having kin contacts with them through their female members. The set of contiguous bands that were linked by customary intermarriage and female exchange was a social unit that some theorists refer to as a *connubium* (Williams 1974). Such a unit was probably also a single speech community during the Paleo-Indian period, but would never have functioned as a single community.

In addition to its areal extent, the Plenge site is extraordinary for the range of fluted point styles that has been found there (Figure 3.8). Virtually every style known for the rest of the Northeast is represented at the site. The deeply

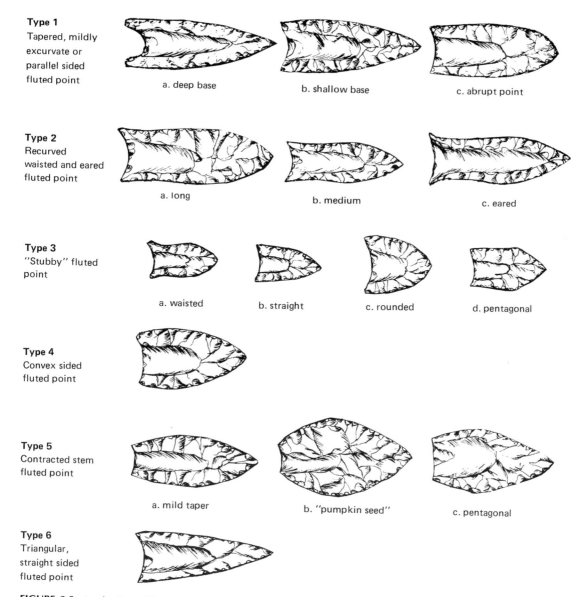

Type 1
Tapered, mildly
excurvate or
parallel sided
fluted point

a. deep base

b. shallow base

c. abrupt point

Type 2
Recurved
waisted and eared
fluted point

a. long

b. medium

c. eared

Type 3
"Stubby" fluted
point

a. waisted

b. straight

c. rounded

d. pentagonal

Type 4
Convex sided
fluted point

Type 5
Contracted stem
fluted point

a. mild taper

b. "pumpkin seed"

c. pentagonal

Type 6
Triangular,
straight sided
fluted point

FIGURE 3.8. A selection of fluted points from the Plenge site showing the wide range of variation within that assemblage. (From Kraft 1973:67.)

concave base of points from the Debert site can be found there, as can the stubby fluted points typical of the Port Mobil assemblage. There are Clovis-like and Folsom-like points, as well as the pentagonal forms that used to be unique to the Reagan site. Narrow-waisted Cumberland-like points are found here too, as are unfluted lanceolate forms. The explanation appears to be that the Plenge site was used repeatedly over several centuries, perhaps for most of the Paleo-Indian period, as stylistic preferences gradually changed. An alternative explanation is that the Paleo-Indian users of the site were eclectic makers of several point styles at once, but our understanding of how people behave generally discourages this interpretation. Another alternative explanation is that the site was used by several different bands carrying different point styles, but this, too, is unlikely because it does not fit with what we know of the seasonal movements of restricted wanderers.

Over 76% of the Paleo-Indian artifacts from the Plenge site are made from the red, brown, or yellow chert that can be found 50–80 km southwest in the Pennsylvania side of the Delaware valley. Another 12% are made of local black chert, and about 6% appear to have been made of cherts from central and eastern New York. The small percentage of imported cherts is additional evidence against the argument that stylistic variety at the Plenge site resulted from its use by several unconnected bands.

The red, brown, or yellow chert is usually called jasper and is a particularly fine grade of chert that Paleo-Indian craftsmen would have been willing to travel some distance to acquire. The deep red color can be achieved by heating the preform or finished artifact, and there is some evidence that this was done as a means to improve the chipping qualities of the material. Both the incidence of heat-caused "pot lid" fractures and color alteration point to the frequent use of heat treatment at the Plenge site (Kraft 1973:62). Few other sites contain lithic materials that are capable of showing evidence of heat treatment so clearly, and in fact the dramatic (even magical) red color that the treatment produced might have loomed as large or larger than technological considerations in the minds of Paleo-Indian knappers.

Ritchie (1957:10–11) once attempted to explain the occurrence of Pennsylvania jasper at sites northward into New York and southern New England as resulting from the northward migration of Paleo-Indians after climatic improvements here. This was another early attempt to explain archaeological remains as the end products of unique events rather than as the by-products of patterned behavior. It is now clear that there is no more reason to accept Ritchie's hypothesis than there is to accept Witthoft's migration hypothesis regarding the origins of the Shoop site occupants. This and several other points already mentioned all support Kraft's impression that the Plenge site was used periodically over an unusually long time span. He regards the unfluted, triangular, and pentagonal Paleo-Indian points from the site as relatively younger than the other styles (Kraft 1973:112).

Farther north and lying closer to the main channel of the Delaware River are the Shawnee–Minisink and Zierdt sites. The Zierdt site is a small and incompletely reported site that has produced a fluted point, knives, scrapers, a graver, and a core (Werner 1964). This small inventory suggests that the site was a small family encampment, not a specialized hunting camp. The Shawnee–Minisink site is a little better known. It produced 27 unifacial artifacts, 7 bifaces, and 6000 waste flakes, as well as an anvil stone and hammerstones. A hearth produced four radiocarbon dates ranging from 9310 to 11,050 B.P. One of these, a date of 10,590 ± 300 (W2994) was from a hearth containing fish bones and charred hawthorn pits. Only one of the bifaces was a fluted point, and the total tool inventory indicates wood- and bone-working as primary activities on the site. Most of the chert was of a local black variety, and the large amount of debitage indicates that tool manufacture was an important activity. The discovery of fish and hawthorn plum remains gives us a rare glimpse of the kinds of gathered foods the Paleo-Indians were utilizing in the course of their seasonal round. The site was probably a briefly occupied work camp of a small band, but it is unclear whether the Paleo-Indians who camped there were a specialized task group or a complete family band (Eisenberg 1978:65–71; McNett *et al.* 1977).

The Port Mobil site lies in the extreme southeastern corner of our area. The site is situated on the west side of Staten Island overlooking the Arthur Kill. Staten Island is actually on the New Jersey side of the Hudson River Channel, but the Arthur Kill estuary and the state boundary that runs along it make the island part of New York. The site is only 3–16 m above modern sea level, but nevertheless would have commanded a splendid view of the countryside to the north, west, and south during the Paleo-Indian period. Even more important for a clear understanding of the site and its location is that prior to 10,000 B.P. the ocean level was perhaps 90 m lower here and the seacoast 100–150 km away from the Port Mobil site (Edwards and Emery 1977; Kraft 1977b). The Hudson River therefore continued to the southeast from its present mouth, running through the narrow, deep, and now submerged Hudson trench. The Arthur Kill was a small freshwater stream, and Staten Island was probably not an island at all. Subsequent rising sea level submerged the sections of continental shelf that had been exposed and drowned the ancient Arthur Kill, Raritan, Hudson, and other streams, turning them into saltwater estuaries.

Much of what is now submerged was probably attractive terrain for Paleo-Indian hunters. Sea level was at a low point in 19,000 B.P., after which it began to rise as continental glaciers melted. However, because the 19,000 B.P. low water was below the lip of the continental shelf, sea level rise for the following 9000 years was accompanied by relatively little lateral inundation. Most of the lateral inundation over the relatively flat continental shelf took place between 10,000 and 5000 B.P. Although Emery and Edwards (1966) have suggested that rich Paleo-Indian sites might have survived the inundation, we have neither the technology nor the funding to go after Paleo-Indian needles in the Atlantic haystack. Even if we did, we would have to deal with the very real possibility that most of the sites were destroyed by daily wave action as the sea level rose.

Port Mobil escaped inundation because at the time of its occupation it was an inland site, not the coastal site it now appears to be. It has produced a relatively simple assemblage that Funk (1972:21) thinks is like that from the Shoop site. This plus the site's location overlooking much of the New Jersey lowlands suggests that it was a small hunting camp. However, the knives, drills, and spokeshaves that were absent at Shoop are present in this assemblage, indicating a wider range of activities at Port Mobil and perhaps its use by complete bands rather than all-male hunting groups. Some of the fluted points from Port Mobil are short and stubby, a style that some have suggested is relatively late. However, Clovis-like, Cumberland-like, and pentagonal fluted points are also in the assemblage, and so far there is little from this or any other site to indicate their temporal order, if any. The North Beach component at Port Mobil, which may be older than the other two components, produced evidence of Clovis-like points, but this is slender evidence on which to establish a relative point chronology.

Chert selection by Paleo-Indians at Port Mobil once again reflects expensive tastes. About 72% of the fluted points were made of red Pennsylvania chert from the Delaware drainage, the remainder mostly from local black chert or Normanskill chert from the middle Hudson Valley (Kraft 1977b:10). The site is littered with a large amount of waste chips relative to finished artifacts. This is further evidence that this was a band habitation site rather than a hunting camp, and it shows that these knappers probably made small points out of preference rather than from a shortage of raw materials. Perhaps most significant of all is the high percentage of red chert points. The Paleo-Indians were terrestrial people, whose movements were probably contained more than facilitated by major streams. We find none of the heavy woodworking tools that are found in more recent sites and that are so suggestive of dugout canoe manufacture. And none of the indicators of the strong riverine orientation that would eventually emerge in the Northeast is present. The Pennsylvania quarries were only 100 km away to the west. The Normanskill quarry was close to twice that far to the north and did not offer chert of a significantly higher quality. As an aside, I have seen little speculation regarding the possibly attractive qualities of the Pennsylvania jasper color. Red ocher would later become a singularly important substance in prehistoric mortuary practices in the Northeast, and the magical connection between the bright red color of a jasper point and a successful kill cannot be denied. Unfortunately neither can it be proved, and we may never be able to explore this tantalizing ideological dimension of Paleo-Indian preferences for the material and the practice of enhancing its color by heat treatment.

From Port Mobil we move up the Hudson drainage into New York's Orange County. The Wallkill River flows northeastward out of New Jersey, through Orange County, and then runs nearly parallel with the Hudson before emptying into it near Kingston. In fact, the Wallkill provides an easy corridor from the middle Hudson valley, linking up with the Musconetcong River corridor and therefore the Delaware valley. We have already seen that the Plenge site lies in the Musconetcong valley, and it may be that this natural corridor linking the Delaware and Hudson was a major reason for its location there. The Wallkill flows through the agriculturally rich "black dirt" area of Orange County, an area that was first a proglacial lake, later a vast bog, and now drained farmland. The ancient bog has produced several extinct mammal finds, including a Pleistocene moose–elk (*Cervalces scotti*) with a radiocarbon date of 10,950 ± 150 B.P. (I-4016). About 30 km downstream to the northeast, a mastodon (*Mammut americanus*) skeleton has produced a radiocarbon date of 10,000 ± 160 B.P. (I-3785) (Funk *et al.* 1970). Thus, the Musconetcong–Wallkill corridor was not just a handy passage from the Delaware to the Hudson, but probably a rich Paleo-Indian hunting ground as well. The most important find in the area thus far has been a limestone fissure on the northwest side of Lookout Mountain, which overlooks the old bog and the Wallkill flowing through it. Dutchess Quarry Cave, as it is called, unfortunately looks straight into prevailing winds as well, so it was not extensively occupied prehistorically. Nevertheless, some important evidence has come out of it. A proglacial lake covered the valley in front of the cave around 15,000 B.P. By 13,000 B.P. the lake was gone and bog deposits had begun to accumulate (Funk, Walters, and Ehlers 1969). It was a tundra environment that attracted both game animals and Paleo-Indian hunters. The lowest productive stratum in Dutchess Quarry Cave produced caribou bones (*Rangifer tarandus*) and a fluted point resembling Cumberland points, which are best known in the Tennessee and Cumberland river drainages far to the southwest. Apart from the Holcombe site in Michigan, in which a caribou toe bone was found (Fitting *et al.* 1966), this is the only known archaeological association of caribou and cultural material south of the animal's present Canadian range except for some puzzling remains at the much later Duxbury site in Massachusetts (Guilday 1968). Although the association is not as direct as one might wish (the point was in the same stratum but not in contact with the bone), the caribou limb bones appear to have been broken for marrow extraction, something that would have required human hands (Guilday 1969). Cumberland points are generally regarded as dating to late in the Paleo-Indian period (Figure 3.9), so a radiocarbon date of 12,530 ± 370 B.P. (I-4137) on the caribou bone came as a surprise. The 370-year margin for error represents a single standard deviation from the mean, so there is a slight chance that the bone could actually date to $12,530 - (3 \times 370) = 11,420$ B.P., but the chances are statistically equivalent that the bone really should date to $12,530 + (3 \times 370) = 13,640$ B.P. Thus, we are stuck with what may be the oldest radiocarbon date on a North American fluted point and possible evidence that we understand the significance of stylistic variation less well than we would like (Funk *et al.* 1970). This situation will prevail unless and until some technical reason to doubt the date is advanced.

Additional caves have been recently found and excavated at Dutchess Quarry. Dutchess Quarry Cave will probably be known as D.Q.C. No. 1 in future publications, since at least cave No. 8 should prove to be just as significant. Cave No. 8 has produced more fluted points, caribou bones, and some other remains that have not yet been assessed by Robert Funk and the excavators.

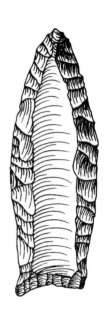

FIGURE 3.9. A sample of three Cumberland points from Missouri and Alabama. Specimens illustrated range in length from 59 to 70 mm. The type is generally regarded as late Paleo-Indian. Shown at actual size. (Drawings from Bell 1960:23.)

With or without the fluted points, the bones in Dutchess Quarry Caves show that Paleo-Indians were probably hunting caribou in the Hudson drainage at a time when our area was sparsely wooded tundra. The main ice front stood on the southern banks of Lake Ontario and the St. Lawrence River, with smaller independent ice caps still surviving in the Green Mountains, White Mountains, and on the Gaspe Peninsula. Although they did not have much longer to live, glacial Lakes Albany and Hitchcock might still have existed at low levels in the Hudson and Connecticut valleys, respectively (Figure 3.10). Lake Fort Ann had ceased to empty into the Hudson River from the Champlain drainage, and retreating ice had by now allowed seawater to inundate that great northern lake basin. Even though the discharge from Lake Fort Ann no longer flowed into the emerging Hudson River, the river was probably still swollen by glacial meltwater. Indeed, the Hudson may well have been a formidable barrier to the terrestrial Paleo-Indians, discouraging any movement eastward into New England except during the winter freeze. Even though the data were not acquired through any rational sampling procedure, it is probably significant that no Paleo-Indian sites and only one stray point of the hundred known for the Hudson drainage come from the part of it that lies east of the Hudson River (Funk 1977a:317).

In some parts of the area the Paleo-Indians would not have found even tundra. The beds of recently drained glacial lakes would have been bare expanses of lake sand, which prevailing winds would have quickly converted into cold deserts of shifting dunes. Those dunes are immobile today around Albany and elsewhere, stabilized by vegetation, but that stabilization took time, and for at least a few centuries dry glacial lake beds were a fit place for neither man nor beast.

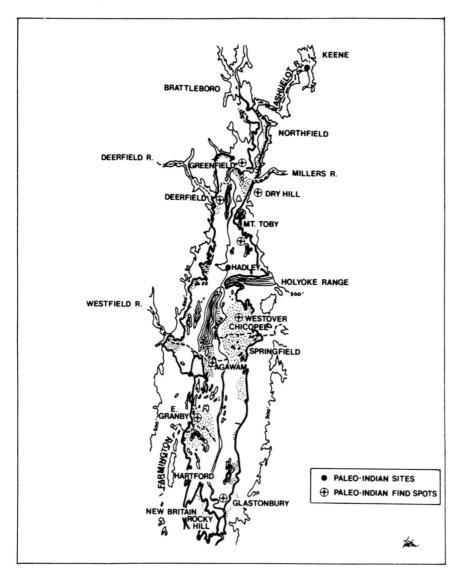

FIGURE 3.10. Paleo-Indian remains in the Connecticut valley. The heavy line indicates the shore of Lake Hitchcock. Lighter lines show the 152.4-m (500-ft) contour and the modern Connecticut River. (From Curran and Dincauze 1977:334.)

To the east, the coast of Maine, like the Champlain basin, was inundated by the sea, and mountainous areas were still capped with glacial ice. What remained was tundra, and the most attractive parts of that may well now lie submerged on the continental shelf. It may well be a long time before we find any evidence elsewhere in our area to confirm or challenge the early date from Dutchess Quarry Cave.

One old sand dune became the site of a Paleo-Indian camp. The 2-km-long dune on the north side of Lake Assawompsett in southeastern Massachusetts developed after the drainage of a much larger glacial lake in the area and attracted both Paleo-Indian and later hunters. The dune stands 12 m above the modern lake and would have afforded a good view of the surrounding countryside as well as access to water and waterfowl under tundra conditions. Only a few Paleo-Indian artifacts have been recovered from five small sections of the site Wapanucket No. 8; most remains date to the Archaic periods (Robbins and Agogino 1964). The small size of the assemblage allows no inferences regarding size utilization apart from the observation that it was probably a temporary camp site. The artifacts themselves, however, are of some interest. Of the six fluted points found, only one is complete. It measures only 3.8 cm long. A second fragmentary point is split lengthwise and allows a length measurement of only 4.4 cm. Thus, the Wapanucket No. 8 fluted points are all of the stubby style already noted at Port Mobil, and which we will see are also present at the Reagan site. This style is thought to be relatively late in the Paleo-Indian period.

Another Paleo-Indian site lies about 30 km north of Dutchess Quarry Cave, also in the drainage of the Wallkill. This is the multicomponent Twin Fields site near Allards Corners. This site is situated on a high sandy bluff overlooking the Dwaar Kill. Collectors have found fluted points on the surface of the site in recent years, and Leonard Eisenberg has excavated there. Only 12% of the total artifact inventory obtained by Eisenberg from Twin Fields is of Paleo-Indian manufacture. Within this subset there were only two fluted points, two small knives, and a small pebble core. The bulk of the inventory consists of unifacial tools. The debitage to artifact ratio is relatively low, 8 : 1, and 95% of the chert material is from the Normanskill chert beds of the middle Hudson Valley. The remaining 5% came from unknown exotic sources. Eisenberg (1978:136) interprets the Paleo-Indian component as "a temporary work camp for the processing of hard plant materials." He sees relatively little evidence for other kinds of activities such as stone tool manufacture, hunting, hide working, or fishing at the site. Table 3.2 shows his inferences regarding Twin Fields and five other Paleo-Indian sites in the Delaware and Hudson drainages.

The West Athens Hill site lies about 110 km north of Dutchess Quarry Cave on a hilltop near the village of Athens, New York. The hill is in the heart of the limestone belt that contains high-quality Normanskill chert, and good supplies of the usually green chert are available on it. In addition, the hill would have offered Paleo-Indians a fine view across the lowlands eastward to the Hudson River and westward to the Helderberg Scarp and the Catskill Mountains. The hill is in fact part of a north–south ridge, another portion of which only 8 km north is the famous Flint Mine Hill chert quarry. Thus, at West Athens Hill the Paleo-Indians had a dual-purpose site, both an elevated hunting station and a quarry site (Ritchie and Funk 1973:9–36).

TABLE 3.2
Major Site Activities Inferred Primarily from Geographical Locations and Lithic Remains (Eisenberg 1978:130)[a]

Site	Stone procure-ment	Hunting	Fishing	Plant procure-ment	Stone tool manu-facture	Bone process-ing	Wood process-ing	Hide process-ing
Plenge	+	+	?	+	+	+	+	+
Shawnee–Minisink	+	−	+	+	+	−	−	−
Port Mobil	?	+	?	−	?	+	+	?
Twin Fields	−	−	−	+	−	−	+	−
West Athens Hill	+	+	−	+	+	+	+	+
Kings Road	+	+	−	−	+	+	−	−

[a] + = present; − = absent; ? = undetermined.

The only radiocarbon date from West Athens Hill came out to A.D. 1650 ± 115 (I-3443), apparently the result of a recent forest fire that penetrated tree roots in the archaeological strata. We do not have any other independent means for dating the site. The fluted points found here are Clovis-like (Figure 3.11), and when we are sure of the temporal significance of this and other styles we might be able to estimate the site's age. Although drills are missing from the assemblage, it does contain knives, spokeshaves, and other implements that suggest that some tool manufacture was carried out here along with quarrying. It appears that Paleo-Indians may have spent more time here and carried on a wider range of activities here than would have been the case if the site were just a hunting station or just a quarry.

The debitage to artifacts ratio at West Athens Hill is 33:1, compared with 2.5:1 at the Shoop site. West Athens Hill was a place where knappers roughed out preforms from quarry blocks and sometimes converted those preforms into finished tools as well, whereas only the latter was carried out at the Shoop site. Curiously, there are finished artifacts but no chips of Pennsylvania jasper, Upper Mercer Ohio chert, Onondaga chert, Fort Ann chert, and a few other exotic materials on this quarry site. It seems very unlikely that any band of Paleo-Indians would have ranged far enough to have quarried all of these materials. Therefore, we have to conclude that some trade in finished products was going on during the Paleo-Indian period. We have already seen that Paleo-Indian bands were almost certainly linked by marriages into larger sets called connubia. I can now broaden the implications of that concept on the basis of evidence from West Athens Hill and suggest that connubia were overlapping and not exclusive sets. A connubium from the point of view of a given band may well have consisted of itself and say six other bands with which it had regular interaction. However, one of the other

FIGURE 3.11. Fluted points and point fragments from West Athens Hill. Shown at actual size. (From Ritchie and Funk 1973:20).

six bands may well have interacted with only some of the others in this set, its own connubium consisting of those plus a few others with which the first band never came into contact. Thus, it is not difficult to conceive of a situation in which artifacts of Upper Mercer chert would have made their way step-by-step through these linkages to West Athens Hill. The ethnographic evidence we have suggests that the most common mechanism for such exchanges among hunter–gatherers is gift exchange, not trade for profit. The establishment of trading partnerships between members of different bands is common and supplements the binding power of intermarriage. In fact, the two may have been closely connected for Paleo-Indians. About half the artifacts made of exotic cherts and found at the West Athens Hill and nearby Kings Road sites are scrapers. These were probably primarily hide-working implements and therefore perhaps women's implements. It could well be that it was women, with their strong blood connections to other bands, who were the primary conduit of interband exchange. Bands that lived in territories poor in fine chert resources would probably have found other materials to exchange for chert, and it is likely that many of the items exchanged were made of materials that have simply not survived archaeologically. Thus, exotic cherts at West Athens Hill and elsewhere provide us with one, but only one, view of a widespread exchange system that was at least as important to the social system as it was to the economic system of Paleo-Indians.

The Kings Road site lies only 8 km north of West Athens Hill. It is not a hilltop site, but rather lies on an almost imperceptible rise in the broad Hudson valley lowland. It is another plow-zone site like Plenge, and the disruption of farming has destroyed most of the site's internal provenience and any possibility of radiocarbon dating. The assemblage is very similar to that of West Athens Hill in terms of the artifact types present and the activities they imply. *Pieces esquillees* are not in the Kings Road assemblage, however, even though a few were found at West Athens Hill. Nevertheless, both sites appear to represent small band encampments visited by whole bands, not just adult male task groups. The location of the Kings Road site may well have been dictated by its proximity to killed game or some other condition of the time that now escapes our understanding, for the low site is some distance from both water and chert. If Pleistocene game animals, particularly caribou, were migrating seasonally through the Hudson Valley, the Kings Road site would have been directly in their path while the West Athens Hill site would have provided a high lookout adjacent to that path. The Kings Road site may have been used only once. If this was the case, we should expect to find more such single occupation kill sites in largely unpredictable locations along prehistoric migratory game routes in the Northeast, but there are as yet few candidates (Funk, Weinman, and Weinman 1969).

Three excavated Paleo-Indian components are known for the Lake Champlain drainage. Two lie below the highest shoreline of the Champlain Sea, the marine innundation that lasted from 12,800 to 10,000 B.P. Neither of these two sites has been radiocarbon dated, but it seems safe to conclude that neither would have been used until land rebound had ended marine inundation and reestablished Lake Champlain as a freshwater lake at or near its present level. Thus, for geological reasons, both sites appear to date near the end of the Paleo-Indian period (Kirkland and Coates 1977). The Davis site lies on a marine clay terrace about 37 m above the present lake level near the village of Crown Point. The assemblage is small, consisting of only a few points and scrapers. Two of the artifacts were made of a jasper-like chert, the source of which is unknown. The others were made of local Beekmantown chert and Normanskill chert. What is most interesting about this small assemblage is that the five fluted points are all of the Clovis-like parallel-sided style like those found at Kings Road and West Athens Hill. This is presumed on geological grounds to be a relatively late site, yet the points are not of one of the supposed late styles. Perhaps Paleo-Indians occupied the terrace after the Champlain Sea had dropped a few meters but well before its 10,000 B.P. disappearance. On the other hand, perhaps this is just another indication that we do not really understand stylistic variation in fluted points.

The Reagan site is the more interesting of the two excavated components in the Champlain Sea basin. It too lies at or just above the limits of the Champlain Sea, on an elevation overlooking the north bank of the Missisquoi River in northwestern Vermont. When Ritchie (1953) first described the site, there was little in the East to compare it with, and, largely because of the unusual triangular, lanceolate, and pentagonal shapes of its fluted points, it remained an enigma for many years. The site was revealed by wind erosion of its fine sand matrix after a protective pine forest was cut down. Once again there is virtually no chance for discovering intrasite relationships or datable carbon. Of the chert materials found at the site, only a small sample of Onondaga chert can be called exotic. The other cherts, basalts, rhyolites, and quartzites can probably be attributed to more local sources. The same is true of the talc pendants found at the site, sources for which occur in several localities in Vermont.

The very diversity of point styles in the Reagan assemblage might argue for their lateness. Funk (1976:229) and others have noted an apparent increase in stylistic diversity in point assemblages near the end of the Paleo-Indian period. This might be a valid observation, but I balk at the common but reckless leap to the conclusion that it necessarily was caused by environmental change, at least so far as that connection has been vaguely described to date. It seems more likely to me that increasing Paleo-Indian population would have produced more bands as old ones grew too large and split, with the necessary consequence that as soon as the habitable portions of North America were filled band territories had to begin to decrease in size. This alone could have produced late Paleo-Indian diversity even if the floral and faunal environments were not changing. In terms of strict logic, we can at this point no more prove that such diversity caused climatic change. However, my caution in this matter will not prevent me from risking a few more elaborate inferences in the next section.

Whatever the reasons, there does appear to be more point style diversity in later Paleo-Indian sites. The Davis site remains difficult to explain as long as it is regarded as a late site. However, Reagan and Port Mobil both exhibit pentagonal, triangular, and lanceolate forms in their assemblages that are generally thought to be late. Although some efforts have been made to link each style with a special function (e.g. Kraft 1977b:12), the evidence is still too slim for us to test such hypotheses. Nevertheless, it is tempting to look for a connection between the disappearance of old styles (particularly larger points) and the disappearance of Pleistocene game animals. As a final note on diversity and change in fluted points in the Northeast, it is possible that each style *does* represent a distinct time period and that what appears to us to be diversity is really evidence of relatively rapid and widespread stylistic change. The several point styles at Port Mobil and Reagan might therefore represent an equal number of separate components that plowing, erosion, and other disturbances have badly mixed. After all, the period is at least 2500 years long, long enough for each of a half-dozen point styles to have a separate life of four or five centuries. Thus, the uniqueness of the Reagan site that has disturbed archaeologists for so long might simply be the result of our failure to discover more sites from one of several Paleo-Indian sub-periods. McCary's (1951) discovery of pentagonal fluted points in the Williamson site in Virginia certainly indicates that the Reagan site need not be regarded as a bizarre fluke and suggests that there might be a widespread style that we still know very little about.

The range of artifacts at Reagan indicates that this was another band camp site located so as to provide its occupants with a superb view to the east, south, and west. Hammerstones, drills, *pieces esquillees*, and awls are missing from the site, indicating that the full range of possible activities was not carried on at the site. This could have been primarily a hunting station at which women were not often found. Although several types of scrapers were present, the absence of drills and awls suggests that clothing manufacture, probably a female activity, was not carried out here.

The Harrisena site lies at the northern terminus of a portage route connecting the Hudson River with Lake George. The site is located on a ridge of sand that was laid down by the waters that drained southward out of glacial Lake Bolton, the high-level ancestor of modern Lake George. The site would have been available for use by the time of the occupation of Dutchess Quarry Cave, but we have no sure evidence that it was. Harrisena was excavated in 1974 and 1975 as part of a larger program to understand the prehistory of the Lake George region. New England and the Maritime provinces of Canada are together a large peninsular area, and the Hudson and Champlain valleys provide a natural corridor for north–south movement across its base. The Hudson River and Lakes George and Champlain are separated by only a few kilometers of low hills in the Lake George region, and there are at least three important portage routes linking the two major drainages there. Investigations at the Harrisena site were therefore part of a larger program designed to understand this important prehistoric crossroad (Snow 1977a).

The two main components discovered at Harrisena date to later periods discussed in Chapters 4 and 7. However, the Early Archaic component contained some remains that might date to the end of the Paleo-Indian period. Two lanceolate point bases were uncovered in a disturbed context. Although they bear no traces of true fluting, each has been thinned by flakes removed from the base upward, a characteristic of many late Paleo-Indian period points. The points might very well date from that time. Unfluted lanceolate points mark the transition from the late Paleo-Indian period to the Early Archaic period in many parts of central and western North America. As a group they often fall under the heading of "Plano" points. A few have been found in scattered surface collections in the Northeast (Ritchie 1971a:117), but for the most part they tend to be restricted to the central Appalachian uplands southwest of our region. Some archaeologists have suggested that the low frequency of these points in our region may have been the result of a population decline after the Paleo-Indian period (for example, Funk 1976:229). Others, such as Wright (1978:72), think that their scarcity is a consequence of a lag in archaeological discovery and recognition. However, it seems just as likely to me that eastern Paleo-Indian technology simply reacted in different ways to the need to readapt. Coe's work in the Carolina Piedmont has shown us that this was almost certainly the case in that area. There the transitional point type is the Hardaway point (Figure 3.12), which Coe (1964) dates to around 9000 B.P. As it happens, the Harrisena site also produced a Hardaway point and a fragment that is probably part of another (Hammer *et al.* n.d.). Harrisena therefore provides data that appear to

FIGURE 3.12. A sample of three Hardaway points first identified by Coe (1964:67). Lengths range from 38 to 50 mm. The type is dated to 8000–10,000 B.P. Shown at actual size. (Drawings from Perino 1968:31, based on Coe 1964:68.)

bridge the 10,000 B.P. time line that separates the Paleo-Indian period from the Archaic.

There are only three poorly known sites in the Connecticut drainage and the adjoining Housatonic drainage that I have lumped with it. One of these is a site near Washington, Connecticut, that is known only by its site number, 6LF21. Moeller (1980) reports that Paleo-Indian artifacts were recovered from 1.0 to 1.5 m below the surface in a thin, sealed layer of less than 40 m² (Figure 3.13). The component has been dated to near the end of the Paleo-Indian period (10,190 ± 300 B.P.). The assemblage contains miniature fluted points as well as one of standard size. There are also scraper, knife, awl, hammerstone, spokeshave, and debitage remains suggesting that the site was occupied by a small but complete family band. Moeller infers a single brief occupation of the site.

Another Paleo-Indian component is known from the town of Hadley, well within the margin of glacial Lake Hitchcock. The site has been destroyed by plowing, and its small known assemblage consists of fewer than a dozen artifacts. All of them are typical Paleo-Indian pieces that do not either singly or as a group add much to our understanding. The third known component in the Connecticut–Housatonic drainage is the Keene site in southwestern New Hampshire. The site is presently being excavated and the results analyzed, but as yet there is little to say about it (Curran and Dincause 1977:334–335).

We come at last to the only site that appears to have been occupied by composite temporary communities of several bands. The Bull Brook site lies near Ipswich, Massachusetts, only about 12 m above modern sea level. The

FIGURE 3.13. Minature fluted points from Site 6LF21, Conn. Left, 21 mm long; right, 25 mm long. Shown at twice actual size. (Collection of the American Indian Archaeological Institute.)

balancing effects of crustal rebound and rising sea level after glacial retreat from this part of Massachusetts were such that the site was probably never submerged, nor was it ever far removed from the coast as was the Port Mobil site. The kame terrace on which the site is located has been heavily mined for sand and gravel in recent years, and the site itself has been mined for artifacts by local collectors. Despite the confusion caused by this destruction, it appears that the Bull Brook assemblage was distributed in 45 concentrations, which averaged 4.5–6 m in diameter, about the size one would expect for a nuclear family encampment. Hearths and burned bone were found at the centers of at least some of these. Most important, the 45 "hot spots" were generally arranged in a large semicircle about 90 m in diameter. Unless this semicircular arrangement was controlled by some natural but now vanished characteristic of the site, we can probably conclude that it indicates that all or most of the concentrations were deposited simultaneously by nuclear families camped together (Jordan 1960). The situation at Bull Brook is clearly different from that found at the Shoop site, where the locations of concentrations were controlled by topography, or at the Plenge site, where plowing has made the discovery of concentrations almost impossible.

Stylistic consistency within the Bull Brook assemblage also argues for a relatively short single occupancy of the site. Although there is some variability, the fluted points in the assemblage are generally analogous to the Clovis-like points found at West Athens Hill. The extreme variability that is so suggestive of repeated occupancy over a long period at the Plenge site is absent here.

At the same time, the Bull Brook assemblage contains virtually the entire range of Paleo-Indian tool classes. There are knives, drills, *pieces esquillees*, end scrapers, side scrapers, awls, gravers, spokeshaves, and hammerstones. However, the range of types within each of these classes is restricted, as is the case with projectile points, further evidence that this site was not used repeatedly over a long period. Thus, Bull Brook appears to have been a site at which the whole range of social and technological activities practiced by Paleo-Indians took place. If we conservatively estimate that each "hot spot" was produced by a nuclear family of five people, we generate a total population of 225 for the site, certainly more than would normally travel together in a restricted wandering pattern of seasonal movement. It seems safe to infer that the site was temporarily occupied by part of a connubium of several related bands and that it was the scene of gift exchange, intermarriage, and other social activities.

Much of the chert in the Bull Brook assemblage appears to be of local origin, although at least some of it is Normanskill chert from the Hudson Valley or red chert from Pennsylvania (Byers 1954, 1956; Jordan 1960). It seems unlikely that the Bull Brook hunters would have ranged far enough westward across several river drainages to have quarried all of these raw materials themselves. We can probably account for them more reasonably by inferring the movement of exotic cherts by means of gift exchanges between members of different bands. Much has been made of the presence of exotic cherts from the west at both Wapanucket No. 8 and Bull Brook, particularly that they are evidence of the eastward trend of migrating Paleo-Indian bands. However, this again is an attempt to use archaeological data as evidence of unique events, something I have already denounced as risky. Paleo-Indians were in southeastern New England for centuries, and it is naïve to assume that our only two excavated sites there might represent their initial arrival. Once again caution compels us to treat the presence of exotic cherts as the result of patterned behavior, most probably gift exchange. It should be no surprise that exotic cherts in southeastern New England came mainly from the west, because there are few attractive chert quarries to the north and none at all to the east and south.

The issue of the first arrival of Paleo-Indians in southwestern New England generally and the age of Bull Brook particularly can be approached more safely from another direction. I have already noted that there are far more Paleo-Indian remains known for the western side of the Hudson valley than for the eastern side, and I have suggested that the late-glacial lakes and rivers that occupied the Hudson drainage may have discouraged the movement of early Paleo-Indian bands from the west into what is now New England. The date of 10,585 ± 47 B.P. for the Debert, Nova Scotia, site is quite firm (Stuckenrath 1966:76). We can safely conclude that any barrier to movement through the Hudson drainage was overcome before that date. The average of three dates run on radiocarbon samples from the Bull Brook site is 8975 ± 230 B.P. (Crane and Griffin 1959:185). However, the samples were collections of scattered and poorly associated flecks that were assayed when the dating technique was still in its infancy. Most archaeologists regard the date as too young. It seems likely that the true radiocarbon age of Bull Brook lies nearer that of the securely dated Debert site and near the end of the 10,000–12,500 B.P. range I have given the Paleo-Indian period.

The Debert, Nova Scotia, site lies well outside our area. But the site has yielded an assemblage more diverse than any of those discussed thus far, and it is the only securely dated Paleo-Indian site in the Northeast. It would be a mistake to forgo discussion of this extraordinary site that lies so near the end of the New England–Maritime peninsula. At the time of its occupation around 10,500 B.P., the Debert site rested on a low hill, surrounded and underlain by tundra and permafrost. Snowfields were visible in the Cobequid Mountains less than 16 km away, and there were active glacial ice caps within 100 km. There had been some sea inundation to the west a thousand years earlier, but, by the time of the site's occupation, most if not all of the inundated land had rebounded and was above sea level. Sea level was still low worldwide, however, and great stretches of Nova Scotia's portion of the continental shelf were exposed.

MacDonald (1968) infers that the Paleo-Indians of the Debert site concentrated on caribou herds that migrated seasonally between the Minas basin to the south and the Cobequid Mountains to the north. It is likely that they exploited other animal and plant resources too, but no remains of any of these were found in the site. Instead, bone, wood, and hide working must be inferred from the presence of tools that were clearly made for those purposes. Stone tools of all Paleo-Indian classes were present at Debert, although limited as to specific type, as was the case at Bull Brook. The deeply indented Debert fluted point, noted elsewhere only at the Plenge site, was the only style found. Tools like fluted knives and scraping planes, which are rare elsewhere, were also found. Thus, MacDonald infers a full range of manufacturing activities despite the low ratio of debitage to artifacts (6:1). Most of the artifacts (75%) were made from local varieties of chalcedony, which have excellent chipping characteristics. None of the remaining lithic varieties in the assemblage appear to have come from any distance. However, to say that the Debert Paleo-Indians used local raw materials is not to say that they had the same immediate access to them that was enjoyed by the inhabitants of West Athens Hill. The debitage to artifact ratio and the general absence of cortex flakes from the site combine to indicate that these knappers quarried stone elsewhere, manufactured blanks at the quarry sites, and carried out only the final chipping stages on the habitation site.

Assemblage concentrations, or "hot spots," like those found at Bull Brook turned up at Debert as well. In this case, however, there were only 11, each generally associated with a hearth. More important, in the Debert case they ranged in size from about 70 m^2 to about 200 m^2. This range is much larger than the 30 m^2 maximum suggested by the diameters cited for Bull Brook. Perhaps the destruction at the Bull Brook site obscured the true sizes of the site's band concentrations. On the other hand, the larger size range at Debert could have resulted from repeated use of the site over a longer occupation period than was the case at Bull Brook. Still another possibility is that social units were substantially different at Debert for one of several possible reasons, among them contrasting seasonality and different ages. Indeed, MacDonald does not see a clear deliberate arrangement of the concentrations like that noted for Bull Brook, and he regards them as representing separate encampments used over a period of several years. Thus, each concentration of remains at Debert probably represents one or a very few temporary encampments by a band composed of more than one nuclear family, perhaps a total of 15–30 individuals (MacDonald 1968:126–134).

The wide range of artifacts in the Debert assemblage indicates that both sexes and all ages were present in the bands that camped there. Thus, the site was not a special-purpose site like some of those already discussed. However, neither was it a site like Bull Brook, where several bands came together in large congregation. It is interesting to note, too, that MacDonald could find no clear evidence for the separation of male and female activities at the Debert site. Debitage, points, and tool preforms, which are usually associated with male activities, are not clearly distributed differently from scrapers and other hide-working tools (usually associated with females). Of course, our observation of male versus female activities in this archaeological context rests on the possibly erroneous assumption that division of labor during the Paleo-Indian period was similar to that of most American Indian hunter–gatherers 10,000 years later. There may be patterns and regularities in Paleo-Indian sites that we have yet to discover. Unfortunately, we must wait until many more undisturbed sites are excavated and the analytical powers of modern computers are brought to bear before we will know for sure.

Having summarized the data base for the Paleo-Indian period in the Northeast, I can now turn to a general statement regarding the cultural system that produced those data. Others have attempted a similar synthesis in the past, usually depending on theoretical writings by ethnologists and ethnographic analogues. Service's (1962) statements on the nature of band organization are often cited. To this I have already added some more recent observations by Williams (1974). Specific ethnographic analogies are drawn more eclectically. MacDonald (1968:129–134), for example, prefers the analogy of the Naskapi–Montagnais of northern Quebec and Labrador. Funk (1976:226–227) uses the analogy of the Nunamiut Eskimo of northern Alaska. Rather than make direct use of any particular ethnographic analogy, I prefer to summarize the Paleo-Indian cultural system in terms of the economic, social, technological, and religious subsystems that I use as descriptive categories throughout this volume. This approach has the advantage of making all periods (including the historic) mutually comparable. The approach also has the advantage of avoiding the possible impression that the Paleo-Indians of the Northeast were more similar to the Eskimo, Naskapi, or some other group than was actually the case.

The continental glacier began to melt back around 15,300 B.P., at which time its front stood on a line running through Staten Island, Long Island, Block Island, Martha's Vineyard, and Nantucket Island. South of these modern islands the continental shelf was exposed to the 130-m isobath below modern sea level, and the exposed shelf appears to have supported tundra, mammoths, mastodons, and other Pleistocene species. There is not now and may never be evidence of Paleo-Indians in the area, but some archaeologists presume that they could have been there.

By 13,000 B.P. the ice had retreated far enough northward to open up vast new tracts of tundra. The front still stood south of the St. Lawrence valley and much of the land marginal to the glacier was still depressed from the weight of ice only recently melted. The result was that meltwater was impounded in glacial lakes that spread out over the middle portions of the Hudson, Connecticut, and other valleys. The levels of these lakes changed rapidly over the course of only a few centuries as the ice front continued its retreat and the earth's crust rebounded upward. We can estimate that Lake Albany began to form about 14,000 years ago but fell to successively lower levels, decanted, and disappeared by no later than 12,900 B.P. In a similar way, rapidly retreating ice and lagging crustal rebound allowed seawater to inundate

PALEO-INDIAN CULTURAL SYSTEM

coastal Maine, a transgression that reached maximum extent about 12,500 B.P., but reversed and retreated rapidly as crustal rebound raised the area out of the sea over the following centuries.

Thus, the first Paleo-Indians into our region, who may have arrived around 12,500 B.P. or even earlier, faced an environment that was changing rapidly. Glacial lake levels everywhere and sea levels in northern New England were dropping so rapidly that the change might have been apparent to bands returning to traditional camp sites near them over several generations. Off southern New England, where crustal rebound was less important, rising sea level led to a transgression of the continental shelf that was particularly rapid after 11,000 B.P. At the same time the tundra landscape began to turn into parkland as spruce, birch, jack pine, and red pine spread out of their refuge areas to the south. These species were established in southern New England and New York by 12,000 B.P. and in Maine by 10,000 B.P. The rapidity of these changes, and the thousands of local catastrophies they imply, must have been a severe hardship for mammoths, mastodons, and many other species. The Paleo-Indians, however, were skilled opportunists, people who traveled light and could quickly exploit game animals caught at a disadvantage. The largest of these species were almost certainly slow reproducers for whom a small increase in death rate could mean a steady population decline.

The Paleo-Indians probably moved in bands that were initially free wandering communities that moved frequently and without restriction, their direction, persistence, and territory covered being controlled mainly by game movements and the abundance of other wild food resources (Beardsley *et al.* 1956:135). Deliberate spacing and territorial restrictions probably developed as those first bands of Paleo-Indians grew and split, or were added to by others drifting in from New England. Bands therefore settled into traditionally held territories within which they moved seasonally. A successful subsistence strategy would have depended on a neighborly maintenance of boundaries, an unconscious practice by many animal species in addition to humans. This more evolved community pattern is called *restricted wandering.*

Despite the scarcity of direct archaeological evidence, our general understanding of hunting cultures is enough to convince me that Paleo-Indians must have hunted smaller game and gathered plant foods when they could. Indeed, most archaeologists have dismissed the old view that Paleo-Indians were big game specialists as too simplistic. Nevertheless, it must be conceded that an environment that was changing as rapidly as this one probably did not offer dependable seasonal supplies of such things as edible plants, shellfish, and fish runs. All such plant and animal communities must become established and thrive in a relatively stable environment before their seasonal availability can be predicted with any security. Even though they appear to have settled into a pattern of restricted wandering, Paleo-Indians must have found seasonal plant and animal resources (which were to become so important in later periods) to be dangerously impermanent and unpredictable. Thus, while they were not exclusively big game hunters, it seems safe to say that they were specialists in that subsistence strategy and filled out their diet in other ways when opportunities arose.

To their restricted wandering settlement pattern, we can add the notion of a *focal subsistence strategy* (Cleland 1976). Put simply, an extreme focal adaptation is one that emphasizes exploitation of a single reliable resource. Its polar opposite is a *diffuse subsistence strategy*, one that emphasizes a complicated exploitation of many resources. We shall see that the Indians of the Northeast alternated between focal and diffuse strategies throughout prehistory, for each presents its own kind of reliability and its own potential for disaster. For the Paleo-Indians, most resources other than big game were too thin or were shifting too rapidly with the evolving environment. It would be a long time before fish runs settled into reliable patterns and probably much longer before plant resources did the same. Thus, the balance of risk and opportunity compelled them to adopt a focal strategy. The tool inventories of focally adapted people are relatively specialized and limited in size, and we have seen that the known Paleo-Indian tool kit was certainly that. People with this kind of adaptation often make up for seasonal variations in their focal resource(s) by developing food storage techniques. It seems likely that, as wanderers, the Paleo-Indians did not have elaborate techniques for preserving and storing food, but instead depended on carrying small amounts of preserved food and making up for seasonal shifts in game by following the moving herds. This pattern is clearly also consistent with the archaeological evidence.

It is interesting to note that today there are generally many more resources at lower latitudes than higher ones and that the relatively few resources in the high latitudes tend to be stable and reliable. Thus, it is no surprise that, among historic hunters, most focal adaptations are found in the middle and higher latitudes. Around 12,500 B.P. continental glaciation compressed environmental zones toward the equator, narrowing the bands of low-latitude environment. At least in the case of North America, most of the habitable part of the continent was made into a set of environments in which focal adaptations were virtually the only option for human groups.

The major disadvantage of a focal adaptation is its rigidity, for it is both specialized and conservative. Focal adaptations do not develop unless the primary resource is highly dependable, but in the long run they may not be. Anyone old enough to read this volume is aware of our own focal dependence on oil and the consequences of having the supply suddenly fall below demand. Thus, a focal adaptation by definition carries the germ of its own disaster. For the Paleo-Indians the disappearance of many large game animals and the floral environments that they had depended on mushroomed into just such a disaster, and the era of widespread adaptive reorganization that followed the Paleo-Indian period was the result.

The hallmark of the Paleo-Indians remains the fluted point. However, it must be remembered that, as sophisticated as these points are in their own right, they are merely the surviving portions of what must have been more complex and elegant weapons. The stone *pieces esquillees*, spokeshaves, scrapers, drills, and other tools in Paleo-Indian assemblages are indirect evidence for equivalent skills in working bone, antler, wood, and ivory. Assemblages from historic Eskimo sites have shown us how minor stone can be in the total tool inventory of a hunting band. There may well have been many artifacts as impressive as fluted points that were made from materials that have since perished. This should be remembered even though we must wait for the lucky discovery of sites where direct evidence has been preserved.

Paleo-Indian bands appear to have maintained an economic subsystem that involved a seasonal pattern of restricted wandering once they became established in the Northeast. It seems likely that each maintained a territory that its members considered their own, moving about within it according to the movements of the big game animals on which they specialized and exploiting other food resources as they chanced upon them. They probably had polite understandings with adjacent bands regarding territorial rights and reinforced those understandings at occasional multiband encampments where gift exchange and marriages took place. It seems likely that gift exchange in this context was primarily responsible for the conveyance of exotic cherts that appear in most Paleo-Indian sites. *Gift exchange*, with its implicit emphasis on reciprocity and strong social overtones, is a much more appropriate label for this activity than is *trade*, which carries too many implications of profit motivation in normal usage. Bull Brook appears to have been a site at which these kinds of activities took place. Nuclear families, each of which typically consisted of a married couple, their children, and perhaps some grandparents or other close relatives, probably traveled together in bands totaling not much more than 50 individuals. Bull Brook could have accommodated five times that many all at once, and it seems likely that this was a temporary rendezvous of several bands of an eastern Massachusetts connubium.

The other sites we have examined appear to fit elsewhere in the standard seasonal round that was so important to the economic subsystem as a whole. The Debert site appears to have been a place used repeatedly over a long period by a single band. The Plenge site was of the same sort, perhaps used off and on through the whole of the Paleo-Indian period, but so badly disturbed that archaeologists have had difficulty separating assemblages. The West Athens Hill and Kings Road sites also appear to have been used by complete bands. Kings Road may have doubled as a kill site, whereas West Athens Hill was important as a game lookout and quarry site as well as a band camp site. In contrast, the Shoop site was quite possibly a traditional game lookout and camp site for an all-male band subset. In sum, the sites suggest that there were at least three community units that split up and recombined as circumstances required: (*a*) a band subset or special task group; (*b*) a complete band of several nuclear families; and (*c*) multiband congregations. The first of these could be either a special task group composed (for example) exclusively of adult males or one or two complete nuclear families. Robert Funk (1972:31) suggests that the Davis and Wapanucket No. 8 sites were occupied briefly by microbands of the latter type.

We have little evidence that would allow us to guess at the form of Paleo-Indian housing. On the basis of analogy with living hunters and some parallel archaeological evidence from the Old World, we can suggest that they lived in temporary skin-covered shelters or simple windbreaks that were large enough to accommodate no more than a single nuclear family. We can only hope that a site will be found in which post holes have been preserved to show us at least the skeletal structure of such shelters.

With the exception of the presumed association of a single point and caribou bones at Dutchess Quarry Cave, we also lack any direct information on Paleo-Indian kill sites in the Northeast. Kings Road is presumed to have been a kill site on the basis of its location alone. This is typical of the entire Eastern Woodland region; huge kill sites containing the remains of dozens of animals associated with Paleo-Indian remains are known for the West, but have not been found in the East. Ironically, many mammoth and mastodon skeletons have been found in the Northeast, but we have yet to find them together with Paleo-Indian remains. Thus, the connection between these early hunters and the now-extinct species is only an inferred one. Spruce wood associated with a mastodon skeleton found at Kings Ferry, New York, yielded a radiocarbon date of 11,410 ± 410 B.P. (Y-460). A mastodon rib from Sheridan, New York, dated only 9200 ± 500 B.P. (M-490). There are other dates on similar elephant remains from Michigan and elsewhere in the East, which together indicate that Paleo-Indians and these now-extinct creatures were contemporaries (Hester 1960). It seems unlikely that they could have ignored each other.

The social subsystem must have been based on the three-tier structure I have already mentioned. The basic unit was probably the nuclear family, the community unit being the band. Multiband congregations should probably be regarded as important but not regular occurrences. It is difficult to infer any additional institutions, although it is tempting to speculate on the development of trading partnerships between males of different bands. We presume that bands were both exogamous and patrilocal, such that people married outside their own bands and women moved to live with their husbands' bands. This would have meant that there were already many close links between women in adjacent bands, but that men lived with their brothers, sons, fathers, and fathers' brothers. Men might have felt close ties to their sisters in other bands, of course, and may well have felt the need to maintain direct links with the males of those bands. Thus, gift exchange, which may have been tied in direct ways to marriage exchange through bride price or other mechanisms, was probably an important social institution.

The technological subsystem has also already been discussed in some detail. However, there are some broader implications that I have left unsaid until now. Clearly Paleo-Indians lavished care on the manufacture of some things while regarding others as unworthy of it. They zeroed in on the best chert and other lithic sources very quickly after entering virgin territory and appear to have exchanged fine raw material with other groups long after settling in. But all of that is based on positive evidence. What we do *not* find in Paleo-Indian sites turns out to be as important as what we do find. Surely they made and used containers, but these must have been of bark, hide, basketry, or some other perishable material. Some historic hunters are known to have used the stomachs of their favorite game as natural containers and their contents as vegetable food. Such containers can be heated over open fires easily, as the parlor trick of boiling water in a paper bag demonstrates. It is clear and significant that the Paleo-Indians could not afford the weight of clay or stone vessels. If the native American horse still survived in the Northeast in this period, it was not (perhaps could not be) used. Even in the Old World only a small minority of the wild horses had any potential for domestication, and it was millennia before people there were ready to try it. Dogs were later used as beasts of burden, but it is likely that Paleo-Indians did not yet have them. Moreover, Paleo-Indians were terrestrial people; their seasonal movements in pursuit of game would not have been facilitated much by boats.

Another important bit of negative evidence is the absence of food-grinding tools in Paleo-Indian sites. This supports the argument I have already made about the unpredictability of wild food plants in this period. Vegetable and other seasonal food supplies must be dependable over the long term so that people can build up a bank of accurate information about location and seasonality. Only then can they settle into a seasonal round involving an annual return to old traditional sites, and only then will they invest in the production of heavy implements that can be left behind and returned to year after year. Thus, the absence of heavy food-grinding tools points to both an erratic pattern of seasonal wandering and a lack of specialization on seasonal plant resources. A similar argument can be constructed to explain the lack of obvious fishing equipment in Paleo-Indian assemblages, but such equipment can be made of perishable materials more easily than food-grinding tools can be, and it is risky to conclude that they did not fish. Indeed, fish bones at the Shawnee–Minisink site indicate that they did.

We do not yet have the kind of direct information on the Paleo-Indian religious subsystem that is known for the analogous Upper Paleolithic of the Old World. Only a few burials are known, none of them in the Northeast, and these have yielded little we could not otherwise guess. Hunters whose movements tend to be erratic often do not practice elaborate burial programs for the dead. Deaths often occur under difficult circumstances, particularly in the winter, and the dead are often simply abandoned or given only minimal attention before the band must move on in its effort to survive. Nevertheless, we can be sure that ideology was as important to these people as it is to all human societies. There must have been oral traditions that had become formalized and loaded with subtle messages over centuries of retelling. In these the hunt and other primary concerns must have loomed large as dominant themes. The giant animals of the Pleistocene would not have been overlooked in these traditions. Indeed, the story of "stiff-legged bear" that is found in more than one Algonquian language might be one such tradition that has survived the millennia. Speck (1935) noted that the creature in this story was huge, stiff-legged, and possessed long teeth, quite possibly a cultural memory of the mastodon.

Much has been made by other archaeologists of presumed late Paleo-Indian sites, the internal diversity they are said to exhibit, and the lack of any clear descendant cultures. Yet, as we have seen, a dozen sites are barely enough to give us some sense of variation in settlement pattern and almost certainly not enough to convey a clear picture of a period 2500 years long. I have suggested that the stylistic diversity seen on some sites could easily be the consequence of the mixing of assemblages deposited in separate occupations over many centuries. Thus, there may have been no more stylistic diversity internal to late Paleo-Indian assemblages than there was in earlier ones. While the Reagan assemblage was once disturbingly unique in the Northeast, it no longer is. Fluted points similar to the pentagonal points found at Reagan have recently turned up at the Plenge site and elsewhere.

END OF THE PALEO-INDIAN PERIOD

The Early Archaic period, which follows the Paleo-Indian, lasted from about 10,000 to 8000 B.P. (8000–6000 B.C.), a period of 2000 years. While it is true that relatively few remains from this period have been recognized in the Northeast, that observation does not necessarily lead to the conclusion that few have been found. The publicity given fluted points since their initial discovery with extinct species in the West has heightened awareness of Paleo-Indians in the public at large, and fluted points therefore do not often pass unnoticed. Diagnostic types for the Early Archaic are not equivalently obvious in private collections. Added to this is the unhappy fact that professionals have excavated few Early Archaic components in our area, a circumstance that has led many of us to look for reasons why there may have been an Early Archaic depopulation here. Ritchie and Funk (1971) have followed Fitting (1968) in suggesting that the evolution of coniferous forests having low food productivity reduced game and human populations during the period. While there may be some validity to this idea, remember that we have only a handful of sites for the Paleo-Indian period and should not necessarily expect to know of many from the Early Archaic, which was of shorter duration. Thus, the lack of clear descendant cultures for Paleo-Indian could easily be the result of our ignorance.

Another serious difficulty that impedes our understanding of these early periods is that forest environments were changing rapidly from the point of view of a given locale. Looked at regionally, whole forests were moving northward, subtly changing their characters as they shifted. The tundra that had dominated our area before 12,000 B.P. gave way to trees after that date, and the tundra that emerged farther north as ice continued to retreat was a high-latitude tundra that was different in character and could not support the same animal populations. Thus, some Paleo-Indian bands may have drifted northward, evolving into the Shield Archaic communities of the Canadian subarctic as they adjusted to an environment that was at once both like and unlike that which they had experienced previously. Late Paleo-Indian communities that remained in our area would have had to adjust to major environmental changes and in doing so would probably have adopted techniques and strategies from communities to the south, where similar pressures would have begun earlier. Given this northward shift of ideas (and perhaps people as well) that probably accompanied rapid cultural evolution, it is not surprising that what little evidence we have shows no gradual shift from the Paleo-Indian to the Early Archaic period.

The next generation of archaeologists faces many unresolved problems, not the least of which is the cargo of preconceptions to which I am undoubtedly contributing here. One such preconception (not mine) is the notion that we should expect to find Plano points in assemblages that are transitional between Paleo-Indian and Early Archaic. What this notion ignores is that Plano points are generally a western phenomenon, and that they are rare east of Ohio, Kentucky, and Tennessee. They are not a necessary intermediate stage between fluted points and the point types of the Archaic period. Indeed, I think that we should be surprised that we have found as many Plano points in the Northeast as we have. The two Plano-like bases and the Hardaway point(s) from the Harrisena site are clues to what may have been a uniquely northeastern transition. But this is a matter for the next chapter.

ARCHAIC
READJUSTMENT

Because Paleo-Indian remains are unique in so many ways and because we have taken so long to recognize the evidence for the sequence of periods we now enter, the notion of a clean discontinuity around 10,000 B.P. has become implicit in much of the literature. Ritchie (1969a:16) voices this view when he says that "early in the postglacial period, Paleo-Indian hunters may have left the Northeast for parts unknown, or they may simply have dwindled in number from an already scanty maximum to a few remnant bands." The latter part of that statement seems to me to be closer to what probably happened, although still somewhat overstated. The Paleo-Indian period ended with a relatively rapid forced readjustment when the focal adaptation of the Paleo-Indians collapsed. It does not necessarily follow that they all left the area or died off in place. There may have been some population reduction during the initial period of readjustment, but there may also have been no setback in slow steady population growth; we simply do not have the data to know one way or the other. What we do have, however, is a clear archaeological discontinuity, for the artifact styles and overall adjustment of Indians during the Early Archaic are indisputably different from those of the preceding Paleo-Indian period.

We have seen that the Paleo-Indian population was small, probably under 25,000. We have also seen that the Indian population of New England was probably larger than has been previously thought by ethnohistorians, perhaps approaching 200,000. While I do not see much evidence of wholesale population losses and replacements over the 10,000 years of prehistory that followed the Paleo-Indian period, neither do I presume a steady in-place growth of the 10,000 B.P. population to A.D. 1600 levels. There appear to be quite real discontinuities in the archaeological record to indicate that growth was by fits and starts, with a few major setbacks. The principle of uniformitarianism and the assumption of continuity, which were so important to the defeat of catastrophism by early evolutionists, have preserved a bit too well into the present century. There is a tendency to presume continuity in archaeological sequences and to presume further that any apparent discontinuity will disappear when missing evidence of transition is eventually found. Clearly, the burden of proof is on any hypothesis that proposes migration and displacement in place of in-place change to account for apparent discontinuities in the record. However, we have by now excavated enough sites to be rather sure that certain discontinuities are real and not the products of incomplete analysis (Funk and Rippeteau 1977:9–11).

Fortunately, we now have somewhat more sophisticated conceptual tools for dealing with discontinuity over time than was once the case. Even if we cannot pinpoint the prehistoric disasters that must have occasionally forced rapid readjustments, we can be sure that they occurred. Winters like that sustained by western New York State in 1976–1977 must have occurred from time to time over the last 10 millennia. Disastrous growing seasons like that of 1816 (the year without a summer) must be an occasional if rare occurrence as well. Unknown prehistoric epidemics would have added to these occasional weather-related disasters. Indeed, there are many plausible mechanisms to account for occasional local or regional population declines through the course of prehistory. Catastrophe theory, a recent branch of mathematics pioneered by Rene Thom (1975), is particularly well suited as a model for such events in prehistory. It is a controversial outgrowth of topology that focuses on a set of elementary catastrophes, only the simplest of which is used here. It may be that further exploration will convert catastrophe theory into a powerful new tool for archaeologists (Woodcock and Davis 1978), but for the moment it is mainly a handy model for illustrating archaeological discontinuity graphically (Renfrew 1978). Figure 4.1 illustrates the collapse of a system using a simple cusp catastrophe as a model. Here one might use the axis A to indicate the degree of focal as opposed to diffuse adaptation. Axis B can be used to indicate degree of resource reliability, and axis C population size. A community tracking from 1

FIGURE 4.1. A simple cusp catastrophe as a model for archaeological discontinuity. A population tracking on the folded surface collapses to a lower level (6) when it reaches a point of instability. See text.

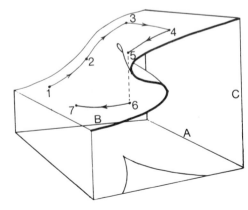

to 7 on the folded surface will reach a point (5) where the subsistence system is no longer stable due to extreme focal adaptation and a decrease in resource reliability. The system will then collapse to a lower population level (6), after which the community may retreat from a focal toward a diffuse adaptation before beginning the cycle again. The process by which a community gets to Point 5 is slow due to the conservatism inherent in adaptation. People rarely invite disaster by leaping to new subsistence strategies, but as Figure 4.1 shows disaster can ultimately occur just the same.

Notice that I am consistently using the focal–diffuse scale to describe overall adaptation. A cultural system cannot be thought of as alternating between focal and diffuse adaptations through the course of a seasonal cycle. Thus, Figure 4.1 shows us that overall adaptive systems have inherent potentials for instability. Looking at the flat surface below the folded surface one can see how that instability projects onto a two-dimensional plane. The system is stable only when the combination of adaptation and resource reliability projects a point onto the area outside the wedge-shaped zone of instability, for within that area the system is in a position analogous to a light switch midway between off and on.

This is a reasonable model for what happened to people in New England around 10,000 B.P. when the Paleo-Indian period ended and the Early Archaic period began. Such a situation is similar to that observed by evolutionary biologists for animal populations that undergo severe depopulations. Often the surviving smaller population of a species is at the margin of the previous distribution. Rapid evolution may occur within the surviving population before it expands once again into the niche of the ancestor population. Even if little evolution takes place within the surviving population, it is apt to be better adapted to the new conditions and therefore not all that similar to the norm of the ancestor population. Thus, even without rapid evolution within the surviving population a new norm has been established. The result of this kind of pulse in the history of a species will be the appearance of evolutionary discontinuity in most if not all parts of its distribution. Similarly, the collapse of a prehistoric population to a new stable level should be expected to produce the appearance of discontinuity in the archaeological record.

EARLY ARCHAIC PERIOD: 10,000–8,000 B.P.

The preceding paragraphs have been designed to show that there need not have been a regional population replacement after 10,000 B.P., even though there may be many examples of apparent replacement at a local level. The period we now find ourselves in I have called the "Early Archaic" despite the developmental stage implications that term once had. This usage is in line with that which has become traditional in eastern archaeology (Griffin 1967), but differs slightly from the new scheme proposed by Stoltman (1978). Stoltman keeps the period's time boundaries, but changes its name to "Transitional I." Regardless of how it is labeled, it is a 2000-year period that is thus far defined mainly by a few widespread projectile point types.

Byers (1959) once suggested that certain crude implements from the Ellsworth Falls site in Maine together with similar materials from the E. D. Prey site in Connecticut might constitute evidence for very early Archaic cultures in the region. Krieger (1964:43) gave the first of these even greater antiquity, making it a component of a hypothetical pre-projectile point stage. Krieger's suggestion is clearly out of the question, because it would require Indians to have lived under glacial ice in Maine prior to the beginning of the Paleo-Indian period. I must also agree with Funk (1976:234) and Ritchie (1969a:32) regarding their possible Early Archaic connections. The presumably early materials at Ellsworth Falls were not distinguished as a separate component at the time of excavation, and there is little to indicate that they are distinct from the cruder elements in the Late Archaic component from the site. Much the same criticism can be leveled at the presumably early evidence from the E. D. Prey site (Ritchie 1969a:33).

Wright (1978:72) has noted growing evidence for a complex of Early Archaic lanceolate points in the Northeast. This includes the scanty evidence for Plano-like points that I mentioned at the end of the previous chapter. At least some of these are similar to Eden and Agate Basin types, which are best known on the Great Plains and the Midwest. Although very scarce in New England generally, Hardaway-like points were found at the Harrisena site near Lake George (Hammer *et al.* n.d.). Hardaway points are best known in the Carolina Piedmont, but related specimens have been found in Illinois, Alabama, and other locations around the Eastern Woodlands (Coe 1964:64–67). All are presumed to date from the Early Archaic period as defined here. Kirk Stemmed (Figure 4.2), Serrated, and Corner-Notched types are also known for the end of the Early Archaic period in the Carolina Piedmont (Coe 1964:69–70, 122). They date earlier at the St. Albans, West Virginia site, where they are associated with a date of 8930 ± 160 B.P. (Y-1538) (Broyles 1966). As we shall see, they are generally later in the Northeast, the available dates falling into the early part of the Middle Archaic period. Whatever their ages, Kirk analogues are found in many parts of the Eastern Woodlands. A series of bifurcate-based types is thinly scattered over southern New England (Dincauze and Mulholland 1977). Analogous types at the St. Albans site are dated there by four radiocarbon dates ranging from 8160 to 8830 B.P. The only date on any bifurcate type in our area is 7135 ± 200 B.P. (SI-2638) from the Harrisena site (Snow 1977a:435). We can probably assume that this indicates a survival of bifurcate-base points into the Middle Archaic period. Finally, Wright (1978) sees growing evidence that there were some Early Archaic side-notched types that might even associate with Paleo-Indian remains.

I have reached a point where a digression into the realm of projectile point types and their significance cannot be postponed. It is a journey not often taken by archaeological authors, and assumptions, both right and wrong, are usually left implicit. My aim is to make my assumptions explicit with regard

FIGURE 4.2. A sample of Kirk Stemmed points. These specimens are serrated examples from Kentucky. Assigned to the Early Archaic in the Southeast; specimens from the Northeast tend to date to the Middle Archaic. Shown at actual size. (After Bell 1960:63.)

to point types and types generally for this and subsequent chapters, because they are fundamental to many important differences of archaeological opinion. In the first place, the spatial boundaries of projectile point types are not necessarily coterminous with social groups. This is a particularly important observation given the wide distributions of the point classes just discussed. Ethnographically observed hunter–gatherers such as the Australian aborigines lived in widely scattered bands, individuals interacting with others of their connubia and not incidentally engaging in the kind of gift exchange I have suggested took place among Paleo-Indians. Individuals exchanged finished pieces as a means of maintaining social connections through reciprocity. In the course of doing this they criticized each other's work either implicitly or explicitly, an activity that enhanced prestige and enforced uniformity in what was considered excellence. It should not be surprising that projectile point styles of striking uniformity are widespread in the Eastern Woodlands even though that uniformity was probably the cumulative result of a complex network of individual exchange relationships (Michlovic 1975). Haas (1958) discovered that Algonquian and Gulf languages are related at a deep and ancient level, and Willey (1958) proposed that Early Archaic period Indians spoke related Algonquian–Gulf languages throughout the Eastern Woodlands. The apparently intrusive Iroquoian and Siouan communities had not yet arrived according to his hypothesis, and local speech communities would have been linked in a regional L-Complex (Hockett 1958:324). In such a complex each of many overlapping connubia would have had the linguistic integrity of a dialect, but this would have been an abstraction of the whole for there would have been no sharp internal linguistic boundaries. Thus, although people from one end of the region might not have been able to understand people from the other end, there was continuity of language between these locational extremes and therefore a medium for the diffusion of particular point styles. We therefore have both the mechanism (gift exchange) and the medium for the broad diffusion of diagnostic projectile point types, and we need not be shocked at the widespread Early Archaic distributions.

A second important principle connected with projectile points is that they do not necessarily occupy short, mutually exclusive time units. The often implicit assumption that they do is part of the bias we have taken on as a consequence of our uncritical borrowing of the stratigraphy principle from geology (Gruber 1978). Artifact types have too often been treated as if equivalent to geological index fossils. The major classes I have described probably overlapped in time, some of them probably used at different times and for different purposes by the same individuals. This leads inevitably to the observation that the point types we take so seriously are only the surviving portions of larger weapons or other tools. We would be foolish to assume that any prehistoric Indian carried only one type of tool requiring a stone point, yet that is exactly what is implied by the assumption that point types should be expected to occupy mutually exclusive time slots. Coe (1964:67) found that three types, the Hardaway Blade, Hardaway–Dalton, and Hardaway Side-Notched, occurred together in some places but had different life spans. The situation is different than it was during the Paleo-Indian period, where diversity is usually more easily explained as a function of stylistic change over time. Beginning with the Early Archaic, point types take on some of the characteristics of modern hats, each made consistently enough to deserve its own name. It is reasonable to presume that a given individual could have made, used, and exchanged two or more such types, each designed as part of a larger, perhaps specialized, tool.

A third principle, which flows logically from the second, is that each point type represents archaeologically a more complex tool type, which in turn had its own function. Stability in the point type form over space and time is probably indicative of stability of the larger complete tool. This in turn implies that the tool was well adapted for some particular purpose or set of purposes. Stated that way, it is easy to see how point types were probably tied to specific subsistence adaptations, even though those specific adaptations have not yet been discovered. Since point types were tied to subsistence strategies, it is also easy to see how a given point type might have a distribution and life span quite different from that of another point type, even though the two might sometimes occur together. We have seen in Chapter 2 that subsistence strategies can vary substantially even within a region as small as aboriginal New England. We should not be surprised, therefore, to find that a point type has a different life span in one region as opposed to another, that certain point types show up only on certain site types, or that certain point types were never used at all in some regions despite their availability. Kirk Stemmed and Kirk Corner-Notched points were used around 9000 B.P. (7000 B.C.) at the St. Albans site. The precedent of this date is so strong that it has led Funk (1977b:23) to say that "there is no convincing evidence for a large time lag in diffusion of early southeastern traits into the Northeast, despite apparently anomalous dates ranging from 5100 to 5570 B.C. [7050–7520 B.P.] for Kirk-like points at Sheep Rock (Michels and Smith 1967), Harry's Farm (Kraft 1975b), and Rockelein (Dumont 1974). These dates seem too young for the Kirk styles." He makes the basic premise held by many archaeologists clear in another place. "Presumably each type occupied its own time level and was shared by all contemporary human groups on a regional or areal basis (despite the seeming coexistence of several types in the Staten Island sites) [Funk 1978:23]." This widely held interpretation implies a preference for the use of a point type as an index artifact over the acceptance at face value of the only radiocarbon dates we have for the type in the Northeast. The interpretation begs the question and is an example of a fallacy that is the Achilles heel of postradiocarbon archaeology. I argue here as I do elsewhere that we cannot dismiss radiocarbon dates without both cause and a plausible explanation for why the dates might be in error. Furthermore, the existence of the radiocarbon dating technique frees us from the need to adopt geological assumptions regarding strata and index types. Looked at in that way, we are able to say without blushing that Kirk points were used about 9000 years ago at the St. Albans, West Virginia site and that analogous points were used 7000–7500 years ago at three sites (at least) in the Delaware and Susquehanna drainages. The problem pointed out by Funk disappears. Thus, we are able to get on with the search for the adaptive significance of the point type and the reasons for the rather different life spans in two different parts of the Eastern Woodlands by putting untenable assumptions behind us.

James Tuck (1974) has attempted to impose order on the Early Archaic period of the Eastern Woodlands by proposing three broad horizons of related projectile point types. To these Chapman (1976) has added a fourth. Both use *horizon* as Willey and Phillips (1958) defined it: a regionally broad, temporally brief unit that assumes that the artifact types defining it have the characteristics of index types. The oldest horizon defined by Tuck is the Dalton, which is identified by Hardaway points along the Atlantic Coast and Dalton points elsewhere. He gives this oldest horizon an age of 9000–9700 years. The second Early Archaic horizon defined by Tuck is the Big Sandy, which is defined by an early form of side-notched points of the same name and dated to about 8500–9000 B.P. Tuck's third horizon is the Kirk horizon, which takes its name from the Kirk Corner-Notched, Kirk Stemmed, and Kirk Serrated points that identify it. He gives the Kirk horizon an age of about 8000–8500 B..P. Chapman (1976) adds a fourth Early Archaic horizon that is really three separate bifurcate-base point horizons defined by the St. Albans Side-Notched, LeCroy Stemmed, and Kanawha Stemmed points, respectively (Figure 4.3). Radiocarbon dates from West Virginia and Tennessee range

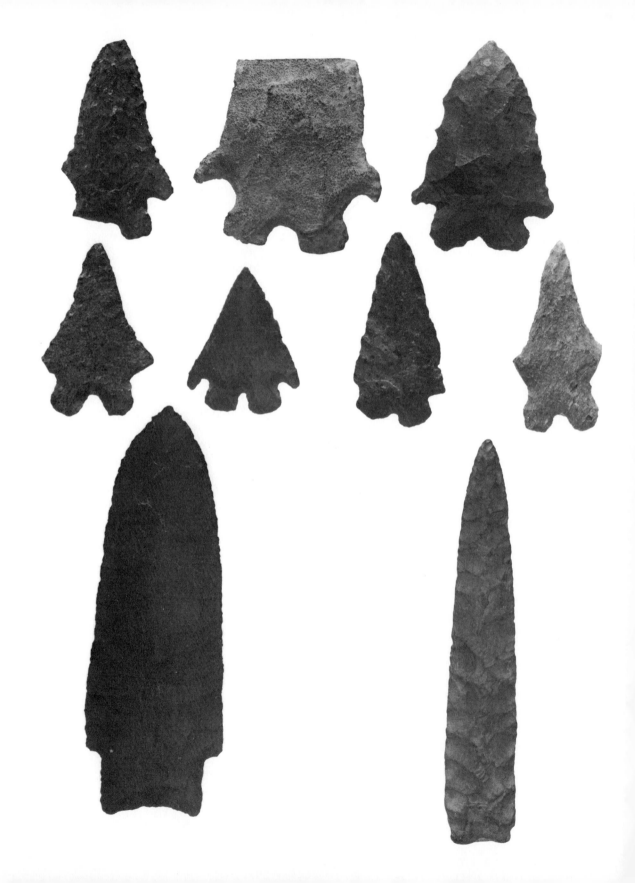

from 8660 to 8830 B.P. for the St. Albans Side-Notched and from 8160 to 8250 for the Kanawha Stemmed type. The LeCroy Stemmed points are thought to be temporally intermediate, so a date of 8920 ± 325 (Gx-3597) is rejected as too old. Whether or not that is appropriate, the three bifurcate-base point types would appear to have overlapping temporal distributions with Tuck's Big Sandy and Kirk horizons.

While the first principle discussed above would allow for the existence of the horizons proposed by Tuck and Chapman, the second two principles place a heavy burden of proof on them. Of the really six proposed horizons, at least two are already questionable because of ill-fitting radiocarbon dates, and I suspect that the others will be also as soon as more radiocarbon dates come in. Tuck supports the dating of his Dalton horizon with two dates from the Stanfield–Worley rock shelter in Alabama. The Big Sandy horizon is also supported by two dates, from West Virginia and Iowa, respectively. Serious problems begin with the Kirk horizon point types, for which several radiocarbon dates are available. Chapman reports nine dates ranging from 8060 to 9435 B.P. for Kirk phase components on three sites. Kirk horizon strata at the St. Albans site yielded three dates ranging from 7900 to 8850 B.P. Four dates noted earlier from the Susquehanna and Delaware drainages range from 7050 to 7520 B.P. Tuck (1974:77) notes that at Russell Cave, Alabama, there are "a number of Kirk projectile points, unfortunately mixed with other artifacts spanning nearly one thousand years from 8560 ± 320 B.P. to 7565 ± 250 B.P." The situation is unfortunate only if we insist that Kirk points must have been widely made and used only for a few centuries before 8000 B.P., an unsupported assumption in my view. Yet it has caused Tuck to imply that there must have been a stratigraphic mixture at Russell Cave, and it has caused Funk to discard all four dates on Kirk points in the Northeast as too recent. Clearly what is most needed at this juncture is a complete reassessment of the formal identification of point types in the Kirk series along with an examination of their spatial and temporal distributions that does not start with such assumptions. Just as clearly, we cannot risk an extension of Kirk index types into New England until we are sure of what it is we are extending. Tuck gets at the heart of the matter by noting that Kirk Corner-Notched points are apparently older than Kirk Stemmed on sites where that relationship can be detected. He regards this as an evolution in style from corner notching to stemmed points, since "there is little difference in either the method of manufacture or in the hafting process between the two forms [Tuck 1974:77]." Clearly the Kirk types represent some sort of developmental sequence and should not be expected to fall consistently into a temporally thin horizon.

FIGURE 4.3. Early Archaic points. Bifurcate points from eastern Massachusetts, except broken specimen from Lake Winnipesaukee, N.H. Upper right specimen, 5.5 cm. All resemble Kanawha points more closely than St. Albans or LeCroy points. Plano points: left (11 cm) from Nichols, N.Y.; right from Hamilton, Mass. Shown at actual size. (Courtesy of Peabody Museum of Salem, Mass.)

The dating of St. Albans Stemmed points is much tighter, because dates on the type all come from two sites in the Appalachian highlands. Two dates on the type range from 8820 to 8830 B.P. at the St. Albans site (Broyles 1966: 40). Three more dates from the Rose Island, Tennessee site range from 8660 to 8800 B.P. The stratigraphically later LeCroy point is dated to around 8250 at St. Albans, but as noted earlier is associated with a date of 8920 ± 325 (Gx-3597) at Rose Island (Chapman 1976:3). This is clearly too old given other evidence internal to the Rose Island site. However, the date has a relatively large error margin of 325 years such that it is within one standard deviation of conforming with the stratigraphic sequence. It is, therefore, a perfectly good date.

The Kanawha Stemmed point is dated to 8160 ± 100 B.P. (Y-1540) at St. Albans (Broyles 1966:40). This date is in line with others from the same site and in line with the site's stratigraphy. However, it is much older than the date 7135 ± 200 B.P. (SI-2638) that probably relates to an analogous bifurcate-base point at the Harrisena site in the upper Champlain drainage (Snow 1977a:435). We therefore have a problem trying to force Kanawha points to fit the horizon concept that is like the one we have with Kirk points. Independent radiocarbon dating in the Northeast puts both bifurcate points and the Kirk series into the first millennium of the Middle Archaic period instead of into the Early Archaic period where they tend to fall at southeastern sites. If this time lag is real, and we must at least proceed as if it is for the present, then it is possible that the Early Archaic in New England was characterized by (a) point types that persisted locally into the Middle Archaic, (b) still undiscovered or unrecognized point types that differ from the above, or (c) nothing at all. At least for the present the first alternative seems the most likely.

While it is difficult to prove the destruction of sites from the erosion and deposition associated with marine and riverine environments, a closer examination of the Fitting hypothesis is possible. Table 3.1 (p. 114) shows in a very general way that the forests of 9500 years ago were still well south of their present positions. Coastal areas of New England, including many now submerged, were dominated by northern hardwood forests, whereas interior parts were dominated by boreal forest. Ritchie and Funk (1971:46) reason that "the forest composition was undergoing a marked alteration from spruce–pine to pine with a significantly lowered carrying capacity for game." Ritchie (1969b:213) argued previously that "the oak–pine and later oak–hickory forest successions which followed from about 4000 B.C., associated with the warmer conditions of the Xerothermic period, restored forest conditions highly favorable to game animals, especially to mast eaters like the deer and turkey, and their associates and predators, including man in the Archaic hunting–fishing–collecting stage, and his radiocarbon-dated appearance at this time is not fortuitous." Ritchie and Funk had reported Early Archaic point types from four sites on Staten Island (Figure 4.4) and concluded that

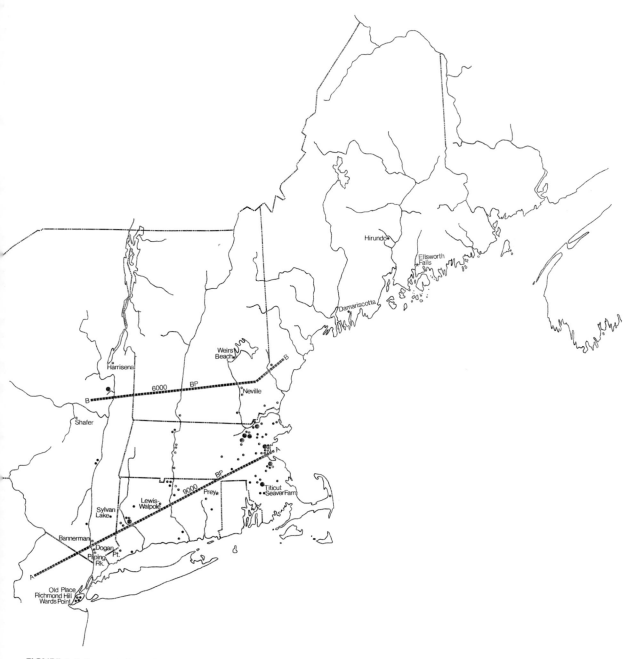

FIGURE 4.4. Some Early and Middle Archaic sites. Small dots indicate single sites; large dots indicate clusters of three or more sites. E. D. Prey and Ellsworth Falls (*) were once but are no longer regarded as Early Archaic. A–A indicates 20% oak isopoll in 9000 B.P. B–B indicates 20% oak isopoll around 6000 B.P.

an adverse environment had prevented Indians of the period from taking up residence farther to the north in the Hudson drainage or elsewhere. One of them, the Ward's Point site, produced two radiocarbon dates, 7260 ± 125 B.P. (I-4512) and 8250 ± 140 (I-5331), the first of which might be another indication that some Early Archaic point types persisted past 8000 B.P. in New England. Both dates are associated with a stratum containing Kirk Stemmed, LeCroy Bifurcated, and Kanawha Stemmed types. The earlier date fits with dates on LeCroy Bifurcated points at St. Albans. The later date is similar to that obtained for Kanawha Stemmed analogues at the Harrisena site as well as being similar to dates on Kirk Stemmed points from the Susquehanna and Delaware drainages. The Richmond Hill site on Staten Island produced a date of 9360 ± 120 (I-4929) associated with Palmer Corner-Notched and Hardaway points, which also date to the beginning of the Early Archaic in the Carolina Piedmont. A LeCroy Bifurcated and a probable Kirk Stemmed point were also found in the deposit. The Old Place site is even more perplexing, producing both Early and Middle Archaic point types along with a date of 7260 ± 140 (I-4070).

The upshot of this complex discussion is that, while there are a few examples of Plano, Kirk, and bifurcate-base analogues in aboriginal New England, they are not abundant and they have not been adequately dated by radiocarbon on sites within the region. Our evidence for the Early Archaic is therefore equivocal and confused by the possibility that some of the types might have persisted into the Middle Archaic period here. Robert Funk has been particularly struck by the scarcity of Early Archaic materials and has come up with two hypotheses to account for it. First, he points out that river floodplains are likely locations for sites of that age, but that deposition and meandering over the last 8000 years could easily have destroyed much of the evidence or buried it under deep layers of alluvium (Funk 1977b:22). The second hypothesis, which will stand either alone or together with the first, was partly William Ritchie's idea. The hypothesis, which Ritchie and Funk (1971) adopted from Fitting (1968), suggests that Early Archaic populations were severely depressed by the low productivity of the forest environment that dominated the region at the time. To these can be added the probability that sea level, which was still rising to its present level, destroyed many coastal and estuary sites during the Early Archaic (Salwen 1975). Around 9000 B.P. sea level was about 25 m below its present stand. By 3000 years ago it was within 3 m of its present position (Salwen 1965:33).

Serious doubt has been cast upon Ritchie and Funk's application of Fitting's hypothesis since it was first stated, primarily as a result of palynological studies. Davis (1967:35–36) has divided the period 9500–7000 B.P. into two subperiods for southern New England, the first dominated by pine–birch–alder and the second by pine–oak. The first environment probably resembled modern northern Minnesota, whereas the second probably resembled modern central Ontario. Farther north, palynologists have determined that the environment around Moulton Pond, Maine, resembled the pine–northern hardwood forests of modern central New England (Davis *et al.* 1975). Thus, the simplified depiction of New England forests during the Early Archaic period as shown in Table 3.1 (p. 114) misrepresents the situation, as more detailed analyses have shown. It may well be that the forests of New England were less productive 9000 years ago than they are now, but the modern analogue forests are hardly a silent no-man's-land. The hypothesis must be revised.

In fact, the evidence for an Early Archaic occupation of New England is growing, the data made ambiguous only by the possible time lag mentioned earlier. The distribution of sites and find spots that have produced bifurcate-base types compares well with the distribution of Paleo-Indian sites and stray finds. Indeed, there are more sites and more stray finds of presumed Early Archaic material on Figure 4.4 than Figure 3.1 shows for Paleo-Indian remains. This is significant, particularly since the Early Archaic is the shorter of the two periods, although this might be balanced by the persistence of some types past 8000 B.P. In addition to the concentration of Early Archaic materials in southern New England, Sanger has orally reported Kirk points from coastal Maine, and Wright (1978) describes several pieces from southern Ontario. The Lewis–Walpole site in Farmington, Connecticut, has produced analogues of Palmer Corner-Notched, Kirk Corner-Notched, Hardaway, and Kanawha Stemmed types. Thus, there can be little question any more regarding the occupation of New England during the Early Archaic. What remains now, however, is a very poor understanding of the cultural system of that period and its adaptation to the environment of the time (Starbuck 1977).

Assessment of the Early Archaic cultural system is very difficult given the small number of data available. Our knowledge of site types and their distributions is clouded by the possibility that they cannot be located through the use of techniques that depend on modern topographic features. Many could be buried under river alluvium or seawater or might have been destroyed completely over time. The central difficulty, as it often is in archaeology, is that we simply cannot estimate the limits or significance of negative data. Most finds of presumed Early Archaic point types are isolated or come from sites at which later components dominate. Thus, we have no recognizable assemblages from which to estimate activities. Worse than that, we do not even have a clear association between site locations and resources. Figure 4.4 suggests a preference for locations near major streams, but this tendency is no stronger than that shown in Figure 3.1 for the Paleo-Indian period and must be regarded as inconclusive. Dincauze and Mulholland (1977:441) regard the Titicut and Seaver Farm sites on the Taunton River in southeastern Massachusetts as together constituting an Early Archaic base camp. Together, the adjacent sites contain a major Early Archaic component defined by bifurcate-base and other diagnostic point types. The dual site lies on the north (outside) bank of a bend in the Taunton River, and, although

Early Archaic Cultural System

there has been a substantial amount of digging, little has been reported regarding intra-site distributions or associations of Early Archaic remains (Robbins 1968; Taylor 1976). The Early Archaic component at the Harrisena site is only slightly better known. This site is the northern terminus of a portage linking the Hudson River and Lake George, a portage only 15 km long that connected primary watercourses of the Hudson and Champlain drainages. Evidence of the Early Archaic period at the Harrisena site includes bifurcate-base points and analogues of Plano and Kirk points. A single bifurcate-base point was found in association with a pit that produced a radiocarbon date of 7135 ± 200 b.p. (SI-2638), one of the Northeastern dates suggesting that some Early Archaic diagnostics may have been used here until well into the Middle Archaic (Snow 1977a). Hardaway-like point fragments were found some distance away from the bifurcate-base materials and the dated pit and may therefore be the result of a separate and earlier brief occupation. The site appears to have been a temporary camp at which some hunting, butchering, and hideworking were carried out. This is suggested by the quantities of points, knives, and scrapers found associated in Early Archaic components. There was no evidence of fishing equipment, and debitage frequency seemed low relative to artifact frequency, indicators that neither fishing nor tool manufacture was important at the site. There was also a curious and statistically significant preference for quartz and quartzite in the debitage even though we found no finished artifacts made of this material (Hammer *et al.* n.d.). It appears from evidence at other sites that these were favored materials for scrapers, which in turn are indicators of hideworking.

So far, then, we have only the base camp on the Taunton River and a portage terminal on Lake George to suggest site types and distributions. Other finds are distributed almost randomly within the area. Clearly we have no means to suggest house types (if any) and their arrangements within communities. Nor can we make many reasonable guesses regarding food resources and their seasonal procurement. Tuck (1974:78) cites some Early Archaic evidence from outside the Northeast that helps here, however. Chipped stone drill bits that are different from Paleo-Indian drills appear to be new additions to the tool kit, and they probably indicate changes in woodworking and boneworking. Large choppers or digging tools probably indicate increased attention to the gathering of tubers and roots. Remains from Russell Cave, Alabama, include evidence for the use of 34 vertebrate species and 5 species of freshwater mollusks, along with a bone fishhook. So the little evidence we do have suggests a broadening of the subsistence base from what it had been during the Paleo-Indian period. This is in line with the hypothetical collapse of the focal Paleo-Indian subsistence adaptation to a more diffuse Early Archaic adaptation, perhaps accompanied by a population decline. Early Archaic seasonal movements were probably more complex due to the broader range of resources utilized, and the kinds of special purpose sites used were probably more varied. Certainly with the forests now reestablished and the role of big-game hunting no longer central to subsistence we should not be surprised to find no evidence of hilltop lookout camp sites in the Early Archaic period. We can only hope that we will eventually find a few intact examples of the kinds of special-purpose sites they did have.

Possible population decline notwithstanding, I see no evidence of a withdrawal of Paleo-Indians and a population replacement by Early Archaic period people. On the contrary, there appears to have been continuity from one period to the next, albeit under possibly reduced circumstances. That being the case, the social subsystem probably remained intact. There was probably a continuation of band organization along with overlapping connubia as the units of band interrelations. Although there is no archaeological evidence to make a convincing argument, there is a general opinion among archaeologists that this was a time during which bands were settling into territories. Certainly the settlement system was one of restricted wandering by this time, a system defined by "communities that wander about within a territory that they define as theirs and defend against trespass, or on which they have exclusive rights to food resources of certain kinds. Movement within the territory may be erratic or may follow a seasonal round, depending on the kind of wild food resources utilized [Beardsley *et al.* 1956:136]." I should guess that by this time movements were not erratic and that the system was trending toward the even more regularized central-based wandering pattern. The social implications of these patterns include the possible development of regional boundaries around sets of bands; that is, interband relations were probably becoming more regularized such that abstract connubia were being replaced by more clearly crystallized and mutually exclusive groupings. Tuck (1974:78) speculates that "it was a time of 'settling in' when an increasing number of food sources began to be utilized, when people became more familiar with their local environments perhaps at the expense of interchange with other groups which were also becoming more committed to 'their own' river valleys, lake systems, or other biological or physiographic areas."

For the period following this one, Dincauze (1976:139) sees a settlement system having a number of special-purpose sites, a system implying "increasing specialization of task locations, increasing complexity of communication networks, and increasing interdependence and diversification of social units." She sees this as paralleling developmental trends observed by Fowler (1959) at the Modoc rock shelter site in Illinois. If we assume that the Early Archaic system in New England was similar to that observed by Fowler in Illinois, and that the developmental trends were general within the Eastern Woodlands, then we can guess that the Early Archaic system here was rather like that in southern Illinois in its general outlines. Fowler sees the system prior to 8000 B.P. as involving fewer special-purpose sites than would be the case in the Middle Archaic. This means that there would have been less elaborate seasonal scheduling and a tendency for a relatively broad range of activities to be carried out at all sites. This makes sense in terms of how we might expect New England cultures to have readapted from a systemic collapse around 10,000 B.P. toward increasingly complex adaptations of the later Archaic periods.

The technological subsystem is defined by the diagnostic artifact types already discussed at some length: rare spokeshave scrapers, drills, choppers, hammerstones, anvil stones, abrading stones, and bifacially chipped celts and adzes (Ritchie and Funk 1971; Ritchie 1971b). The last, along with the drills, suggest increased attention to woodworking. The anvil stones were probably important for processing nuts. In addition to the general forms of points produced during this period, Early Archaic points often have serrated edges. Moreover, resharpening while the point was still hafted often produced concave sides and steeple shapes, as well as asymmetrical beveling which gives the point a parallelogram cross section. Fitzhugh (1972) sees bifurcate-base forms moving into New England only after about 9000 B.P., an interpretation that is consistent with the late dates available for these points but which might be contradicted by future discoveries. Certainly the Kirk Stemmed, Kanawha Stemmed, LeCroy Bifurcated, Hardaway, Plano, and Palmer analogues in New England each had its own history, and it seems likely to me that each represents a separate complex tool type. It is probable that both time and tool function were significant determinants of type forms and that neither should be assumed to have had overriding significance.

I see much less evidence of the regional exchange of exotic chert types or anything else for this period when compared to the preceding Paleo-Indian period. This may be further evidence of growing regional diversity, reduced population, or both. At the same time there seems to have been a growing preference for quartz and quartzite as raw materials for scrapers. Overall the evidence is for a possible increase in the range of nonlithic raw materials, a reduction in the range of exotic lithics, an increase in the range of tool types made of stone, and a presumed increase in the range of subsistence activities indicated by the tool remains. Given the increase of tools designed for working wood, antler, and bone, we may be able to infer an increase in the number and range of things made from these materials, but poor preservation makes it difficult for us to obtain direct evidence to support that notion.

We have no evidence on which to base an assessment of mortuary site types and burial programs apart from the pit at the Harrisena site. The pit might have been a burial pit, but no trace of a burial was found, not even tooth enamel. Unfortunately, we must wait for concrete evidence for the Early Archaic religious subsystem.

MIDDLE ARCHAIC PERIOD: 8,000–6,000 B.P. We know more about the Middle Archaic period than the period preceding it. As I use it here this period begins 1000 years earlier and ends 2000 years earlier than proposed by Willey (1966:249) some years ago. It is closer to

Stoltman's (1978) proposed "Meso-Indian" period, but ends 1000 years earlier. It is exactly equivalent to Griffin's (1967) Middle Archaic. Readers who find the Christian calendar a more meaningful frame of reference should note that the period falls roughly between 6000 and 4000 B.C. In a worldwide context, this was a period in which copper replaced stone in the Mediterranean area, corn began to be cultivated in Mexico, Egyptians began to engage in sea trade, and megalithic construction began in northwestern Europe.

The coastline was still some distance from its present location and sea level was still rising rather rapidly. The result is that many coastal sites of the period were later destroyed or submerged, and what we know of the Middle Archaic has a heavy interior bias. We have good evidence for the period from the Neville site at Manchester, New Hampshire, the Hirundo site near Old Town, Maine, and the Harrisena site near Lake George, New York. Of these, the most significant work thus far has been that carried out by Dincauze (1971a, 1976) on the Neville site remains. The Neville site is located at Amoskeag Falls on the Merrimack River very near the line I have arbitrarily drawn to separate the upper from the lower Merrimack drainage. The river had eroded down to the sill of the falls, taken on many of its modern flow characteristics, and become seasonally clogged with migratory fish by 8000 years ago. Mercury concentrations in the Middle Archaic strata deposited after that date indicate that the Indians were harvesting this seasonal resource. Dincauze concludes that the site was a late spring–early summer base camp during the period.

The deciduous forests of southern New England were already well developed by 8000 B.P. A line separating a southern zone in which oak pollen made up more than 20% of the whole from a northern zone in which it made up less than 20% ran from Tappan Zee on the lower Hudson to the site of modern Boston 9000 years ago. This 20% oak isopoll moved north to about the northern boundary of Massachusetts by 8000 B.P. and to the location shown in Figure 4.4 by 6000 B.P.; there it has stayed. The eastern end of the line curved northeastward, crossing the Merrimack around Manchester and continuing parallel to the general trend of the coastline through northern New England (Dincauze and Mulholland 1977:448). This, too, has changed little in subsequent centuries. The frequencies of other species have changed, however, and there has been a long and complex evolution of New England's forests. Some species migrate more rapidly than others, and many are adapted to soil conditions that took a long time to develop after deglaciation. For example, the relative rise in some types of conifer pollen through the Middle Archaic period may well have resulted from the progressive growth of bogs, in which some species flourish (Wright 1971:451). Edaphic conditions like this one are so important to the evolution of forests that it is very risky to infer climatic episodes from pollen frequency profiles. It is downright absurd to crawl farther out onto the limb and use such inferred minor climatic episodes as explanations for changes in the archaeological record. Not only can we not be sure that a hypothetical climatic period really existed, there are no precise mechanisms to show how any such period might have caused human culture change. What we are left with is the observation that the frequency of oak pollen from the Middle Archaic on is an indicator that conditions were not all that unfavorable for the last 8000 years at least, but that there may have been minor fluctuations in moisture and average temperature during that time. Furthermore, we are rather unsure of the succession of those fluctuations and do not have the faintest idea how they (if they occurred at all) may have affected human adaptations.

The primary Middle Archaic complex at the Neville site has the Neville point as its most important diagnostic type (Figure 4.5). The point type is similar to the Stanley Stemmed point of the Carolina Piedmont, differing from it only by being generally a bit smaller. Indeed, the close correspondence between Dincauze's Neville site and Coe's (1964:14–55) Doerschuk, North Carolina, site has been the main ingredient in Dincauze's (1976:140–142) proposed "Atlantic Slope" culture area for the Middle Archaic. Materials from Middle Archaic assemblages within this province resemble each other and contrast with those from the Mississippi and Gulf drainages westward. Thus, in this period New England was beginning to take on a regional appearance, although still as part of a larger coastal province. The Neville complex includes the Neville point, large flake scrapers, as well as small quartz crystal scrapers, wedge-shaped flake knives, and chipped-stone perforators with Neville-like bases. Together, a dozen radiocarbon dates from the site indicate that the Neville complex had a life span of perhaps about 8000–6500 B.P. Curiously, the Stark complex was added to it sometime after 7000 B.P., although this, too, terminated by 6000 B.P. Although those who equate complexes with prehistoric cultures are apt to be disturbed by this apparent miscegenation, Dincauze is not. The Stark point is analogous to the Morrow Mountain point of the Carolina Piedmont and the Poplar Island type of the closer Middle Atlantic region. The rest of the Stark complex differs in small ways from the Neville complex. Perforators have bases that mimic Stark rather than Neville point bases, and winged spear-thrower weights are present along with full-grooved axes. The latter ground stone implements are significant in their implications and are found as early at this site as anywhere in the Eastern Woodlands. Those implications are discussed in the following paragraphs.

As the Neville complex faded in importance prior to 6000 B.P. it was replaced by the Merrimack complex. The Stark complex did not disappear but coexisted with the Merrimack complex just as it had with the later history of the Neville complex. Merrimack Stemmed points are square-stemmed points generally similar to the Neville points, but in fact are not similar to the earlier type technologically. In terms of technology Stark points are intermediate between the other two, providing a kind of bridge between the Neville and Merrimack types. Merrimack complex perforators have rather unspecialized bases, but in other respects the artifacts of this complex are not much changed from what went before. Overall the picture conveyed is that

FIGURE 4.5. Middle Archaic points from New England. Upper left point is 6 cm in length. Top row, Neville points; middle row, Stark points; bottom row, Merrimack points. Shown at one-half actual size. (Courtesy of Peabody Museum of Salem.)

of an evolving culture that adopted and abandoned point and other types, presumably as they adopted and abandoned the more complex tools of which they were parts. Dincauze (1976:122) even holds open the possibility that there was no distinct and separate Stark complex, only Stark elements in an evolving continuum. Whatever the specific case, the sequence ended at the Neville site around 6000 B.P. for reasons we cannot yet understand.

Middle Archaic levels at the Neville site contain ample evidence of hide-working, knapping, woodworking, and the harvesting of migratory fish. At that time the site was clearly a base camp in which a variety of activities were going on, not simply a fishing station. Smaller lakes and streams in the lower Merrimack drainage have produced sites containing Neville and Stark points in association with somewhat different assemblages. These assemblages contain semilunar ground stone knives, plummets (probably net sinkers), and gouges (Figure 4.6). The last are probably evidence that dugout canoes were being made and used at these sites. Neither boats nor nets would have been necessary to take fish at the Neville site's Amoskeag Falls, but both would have been useful on small lakes. The semilunar knives (or ulus) are further evidence that other kinds of activities were going on at these sites, although the specifics remain unclear.

It is interesting that, unlike the very widespread Neville and Stark point types, the Merrimack point appears to be restricted to the lower Merrimack drainage (Dincauze and Mulholland 1977:442). This could signify an intensification of regionalism to the point of introversion just prior to the gap that appears around 6000 B.P. Dincauze (1976:137) has suggested that there may be some climatic fluctuation that could explain it, but such an event could be so sudden and short term that it would not show up in palynological studies. Whatever the cause, a repeat of the systemic collapse of 10,000 B.P. could well have occurred, followed by a cultural readjustment that took the Middle Archaic people of the Merrimack to other sites and onto new schedules for the next 1000 years.

In at least some other parts of aboriginal New England the latter centuries of the Middle Archaic saw more intensive human activity. Funk (1976:168) has dated a Middle Archaic feature at 6560 ± 100 B.P. (Y-1655) at the Sylvan Lake rock shelter site in the lower Hudson drainage. There appears to be continuity of occupation after that, the next date coming at 5670 ± 80 (Dic-208) for some Late Archaic remains. As we shall see, dates of similar age mark the beginnings of intensive exploitation of oyster beds along the lower Hudson, a practice that has its roots in the Middle Archaic. At the same time, evidence at interior sites appears to be laying the foundations of the subsequent Late Archaic period. Distinctive points of the Otter Creek type have been dated to 6290 ± 100 B.P. (Dic-218) at the Shafer site in the Mohawk drainage (Wellman 1975). In these early appearances, the Otter Creek point seems to stand alone without the complex of other artifact types such as gouges, plummets, and ground slate items with which it associates in the Late Archaic (Funk 1977b:24). As we shall see in the next chapter, the complex is central to the Late Archaic Vergennes phase, which appears to have its greatest expression in the Champlain drainage. Ritchie (1971b:3) has long seen all of this as having originated to the northwest of New England in the lower Great Lakes region. In this he has been echoed by several others such that there is a consensus for the view even while the evidence for it may

FIGURE 4.6. Semilunar knives (*ulu*s) of ground slate from Essex Co., Mass. Specimen on bottom was holed for hafting. Shown at three-quarters actual size. (Courtesy of Peabody Museum of Salem.)

be slipping away. Ground slate seems to have a northern distribution and northern origins, but the Otter Creek point is a notched point that may derive from the midcontinental region to the west. Meanwhile, plummets, gouges, and ulus are already known from Middle Archaic sites in at least the Merrimack drainage (Dincauze 1976:136, 141). Once again we have a situation that demands we look at the time–space distributions of artifacts individually. Otter Creek points in Middle Archaic contexts herald the coming Late Archaic period, but they also signify the adoption of a new implement which in turn probably signifies some as yet unknown revision of the subsistence adaptation.

Coastal adaptations generally and the exploitation of shellfish in particular have been the focus of recent controversy in New England archaeology. I should say at the onset that I think that the abundance of prehistoric shellfish refuse and the controversy itself have combined to exaggerate the importance of this food resource to Indian populations. Much of the weight of an oyster is shell and the meat it yields is not all that nutritious, yet the bulky shell preserves better than the evidence of any other aboriginal food-getting activity. Nevertheless, the controversy is an interesting one because it illustrates the fundamental difference between Flannery's law-and-order and Serutan archaeologists (see Chapter 1), and it exemplifies the difficulty inherent in the use of negative data. Regardless of theoretical position, all archaeologists engaged in the debate are obliged to explain the nonexistence of evidence of shellfish utilization in certain places and periods.

Shellfish are tasty, especially with drawn butter, but are an inefficient source of food. Their caloric value is low and they are deficient in several compounds necessary in human diets. A pound (454 g) of shellfish meat yields only about 400 calories (White 1974:72), and four times that much would have to be consumed per day by the average adult if nothing else were eaten. As Brennan (1974:85) notes, this would mean that about 250 oysters per person per day would be required to sustain daily caloric requirements. Clearly oysters, and shellfish generally, could not have been more than a supplementary part of the diet for most people most of the time. My own analysis of the Damariscotta, Maine, oyster middens supports Brennan's view. The Damariscotta middens were once one of the world's largest accumulations, before much of the shell was hauled away for commercial use. Goldthwaite's (1935) most liberal estimate of the total number of oysters in the middens at Damariscotta in A.D. 1600 is 198,600,000. My conservative estimate of their age suggests 1600 years of accumulation. That gives us a maximum harvest of 124,125 oysters per year. Purchas's (1625) figures indicate an A.D. 1600 population of at least 800 people in this coastal drainage. That gives us only about 155 oysters per person per year. We could multiply that figure by 10 and still not have the staple food resource that some presume shellfish to have been. Nevertheless, if one takes a techno-environmental determinist approach to the problem, the very existence of shellfish means that they must have been exploited. Thus, we have Brennan's (1974:81) statement that the idea the shellfish might not have been used in northern New England while people in the Hudson drainage were gathering oysters "is a view absurd on its face." His is a very strongly held opinion, but others are willing to go even farther out on this limb: "Indeed, it seems inconceivable to me that early man would bypass shell fish as a food source—it's such an easy way to make a living! [Newman 1974:136]." The latter quote displays unfamiliarity with the nutritional value of shellfish, the archaeological record, and the ethnohistorical literature. We have seen (Chapter 2) that most of the historic Indians of northern New England did not practice horticulture for good and sufficient reasons even though it was available and marginally productive. The Indians of northern New England did not normally eat dogs, mink, otter, fisher, skunk, or each other except during periods of starvation, when everything was eaten (Speck 1940:97). Champlain (Grant 1907:55) notes that in the St. Croix drainage shellfish were used only when there was no hunting, although they harvested them from time to time in the summer as well. My point is that, taking a systems perspective, it is reasonable to conclude only that shellfish were used (without butter) by some Indians in some seasons during some periods of prehistory, but we cannot presume that the simple existence of shellfish caused them to be an important food resource. All of the sketches of historic cultures in Chapter 2 reveal complex seasonal schedules that would not be much illuminated by an archaeological obsession with the shell middens to which most of them contributed.

My perspective and the conclusions that result have been vividly condemned on several occasions (Newman 1974; Braun 1974; Brennan 1974, 1976). Perhaps the most colorful attack comes from Brennan (1976:112), who asserts that "no aspect of northeastern archaeology has been the subject of more sophistical, sociolistic interpretation than the harvesting of these easily acquired dietary resources." Powell (1977) has wondered about the uncertainties that must lurk under this verbal camouflage. Those who penetrate the meaning of *sophistical* far enough to discover that it refers to the Sophist philosophers of ancient Greece will probably also discover that their ill repute is due largely to the fact that most of what we know about them comes from the writings of their opponents. While arguments presented in this volume often reflect the skepticism (even iconoclasm) of the Sophists, they do not contain the deliberate and subtle fallacies that Plato and others claimed were part of the Sophist tradition.

In addition to the theoretical components of the controversy, there is the practical difficulty of rising sea level. Although the most rapid rate of rise occurred during the Paleo-Indian and Early Archaic periods, the sea has risen more or less steadily throughout prehistory in New England. The rates have been complicated at various points along the coastline by isostatic rebound of the land, as we saw in Chapter 3, and tectonic movement of the land as well.

Nevertheless, as a general rule, we can assume that many coastal sites, even relatively recent ones, have been inundated and destroyed by rising seas. This means that if one contends that shellfish gathering or some other activity did not go on at a particular time and place, or alternatively that it did but the evidence has been destroyed, one is necessarily dealing with negative evidence. This problem is not as serious along the Hudson estuary as it is elsewhere. The lower Hudson is a fjord, or at least it was until sea level approached its current high level. It is the world's lowest latitude fjord and one of only a few known to have existed on the Atlantic coast of the United States. Somes Sound on Mount Desert, Maine, is another candidate. Sites of most periods of prehistory can be found perched atop the steep walls of the Hudson fjord, above even today's high sea level. Thus, evidence of early shellfishing has been preserved here while possibly being destroyed in many other locations in aboriginal New England.

However, even the lower Hudson sites are not without their problems. Louis Brennan has excavated middens there for several years, during the course of which he has assembled an impressive series of radiocarbon dates (Brennan 1977a:412). The oldest of these is a date of 6950 ± 100 B.P. (L-1381) on shell from the base of the Dogan Point midden, a date that would indicate a Middle Archaic period beginning for shellfish exploitation there. There are few diagnostic artifacts in the middens, few artifacts of any kind for that matter, strong indication that these were refuse heaps upon which people did not live and work. Disturbingly, however, diagnostic artifacts when they do occur do not match well with radiocarbon dates derived from shell samples found in direct contact with them (Brennan 1974, 1977b). Brennan is not the sort of archaeologist who discards unexpected radiocarbon determinations as bad dates; rather, he reports and tries to explain them. Table 4.1 lists a series of his radiocarbon dates along with the ages he rather courageously admits to having expected for the samples. In every case he based his expectation on diagnostic artifacts found in association with the sample, that is, artifact types that have been consistently dated at other sites in the Hudson drainage. Brennan has many other radiocarbon dates, none associated with diagnostic artifacts that would allow him an

TABLE 4.1
Expected and Reported Dates on Samples from Shell Middens in the Lower Hudson Valley

Site	Reported date (B.P.)	Expected date (B.P.)
Piping Rock	3750 ± 150 (Gx-3371)	1500–2000 (Brennan 1974:89)
Dogan Point	5075 ± 160 (Gx-1919)	3000 (Brennan 1974:87)
Dogan Point	5095 ± 130 (Gx-2324)	3000 (Brennan 1974:87)
Piping Rock	5135 ± 155 (Gx-3238)	3500 (Brennan 1974:87) or 2500 (Brennan (1977a:427)

independent test for accuracy. However, in the four cases where he was able to carry out a clear test, he found the shell dates to be on the order of 2000 years too old. There are two possible explanations, each with its own special implications for prehistory. First, there could be some consistent error factor involved in dates derived from carbonate in oyster shells from the Hudson. We now know that consistent error factors exist in radiocarbon dating that are linked to the carbon-bearing substances being dated and are quite independent of the general deviation of radiocarbon dates from true calendrical age (Stuckenrath 1977). However, to accept this possible explanation, we must reject the finding of Stuiver and Borns (1975) that marine shell dates are fully reliable. Either that or we must assume that sample pretreatment procedures on these dates were not as thorough as those designed and used by Stuiver, or that some other similar unknown factor caused these dates to diverge from what was predicted. The second possibility is that there was some complicating factor in the deposition and preservation of the shell and associated diagnostic artifacts. Brennan (1977b) favors this kind of explanation, specifically that weathering, settling, and decomposition of the shell matrix caused the diagnostics to migrate downward into lower layers of the shell middens. This hypothesis is strained though plausible. It seems strange that all of the unexpected dates should differ from what was predicted by such a consistent margin. I think that this issue remains open and that we must accept the possibility that all dates on oyster shell from the Hudson might be consistently too old. If this is the case, then the 6950 B.P. date for the base of the Dogan Point midden could be perhaps 2000 years too old, putting the beginning of shellfish utilization there into the Late Archaic instead of the Middle Archaic period and most of the early intensive use well into the Late Archaic. Like Brennan, I am inclined to take the reported dates at face value for the moment. Whatever explanation for the discrepancy eventually prevails, there appears to be clear evidence that shellfish collecting was a subsistence activity of the Middle Archaic, at least in its later years.

Once again, however, theoretical perspective intrudes into interpretation. Brennan favors the mechanism of migration of diagnostic artifacts into older strata because he favors an age of at least 7000 years for shellfish utilization. If he accepted the possibility of consistent error in radiocarbon dating of oyster shell carbonate, then he would have to accept the possibility of a true age of only 5000 years for the base of the Dogan Point midden. Indeed, he feels that the community responsible for the midden was driven up the bank by rising sea level and that there were once even older middens where the river now flows. He concludes that there were probably oysters in the Hudson 12,000 B.P. Because his position is at the law-and-order end of Flannery's spectrum, he concludes that, ipso facto, Indians must have been harvesting oysters 12,000 years ago. Students of elementary logic will recognize the fallacy of *petitio principii* here, for that which is to be proved is clearly taken for granted by Brennan.

The fully credible estimate of Edwards and Merrill (1977:31) is that "some [shellfish] species such as the oyster became relatively abundant as far north as Georges Bank by 10,000 B.P." Even then, once again taking a systems perspective, there might have been no compelling reason for people to adopt them as a food resource. Brennan's data suggest that relatively large oysters, creatures up to 40 years old when harvested, were discarded in middens 5200–6000 years ago, with a possible hiatus around 5500 B.P. He suggests that "fluctuations in size may have been due to aboriginal exploitative practices or to climate and geology. Most probably they were due to all three factors [Brennan 1977b:127]." His view that shellfishing must predate this "giant oyster" period prevents him from advancing an alternative explanation. Unusually large oyster valves were found at the base of the Damariscotta, Maine midden, too, in bottom layers only 2000 years old. My interpretation was and still is that these were mature oysters taken from previously unused beds. Such giant oysters can be harvested only once, after which Indians typically settled into a steady harvesting of oysters after they reached suitable size, or an age of about 7 years (Snow 1972:216). Although Brennan (1977b: 126) does say that the large valves might have resulted from the opening up of virgin beds by shoreline shift, or that the Indians could have promoted their growth by not eating oysters for a generation or two, he stops short of saying that this could be evidence of the inception of intensive shellfishing as such. Yet his date of 6950 for the base of the Dogan Point midden stands alone. The next oldest date is 6150 ± 120 (Rl-177) from the Bannerman site. Two dates, 5850 ± 200 (Y-1315) and 5650 ± 200 (L-103E), define the lowest horizon within which Brennan identifies very large oysters. Taken together, I think that we have clear evidence that the Middle Archaic was the period in which Indians began exploitation of oysters along the Hudson and that intensive exploitation began in the Late Archaic, at which time the Indians stepped up their harvesting of previously underused beds.

Middle Archaic Cultural System

Figure 4.4 shows the distribution of Early and Middle Archaic sites and isolated finds in southern New England. To these can be added a single Neville point from the Harrisena that I originally took to be a much later Snook Kill point (Snow 1977a:436), a tiny Neville component at the Hirundo site in Maine (Sanger et al. 1977:464–465), and another at Weir's Beach, New Hampshire (Bolian 1977). Dincauze sees the Neville site as a base camp and a fishing station, a more broadly defined site type that we find at fishing stations in later times. Funk (1977b:25) also sees sites as being oriented to migratory fish and other aquatic resources during the Middle Archaic, although his interpretation is in part the result of his view that the forests of the region were not very productive at the time. If, as Funk thinks, forest resources were thin, particularly in the winter, then the beginnings of shellfishing observed along the lower Hudson might have been the sort of starvation-induced wintertime activity observed by Champlain in the seventeenth century. There is, of course, no reason why the Indians of this period would have avoided oysters and other shellfish at other times of the year, although these resources could never have amounted to more than a dietary supplement. Thus, shellfish-gathering sites were special-purpose sites that were probably used by single-family bands. The small freshwater sites noted in the lower Merrimack drainage by Dincauze were probably also special-purpose sites. Fishing equipment and heavy woodworking tools at these sites probably indicate the construction and use of dugout canoes, a practice that continued into the next period.

While Ritchie maintains that the forests were too unproductive to allow more than occasional upstream forays into the interior, Funk is inclined to see both Early and Middle Archaic settlement as year-round (Funk 1977b:25). The difference of opinion seems to force a choice between no people at all living in a given drainage as opposed to a perpetual, sparse population living throughout it, an unrealistic choice that neither endorses. The shreds of evidence currently in hand would suggest base camps at sites where migratory fish could be taken in large numbers, summer camps on freshwater sites, and probably winter hunting camps at interior locations. Shellfish could have been harvested at almost any time of the year, perhaps initially on occasions when other supplies were short. The scarcity of pitted stone anvils suggests that nuts were not yet a major dietary component. All of this indicates a continued broadening of the diffuse adaptation of the previous period and a continuation of the trend from a restricted wandering pattern toward central-based wandering. We have no bone remains from which to judge hunting, but we can presume that these people hunted deer, possibly moose and caribou, and the other modern species that by this time predominated in New England.

Bands and sets of bands continued to settle into territories. The restricted distribution of Merrimack points might point to a culturally significant set of bands for the Merrimack drainage. Abstract connubia may well have disappeared by now, replaced by clearly bounded sets of bands, incipient tribes as defined in Chapter 1. Base camps were probably inhabited by composite bands, whereas special-purpose camps were used by single-family bands. Unfortunately, we have no data at all on houses and cannot do more than guess at their sizes and forms. They must not have been large substantial structures, and something like the single-family wigwam of historic times would be the most we should expect to have existed.

If our assessment of the probable Early Archaic settlement system is correct, then the Middle Archaic system probably involved more elaborate and more carefully planned seasonal scheduling than previously. The ranges of activities carried out on special-purpose sites continued to narrow while the numbers and kinds of such sites utilized within a round continued to increase.

The technological subsystem includes celts and gouges, both evidence of heavy woodworking, which in turn implies the use of dugout canoes. Full-grooved axes are new and further evidence for the importance of heavy woodworking. Notched net sinkers and plummets appear for the first time, carrying with them implications for an elaboration of fishing techniques. Funk (1978:25) sees notched pebble net sinkers as an important new element in the Middle Archaic tool inventory. Brennan, however, considers the number he has found (10) to be small, and on the basis of one find of a cluster of three concludes that they were probably bolas stones (Brennan 1974:91). The bola was a common weapon on the Pampas of Argentina, but it was unknown to any historic culture of the Eastern Woodlands. There is little reason to interpret notched pebbles as bolas stones under these circumstances and good reason to accept Funk's interpretation.

Semilunar knives or ulus are also introduced, while knives and scrapers continue from the previous period. The various diagnostic point types of the period suggest unknown tools and weapons that may have had specialized uses. Perhaps the most interesting new addition is the winged spear-thrower weight (Figure 4.7). The function of this distinctive artifact has not always been clearly understood. For a long time examples of it were referred to as "banner stones," a name that implies some sort of vague and exotic ceremonial use. "Ceremonial objects" is what archaeologists call things whose real functions are not understood. More recent research has shown that banner stones were in fact spear-thrower weights (Palter 1976). Most ethnographically known spear-throwers are rigid, or at least flex only a little, a trait that we infer characterized Paleo-Indian spear-throwers as well. Attaching a weight to a rigid spear-thrower does nothing to improve its performance, since the inertia of the weight must be overcome and that effort offsets any momentum advantage in the latter part of the throwing action. It would hardly seem likely that an Archaic hunter would attach a functionally useless stone to his spear-thrower merely for the magical properties of its heavy wings. A clue to the real function came from Late Archaic winged weights that have long holes drilled through their center sections, through which the shaft of the spear-thrower was apparently inserted. The holes are often not much more than 1 cm in diameter, and a rigid shaft of that diameter will snap on the first throw. The answer would appear to be that these hunters were not using rigid spear-thrower shafts. Indeed, there is some evidence from Florida that ironwood was used in the production of spear-throwers. Ironwood preserves very poorly once in the ground, but while still fresh is hard, resilient, and flexible. When used with a weight, winged or otherwise, the flexible spear-thrower has a snap that makes it a much more effective propelling device than the rigid spear-thrower. In later periods the hunters of the Eastern Woodlands made weights in other shapes as well, including the artifacts archaeologists call boatstones and birdstones. Like the radiator caps of twentieth-century automobiles, spear-thrower weights had a practical function but soon took on decorative functions and the magical properties of flight. The hunters of the Middle Archaic not only anticipated flexible fiberglass fishing rods, golf clubs, and even vaulting poles, they also anticipated the artisans of Detroit.

FIGURE 4.7. Ground stone spear-thrower (atlatl) weights. Drilled and polished specimens from the Middle and Late Archaic periods. Shown at three-quarters actual size. (Courtesy of Peabody Museum of Salem.)

The rather uninspiring range of raw materials used by most people during the Middle Archaic suggests that there was little trade to bring exotic cherts and other materials from distant sources. This in turn is further evidence of settling in and the development of social boundaries. Dincauze (1976:96) sees a reversal of this pattern of isolation after the end of the Middle Archaic period, but not until then.

As before, we have no evidence at all regarding mortuary sites and burial programs. Yet far to the north on the Labrador–Quebec coast Indians were already building stone mounds over the graves of their dead, perhaps the earliest stirrings of a mortuary tradition that would eventually spread over the Eastern Woodlands. The Middle Archaic hunter–gatherers of the subarctic coast dug flat-bottomed burial pits a meter deep and 8 m in diameter, filled the pits over extended burials, and constructed a mound of boulders over the pit fill to a height of .5 m or more. The best-known example thus far contains only a single extended face-down burial with its head oriented to the east (McGhee and Tuck 1975:85–94; Tuck and McGhee 1976). This burial was accompanied by grave goods that included a walrus tusk, two large stemmed quartzite knives, an oval knife of the same material, graphite pebbles, a caribou antler pestle, a bone or antler pendant, a bird-bone whistle, a harpoon line holder made of antler, a caribou antler head for a toggling harpoon, and stemmed and socketed bone points, some of which were part of a cache also including chipped stone points. Red ocher (hematite) was smeared on much of this. The site is L'Anse Amour, and the Middle Archaic age of the first radiocarbon date obtained from it so astonished the investigators that a second run was made at a different laboratory. The first date of 7530 ± 140 B.P. (I-8099) was supported by an only slightly younger determination by the Smithsonian Institution laboratory. The burial mounds are the oldest known anywhere in the world, and their discovery destroys the arguments of those who insist that American Indians must have gotten the idea from outside. The toggling harpoon head is also the oldest known and shows that American Indians were making and using this sophisticated weapon long before the Eskimo (who are usually credited with having invented it) reached the New World. Finally, the burial program at L'Anse Amour laid the foundations of a mortuary complex that flourished along this same stretch of coast and into northern New England during the Late Archaic. Whether we will eventually find similar Middle Archaic burials of people pressed face down into the earth under a boulder mound that was both a memorial and a prison is hard to say. For the moment it appears unlikely that we will.

LATE ARCHAIC
FLORESCENCE

We now pass into what is at once one of our most fascinating and most confusing periods. Late Archaic sites interested archaeologists long before they were recognized as such, and there is a body of literature stretching back a century that in one way or another deals with Late Archaic data. A major difficulty is that ideas about archaeology and prehistory have changed and matured through the course of this century, and old reports must be evaluated in terms of the hidden assumptions and mind sets of the decades in which they were written. In addition, widely accepted generalizations once established tend to be perpetuated long after the assumptions underlying them have been superseded. Thus, the beginning student is confronted by a bewildering array of anachronisms, some of which are still legitimatized through continued use. A summary of the history of research of the Late Archaic will help to unravel part of this Gordian knot, but as we shall see the sharp edge of a relatively new paradigm is necessary to cut away its last strands.

As used here, the Late Archaic period lasted from about 6000 to 3700 B.P. Beginning with this period it is convenient to think in terms of the more familiar Christian calendar, conversion to which puts the period at about 4000–1700 B.C. The period was nearly as long as the Paleo-Indian period, and two centuries longer than either the Early or the Middle Archaic periods. During its course in the Northeast, independent developments in the Old World passed through what is often called the Copper Age and nearly through the Bronze Age. The plow was developed in the Near East, pyramids were built in Egypt, horses were domesticated in Asia, and construction began at Stonehenge, England. Also during this period early Eskimo bands began pressing into what is now Alaska from Siberia, the last major population to enter the New World prior to the historic European invasion.

CHAPTER 5

We have already seen that significant cultural diversification was beginning within the region by the end of the Middle Archaic. This diversification continued into the Late Archaic. The diversity and its relationship to the dimensions of time and space are only now beginning to be clearly perceived, and many of the published generalizations of the past are based on serious mistaken perceptions. The story of those mistaken perceptions will be much clearer if preceded by a summary statement of how the Late Archaic is perceived today. James Tuck (1978a) has summarized the Late Archaic of the region in terms of three major traditions into which all of the confusing fragments of archaeological data can be classed. The first of these he calls the "Lake Forest Archaic." Evidence of this Late Archaic tradition can be found primarily in the maple–beech and the maple–beech–hemlock forests of the Champlain drainage and the drainage basin of the Great Lakes and St. Lawrence River generally. It includes such familiar archaeological complexes as the Laurentian and Old Copper. The second major tradition is the "Maritime Archaic," which occurs in the drainages of Maine and New Brunswick, as well as in the other Maritime provinces, Newfoundland, and around the shores of the Gulf of St. Lawrence. The striking red ocher burials of this tradition constitute its most familiar characteristic, although we now know much more about its other equally interesting subsystems. Finally, Tuck defines a third "Narrow Point" tradition for the deciduous forests of southern New England, the piedmont and coastal plain as far south as North Carolina, and the interior states of Ohio, Indiana, and Illinois. The quotation marks are the consequence of uncertainty about a proper name for this tradition. Tuck and others have provisionally named the tradition for a shared characteristic of the projectile point types that are considered diagnostic of it. As we shall see, many names have been proposed for the tradition, but none has been fully satisfactory, largely because they have typically been borrowed from a set of existing physiographic terms, none of which correspond to the large region in which the tradition flourished (Figure 5.1). Tuck is on the right track when he suggests names for the first two traditions that reflect their adaptations, as much as geographic or physiographic correlates, and I propose that the same logic be extended to the third tradition. If this is done, a fairly obvious choice is "Mast Forest Archaic." The term has nothing at all to do with ships, but refers collectively to the nuts produced by the oak, chestnut, hickory, beech, and other species that dominated these forests. It may eventually be necessary to add the adjective "Northern" to the term to distinguish this Late Archaic tradition from those that occupied mast forests farther south, but for present purposes the term is long enough.

James Wright (1972a) has defined a fourth major tradition for the period that has some bearing on New England. This is the Shield Archaic, which takes its name from the Canadian Shield region that it largely occupied. Its distribution lies north of the Lake Forest region, but extends southeast to the Gaspe Peninsula of Quebec. David Sanger (1971a) has found traces of it in

FIGURE 5.1. Late and Terminal Archaic sites.

the northern portion of the St. Johns drainage, but it makes no other appearance in our region.

The real problem with the three traditions lies not with their names but with the tradition concept itself and its application. "Tradition" has always been used in a variety of ways (Willey and Phillips 1958:34–37), but it has in recent years been often used in two senses: first to refer to whole cultural traditions and second to refer to narrow artifactual traditions. Because archaeology deals largely with artifacts and because archaeologists have not often explicitly dealt with whole cultural systems as I am attempting to do here, traditions have in fact tended to be technologically defined even when the intent was broader. The most extreme (and most unfortunate) expression of this tendency has been the practice of defining traditions in terms of single artifact classes. The provisional designation of the Mast Forest Archaic as "Narrow Point" is revealing in this regard. In fact, this tradition has more often than not been identified by the presence of one or more of several narrow stemmed projectile points rather than any broader assessment of the tradition's economic adaptation or other aspects of its cultural system. Even when more than one artifact class is used to define a tradition such as this one, the resulting complex tends to take on separate reality. The tradition is deemed to be present at a site if all the parts of its complex (defined earlier on the basis of the assemblage at some other site) are present, but it is not fully present if they are not. This practice gives special importance to artifact associations that may well have been more casual than our definitions will allow. Moreover, the practice impedes our understanding of both adaptation and the often separate distributions and life spans of types within different artifact classes. All of these difficulties have contributed to the general confusion that surrounds the Late Archaic in the published literature, and all of them must be borne in mind through the discussion that follows. As one means of getting around some of the problems implicit in the tradition concept and at the same time promoting a systems perspective, I treat the Maritime, Lake Forest, and Mast Forest themes as adaptations rather than traditions.

MARITIME ARCHAIC ADAPTATION

The artifact types that characterize this Late Archaic adaptation are similar to those of the Lake Forest Archaic, but its distinctive maritime flavor is unmistakable. Evidence of it has been found in the drainages of Maine and New Brunswick, from the Androscoggin eastward, through the Maritime provinces, and along the coasts of Quebec, Labrador, and Newfoundland that border the Gulf of St. Lawrence. It was originally known mainly from a long series of excavated cemetery components that were for many years attributed rather curiously to the "Red Paint People," much as midwestern burial mounds were attributed to the "Mound Builders." These terms, which now seem rather innocent, long carried the connotations of mysterious lost races, from which myths sprouted that were at best misleading and at worst justification for anti-Indian racism. By the 1940s it was clear that the Red Paint sites were Archaic period cemeteries and, as such, special-purpose sites used within a broader adaptive framework. Byers (1959:255) defined a very broad "Boreal Archaic" to include both the Lake Forest Archaic and the Maritime Archaic as used here. He went on to suggest a "Maritime Boreal Archaic" for Maine northeastward, but the suggestion was lost amid general objections to the concept of a Boreal Archaic. "Boreal" had already been adopted by ecologists to describe northern subarctic forest, an environment that is approximated only in high mountainous parts of our region. James Tuck (1971a:350) revived the term in part by defining the Maritime Archaic after his discovery and analysis of an important cemetery component at Port au Choix, Newfoundland.

The materials from the Port au Choix site were found to be similar to those known for decades from Maine. The earliest radiocarbon date from Port au Choix converts to 2340 B.C., younger than some dates from Maine but well within the Late Archaic period. Although it lies far outside the region defined for this volume, the site is important because it produced the only preserved substantial skeletal material known for any Maritime Archaic site. Tuck uncovered 53 burials in 1968 and James Anderson eventually analyzed 99 individuals. Most burials were covered by one or more layers of limestone rocks in sandy soil containing crushed shell. This acid-neutralizing matrix explains the remarkable preservation of the skeletons and the usually perishable artifacts that accompanied them. There was no special burial orientation and no evidence that the Indians discriminated in their burial practices on grounds of age or sex. The 99 individuals were almost evenly divided between male and female, and the relatively large number of newborn and infant burials suggests that no one was excluded from burial on the basis of age. The individuals were about evenly divided between adults and sub-adults. Red ocher accompanied every burial, and most were accompanied by artifacts of stone, tusk, antler, and bone. Only the red ocher and stone artifacts are typically found in Maine cemeteries. There seems to have been no distinction made by age or sex when mortuary offerings were made. Children of either sex were as apt to be accompanied by various tools and weapons as adults of either sex.

Grave offerings included long slender slate bayonets like those sometimes found in Maine (Figure 5.2). However, Tuck also found similar forms made of bone. Shorter ground slate points were also mimicked in bone. Harpoon heads of both toggling and barbed varieties were made of bone or antler. Implements that appear to have been foreshafts were made from whalebone. There were bone daggers and one made of walrus tusk that fitted a fragmentary antler sheath. Heavy woodworking axes, adzes, and gouges like those frequently found in Maine were also found at Port au Choix. Ground beaver incisors were mounted in antler handles and were apparently used rather like the historic "crooked knives" of the northern woodlands. Other tools included caribou and other mammal bone awls, bone splinter needles,

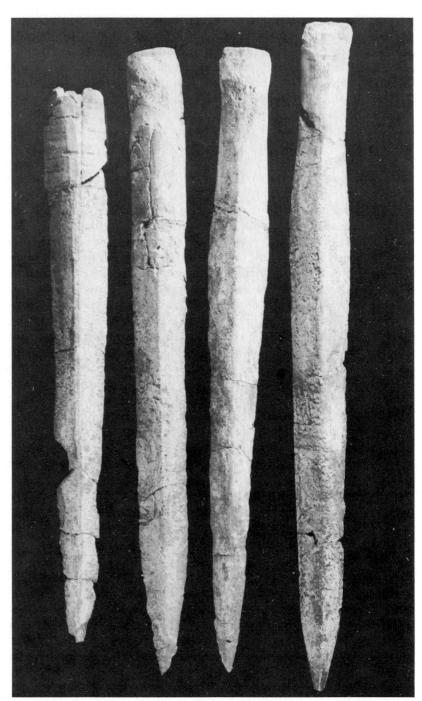

FIGURE 5.2. Bone daggers 22–24 cm long from Burials I and II, Grave 5, Nevin site, Maine (Byers 1979). Shown at three-quarters actual size. (Collection of R. S. Peabody Foundation.)

combs, hairpins, tubes, whistles and pendants of bone or antler, and beads and pendants of shell, teeth, claws, and bird beaks. Bird effigies were sometimes carved onto tools and there are two carved stone killer whale effigies. Finally, there were crystals of calcite, quartz, and garnet along with nodules of white quartz.

Tuck (1971a:350) infers that caribou were an important component in the diets of the people who buried their dead at Port au Choix and for the Maritime Archaic generally. Caribou still live in large numbers on Newfoundland and were found in early historic times in interior Maine and the Maritime Provinces as well. Sea mammals must also have been important, especially the harbor seal, which can still be found in substantial numbers along the Maine coast and northward. Bone and slate bayonets (Figure 5.3) were probably used to take caribou while seals were typically harpooned. Tuck infers that migratory fish such as salmon were too important a resource to have been ignored and that birdbone implements and bird effigies are ample evidence of the importance of sea birds. Sea ducks, murres, and the now extinct great auk were all hunted.

Of all the Late Archaic sites excavated within Maine and New Brunswick, few contain artifact inventories comparable to that of Port au Choix. Byers (1959:250) reported three coastal Maine sites containing bone tools and swordfish swords (Figure 5.4). The latter occurred only in Late Archaic contexts and were often worked into bayonets and engraved with elaborate geometric incised decorations. Bourque's (1975) more recent work at the Turner Farm site confirms Byers's observation. All three of the sites mentioned by Byers, Waterside, Tafts Point, and Nevin, as well as the Turner Farm site, have lenses of shell that neutralized natural soil acidity and allowed preservation of bone and other perishable material. Nevin and particularly Turner Farm are also more than just shell middens, for both appear to have served as coastal encampments where a variety of activities were carried out. Occupation 2 at the Turner Farm site began around 2600 B.C. and lasted until the end of the Late Archaic (Bourque 1976). The artifact inventory includes bone daggers, both foreshafts and bayonets of swordfish sword, barbed and toggling harpoon heads of bone and swordfish sword, bone fishhooks and needles, and carvings in bone. In addition, there were chipped stone points of stemmed and expanded stemmed types, the latter easily described as having broad and shallow side notches. There were also plummets, adzes, gouges, and whetstones like those found in interior cemetery sites.

Some sites have also produced semilunar knives of slate or other fine-grained stone. The semilunar knife survives in Eskimo technology, and for that reason it is often called the *ulu*, an Eskimo word for "woman's knife" (Figure 5.5). Many sources report the use of this tool. For the most part, Eskimos used the ulu for gutting and cutting up fish and for dressing sea mammal skins. It was occasionally used for other more general purposes as well, but there seems to be a clear link between the ulu and maritime

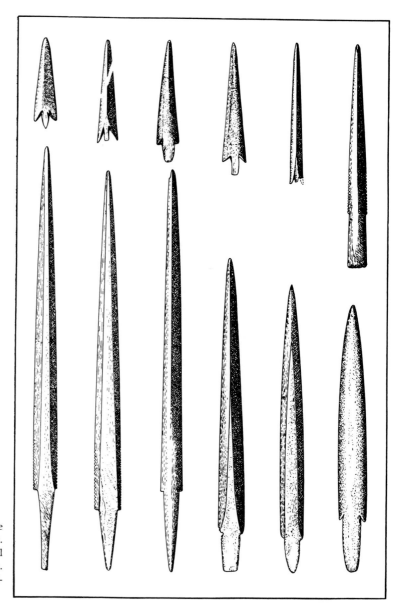

FIGURE 5.3. Late Archaic ground slate points from the Maine Maritime Archaic. Sizes range up to 35-cm bayonets, and all have bone or swordfish bill analogues. Shown at one-third actual size. (After Willoughby 1935:57.)

resources. Their distribution reinforces this apparent functional link, because ulus seem to be most frequent in coastal drainages and in the lower Great Lakes region (Turnbaugh 1977). The coastal distributions of most seal species end north of aboriginal New England, but that of the Harbor Seal (*Phoca vitulina*) includes the Atlantic coastline as far south as Chesapeake Bay and Lake Ontario as far as Niagara Falls. The word for Harbor Seal has been reconstructed for proto-Algonquian (Siebert 1967:19), indicating that it has

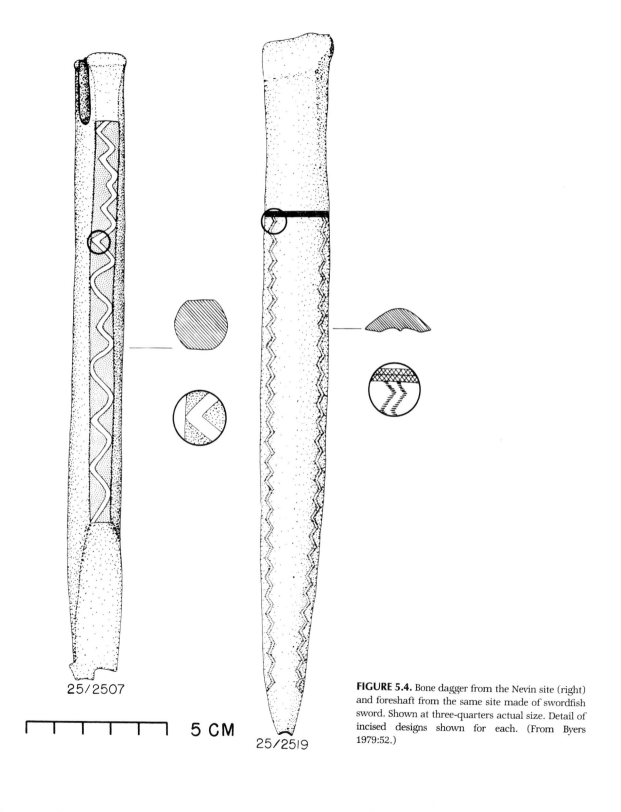

25/2507

5 CM

25/2519

FIGURE 5.4. Bone dagger from the Nevin site (right) and foreshaft from the same site made of swordfish sword. Shown at three-quarters actual size. Detail of incised designs shown for each. (From Byers 1979:52.)

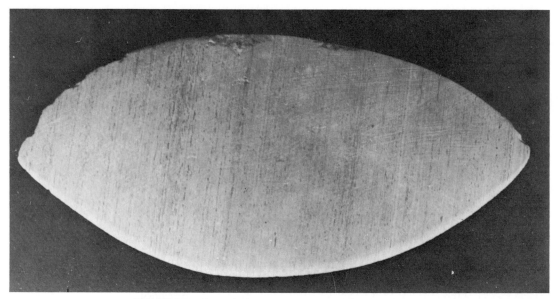

FIGURE 5.5. Elliptical *ulu* from Burial 3, Wapanucket No. 6, 19 cm long. Shown at three-quarters actual size. (Bronson Museum collection.)

been important in the vocabularies of northeastern Algonquian languages for at least 3200 years and probably much more (Snow 1976a:345). The migratory fish of the North Atlantic favor streams that enter the sea along the same stretch of coastline. We have already reviewed archaeological evidence of their importance to Indians in the Archaic periods. Much more work has to be done before this hypothesis linking ulus to maritime resources is adequately supported, but the preliminary indications are encouraging.

Bourque's (1975, 1976) work at Turner Farm has done much to clarify the nature of Late Archaic exploitation of coastal resources (Figure 5.6). Turner Farm is only one of several coastal Maine sites that has survived rising sea level over the past several thousand years by virtue of protected placement atop rocky promontories. Because of the rocky character of the Maine coast, sea level has come up in many areas without much lateral inundation, and sites like Turner Farm were never far from shore during or after the Late Archaic. Salwen's (1965) hypothesis explaining the lack of Late Archaic shell middens in southern New England and Long Island as the consequence of inundation and erosion therefore does not apply well in Maine. At Turner Farm and some other coastal sites such as Goddard, Nevin, Taft's Point, Basin, Waterside, and Stanley, shellfish are present in Late Archaic levels but appear to be relatively less important than later on (Bourque 1975:41). Instead we often find the remains of swordfish and other large marine game, in the case of the Stanley site associated with a point or knife made of native copper (Figure 5.7). The point is that Late Archaic coastal adaptation was

FIGURE 5.6. Gaming or magical bones found together at the Turner Farm site, Maine. Shown at three-quarters actual size. (Photo by G. Hoagland. Courtesy of Maine State Museum.)

patterned differently from what would come later. For reasons of availability, preference, or both, shellfish were less important than other resources at this time. This observation is a reminder that debates on the presence or absence of shellfishing (or any other resource activity), like the one discussed in the last chapter, need to be approached with caution.

Of all the remains in the coastal sites of the Maritime Archaic, those of swordfish (*Xiphias gladius*) are perhaps the most provocative. Porpoise, seals, whales, and black fish are sometimes found beached, but the swordfish is a pelagic fish that virtually never floats to shore. Moreover, it is found off the coast of Maine only during the summer, and the remains we have found must come from fish that were speared or harpooned while they sunned themselves at the surface in quiet water. The sharp dorsal fin of the swordfish is still frequently seen off the coast of Maine, but the local folklore is liberally salted with stories of punctured dories and other near-fatal encounters with the creature. If Late Archaic Indians were taking this fish, as they must have been, they must also have been rather skilled sea hunters.

Added to faunal remains that indicate sea hunting are the porpoise and killer whale effigies (Figure 5.8) that sometimes turn up in cemeteries in both Maine and Newfoundland (Bourque 1971:228; Tuck 1971a:348). Given the formidable nature of these animals (especially the swordfish), and the sizes and frequencies of the heavy woodworking tools found in both habitation and cemetery sites, I conclude that sea hunting was carried on by relatively large bands of men in relatively large dugout canoes. We have been accus-

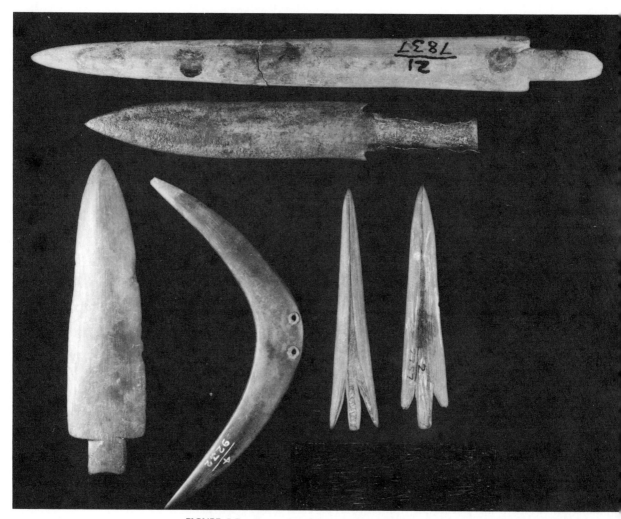

FIGURE 5.7. Top, a slate bayonet above a native copper spear point from Caldwell's I., Friendship, Maine. Bottom, left to right, slate spear point, slate pendant, and two slate points from Warren, Maine. Shown at three-quarters actual size. (Photo by Bruce Bourque. Collection of the Museum of the American Indian, Heye Foundation.)

tomed to thinking of Archaic dugouts in terms of the small eastern dugouts of the early historic period, rather than the historic Northwest Coast dugouts that they probably resembled more closely. Various trees, particularly the white pine, grew large enough in Maine to have provided logs of more than adequate size. Moreover, the locations of Archaic sites in large open lakes and along relatively large and navigable streams also support the hypothesis that travel was usually by large dugout canoe. This site preference has already been noted by Tuck (1971a:352), although he has used it to argue for

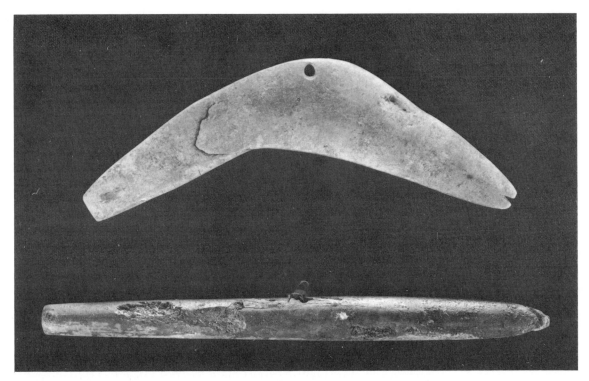

FIGURE 5.8. Top, zoomorphic slate pendant, 164 mm long. Bottom, holed slate bar pendant, 190 mm long. Both from Turner Farm site, Maine. Shown at three-quarters actual size. (Photo by G. Hoagland. Courtesy Maine State Museum.)

a strong marine orientation rather than as a consequence of the use of large dugouts.

Like Tuck, I see the interior component of the Maine Archaic subsistence system as one dominated by caribou hunting. The woodland caribou (*Rangifer tarandus caribou*) lived in Maine at the time and was well adapted to the mature coniferous forest of the area. The 7000–4300 B.P. forest contained pine, hemlock, spruce, and a few hardwoods and upon reaching maturity would have supported the heavy lichen growth that is essential for the caribou diet. Today, the mean annual total snowfall for almost all of northern New England is almost 2 m (Lull 1968:21), too deep for the wapiti. Thus, the area may never have supported many wapiti, and the moose population of 3000 B.C. was probably relatively low as well. The environment was not at all favorable for white-tailed deer. Thus, it is likely that the caribou was the most important big game animal during the Late Archaic. Woodland caribou do not move in herds of thousands like the barren ground caribou, but they are more gregarious than the solitary moose, and it seems likely that they would have been hunted by relatively large bands of Indians.

Such a hunting band could easily kill a dozen animals with lances in the water, in deep snow, or by forcing them to run close to a stout fence designed to protect the hunters but not the caribou. The last technique is recorded for the historic Beothuk, who relied heavily on woodland caribou (Oswalt 1966:76–77).

Only a few interior Late Archaic habitation sites have been investigated. The best known is the Hirundo site, which has been the focus of an interdisciplinary investigation by scholars from the University of Maine (Sanger *et al.* 1977). Like other interior sites, this one lacks shell and therefore preserved organic remains. Comparison with coastal sites must therefore be confined to lithic artifacts, but even then there are some surprises. Ground slate points are present in the Hirundo assemblage, but absent at Turner Farm. Gouges occur in both assemblages, but are stylistically dissimilar. While chipped stone points are stemmed or eared-stemmed at Turner Farm, they are more decidedly side-notched at Hirundo (Sanger *et al.* 1977:468). There appears to be no simple explanation for the differences. The sites appear to be contemporaneous, or nearly so, and they are separated by fewer than 100 km (by river) within the Penobscot drainage area. Hirundo is located on Pushaw Stream, a tributary of the Penobscot, and was probably an anadromous fishing station. It may be that the activities carried out at this site were sufficiently different from those that went on at Turner Farm to produce the contrast in assemblages.

My own excavations in a small habitation site adjacent to the Hathaway cemetery site produced materials similar to those found at Hirundo. Here again we have an interior site on a tributary of the Penobscot, the Passadumkeag River. The site was probably an anadromous fishing station and is situated at a point where the Passadumkeag emerges from a large bog. It may be that the bog had much more open water during the Late Archaic, but we cannot be sure. We do know that the forest environment was dominated by hemlock, birch, and white pine at the beginning of the Late Archaic and that northern hardwoods became more important as the period neared its end (Davis *et al.* 1975). Bourque (1975:42) has pointed out that interior Late Archaic sites tend to divide between those on easily traveled major river channels and those on relatively shallow and rapid channels. He places both Hirundo and Hathaway in the latter category, but it should be noted that even these sites are on streams that are placid when compared to the fast and steep streams of upper tributaries. Bourque therefore could have defined at least one more stream category, one having no associated Late Archaic sites at all.

Overall, the forest type, site locations, and assemblage constituents are all consistent with the view that Late Archaic populations were adapted to both caribou hunting on the interior and sea hunting at coastal sites. Travel was probably by dugout canoe, and upper tributary areas were probably penetrated only by hunters moving on foot. Primary sites were located where they could be reached by dugout. Interior and maritime hunting probably alternated seasonally, with sea hunting being primarily a summer pursuit. Roughly the same social organization would have been necessary for both activities, so that they functionally reinforced as well as seasonally complemented each other. I hypothesize that caribou hunting and sea hunting in large dugouts are both consistent with relatively larger bands of hunters than were called for in later periods. Fall and spring anadromous fishing stations could also have supported relatively large population concentrations. Added to this system was the elaborate mortuary subsystem for which the Maritime Archaic is so well known. We have seen in a brief way with the Port au Choix case what one unusually well-preserved example looked like. To understand fully the less well-preserved but more numerous cases from Maine, as well as to understand the published interpretations of them, an excursion into the history of New England archaeology will be necessary.

The popular mythology that accumulated around the Late Archaic cemetery remains of northern New England has only recently been surpassed in bulk and absurdity by the currently popular Celtic craze. These pseudoscholarly fads have common themes and similar life spans, something that is already appreciated by social psychologists. Where people now see evidence of pre-Columbian Celtic visitors, a few years ago they saw irrefutable evidence of Vikings. To these we could add attempts to prove linguistic links between the Algonquian languages and Norse and even Portuguese. None of these has generated quite as much nonsense as the mound builder mythology of midcontinental America, but they stand out in the context of New England prehistory.

Rise and Fall of the Red Paint People

The Red Paint mythology was stimulated first by controversy among scholars. Once it became the subject of popular writing it took on some of the characteristics of the great spate of supposed Viking finds that occurred in the nineteenth century. The scholarly controversy is well documented, but the popular mythology that it spawned has come to me largely through old newspaper accounts and by word of mouth. Nevertheless, it is a good case study that shows both the growing pains of scientific archaeology and the structure of archaeological mythology. I hope that the summary that follows makes that distinction clear.

Interest in Maine's Late Archaic cemeteries surfaced in the 1880s. Augustus C. Hamlin, a Bangor physician who was active in the local historical society, contacted F. W. Putnam of Harvard's Peabody Museum at a meeting of the American Association for the Advancement of Science. Hamlin mentioned numbers of stone tools that he had found associated with deposits of red ocher near the shore of Alamoosook Lake. He had heard of the tools from Foster Soper, a friend of the landowner. Unfortunately, the landowner, Elijah Emerson, steadfastly refused to let anyone excavate there. Through Soper, Hamlin eventually received permission to dig on Emerson's land, but for a single day only. Not dismayed by the time limit, Soper and Hamlin hitched up oxen and plow and spent the day plowing up what later proved to be a prehistoric cemetery. Their efforts yielded 99 implements but precious little information. After a rain, a man named Marks was able to find 20–30 more implements on the same field (Moorehead 1922:34).

Putnam's interest in Hamlin's material was aroused, and he accordingly sent one of his assistants, Charles C. Willoughby, to investigate the sites in the vicinity of Alamoosook Lake in 1892. Willoughby's excavations at the Orland site equaled and probably surpassed even Putnam's expectations. His work was conducted with precision and care that exceeded that of many other archaeological undertakings of the day. In recognition of his performance in the field, Willoughby was made Assistant in the Department of Anthropology of the Chicago Exposition of 1892–1893. He went back to work on the sites around Alamoosook Lake in 1894. The sites he excavated were described in detail and published in 1898 in the first volume of the *Archaeological and Ethnological Papers of the Peabody Museum* (Willoughby 1898). In his report Willoughby suggested that the burials must be old because of the almost complete absence of skeletal material. He went on to compare their contents with Eskimo and Beothuk material culture, but cautiously withheld any conclusions. In later years, however, he became more inclined to believe that there was a connection between these sites and the Beothuk. Accepting Powell's judgment that the Beothuk did not speak an Algonquian language, he concluded that the "Red Paint" remains were left by someone other than the ancestors of modern Algonquian speakers.

In 1912, Oric Bates and H. E. Winlock wrote a two-volume thesis on Maine prehistory as part of their anthropological studies at Harvard. It contains what appears to be the first use of the term "Red Paint People" in print. The label contains the implications that the use of red ocher set these people apart in North American archaeology and that, being people, they were not necessarily American Indians.

Moorehead came on the scene in 1912 with the first of a long series of survey trips in Maine that were to continue over the following 8 years. He was more interested in surveying unexplored regions with quick excavations than following out specific archaeological problems to satisfactory conclusions. He amassed mountains of unanalyzed data, sometimes making casual observations, the significance of which only became clear after someone else followed up his work. His article entitled "The Red Paint People of Maine" appeared in 1913 and sparked immediate controversy. Moorehead's primary point in this article was that the burial complex first defined by Willoughby and named by Bates was different from modern Algonquian tribes and substantially older as well. He declined, however, to support J. P. Howley's hypothesis that the Beothuk were the modern descendants of the people responsible for "Red Paint" burials (Howley 1915; Moorehead 1913:39–41).

David Bushnell immediately attacked Moorehead's contention that the burials were different from historically known burials in content and age. He argued that the use of iron oxide was not confined to Maine and probably occurred in every state east of the Mississippi. He added that the ground containing the burials is always moist and that this should account for the lack of skeletal material, a feature that Moorehead thought indicated great age (Bushnell 1913). He concluded that the graves were no different in form or content from recent Iroquois or Algonquian burials, but in his haste to make his point, he missed several significant differences, including strong evidence that each of Moorehead's interments was followed by the burning of a large fire over the grave.

In the following year, Clarence Moore published a similar attack on Moorehead. He noted that, with the exception of the Ozark cave sites, Moorehead found the Maine "Red Paint" sites of greater interest than anything else recently found in the United States. He sarcastically added that Moorehead also excavated the Ozark sites and implies that this might be a significant factor influencing his judgment. Like Bushnell, he pointed out the use of iron oxide in other areas, particularly in Florida where he had some personal experience (Moore 1914).

Moorehead's reply to Bushnell was written before he had a chance to read Moore's comments, and the battle began to take on some of the confusion of a contest between blindfolded prizefighters. The argument of the reply revolved around Moorehead's indignation regarding Bushnell's presumptuous comments on an area he had never visited and archaeological materials he had never seen. This would not necessarily be a valid argument under other circumstances, but in this one Moorehead had a point. After enumerating the number of burials he had personally unearthed (197) and the time he had spent with contemporary Indians (many months), he declared that he, at least, saw a difference. He noted, too, that he was aware of the use of iron oxide in other regions, but insisted that other "culture types" such as special forms of gouges, plummets, and adze blades did not occur in these other cases (Moorehead 1914:360). He also discounted moisture as a cause of rapid skeletal deterioration and pointed to the deterioration of some of the stone tools as further evidence of great age. With a few additional but peripheral points, Moorehead rested his case. The argument doubtless pleased those archaeologists who regarded experience regardless of its quality as superior to the most logical and explicit scientific argument. As it happened, Moorehead this time had logic and the weight of evidence on his side as well.

Bushnell and Moore fired their final salvos together in 1915 with a double-barreled but considerably weaker blast. Yes, the graves were different, said Bushnell, but not veiled in mystery. He continued to insist that they were recent and ended with a charge that Moorehead had failed to understand both Bushnell's argument and his (Moorehead's) own data (Bushnell 1915). Moore belatedly added the only unquestionably valid charge against Moorehead by pointing out the hopeless inadequacy of the term "Red Paint People," a point that should have been made long before (Moore 1915). Moore continued to doubt the validity of the complex as an example of an early prehistoric culture, but his argument, like Bushnell's, was weaker than in 1913. Just as the real problems were being approached, both sides gave up the battle and left the field open for popular speculation. Moorehead never replied directly to the last charges made by Bushnell and Moore. As things were beginning to settle down, however, Willoughby jumped into the fray by publishing an article in defense of Moorehead (Willoughby 1915). In this, he refuted statements made by Bushnell, and with long quotes from a journal of Plymouth pilgrims showed that burials there were different in many ways from "Red Paint" burials. With this, the debate closed and was not reopened by professionals for 25 years.

In 1922, Moorehead published his *Report on the Archaeology of Maine*, a summary of his work to that date. With that, he turned his attention elsewhere. During the period that followed there were three publications from Walter B. Smith. Smith was an amateur who had accompanied Moorehead on some of his expeditions. His 1929 publication of *The Lost Red Paint People of Maine* did much to stir popular interest. In this monograph he advanced the hypothesis that these now vanished people might have lived along the coast when it extended much farther into what is now the Gulf of Maine. He suggested that most of them were killed when great tidal waves [tsunamis] inundated and permanently covered the land to the present coastline. He cited landlocked salmon in some Maine lakes as evidence of the great wave and suggested that the later Indian populations might have been paddling around offshore in canoes only to find themselves suddenly deposited on land as a replacement population. It would have been the fastest and cleanest population replacement in the history of the world, a hypothesis that appealed to popular preferences for catastrophic explanations and would thereby withstand evidence to the contrary for many years.

Willoughby published his *Antiquities of the New England Indians* in 1935, and in that same year Moorehead died. As these men left the scene, Hadlock (1941) made a half-hearted attempt to clarify the old debate. Hadlock and Stern (1948) worked together at the Hathaway site a few years later, a site originally excavated by Moorehead in 1912 that I would also excavate in 1968 and 1969. Benjamin Smith (1948) published a description of artifacts from sites of the Moorehead complex at about the same time, but little new work was done for the following 20 years. Apart from a summary article by Byers (1959), the subject fell by default into the hands of the popular press.

A December 10, 1967 article by LaRue Spiker in the *Portland Sunday Telegram* breathlessly announced that "some archaeologists believe these early Maine people came we know not whence, then disappeared for reasons unknown and that their culture was distinct from that of the northeastern woodland Indians." It quoted Moorehead as saying "I have never before examined places appearing so old the implements and the ochre were the only positive evidences that primitive excavation had been made." And Walter Smith was made to add to the mystery with a reference to "a few things we think we know about them and more that we don't know." We are told that the complex was by now dated by radiocarbon, but the story is not affected by their repetition. Meanwhile the Celtic craze was already beginning, the Pattee farm in North Salem, New Hampshire, having been already declared an Irish monastery. The idea spread to Maine where nineteenth-century lime kilns suddenly became megalithic tombs, and one in particular was made to carry the weight of two myths at once when it was declared the tomb of the lost Red Paint prince. The attribution was modified only slightly for inclusion as "caves used by Red Paint People, Maine's earliest inhabitants" on a 1955 map published by the National Geographic Society. The W.P.A. publication entitled *Maine: A Guide Down East* is a possible source for this, for in it we are told that the structure is a "Red Paint (Indian) Vault" (Byers 1953:2).

Plummets from Late Archaic sites became the subject of a subcontroversy (Figure 5.9). To some they were bolas stones, to others something else. One man insisted that they were goose killers, used singly on the ends of long thongs by Red Paint hunters sneaking through the marshes of coastal Maine. Another followed a lead originally published by Willoughby by insisting that they were used as fish bait. When smeared with tallow they were presumably irresistible to trout, who were unable to unlock their jaws from the plummets once they had seized them. Just which fish were supposed to have gone after the football-sized plummets found in sites near fast water was never explained. That they were probably net sinkers was an explanation too mundane to be taken seriously.

The new surge of research that began in the late 1960s put an end to Red Paint princes sleeping eternally in lime kilns while their subjects drowned under cataclysmic waves of seawater. It put an end to an exotic race of hunters stalking the marshes with stone goose killers, and it put an end to Beothuks in New England. What we are left with is considerably less titillating, but less ridiculous as well. In any event, it has been replaced by the Celtic revival. We can only guess what will replace this most recent madness when it is discredited in its turn.

Moorehead Complex

The excavation and analysis of coastal and interior habitation sites have given us a more balanced view of the Maritime Archaic. No longer do archaeologists attempt to assess the whole cultural system on the basis of evidence from cemeteries alone. Just the same, interest in the mortuary sites has continued, and recent excavation of cemetery remains that fall into what we now call the Moorehead Complex has clarified the inner dynamics of this mortuary subsystem.

The Hathaway cemetery site was hastily excavated by Moorehead in 1912 and reexamined by Wendell Hadlock and Theodore Stern in 1947. I returned to the site in 1968 and 1969 in order to obtain new data and clarify the results of the two previous excavations. Like many Moorehead Complex sites this one

FIGURE 5.9. Plummets. Left, Hathaway site (67 mm); center, Haskell site (74 mm); right, Haskell site (114 mm). Shown at actual size. (Collection of R. S. Peabody Foundation.)

was situated on a gravel knoll overlooking a lower tributary of the Penobscot. This particular knoll is the end of an esker that was breached by the Passadumkeag River shortly after deglaciation. Excavation of a series of burials and reanalysis of those excavated in 1912 and 1947 revealed a set of four separate components, only two of which applied to the Maritime Archaic. Two recent burials from the Hathaway IV (late prehistoric) component contained organic remains, but the earlier components were all devoid or nearly devoid of human skeletal remains or other organic material. We discovered that all of the shallow red ocher burials removed by Moorehead in 1912 and one of those we uncovered belonged to the oldest component (Hathaway I) (Figure 5.10). Carbon from Burial 40 yielded a date of 5165 ± 185 B.P. (SI-878), which puts this earliest known Moorehead Complex component at about 3200 B.C. Several other shallow burials we excavated contained

FIGURE 5.10. Left, greenstone gouge (30 cm) and adze (27 cm). Right, diabase adze (23 cm) and two gouges (16 and 15). All from Hathaway site, Maine. Shown at one-half actual size. Greenstone artifacts date from early in the period (Hathaway I); diabase specimens are late (Hathaway II). (Collection of the R. S. Peabody Foundation.)

materials similar to those found in another section of the cemetery in 1947. None of the burials in this second component (Hathaway II) was directly datable, but an analogous component was dated at Cow Point, New Brunswick, at 3630 ± 135 (SI-988) and 3835 ± 115 (SI-989), or around 1800 B.C. Curiously, the two Late Archaic components at Hathaway are both repeated at Cow Point. Cross dating in both directions allows us to place the earlier components at both sites at around 3200 B.C. just as both later components can be dated at 1800 B.C. These two dates would appear to bracket almost the entire lifespan of the Moorehead Complex, and between them can be arrayed all of those burial data that were collected before the advent of modern dating and other analytical techniques. The earlier components at both sites produced burials so shallow that primary interments like those found at Port au Choix seem unlikely. Bundle burials of disarticulated skeletons seem more likely in at least some of these cases. Grave goods tended to include holed whetstones that Moorehead used to refer to as "Passadumkeag problematicals" (Figure 5.11), stemmed and lanceolate points, plummets, fire kits, and gouges made of a distinctive green metamorphosed volcanic rock. Gouges and adzes from the later Maritime Archaic components at both Hathaway and Cow Point tended to be proportionally thicker and made from diabase-related rock. Fire kits of pyrite and chert, plummets, and stemmed points were found in the later components as well as the earlier ones, but to them were added finished points of a distinctive translucent quartzite called Ramah chert (Figure 5.12). This material occurs naturally only in Labrador, and the presence of finished specimens in Maine cemeteries is clear evidence of long-distance exchange during the Late Archaic, at least within the Maritime Archaic (Sanger 1973; Snow 1975).

Seriation of otherwise undated Moorehead Complex cemeteries between the brackets provided by the Hathaway and Cow Point sites gives us some idea of the changes that took place in the complex over time. Plummets, fire kits, and various stemmed points occur throughout, but holed whetstones and lanceolate points drop out a few centuries into the 1400-year life of the complex. There is a phasing out of thin greenstone adzes and gouges and an overlapping phasing in of thicker diabase forms through the middle centuries. During the same middle centuries notched points analogous to Otter Creek points and other types of the Lake Forest Archaic show up along with simple slate points and carved effigies. Faceted slate points, which evolve into long bayonets, and exotic Ramah chert points show up in the middle centuries as well (Figure 5.13) but have more staying power, lasting until the end of the complex after 1800 B.C. (Snow 1975:56).

The end of the Moorehead Complex can best be viewed as a consequence of changes in subsistence adaptation. The decline in heavy woodworking tools, slate bayonets, and plummets after the Late Archaic period all point to a decline in dugout canoe manufacture, and probably shifts in hunting patterns. Swordfish remains disappear from coastal sites and it may be that

FIGURE 5.11. "Passadumkeag problematicals" may have been whetstones. Left, Hathaway grave 153 (26 cm); center, Hathaway grave 141 (19 cm); right, Hathaway grave 152 (39 cm). (All from the collection of the R. S. Peabody Foundation.)

interior hunting shifted to moose and other more modern game. Shellfish gathering became more important and interior travel and hunting may well have come to involve birchbark canoes. With these shifts traditional tool forms, which we have come to recognize as constituents of both camp sites

FIGURE 5.12. Ramah chert point (96 mm long) from Grave 170, Haskell site, Maine. Shown at actual size. The material is actually a translucent quartzite. Left, front lighting shows surface texture. Right, back lighting reveals internal gray coloring. Lobate stemmed form anticipates Adena points of the following period. (Collection of the R. S. Peabody Foundation.)

FIGURE 5.13. Ramah chert artifacts from Maine. Left, three points from Indian Island, Old Town (collection of the Museum of the American Indian, Heye Foundation). Right, points from the Orland site, largest 8.6 cm (collection of the American Museum of Natural History, New York City). Shown at one-half actual size. (Photos by Bruce Bourque.)

and grave lots, fell into disuse. Under the circumstances, the mortuary subsystem was forced to change in response to shifts in the other subsystems, and the complex as it had been previously defined came to an end.

Cemetery sites dominated archaeological attention for many years, but it is now clear that there are also coastal and interior habitation sites. The latter are usually situated at strategic points on main river courses or the lower portions of primary tributaries. They are rare or unknown along more remote upper tributaries. Little is yet known about house types or their distributions within settlements. The house outlines uncovered at Wapanucket No. 6, Massachusetts, appear attributable to the Mast Forest Archaic or the subsequent Terminal Archaic period (Robbins 1968).

Remains in coastal camps indicate that maritime hunting was an important summer activity. Swordfish were apparently taken with spears or harpoons from large dugouts, and marine mammals (especially the harbor seal) were probably taken in the same manner. Shellfish were apparently utilized occasionally, but were not an important constituent in the diet. Spring and fall were probably spent at anadromous fishing stations on main streams. Although there is direct evidence only from Newfoundland, it seems likely that all the communities of the Maritime Archaic were spending some time hunting caribou. This activity probably dominated in the winter months.

The household unit was probably still a nuclear family or a small extended family. The band, however, could easily have been substantially larger than was the case in earlier periods. Maritime hunting, caribou hunting, and the harvesting of fish runs are all activities that could have supported relatively large communities. While the historic pattern in northern New England was for people to live in even larger semipermanent communities and split up into small family bands for excursions to special-purpose camps in the summer and winter, Late Archaic communities could have remained at an intermediate size for the entire year. The adaptation was diffuse and the community pattern classifiable as central-based wandering. However, there may have been no tendency for the community to fragment and reassemble by season and it may well be difficult to decide which of a small number of seasonally occupied sites was the central base.

The technological subsystem is defined by distinctive adzes (Figure 5.14), gouges (Figure 5.15), axes, plummets, fire kits of pyrite and chert, and implements of slate, chipped stone, antler, bone, and swordfish sword. Chipped stone points tend to be stemmed or expanded stemmed types, with broad side-notched types sometimes appearing as well (Figure 5.16). Knives and bayonets of ground slate mimic examples made of bone, antler, and swordfish sword. Sanger's (1975:62) evidence from Hirundo suggests that the side-notched points and ground slate semilunar knives are present in the early part of the period, but disappear near its end. Gouges tend to be deeply grooved early and more shallowly grooved late in the period. Data from Hirundo and elsewhere suggest that ground slate points are simpler in earlier

Maritime Archaic Cultural System

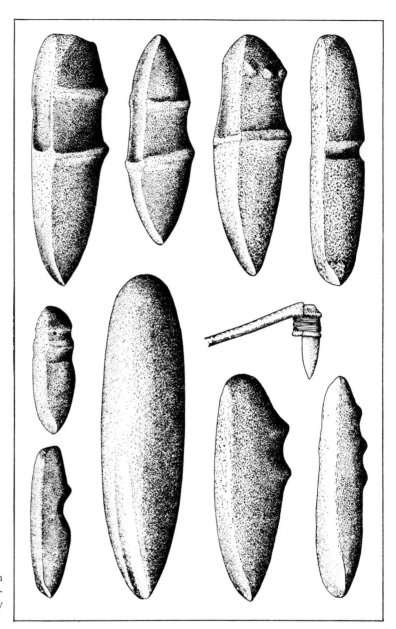

FIGURE 5.14. Adze heads from eastern Massachusetts and Maine. Shown at one-third actual size. (After Willoughby 1935:34.)

centuries, long slender bayonets being late. Spear-thrower weights, which are already present in Middle Archaic sites in Massachusetts and which occur in Lake Forest Archaic sites, are not at all frequent in the Maritime Archaic.

The predominant raw material in most Maine sites is Kineo felsite, a distinctive tough volcanic material that can be quarried only in a few places in the vicinity of Moosehead Lake. Nodules are available from glacial deposits

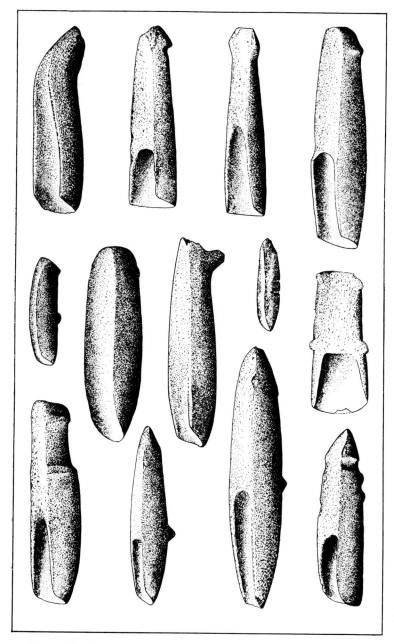

FIGURE 5.15. Gouge heads from eastern Massachusetts, New Hampshire, and Maine. Shown at one-third actual size. (After Willoughby 1935:35.)

to the south, but these are not often suitable for working. Perhaps more important is the appearance in northern New England of finished points made of Ramah chert (Figure 5.17). This material is available only in Labrador, and finished pieces made from it are clear evidence of a broad system of exchange within the Maritime Archaic. Things such as semilunar

FIGURE 5.16. Late Archaic projectile points from the Turner Farm site, Maine. Bases sometimes seem to be a compromise between the stemmed and side-notched forms of the period. Shown at actual size. (Photo by G. Hoagland. Courtesy of Maine State Museum.)

knives, gouges, and adzes were already present in New England during the Middle Archaic, but it seems likely that ground slate points and the artifacts of bone, antler, and swordfish sword that they mimic were introduced from farther northeast. The rich nonlithic tool industry includes toggling and barbed harpoons, needles, and awls as well, further evidence of a maritime

FIGURE 5.17. Ramah chert artifacts from Rattlers Bight, Labrador, near the northern source of this exotic material. Shown at one-half actual size. (Photo by William FitzHugh.)

5 CM.
2 IN.

orientation and links to the northeast. Overall, we are left with the impression of communities of skilled sea hunters stretching from northern New England to Newfoundland. Travel and marine hunting were probably facilitated by large dugout canoes, and the distribution of exotic Ramah chert within the region combines with evidence from the religious subsystem to suggest that the communities of the Maritime Archaic were self-consciously distinctive within the range of Late Archaic societies.

The religious subsystem is very well known due to a long series of excavations at cemetery sites. Clusters of individual burials usually occur on gravel knolls overlooking large rivers or their primary tributaries. Burials are typically accompanied by red ocher and grave goods, the latter not significantly clustered for reasons of age or sex (Figure 5.18). Burials were probably either primary interments or bundle burials. Skeletal evidence has not survived as more than a few fragments in sites excavated thus far in New England. However, Port au Choix, Newfoundland, has provided well-preserved remains. It would appear from the information uncovered there that the dead were buried soon after death and that treatment was uniform for all members of the community. It may be that primary burials were the rule at cemeteries near sites occupied during the summer. Bundle burials may have been the result of saving the remains of those that died during the winter for burial in the spring. The Hathaway site, a cemetery site adjacent to a fall–spring fishing station, contained what may well be both primary and bundle burials, a pattern that we should expect at such a site.

Overall, the cultural system contains elements suggesting development out of local Middle Archaic developments, with the addition of maritime elements from farther northeast. The "Red Paint" cemeteries define a strong religious subsystem that might also have its antecedents to the northeast. The mound burial at L'Anse Amour, discussed in the last chapter, reveals the use of red ocher by maritime hunters of the Labrador coast during the Middle Archaic period, and it is difficult to see the Maritime Archaic as anything but a continued florescence of that ancient tradition.

LAKE FOREST ARCHAIC ADAPTATION

The Late Archaic is a period in which prehistory takes on many local expressions, and developmental themes interact as a series of confusing cross currents. There are more sites known for this period and their contents are more varied than in previous periods. Moreover, these have been recognized for many years, so that we have accumulated a variety of interpretive models that tend to be mutually incompatible. Tuck's (1978a:30–32) Lake Forest Archaic eliminates much of the confusion by simply raising the level of abstraction, but internal confusion remains, and to understand it some further review of the history of archaeological research is necessary.

William Ritchie published his perspective on Northeast prehistory in 1938, a perspective structured to some degree by his specialization in the prehistory of interior New York. For 40 years he has maintained a view of the Late

FIGURE 5.18. Points from Burial 40, Hathaway site, Maine (Snow 1969:78), 107 and 125 mm long. Both are made of friable stone for use as grave goods only. Shown at actual size.

Archaic that has phases of a "Laurentian" tradition at its heart. He sees the tradition "as having its immediate source in the Lake Forest belt lying adjacent on the south to the Great Lakes and extending eastward across lower Canada, with major centers in the Ottawa and St. Lawrence valleys, into the Canadian Maritimes and upper New England [Ritchie 1971b:3]." He also believes that "its most diagnostic traits, occurring in considerable morphological variety, comprise the gouge; adze; plummet; ground slate points and knives, including the semi-lunar form or ulu, which occurs also in chipped stone; simple forms of the bannerstone; a variety of chipped-stone projectile points, mainly broad-bladed and side-notched forms; and the barbed bone point [Ritchie 1969a:79]." Ritchie sees the tradition as containing separate phases, most notably the Vergennes, Vosburg, and Brewerton, which are defined primarily by different diagnostic projectile points (Figure 5.19) and occupy contrasting time–space positions in the Late Archaic.

Ritchie responded to Byers's suggestion that we could talk in terms of a Maritime Boreal Archaic and a Laurentian Boreal Archaic by pointing out that the boreal forests of Canada were the setting for J. V. Wright's (1972a) Shield Archaic. The Laurentian was set not in a boreal forest, but rather a

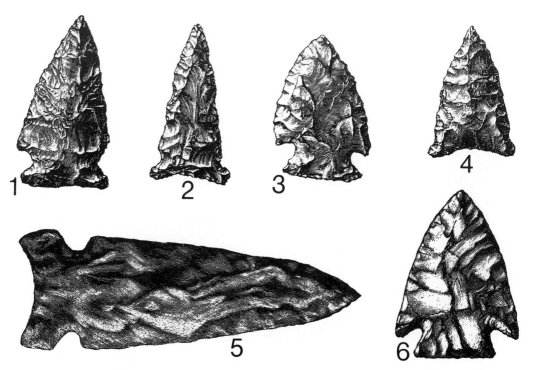

FIGURE 5.19. Point types of the Lake Forest Archaic. Brewerton series: 1, Side-Notched (closely related to Sylvan Side-Notched); 2, Eared-Notched; 3, Corner-Notched; 4, Eared-Triangle. Other types: 5, Otter Creek; 6, Vosburg. Shown at actual size. (From Ritchie 1971a. Courtesy of New York State Museum and Science Service.)

"lake forest" consisting of "conifers—white, red and jack pine, and hem-lock—and stands of northern hardwoods—beech, sugar and red maple, yellow birch, white and red oak, white ash, and basswood, as the principal climax association [Ritchie 1969a:82]." The environment he describes falls in a wide belt from the upper Great Lakes to the Maritime Provinces and is therefore much more widespread than the prehistoric complex he defined as Laurentian. Moreover, it has become clear in recent decades that the lake forest zone outside the distribution of Laurentian was the setting for related cultural developments that, while they could not be defined as Laurentian proper, showed clear technological connections. It was, therefore, a zone within which Late Archaic adaptation took similar form. From the Old Copper sites of the upper Great Lakes to the Maritime Archaic sites of northern New England there appears to have been a Late Archaic cultural continuum, the local expressions of which vary from place to place. We have seen that one part of this larger whole has already been defined separately as the Maritime Archaic. The rest of it Tuck suggests we leave as a broadly defined Lake Forest Archaic, only part of which can be equated with Ritchie's Laurentian.

Unfortunately, because it has been around for four decades, there has been ample opportunity for archaeologists to use the Laurentian in unproductive ways. Just as there has been a tendency for many years to think of artifact types as normative realities, there has also been a tendency to think of complexes like Laurentian as if they were normative concrete realities. Archaeologists have sought to verify the presence or absence of the entire complex in various parts of the Northeast, ignoring the tendency for artifact types to have lives and distributions of their own. Thus, evidence for the Laurentian has been found in many contexts well outside the distribution originally defined by Ritchie, but in nearly all cases not as a complete complex. Tuck (1977:32) has good cause to lament that "it seems that as used today by most researchers 'Laurentian' actually refers to some nebulous group of archaeological cultures scattered over much of the Northeast, dating from the Middle and Late Archaic periods, and characterized by a variety of artifact complexes some of which include broad notched or narrow notched and stemmed projectile points, scrapers (on occasion), celts, gouges and ground slate points or knives (sometimes), and at one time or another, practically any other non-ceramic artifact ever recovered in the Northeast." Such a broad definition dilutes the Laurentian and renders it useless. How-ever, if the broader cultural context is thought of as a Lake Forest adaptation then the problem disappears. Laurentian becomes a specific local adaptation involving a specific set of artifact types. Other local adaptations share some but not all of these, depending on their specific natures as adaptations. Sanger (1975:72) has pointed out that materials from the Hirundo, Maine, site are more similar to Laurentian materials from the Champlain drainage than to Maritime Archaic materials from Newfoundland. While this observa-tion might inspire some archaeologists to debate whether the Hirundo assemblage properly belongs in the Maritime Archaic or the Laurentian, such a debate would be fruitless and unnecessary. The Laurentian is one variation on the Lake Forest theme, which in turn appears as a broad interior adaptation. Similarly the Maritime Archaic is a related and reasonably coherent coastal adaptation. It should be no surprise that Maine sites that we classify for convenience in the Maritime Archaic have traits in common with a Lake Forest variant in the Champlain drainage. Thus, the search for good Laurentian sites is a fool's errand except within the distribution defined by Ritchie, and the thrust of archaeological research has turned as it must to an exploration of variations in local adaptation within the broad Maritime–Lake Forest Archaic continuum. "The time has come in the far northeast to concentrate on explaining the differences between the various synchronous components. Undoubtedly, it will entail a much greater effort than that previously expended on analysis, but the end product holds so much more promise for the anthropologist [Sanger *et al.* 1977:468]."

The broad-bladed side-notched points that typify Laurentian are called Otter Creek points in the Champlain and adjacent drainages. Analogous types from sites like Wapanucket No. 8 in Massachusetts (Robbins 1968:31–37) and Hirundo, Maine (Sanger *et al.* 1977:466), lack type names but appear to have been parts of the same tradition. Such point forms have analogues far to the west and south, into the Mississippi drainage. Points like the Big Sandy type are supposed to be more than 6000 years old there, but we have already seen that Otter Creek points date to about 6300 B.P. in the Mohawk drainage. At this time we cannot say that the point tradition began in the Midwest and spread to the Northeast, only that it has its roots in the Middle Archaic over a broad portion of the Eastern Woodlands. There is at present no good evidence to suggest that the point tradition expanded from the Midwest into the Northeast, and, even if there were, a single point tradition is insufficient grounds on which to hypothesize the movement of a whole cultural system. I doubt that there will ever be grounds to argue "that 'formative Laurentian' people moved into the upper St. Lawrence–Great Lakes region from the south and west [Tuck 1977:39]." What we have with Laurentian is a local Lake Forest adaptation that draws on a point tradition having parallels to the Southwest and a ground slate and bone tool industry that probably originated on the coast of the far Northeast during the Middle Archaic.

Although Ritchie has in recent years come to think of Laurentian as a tradition having at least three phases, one of them does not fully qualify. Ritchie (1969a:84–89) has called one the Vergennes phase, and it contains all of the traits listed earlier as diagnostic of Laurentian. Otter Creek is the diagnostic point type, and the phase is found in the Champlain drainage and the upper Hudson drainage. The KI site in Vermont allowed the first clear description of the phase, and the Otter Creek site, also in Vermont and still undergoing investigation, will probably define that description more sharply. The Brewerton phase is found in central New York, in the Lake Ontario drainage and therefore outside our area. It is characterized by projectile point types in the Brewerton type series. The remaining phase is the still hypothetical Vosburg phase of the Mohawk and middle to lower Hudson drainage. Funk (1976:244) indicates that "the evidence justifies our acceptance of the trait list suggested by Ritchie (1965:83–84) for the Vosburg complex. Two traits, however, on the original (1944) trait list—grooved shaft rubbers and sinewstones—were not found on the sites later investigated by Ritchie (1958) or reported here by the writer [Funk], and should probably be dropped from the inventory." Ritchie (1969a:83) says that "the chief distinctions between the Brewerton and Vosburg phases are the absence from assemblages attributed to the latter of native copper tools and ground slate double-edged knives or points, and the presence in much greater numbers of the slate semilunar knife or ulu. To this, of course, must be added the diagnostic Vosburg point and probably winged spear-thrower weights and plummets. But the last three artifacts are rarely in association with Vosburg points and could be intrusive from other components on most of those few sites where they have been found together. The upshot is that, after years of searching, Funk, Ritchie, and others have still not isolated Vosburg components that are pure enough to meet their high standards, and the Vosburg complex remains a frustratingly amorphous concept.

So it seems that Vosburg may not exist except as a variation on the Lake Forest Archaic theme. As we shall see, the lower Hudson drainage was within the area dominated by a third major Late Archaic adaptation, and we should probably not expect Laurentian traits to turn up in the marginal zone of adaptation between this and the Lake Forest zone. Again, the future of archaeological research in the Northeast will depend on the general adoption of Sanger's advice that we search for the reasons for local variations in adaptation, not the replication of conceptually entrenched complexes.

That part of the Lake Forest Archaic that falls within our region is less well known than the Maritime Archaic. The settlement pattern would again seem to be central-based wandering, but site types and their distributions are poorly understood. Ritchie and Funk (1973:340) report that most known Vergennes phase sites are small camps. They suggest that bands lived primarily by hunting and occupied back-country hunting camps during the fall and winter. They may have reassembled in larger groups at fishing stations on lakes and major streams during the spring and summer. I would add to this that the tool inventory, borrowing as it does from the Maritime Archaic to the northeast, suggests that Lake Champlain was exploited like an inland sea. Anadromous fish runs were heavy in aboriginal times, and the presence of harbor seals here and into Lake Ontario would have allowed an adaptation approximating that of the Maritime Archaic in some ways. Indeed, a major feature of the Lake Forest Archaic is that it flourished in the St. Lawrence drainage, and participating communities had access to the large lakes of the system. However, the entire Lake Forest Archaic has an interior flavor, and the farther removed from the related Maritime Archaic one becomes the

Lake Forest Archaic Cultural System

stronger that flavor seems to be. In the Champlain and upper Hudson drainages, and probably in the upper Connecticut as well, seasonal movements may have focused on winter caribou hunting, spring and fall fish runs, and an especially diffuse summer pattern of hunting, fishing, and gathering.

The household and settlement social units can only be guessed at. I suspect that at least the settlement unit was smaller than that of the Maritime Archaic. The latter people could have lived year-round in relatively large groups, but the communities of the Lake Forest Archaic more probably had to break up into smaller bands at various times.

Gouges and adzes are again suggestive of dugout canoes. Ground slate knives, including the ulu, might be associated with migratory fish runs and seal hunting. The spear-thrower weight (banner stone), which is not widely distributed within the Maritime Archaic, might combine with the distinctive broad side-notched points to suggest a weapon distinctive from those used to the northeast. Raw materials used were generally simply those that were available locally. Ramah chert did not find its way this far west or south. However, the Lake Forest communities of New England were relatively close to the Old Copper industry at the other end of the cultural continuum in the upper Great Lakes. Copper gouges and points have been found in Lake Forest Archaic sites and occasionally even in Maritime Archaic sites. Although not abundant, native copper does occur in the Northeast, so it is not yet certain that these items came from the west by way of some system of exchange.

It is important to remember that the Late Archaic makers of copper tools were not practicing true metallurgy. The copper was not extracted from ore, but was dug up as large nuggets or lumps of native copper. The lumps were beaten into shape and annealed by repeated heating and plunging into cold water. Without annealing the copper would have become brittle and resistant to shaping. Heat treatment of chert to make it easier to work was probably a chert knapper's technique from the Paleo-Indian period on, so the annealing of copper was not necessarily the inspired innovation it might seem to have been. Late Archaic Indians probably regarded copper as a kind of malleable rock, desirable but scarce. While the smiths of the Old World went on to discover how to extract copper from ore at about this same time, the Indians of the Lake Forest did not, and what might have become independent technological development was stillborn.

At least in New England, the Lake Forest Archaic reveals its relative poverty in its religious subsystem. The gaudy red ocher burials of the Maritime Archaic, which gave ideological expression to that whole adaptive system, are missing from the Lake Forest Archaic. Cemeteries are almost unknown, although Ritchie (1969a:92) reports scanty evidence from two Brewerton sites. I have seen evidence of a possible cemetery on the Hudson River in its upper drainage area, but the site was destroyed by road building decades ago, and all that remain are a few Late Archaic drill bits and a leaf-shaped knife, all bearing traces of red ocher. It may be that we may yet find an echo of the Moorehead Complex in the Lake Forest Archaic, but present evidence is not encouraging.

The third major regional expression of the Late Archaic extends from the Merrimack drainage across southern New England through the lower Connecticut and Hudson drainages. It dominates the Delaware and Susquehanna drainages as well as the coastal drainages as far south as North Carolina. Westward it extends across the basins of Ohio River tributaries draining the states of Ohio, Indiana, and Illinois, and even beyond these to the southern shore of Lake Erie and southern Michigan (Tuck 1978a:29). I have suggested that we call this vague and widespread adaptation the Mast Forest Archaic, partly as a means to make it equivalent to the Maritime Archaic and the Lake Forest Archaic. At the moment it is defined archaeologically by a series of similar projectile point types and an ill-defined impression that the sites producing them share a common adaptation. Even if one leaves aside the complexes found in the Ohio and Great Lakes drainages and concentrates on the expression of this adaptation in the Northeast, the picture seems vague and confused. This is in large part due to the failure of any name for it to gain general acceptance, despite the large number that have been proposed by different archaeologists. Tuck's "Narrow Point," enclosed as it is within equivocal quotation marks, is a provisional name at best. It is only one of several permutations based on the series of diagnostic point types (Figure 5.20). Others include "Small Stemmed Point," "Narrow Stemmed Point," "Small Point," "Narrow Point," and so on.

Even if we avoid the trap of naming a whole cultural adaptation after a single artifact class, we find terminological confusion surrounding this regional expression of the Late Archaic. Byers was one of the first to recognize that there was such an expression in southern New England and southward along the Atlantic coast. He suggested we refer to it as the "Coastal Archaic" (Byers 1959:236–243). However, as he defined it, the unit appeared to exclude interior connections and explicitly included elements of the Terminal Archaic period that come after 1700 B.C. Like his "Boreal Archaic," the term never caught on. Funk (in Ritchie 1969a:144) has proposed the term "Appalachian tradition," and Brennan (1967) has long referred to much the same collection of complexes as the "Taconic tradition." Kinsey (1971) would include much of this and some Middle Archaic material in a "Piedmont tradition," and Dincauze (1975a:24) would lump much of the same evidence under the heading "Atlantic Slope Archaic." All of these have failed to catch on in part because each refers to a physiographic province that corresponds to only part of the overall distribution of these related complexes.

Clearly, we have passed the point at which Late Archaic taxonomy was transformed from a set of illuminating generalizations into a thicket of competing abstractions. Even though he could easily do so, Sanger (1975:72) has declined to offer another term or two from his own perspective because "taxonomic terms, even when clearly labelled as 'working hypotheses,' have a habit of getting firmly cemented in the literature." Nevertheless, "terminological confusion cannot obscure the essential historical unity lurking behind these several cultural manifestations [Dincauze 1975a:24]." The message implicit in both of these quotes is that, by discussing the period in terms of

MAST FOREST ARCHAIC ADAPTATION

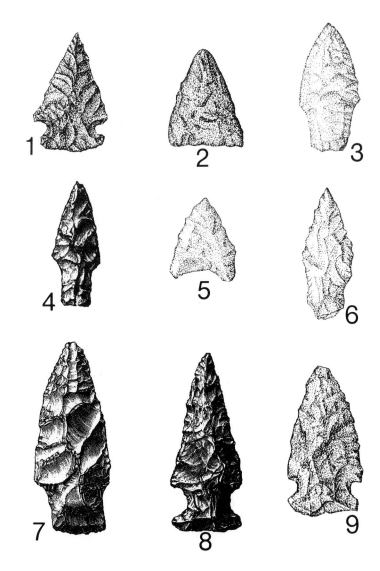

FIGURE 5.20. Point types of the Mast Forest Archaic: 1, Vestal Notched; 2, Beekman Triangle; 3, Wading River; 4, Lamoka; 5, Squibnocket Triangle; 6, Squibnocket Stemmed; 7, Bare Island; 8, Normanskill; 9, Sylvan Side-Notched (closely related to Brewerton Side-Notched). (From Ritchie 1971a. Courtesy of New York State Museum and Science Service.)

drainages or sets of contiguous drainages, we can avoid much of the confusion that arises when abstract traditions and complexes begin to take on more importance than they deserve. In this way we can get at the historical unity of the period without perpetuating or adding to the taxonomic babble. Once again, such terms had their greatest utility in pre-radiocarbon days when contemporaneity had to be inferred on the basis of formal similarities. That need has disappeared, making most of them at best superfluous in archaeological synthesis. All we need is a very general Mast Forest Archaic category to include the continuum of related Late Archaic complexes in southern New England, southern New York, and beyond (Figure 5.21). For

FIGURE 5.21. Points of the Mast Forest Archaic. Top row, Squibnocket Stemmed; second row, Squibnocket Triangular; third row, Bear Creek points; bottom row, Wading River points. The point at top left is 5 cm long. Shown at actual size. (Courtesy of the Peabody Museum of Salem.)

present purposes that continuum includes the Sylvan Lake complex of south-eastern New York and eastward, the Squibnocket complex of southeastern New England, the River phase of the upper Hudson, the Lamoka phase of central New York, and the Bare Island complex of the Mid-Atlantic region.

Terminological confusion has been only one of two major problems surrounding Mast Forest Archaic complexes in the Northeast. The second problem, like the first, stems in large part from the history of archaeological research and the consequence of past working assumptions. As was so often the case, William Ritchie led the way with his research on the Lamoka complex in central New York. In his major synthesis of New York prehistory, Ritchie (1969a) places Lamoka at around 2500 B.C. on the basis of an unusually long series of radiocarbon dates from the Lamoka Lake site. Brewerton materials, which I have made part of the Lake Forest Archaic, tended to date about five centuries younger. Since the spacial unit of analysis was central New York, Ritchie reasonably concluded that Lamoka and Brewerton were related sequentially within that area. He did not analyze the Susquehanna and Ontario drainages separately for the purposes of his synthesis. Problems with the proposed sequence began to arise almost immediately. The O'Neil site on the Seneca River in the Ontario drainage produced Brewerton remains stratigraphically below Lamoka, and Ritchie had to resort to soil creep and other disturbing mechanisms to account for the stratigraphic reversal of the expected sequence (Ritchie and Funk 1973:74–95). Funk (1976) found the same disconcerting reversal at Sylvan Lake Rock Shelter and other sites in the Hudson drainage. Ritchie's (1969b) investigations on Martha's Vineyard and other work in southern New England suggested that the expected sequence was reversed there too. Still other newer data support Ritchie's original suggested sequence. According to Dincauze (1971a), the Middle Archaic Merrimack complex (see Chapter 4) may have evolved directly into the Mast Forest Archaic complexes of southeastern New England, although she has more recently disowned that idea (Dincauze 1976:128).

All of this and much more has been detailed by Funk in his effort to advance "a hypothetical scheme in which Brewerton culture actually precedes, rather than follows, Lamoka where the ranges of the two cultures overlap [Funk 1976:272]." In fact, Funk approaches but does not quite reach the best solution to the problem in the last portion of the quote. Lamoka and other complexes of the Mast Forest Archaic do not extend into Canada, and the Lake Forest Archaic complexes are rare or incomplete in southern New England, Long Island southwestward. They overlap in a belt that tracks west to east across New York and the middle Hudson, Connecticut, and Merrimack drainages. In New England this is roughly along the 20% oak isopoll discussed in Chapter 4. Both Ritchie and Funk have stressed "the concentration of Lamoka and Brewerton manifestations within separate, though broadly overlapping, ranges [Funk 1976:275]." Funk further suggests that the Lake Forest Archaic and the Mast Forest Archaic could be equally old in their respective core areas and that "during an undetermined period of coexistence, the boundaries between group territories would have shifted repeatedly, with occasional incursions by one group into the other's territory [1976:275]." Thus, the solution is at hand but not yet fully grasped, for the sequence problem persists only if we insist that Lake Forest Archaic complexes must always either precede or follow Mast Forest Archaic complexes. Such an insistence is based on the anachronistic notion that point types and complexes that travel with them must necessarily behave as widespread horizon styles, a fallacious assumption that I attacked in the last chapter. If that assumption is abandoned, then it is possible to take the last step on the logical path Funk has cleared. I propose that we stop thinking of a belt of overlap or even a belt of transition between the two zones of adaptation and begin treating it explicitly as a marginal belt of tension between two coeval zones that persisted throughout the Late Archaic. This is the conceptual blade that cuts through the last strands of the Gordian knot that has bound the Late Archaic for so long. Both Ritchie and Funk can be right in the context of this framework, for each is dealing with a local sequence within the tension zone. Furthermore, we no longer need to press a fruitless search for a full-blown Laurentian complex on Long Island or a Lamoka-related complex in the Champlain drainage (Wyatt 1977), for we no longer expect either to behave as a temporally thin, spatially widespread horizon.

Thus, west of our region in central New York, the large central base camp site of Lamoka Lake in the upper Susquehanna drainage was probably occupied for a time around 2500 B.C., while both older and younger sites of the Lake Forest Archaic characterize the Lake Ontario drainage. In the upper and middle Hudson drainage the Late Archaic period began with the Vergennes phase, a variant of the Lake Forest Archaic and prime example of the Laurentian. Vosburg points appear in the middle of the period in this area, but there is insufficient evidence to infer the existence of a Vosburg phase equivalent to Vergennes as a whole cultural system. Instead the middle part of the period appears to have witnessed an expansion northward of the Mast Forest adaptation, displacing the Lake Forest. By 2200 B.C. the Sylvan Lake complex of the Mast Forest Archaic was well established in the entire Hudson drainage. The Mohawk tributary drainage went through the same transition from Lake Forest to Mast Forest adaptation, although the evidence for the change is less well developed. During the last 500 years of the period the middle and upper Hudson and the Mohawk drainages were dominated by the derivative River phase, the hallmark of which is the Normanskill point. Funk (1976:261–263) has tentatively identified a still later Late Archaic complex called "Batten Kill." However, this complex is defined primarily by the appearance of Genesee points, and we should probably look on it as simply the introduction of a single new tool type into an otherwise unchanged adaptation. Moreover, the similarity of the Genesee point to the Snook Kill and the time of its appearance suggest that it should be discussed in the context of the Terminal Archaic.

FIGURE 5.22. Effigy pestle made of graywacke from the Bent site. Shown at one-half actual size. (From Ritchie and Funk 1973:69. Courtesy New York State Museum and Science Service.)

A similar sequence of events appears to have occurred in western Connecticut and Massachusetts. Otter Creek points and other traces of the Lake Forest adaptation appear by 3500 B.C. and phase out with the appearance of Mast Forest types after at least 2600 B.C. (Dincauze 1975a:24; Swigart 1974:23). This relationship, which repeats that observed by Funk in the Hudson drainage, leaves open the possibility that the entire Mast Forest adaptation was intrusive "from the lower Susquehanna region into southern and eastern New York, New Jersey and southern New England," as Ritchie (1969b:219) has suggested. Dincauze (1975a:24) allows for that possibility, but points out that the available data are also consistent with an in-place development. My own view of this and similar issues is that the burden of proof clearly rests on any hypothesis favoring migration over in-place development. In the present case we must assume the latter until such time as the data are no longer consistent with it and require us to opt for Ritchie's hypothesis.

The principal Mast Forest complex of southeastern New England is the Squibnocket, which Ritchie (1969b) defined on the basis of excavations on Martha's Vineyard. The occurrence together of artifacts of both the Mast Forest and Lake Forest adaptations has led both Dincauze (1975a:25) and Ritchie (1969b:214) to suggest the coexistence of the two "traditions" during at least part of the Late Archaic in southeastern New England. Again, it is important not to view this as evidence of two separate cultures sharing the same environment, but rather the eclectic adoption of tool types from a variety of sources by a single Late Archaic culture. Thus, we find assemblages from Late Archaic sites that contain narrow stemmed points, adzes, plummets, gouges, ulus, and spear-thrower weights, clearly a single complex in the eyes of those who used it. Conversely, Brewerton, Vosburg, and Otter Creek point types occur in Mast Forest site contexts, but that is not to say that the Vergennes phase or any other version of the Laurentian as defined for the Lake Forest Archaic is present here.

Thus, the most immediate problem of the Late Archaic becomes the need to identify the adaptive contrasts between the Lake Forest and the Mast Forest adaptations rather than their relative ages. Unfortunately, collective attention has been so concentrated on the latter false issue that little has been accomplished in this regard. Nevertheless, some major points of contrast with the other two major adaptations are discernible. While the Mast Forest complexes often contain pestles (Figure 5.22), manos, and shallow mortars, these grinding implements are typically absent from Lake Forest complexes. The implication is that people within the Mast Forest adaptation made greater use of vegetable foods that required preparation through grinding. While "seeds, nuts, berries, roots, [and] dried meat were probably reduced with these sundry implements, the evidence indicates that acorn meal formed the principal item [Ritchie 1969a:62]." Throughout the Mast Forest zone of southern New England, deer predominated as the major game animal (Ritchie 1969a:58–59, 1969b:215). While fishing with hook and line, nets, and perhaps weirs and traps was characteristic within the Mast Forest adaptation, the "cultures of the Lake Forest Archaic seem to have confined their fishing implements primarily to harpoon, leister points, and the gaff, which need not be used with hook and line [Tuck 1978a:30]." Thus, there were sharp differences in terms of equipment and methods, and we can infer differences in seasonality and species exploited as well. It is likely that the famous Boylston Street fishweir in Boston was built during the Late Archaic (Dincauze 1973; Johnson 1942; Ritchie 1969b:57).

The people in the New England variants of the Mast Forest adaptation also had access to shellfish. Their tool complexes are found in the lower drainages of rivers like the Hudson, Connecticut, and Merrimack, and throughout southeastern New England, always within easy reach of shellfish resources. I have already discussed the issues surrounding the beginnings of shellfish exploitation (Chapter 4). While practiced by the bearers of the Maritime Archaic, shellfish gathering appears to have been less important than sea hunting in Late Archaic Maine and New Brunswick. Shellfish appear to have been more important to the Mast Forest adaptation of southern New England. Ritchie (1969b:233) has asserted that the quahog (*Venus mercenaria*) was more important to Late Archaic gatherers than the soft-shelled clam (*Mya arenaria*) because the former were a more obvious resource than deep-burrowing clams in the early days of shellfishing. Braun (1974) has disputed this interpretation on the basis of relatively new information from the Boston area regarding changes in sea level, temperature, and consequent abundance of various shellfish species over the last 4000 years. In this he indirectly supports Salwen's (1965) thesis that evidence of early shellfishing has been destroyed along much of the New England coast by rising sea level, and that the same factor has caused shifts in species distributions and therefore their frequencies in the strata of certain sites. While all of these factors are significant, they do not assist us in our efforts to reconstruct adaptive systems. The availability (or lack of it) of each species is determined by environmental conditions, and in turn determines the limits for human exploitation. Yet within those broad limits to adaptation human populations have considerable latitude, and environmental determinism does little to illuminate how those choices were made. "The time has passed for blanket statements claiming a late onset of shellfish gathering [Bourque 1975:41," but it is just as clear that we have far to go before we understand how each adaptive system integrated this activity into its overall subsistence pattern.

On the lower Hudson estuary, at least, oysters were gathered throughout the Late Archaic. As we have seen, intensive exploitation of oysters began there at the beginning of the Late Archaic, a beginning marked by two dates that convert to 3900 B.C. and 3700 B.C., respectively. The oyster valves in these lowermost strata from the Kettle Rock and Dogan Point middens are large, probably as a consequence of harvesting from previously unexploited beds. A second horizon in which oyster valves are large but not as large as in the first horizon is dated by a cluster of four dates from Dogan Point and Piping Rock to around 5100 B.P., three of which seemed too old when compared to associated diagnostic artifacts. Another set of three dates from two sites clusters around 4725 B.P. (Brennan 1974:86–87), suggesting an episode of heavy harvesting separated by episodes of disuse, but the data are too few to allow this to be more than a conjecture. By the end of the Late Archaic period, around 1700 B.C., the oysters of the Hudson had been reduced by falling salinity to such a small size that they were useful only as unshucked stew ingredients.

Mast Forest Archaic Cultural System

Site types include coastal sites in which shellfish remains are abundant, such as Ritchie's sites on Martha's Vineyard, the Wading River site on Long Island, and Brennan's Hudson River sites. We can assume summer occupation of these sites and perhaps the use of some of them for emergency shellfishing in the winter. There are also spring and fall fishing stations, such as the Neville site on the Merrimack, and winter camps in back country, like the Sylvan Lake Rock Shelter. The Bent site on the Mohawk river appears to have been a central base camp, suggesting that by the latter part of the Late Archaic at least Mast Forest-adapted people in this drainage were settled into a true central-based wandering system. The Bent site, which Ritchie and Funk (1973:52–70) assign to the River phase, covers about 2 hectares (5 acres), but, although scattered post molds were found, house forms could not be discerned. The fall –winter Pickle Hill site produced a possible house outline 4.5 × 3 m in size and evidence of acorn roasting (Weinman *et al.* 1967). The best evidence for housing found thus far are the three round house outlines discovered at Wapanucket No. 6, Massachusetts (Robbins 1968:12). Each of these houses, one of which had a cache of Squibnocket complex points under the floor, has a spiral outline, such that the doorway was formed by an overlapping wall. Each house would appear to have been sized for a single nuclear or small extended family.

Sites, and therefore community sizes, are not large, but they are numerous and occur in a wide variety of local settings. Dincauze (1975a:25) interprets this as indicating a very diffuse adaptation, a relatively dense population, and a complex pattern of seasonal movement.

The technological subsystem also reflects a diffuse adaptation. Projectile points of narrow stemmed types were apparently used on weapons propelled by weighted and flexible spear-throwers (Figure 5.23). Weighted spear-throwers were apparently less important or absent from the Maritime and Lake Forest complexes. Adzes and gouges suggest the use of dugout canoes, and plummets, notched net sinkers, ulus, and bone hooks indicate that fishing was important. We have seen that weirs were also used in fishing, and the overall impression is that Mast Forest Archaic communities exploited a broader range of fish resources than did the people of other Late Archaic

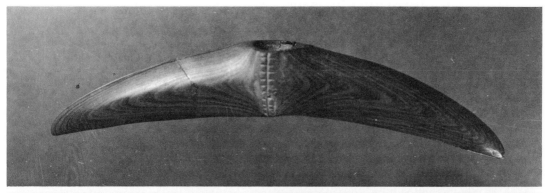

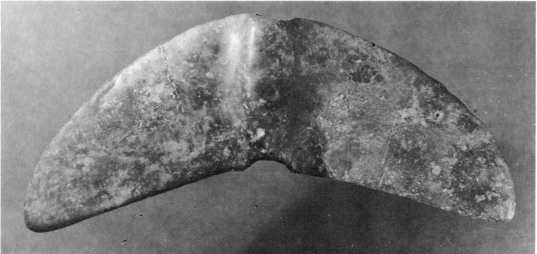

FIGURE 5.23. Winged spear-thrower weights from the Bronson Museum, sometimes called "whaletail" forms. Top, 17 cm long; bottom, 18 cm long. Shown at three-quarters actual size.

adaptations. Furthermore, the presence of food-grinding implements in these sites argues for an exploitation of a broad range of vegetable foods, particularly acorns and other Mast Forest nuts. Dincauze (1973, 1974) has noted a tendency for a rather parochial use of raw materials, communities often using only those materials immediately available within local stream drainages. Thus, there is less evidence for regional exchange of raw materials or finished products in the Mast Forest Archaic than in the rest of New England. Indeed, the intraregional diversity of this adaptation has been a major factor in the interpretive confusion that has prevailed for so long.

Mortuary sites associated with the Mast Forest Archaic are so far well known only in the Taunton River drainage of southeastern New England. Feature No. 206 at the Wapanucket No. 8 site has yielded 11 cremation burials within a larger pit and a date of 4290 ± 140 B.P. (2340 B.C., Gx-1104).

The cremations were associated with large stone slabs, gouges, whetstones, points of the Squibnocket complex, and red ocher (Robbins 1968). A similar but somewhat older cemetery has been excavated at the Bear Swamp site in Berkley, Massachusetts (Staples and Athearn 1969), and Dincauze (1975a:29) has reported a primary burial with red ocher and diagnostic artifacts from a shell midden on Boston harbor. So far it appears that cremation was the usual rule, a marked contrast with the burial programs of the Maritime Archaic. Moreover, the large pit with the 11 individual cremation burials at Wapanucket appears to have had either a fence or a roofed structure around it, something not observed in the Maritime Archaic.

LINGUISTIC PREHISTORY

There is general agreement among Northeast archaeologists that Algonquian is the older language phylum of the region and that Iroquoian speakers intruded at some point in prehistory. Beyond that statement unanimity disappears. Douglas Byers once suggested that Iroquoian was carried into the Northeast by the bearers of the Lamoka complex, a suggestion that Ritchie regarded as "dubious in the extreme" (Byers 1961:49; Ritchie 1969a:105). Tuck has argued more recently that the distribution of broad side-notched points in the Eastern Woodlands argues for an origin of Laurentian culture to the southwest of the area defined for it by Ritchie and that the bearers of this variant of the Lake Forest Archaic were early Iroquoian speakers (Tuck 1977:39). James Wright (1972b) sees continuity over time from the Lake Forest Archaic (or at least its Laurentian variant) to the Ontario Iroquois and therefore shares Tuck's view. Sanger (1975:73) extends this identification to the Maritime Archaic by speculating that "the inhabitants of Maine around 4000 B.P. spoke a language more closely akin to Iroquois than Algonkian."

Tuck's hypothesis is weak because it equates a major migration with the presumed movement of a single artifact class, broad side-notched points. It has been weakened further by the recent dating of Otter Creek points in the Mohawk drainage that makes them at least as old there as analogous points are elsewhere in the Eastern Woodlands. The evidence is no longer wholly consistent with the hypothetical movement of broad side-notched points from the interior into the Northeast. At the same time, Wright's and Sanger's views are based largely on general impressions and remain undeveloped as hypotheses.

The primary difficulty with any hypothesis regarding a Late Archaic introduction of Iroquoian langauages into the Northeast is that the period is too early to fit the independent evidence of linguistics. Floyd Lounsbury (1961:11), whose views in such matters are widely respected, estimates that proto-Cherokee and proto-Northern Iroquoian split 3500–3800 B.P. (1500–1800 B.C.). He has more recently extended this to "as much as four millennia [Lounsbury 1978:336]," but even this would appear to be too late to allow the proto-Northern Iroquoians to appear in the Northeast during the Late Archaic in the context of any of the three major adaptations discussed in this chapter. In addition, it seems likely that proto-Algonquian did not begin to break up into well-defined separate speech communities until around 4000 B.P. (Snow 1975).

A close examination of reconstructed proto-Algonquian words for key plants and animals indicates that its homeland was somewhere (perhaps everywhere) within the Lake Forest, Maritime, and Mast Forest regions as defined in this chapter. Because both species were known to them, we can be sure that speakers of proto-Algonquian did not range very far south of the distribution of tamarack trees or very far north of the distribution of beech trees. The zone of overlap is very close to the combined distribution of the Lake Forest and Maritime Archaic adaptations. Eastern Algonquian languages have not figured importantly in the reconstruction of proto-Algonquian words, so it may be that we have not given sufficient attention to the possible extension of the range of the protolanguage along the East Coast.

There is at this time no convincing evidence to indicate that Iroquoians were present in the Northeast during the Late Archaic. In addition to the lack of linguistic evidence, analysis of skeletal remains by contemporary osteologists has yet to yield any evidence of anything but a single biological population for the period. The best current hypothesis is one favoring the identification of all three major adaptations described in this chapter with Algonquian. The southern distribution of the Mast Forest Archaic along the coast is consistent with the historic distribution of Algonquian languages as far south as North Carolina. Moreover, the identification of any one of the three adaptations with Iroquoians would require not only a migration into the Northeast, but a subsequent retreat to the central and western New York, southern Ontario distribution of historic Iroquoians. The hypothesis therefore carries the burden of not one migration but two or more, too much for current linguistic or archaeological data to support.

As we shall see, both linguistic and archaeological data support a Terminal Archaic period intrusion of Iroquoian speakers. While there were marked differences in adaptation during the Late Archaic, we have seen that contrasts between whole cultural systems were somewhat blurred. In southeastern New England, where we might expect to see sharp contrasts, we instead see an eclectic blending of adaptations, and we must wait a few centuries for the necessary indicators of migratory intrusion to present themselves.

TERMINAL ARCHAIC

The period that I have chosen to call the Terminal Archaic spans the millennium from 1700 to 700 B.C. It contains what some archaeologists prefer to call the Transitional Period as well as centuries both before and after it that they might consider more appropriately assigned to Late Archaic and Early Woodland periods. The Transitional was first used as a period by Witthoft (1949) in an early chronology for Pennsylvania. Ritchie (1951) tentatively adopted the term 2 years later and still later made it central to his chronology for New York. By the time of Ritchie's 1965 summary of New York State prehistory, the Transitional had taken on the explicit characteristics of a stage as well as a period, and he defined it as "essentially preceramic" and marked by "carved soapstone vessels, together with new varieties of projectile points, including both broad 'semilozenge' and narrow 'fishtail' forms [1969a:150]." The stage/period was seen as technologically transitional from the preceramic Late Archaic to the ceramic Early Woodland via an episode of soapstone vessel manufacture.

Ritchie has defined his Transitional period as being only 3 centuries long, from 1300 to 1000 B.C. Defined that way, the period is marked at its beginning by broad point types, but at least some of these types also thereby characterize the last centuries of the Late Archaic (Kinsey 1968). Taken together, the various broad point types have been classified as constituting the "Susquehanna tradition" (Witthoft 1953). Yet the absence of soapstone from the earlier phases containing one or more of these related point types has caused them to be left out of the period by definition. In addition to including only part of the Susquehanna tradition, the Transitional, originally defined prior to the advent of radiocarbon dating, turned out to be unexpectedly brief as well. My solution has been to recognize the essential unity of the Susquehanna point tradition and move back the beginning date of the period to 1700 B.C. so that all its diagnostic types are included. As I will explain later, other considerations have caused me to move the end date up to 700 B.C. and to abandon the options of both cultural transition and evolutionary stage in its redefinition as the Terminal Archaic period.

The earliest point type in the Pennsylvania variant of the Susquehanna tradition is the Lehigh type. The Lehigh in turn is analogous to and generally regarded as derivative from the Savannah River point of the Carolina Piedmont. Coe (1964:118) dates the Savannah River point to around 1950 B.C., although more recent date determinations have cast some doubt on the temporal priority of the Savannah River type (T. Cook 1976:351). Regardless of derivation, the Lehigh point was made and used around 1700 B.C. and has analogue types in the Koens–Crispin type of the Delaware drainage, the Snook Kill type of eastern New York and western New England, and the Atlantic type of eastern New England (Figure 6.1). Independent dates on several specimens of these types are with few exceptions consistent with a period boundary of 1700 B.C. (Dincauze 1975a:29; Swigart 1974:25). Another apparent analogue is the Genesee point, which is found primarily in central and western New York, but which is also occasionally found in the Hudson drainage and other parts of eastern New York and western New England. They were once thought to relate to the Late Archaic period, but "recent discoveries in eastern New York have strongly indicated that Genesee points pertain, not to the Laurentian tradition, but to a very late Archaic horizon which post-dates the River complex and precedes the introduction of soapstone vessels [Funk 1976:261]." Funk further associates the Genesee with broad points of the Susquehanna tradition, but with nothing else that could not be considered standard Archaic equipment. Funk (1976:261–263) has tentatively defined this association as the "Batten Kill" complex. However, I see the complex as basically an early variation on the Susquehanna theme. Genesee points are often large, sometimes twice as long as Snook Kill points, yet there are morphological similarities between the two and intermediate forms as well. Funk is probably correct in seeing close formal connections between the two types, and Ritchie is probably correct in seeing the differences between them as primarily functional. Many of the larger Genesee points would have served much better as knives than as projectile points. The problem awaits the application of wear pattern analysis to both types by some enterprizing scholar. In the Susquehanna River drainage the Lehigh point is followed in time by the Perkiomen point, which is found sporadically in the Hudson, Housatonic, and Connecticut drainages as well. The Perkiomen is followed in time by the Susquehanna Broad type, which is found primarily in the Susquehanna drainage and is more thinly scattered eastward into western New England. The eastern New England analogue of the Susquehanna Broad is the Wayland Notched point (Dincauze 1968:25–26) (Figure 6.2). The end of the Susquehanna tradition is marked by the Dry Brook point type in the Susquehanna drainage and by the analogous Coburn

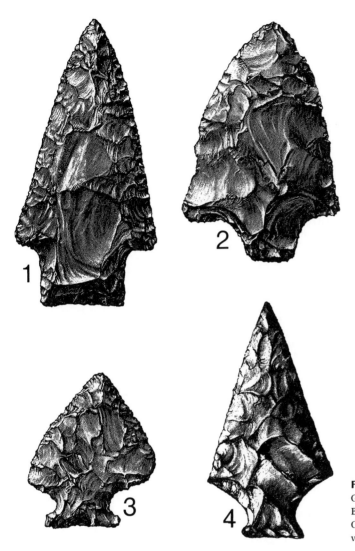

FIGURE 6.1. Some Terminal Archaic point types. 1, Genesee; 2, Snook Kill; 3, Perkiomen; 4, Susquehanna Broad. Shown at actual size. (From Ritchie 1971a. Courtesy of New York State Museum and Science Service.)

point in eastern New England (Dincauze 1975a:27). These last Susquehanna tradition types appear to have been made around 1250 B.C.

Thus, the Susquehanna tradition dominated the first half of the Terminal Archaic period. There are older dates for some of the early diagnostic types that might lead us to prefer an earlier beginning date for the period (Kraft 1970a:59), but these initial indicators from outside our area to the south have to be balanced against the delayed conclusion of the Late Archaic in northern New England. A date of 1700 B.C. remains the best current compromise for the period boundary in our region as a whole.

FIGURE 6.2. Terminal Archaic points from southern New England. Upper left point is 13 cm in length. Top, Atlantic points; middle, Susquehanna Broad points; bottom left, three Mansion Inn blades; bottom right, two Wayland Notched point. Shown at one-half actual size. (Courtesy of Peabody Museum of Salem.)

I have mentioned most of the point types that have been defined for the Susquehanna tradition to date, but there may be as many more types as there are archaeologists to name them. The variable of time, place, and raw material produced many variations on this essentially unified theme. It is important, therefore, that despite the number and variety of its constituent types, the Susquehanna remains a point tradition and should not be regarded as a whole cultural system persisting over five centuries. As we shall see, this caution is crucial for the resolution of a current controversy surrounding the nature of the spread of Susquehanna types into New England.

The latter half of the Terminal Archaic period is characterized by elements of the Orient complex, first defined on Long Island. The primary diagnostic is the Orient Fishtail point type (Figure 6.3), a narrow point that is usually made of quartz or quartzite. The favored form and materials are reminiscent of the narrow stemmed points of the Mast Forest (Late) Archaic, and there is evidence from southeastern New England that Orient points derive from that tradition (Dincauze 1975a:27). Moreover, this point tradition continues after the Terminal Archaic in the form of Rossville and Lagoon point types (Ritchie 1969b:224). Thus, it may well be that, while the Susquehanna point tradition flourished for only 5 centuries, the Mast Forest Archaic persisted into, through, and beyond the Terminal Archaic. In this sense, Orient points can best be thought of as an evolutionary variant of a longer tradition. Orient was therefore not an isolated horizon style.

Orient points are distributed primarily over Long Island, the Hudson drainage, and the drainages of southern New England. This is roughly equivalent to the distribution of the Late Archaic Mast Forest adaptation in New England. However, the diagnostics of the Mast Forest adaptation were

FIGURE 6.3. Orient Fishtail point. Shown at actual size.

entirely replaced by elements of the Susquehanna tradition in central New York and westward. We shall see that this new contrast between southern New England and central New York, which did not exist in the previous period, has implications for the cultural history of the whole Northeast.

Orient points and later types in the Susquehanna tradition are associated with soapstone vessels, which in turn were the primary diagnostic of the now-discarded Transitional stage. The bowls are usually oval to rectangular in shape, with flat bottoms and lug handles at the ends. They range in size from around 14 to 46 cm in length. The form suggests that the vessels were modeled after wooden prototypes. The bowls do not resemble the ceramic vessels that were being made in the Southeast by this time. The wooden prototypes, if they existed, have not survived archaeologically as far as we know, but there are examples of early historic wooden bowls that have generally the same shape and lug handles. Many soapstone bowls show cracks, lacing holes, and other signs of long use (Figure 6.4), and those that were used as grave goods were often "killed" by being deliberately smashed or holed. Not surprisingly, soapstone vessels are most frequently found in sites nearest the primary quarry sources of southeastern Pennsylvania and southern New England. The finished vessels are heavy and sources of the material (steatite) are not found elsewhere in the Northeast. Bowls from southern New England tend to be smoothed inside and out and have rounder bases than the less finished specimens derived from quarries in southeastern Pennsylvania (Ritchie 1969a:171).

Steatite bowls and fragments of them tend to be found in base camp sites along major streams, where canoe transport made use of the heavy vessels worthwhile, not with Orient and other associated points in more remote sites. Clearly the people who made, used, and traded these vessels had reached a point in the evolution of their settlement and subsistence systems where the use of heavy cooking vessels was advantageous. The innovation anticipated the introduction of ceramics at the end of the period. In fact, the steatite vessels were once thought to be evidence of the independent invention of ceramics in the Northeast. Marcey Creek Plain, a crude early form of pottery from the Potomac drainage that used crushed steatite as temper, was regarded as intermediate between the stone vessels and later more sophisticated ceramics. However, we now know that pottery was being made in the Southeast prior to 2000 B.C., and we no longer need independent invention as an explanation. Perhaps we have taken invention too seriously as a mechanism for change in any case. The stimulus of ceramics in some other part of the Eastern Woodlands could have inspired the beginnings of the steatite industry even though the immediate prototypes were probably wooden. Alternatively, the Terminal Archaic people of the Northeast may have reached a point in their cultural evolution where the use of stone bowls was advantageous and someone simply took advantage of the obvious. Certainly they would not have adopted stone vessels were they not ready to do so no matter how strong the stimulus, and it seems unlikely that they would have

FIGURE 6.4. Top: steatite bowl from Truro, Mass., 27 cm long. Shown at one-third actual size. (Bronson Museum). Center: large steatite bowl with notched decoration and mending holes, not to scale (Haffenreffer Museum). Bottom: steatite bowl with single lug, not to scale (American Indian Archaeological Institute).

gone long without having such a simple idea themselves once they were ready. The cultural system(s) of the Northeast reached a level of development during the Terminal Archaic that made the adoption of stone vessels advantageous. Whether the tiny flash of insight that led to their adoption came from within or without seems almost irrelevant when seen in that light. The replacement of steatite with ceramic vessels is a somewhat different matter, for pottery implies skill and knowledge about the properties of clay and how to take advantage of them. Yet even in this case it hardly seems relevant to spend as much time as archaeologists have debating whether the idea was homegrown or came from some outside source. We can at least discard McKern's (1937) hypothesis of an Asiatic origin and Kehoe's (1962) hypothesis of a transatlantic European origin for Northeast ceramics and concentrate on connections internal to North America.

Early ceramic bowls of the Marcey Creek type mimicked earlier steatite bowl forms. Examples have been found as far north as New Jersey. In our area the earliest ceramics make a clear break with the earlier soapstone technology, although a few sherds with crushed steatite tempering have been reported from the Connecticut drainage (Weeks 1971). The earliest specimens in Orient sites are pots with conoidal bases, which were built from coils of clay and malleated with cord-wrapped paddles on both interior and exterior surfaces. Ritchie (1959:39, 66–67) has named this initial type "Vinette I." Clay is available nearly everywhere while soapstone is not, so it is no surprise that this initial ceramic type is more widespread in aboriginal England than stone bowls. Crude as it is, Vinette I pottery represents a quantum leap of technology catching up with a new medium. This is not unusual in technological advances, and the result in this case was a much better vessel than would have been obtained by simply copying old steatite bowl forms in clay. While some archaeologists still see Vinette I as having been introduced from the North (Tuck 1978a:39), I think it more likely that its production in the Northeast was stimulated by prototypes to the South.

BURIAL CEREMONIALISM OF THE TERMINAL ARCHAIC

We saw in the last chapter that the people of the Late Archaic Mast Forest adaptation practiced cremation and were known to bury cremated remains in communal pits, often with red ocher and a few grave goods. These practices continued with some modification into the Terminal Archaic period. Cemetery features at Watertown, Massachusetts, include cremated bone, artifacts that are often broken and damaged by fire, and red ocher in some of the secondary pits (Figure 6.5). As earlier, the pattern is for there to be a large communal pit with several secondary pits for individual cremation burials. Although not all of the pits contain red ocher, nearly all have a basal fill of black, greasy soil that resembles rich midden soil, perhaps redeposited cremation residues (Dincauze 1975a:29). Ritchie (1969a:175–178) has observed much the same sort of evidence at Orient sites on Long Island. Although the Orient sites yielded both cremation burials and primary inter-

FIGURE 6.5. Shattered projectile point preforms from a single cremation burial, Turner Farmsite, Maine. Shown at one-half actual size. (Photo by G. Hoagland. Courtesy of Maine State Museum.)

ments, the use of red ocher, communal pits, deliberately broken artifacts, and ritual fireplaces is consistent with general practice during the period.

My own work on a Terminal Archaic cremation burial at the Eddington Bend site on the Penobscot River in Maine yielded similar results. The pit contained cremated bone, a basal fill of black soil, and broken artifacts of the Susquehanna tradition. A charcoal sample taken in 1970 yielded a radiocarbon date of 1480 ± 145 B.C. (SI-789) (Snow 1975:53). This and other supporting information from Maine is interesting because it suggests that, as the Maritime Archaic waned in northern New England around 1700 B.C., ceremonial practices of the southern New England Mast Forest Archaic spread north to fill the void, carrying with them the new projectile point types of the Susquehanna tradition. I see no reason to regard the mortuary subsystem as part and parcel of the Susquehanna tradition, for the latter is basically a point tradition from farther south and the former has clear roots in the Late Archaic of southern New England. Thus, while only the point types of the Susquehanna tradition are genuinely new in southern New England, the Terminal Archaic of Maine saw the introduction of both new artifact types and a new mortuary subsystem. To explore the significance of this contrast fully, we must return to a discussion of the Susquehanna tradition and the means by which it made its appearance in the Northeast.

EXPANSION OF THE SUSQUEHANNA TRADITION

One of the most interesting current debates in Northeast archaeology has to do with the nature of the Susquehanna tradition and the mechanism of its expansion into the region. We have seen that Orient Fishtail points appear to derive from types present in the earlier Mast Forest Archaic, although the connection over time is obscured by the dominance of Susquehanna tradition types in the region during the first half of the Terminal Archaic. We have also seen that mortuary practices of the period apparently derive primarily from those of the earlier Mast Forest Archaic. Nevertheless, the appearance of point types of the Susquehanna tradition creates an abrupt change in archaeological continuity, and the mechanism of that appearance is the point at issue.

Dincauze (1975a:27) notes that Susquehanna point types "spread at least as far north as the central Maine coast. No mass migration was involved, but rather an infiltration of small groups of people whose industrial traditions were markedly different from those of the resident populations. No evidence of assimilation of either group by the other has been found." Ritchie agrees with this hypothesis of peaceful coexistence: "That the appearance of this tradition did not 'swamp out' the 'small point' tradition is obvious from the continuum of points of the latter tradition in and above the strata where Susquehanna traits occur on the Martha's Vineyard stations [1969b:219]." Both Dincauze and Ritchie therefore interpret the evidence as indicating the coexistence of small communities of two different cultures in southern New

England during the Terminal Archaic period, a situation that has few parallels in the ethnohistorical record.

Rouse (1958) has suggested that there are five archaeological criteria that must be met before a prehistoric migration can be inferred. To meet those criteria the archaeologists must

1. identify the migrating people as an intrusive unit in the region it has penetrated,
2. trace this unit back to its homeland,
3. determine that all occurrences of the unit are contemporaneous,
4. establish the existence of favorable conditions for migration, and
5. demonstrate that some other hypothesis, such as independent invention or diffusion of traits, does not better fit the facts of the situation [64].

To these Sanger (1975) has added that one should

6. establish the presence of all cultural subsystems and not an isolated one such as the mortuary subsystem [73].

Looking at the problem from the perspective of Maine, Sanger concludes that each of the six criteria can be met for the Terminal Archaic in Northern New England: "The homeland can be identified; the chronologies are right; the environmental conditions for population movements are favorable . . . ; there is no evidence for an independent *in situ* development; and the numbers of traits including all subsystems examined suggest strongly actual population movement [1975:73]." The view is supported by Bourque, whose work at Turner Farm and elsewhere suggests genuine site-unit intrusion from the outside: "The intrusion of the Susquehanna tradition into central Maine seems, at this time, to represent the migration of substantial new populations into the area from southern New England [Bourque 1975:43]" (Figures 6.6 and 6.7).

Turnbaugh (1975) has a much wider perspective on the problem. He sees the broad point types of the Susquehanna and related traditions as representing implements adapted to the exploitation of migratory fish in the main Atlantic coast river systems. The evidence for this is found primarily in the distribution of the point types, which generally conforms to those portions of the coastal drainages that are open to migratory fish, particularly common shad (*Alosa sapidissima*). The technological advantage, facilitated by ecological and social factors, therefore led to the expansion of people carrying points of the Susquehanna tradition into the Northeast. "The appearance of the broadpoints seems to represent an abrupt cultural discontinuity. This broken sequence could be accounted for either by trait diffusion or by migration (the actual movement of people into the area). The migration hypothesis is favored in this instance, although no *major* population movement is necessarily implied [Turnbaugh 1975:57]."

FIGURE 6.6. Points of the Susquehanna tradition series from the Turner Farm site, Maine. Shown at three-quarters actual size. (Photo by G. Hoagland. Courtesy of Maine State Museum.)

Publication of Turnbaugh's hypothesis was followed almost immediately by a rebuttal by Thomas Cook (1976). Cook approached the problem by examining overall "Broadpoint Culture" in terms of 7 biocultural dimensions and 14 subcategories. The 14 subcategories are similar but not equivalent to the 14 categories I have adopted for use in this volume. Moreover, where I have discussed aboriginal cultures in terms of social, economic, technological, and mortuary subsystems, Cook discussed "Broadpoint Culture" in terms of stylistic, technological, adaptational, trade, mortuary, biological, and sociocultural dimensions. Nevertheless, the two approaches are similar enough to produce very similar results. "This dimensional analysis of Broadpoint Culture, as defined by Turnbaugh, did not exist. Moreover, the migration claimed by Turnbaugh on the basis of radiocarbon dates cannot be substantiated [Cook 1976:350]." Cook concludes that the widespread distribution of Susquehanna and other broad projectile point types was the

FIGURE 6.7. Points analogous to the Genesee and Snook Kill types of the Hudson drainage. Turner Farm site, Maine. Shown at one-half actual size. (Photo by G. Hoagland. Courtesy of Maine State Museum.)

consequence of a minor technological innovation that was adopted by a variety of local cultures along the Atlantic seaboard during the Terminal Archaic. The cultures that adopted the broad point types are simply too diverse in terms of other dimensions to allow them to be lumped as a single "Broadpoint" culture.

Cook's argument is very strong. There seems to be little evidence for migration in the overall spread of broad points along the Atlantic seaboard. Despite what she says elsewhere about small groups of immigrants, Dincauze (1972:59) also says that "Atlantic [phase] site locations and artifact inventory indicate a basically Archaic life style of mobile foraging, not obviously different from that of the preceding Squibnocket complex." In other words, there was no dramatic systemic change between the Late and Terminal Archaic periods in southeastern New England. But this does not square well with the equally strong arguments in favor of migration advanced by Sanger and Bourque. The solution seems to be that while migration cannot serve as a mechanism for the spread of broad points generally, it does fit the specific case for northern New England. While Orient points and mortuary practices in southern New England point to continuity from the Mast Forest Archaic through the Terminal Archaic period, the break between the Late Archaic and the Terminal Archaic periods in northern New England is sharp. The evidence is consistent with the adoption of broad point types of the Susquehanna tradition by people of the Late Archaic Mast Forest adaptation in the Hudson drainage and eastward through southern New England. This probably represented a technological advance that was part of an overall systemic advance that eventually facilitated the adoption of first soapstone vessels and later ceramic vessels. Meanwhile, in northern New England the Maritime Archaic appears to have undergone a debilitating readjustment at the end of the Late Archaic and either withdrew or was forced northeastward by the now dominant cultures of southern New England. The Terminal Archaic descendants of the Mast Forest Archaic flourished and expanded into northern New England, driving north the band of cultural transition that had stretched from east to west across the middle of the region in the Late Archaic. It may be that some local groups in northern New England were absorbed rather than displaced by the advancing southern cultural system, but the change was pervasive nonetheless. While there was continuity from the Late through the Terminal Archaic in the south, the change in the north at the period boundary was abrupt and complete.

Acceptance of a local migration hypothesis for New England while rejecting it for the East Coast generally leaves some untidy loose ends in Massachusetts and Rhode Island. A necessary correlate of the hypothesis is that there was significant population growth in southeastern New England while there was a decline through emigration or depopulation in northern New England. Expansion of the southern New England population northward and eastward into Maine would have entailed some change in the donor area as communities grew and split. This may explain the confusion in the archaeological record that Dincauze and Ritchie have each tried to interpret as the coexistence of small groups of people from different cultural backgrounds. Their scenario is unlikely, and any hypothesis that depends on it is equally unlikely. We will have to find a better model to explain the ferment of the Terminal Archaic in southeastern New England and the confusion it left in the archaeological record.

We cannot at the moment say much about the consequences of Terminal Archaic population dislocation for the historic people of New England. It may be significant, however, that the Micmac language "has undergone an extensive grammatical evolution that differentiates it from Maliseet–Passamaquoddy and the Abenaki languages [Goddard 1978a:76]." It may be that the depth of the division between Micmac and the other Eastern Algonquian languages of New England has something to do with the events of the Terminal Archaic, but much more will have to be done archaeologically with regard to cultural continuities in the prehistory of the Maritimes before we can devise reasonable hypotheses. We are on surer ground both archaeologically and linguistically to the west in New York.

Ritchie and Funk (1973:72) note that known Orient components are nearly all located near the seashore or major rivers, usually at locations that are protected from prevailing winds. Orient sites have so far not produced post molds or other evidence of house forms or distribution within settlements. Coastal site locations would suggest some dependence on fishing, but neither fishing gear nor fish remains have been found in these sites. Shellfishing was important, and the shell refuse in coastal sites should have preserved evidence of fishing if it was deposited in the first place. There is clear reliance on quahog and oyster, their importance relative to each other depending on local growing conditions (Salwen 1962). There was reliance on deer, turtle, and various birds as well (including turkey). Without question, hickory and other nuts were used too.

TERMINAL ARCHAIC CULTURAL SYSTEM

Seasonal movements probably took these people to interior camps during the cold months. Because Orient was originally defined on the basis of Long Island excavations, materials from these sites, which were probably occupied only during the summer, came to epitomize the phase definition. Because of this, Ritchie and Funk (1973:73) refer to Orient components in the Hudson Valley only as "Orient-like." I think it much more likely that these freshwater sites represent special-purpose sites of the same cultural system, not just the sites of interior cousins of fully fledged Orient people. Funk's (1976:266) inference that camps on bluffs along the Hudson were occupied during the winter is probably correct. Riverbank sites such as that at Schuylerville (Brumbach 1978) were probably spring–fall fishing stations at which migratory fish were harvested. Thus, the absence of fishing equipment at coastal sites probably indicates a clear separation of activities by season and by site location. That is, fish were taken during the fall and spring at sites where major tributary streams enter the Hudson, but were not taken at either coastal locations during the summer or at winter camps. Overall the subsistence system was therefore diffuse and carefully scheduled, a continuation of the pattern observed for the Mast Forest adaptation of the preceding period.

Little can be said of the social subsystem on the basis of present evidence. We can infer the continuation of a central-based wandering system of the preceding period. The household unit probably continued to be the single nuclear or small extended family, and the settlement units probably continued to be small but numerous.

The technological subsystem included the diagnostic steatite bowl (Figure 6.8). The bowls of aboriginal New England were smoothed both inside and out and in that regard contrast with those of central New York and the Susquehanna drainage generally. New England bowls were probably quar-

FIGURE 6.8. Trilobate steatite bowl. Shown at one-half actual size. (Courtesy of the Peabody Museum of Salem.)

ried from outcrops in Rhode Island and Connecticut. As elsewhere, the adoption of the bowls may have been stimulated directly or indirectly by ceramic industries far to the south, but the precise origin of the innovation is less important than its significance for the rest of the cultural system. The people of the Terminal Archaic period had clearly reached a level in the development of their system that allowed for and even encouraged the use of heavy cooking vessels. Their use implies that transportation from one site to another was easy enough and regular enough to permit such baggage. Most such movements must have been along mainstreams in reliable boats. Back-country sites are rare and soapstone bowl remains are never found far from main streams. Finally, all of this might indicate improved food preservation and storage techniques during this period, which in turn reduced the need for mobility during lean months.

Other artifact types include the Orient Fishtail point of the latter part of the period. This type or its immediate antecedents were probably temporarily submerged by Snook Kill, Atlantic, and other popular broad-stemmed types of the Susquehanna tradition during the first half of the period. Susquehanna Broad points and other diagnostics of the central New York Frost Island phase appear only sporadically in the Hudson drainage and eastward. Although Funk (1976:266) suggests that Frost Island components may yet be found in the Hudson Valley, I think it very unlikely, for these are primarily the remnants of another separate cultural system.

In the Hudson drainage, points of the Susquehanna tradition tend to be made of local cherts. Dincauze, however, remarks that points of the intrusive tradition tend to show "an orientation toward the lithic resources of the Piedmont province: fine-grained igneous rocks, slates and other argillaceous stones [1975a:27]." Orient points tend to be made of quartz or quartzite, as were the narrow stemmed point types of the earlier Mast Forest Archaic and the successor Lagoon and Rossville points of the period following 700 B.C.

The religious subsystem clearly derives from that of the preceding Mast Forest system. Large pits contain smaller secondary pits that in turn hold cremations and lenses of greasy black soil. Grave goods include red ocher, soapstone pots, fire-making kits, paintstones, gorgets, and projectile points. Pots are often deliberately holed, and all classes of grave goods are frequently broken and/or damaged by fire. We can infer burial programs that involved cremation or at least ceremonial fires, as well as the ceremonial killing of objects placed in the graves. The spread of these practices northward with an expanding population of southern New England people produced a striking discontinuity with earlier Maritime Archaic practices in Maine, a discontinuity that can be observed in other cultural subsystems, too, as we have already seen.

TERMINAL ARCHAIC IN NEW YORK

I have already noted that the Terminal Archaic in central New York is marked by significant departures from the Mast Forest and Lake Forest adaptations that characterized the preceding Late Archaic. The dominant phase of the early centuries of the Terminal Archaic is the Frost Island phase, characterized by Susquehanna Broad points, steatite vessels, and both Marcey Creek and Vinette I ceramics at some later sites. The mean of a sample of six radiocarbon dates on the phase is 1463 B.C. and the range is 1595–1290 B.C. The few burials we have found indicate that Frost Island burial programs involved cremation, but without the elaborate use of grave goods, red ocher, and communal pits of the Mast Forest Archaic and succeeding Orient culture of New England (Ritchie 1969a:163).

Frost Island steatite bowls tend to be unsmoothed on their exterior surfaces and in this and other respects resemble the bowls of southeastern Pennsylvania rather than southern New England. The implication is that trade and travel connections of the Frost Island phase were with the region to the south, primarily along the Susquehanna River. Indeed, the points and bowl fragments diagnostic of Frost Island are found primarily along the banks of the Susquehanna and its major tributaries and through the Finger Lakes (Lake Ontario drainage) district of New York. "Everywhere throughout its range the sites occupy a riverine setting, never far from the main stream, in fact usually upon the bank of the first terrace or the higher portions of the flood plain. Sites are small, indicative of mere camps, but they may overlap extensively [Ritchie 1969a:157]."

To the degree that we are able to compare them, the Frost Island cultural system shows significant contrasts with both the Mast Forest and Lake Forest systems that preceded it in central New York. The site distribution and inferred food resources are more strikingly riverine for Frost Island, perhaps further indication of the technological significance of the points of the Susquehanna tradition. The Frost Island system seems neither as diffuse as the preceding Mast Forest system nor as adapted to northern resources as the Lake Forest system. Technologically the broad stemmed points of the Susquehanna tradition contrast with the narrow stemmed points of the Mast Forest and the broad notched points of the Lake Forest, both in form and in preferred material. Most Susquehanna Broad specimens from central New York are made of impure calcareous chert that tends to leach to a light porous condition with time (Ritchie 1969a:159). In contrast with southern New England, there is no evidence in central New York for the persistence of narrow stemmed types through and beyond the Terminal Archaic. Adzes tend to be chipped and partially ground in Frost Island, in contrast to the more fully ground specimens of the Late Archaic. Frost Island steatite bowls are, of course, completely new. Finally, I have already noted the significant points of contrast between Frost Island mortuary site types and burial programs, and those of the Mast and Lake Forest systems.

Once again we appear to have evidence of population movement. The Frost Island phase seems to represent a complete cultural system that contrasts in most respects with those of the preceding period in central New York. Its connections, as evidenced by both point types and steatite bowls, are with the lower Susquehanna drainage in southern Pennsylvania. All dated components fit within a relatively narrow time range, and both the technological advantage implied by the broad points and the available environmental data indicate that there were favorable conditions for migration. Independent invention is out of the question and diffusion seems inadequate to explain such a sharp and pervasive change from the Late to the Terminal Archaic. Finally, to the degree that we are able to examine them, all four subsystems of Frost Island appear to contrast with those of the Mast and Lake Forest systems. The criteria for migration are all met.

However, we are still left with the need to explain why the carriers of the Frost Island system should have been able to displace the previous inhabitants of central New York. There are clues in the apparently less diffuse subsistence pattern and the strong riverine orientation. As with Orient, the use of steatite in this system implies less need for mobility, particularly in winter months, and by further inference the possibility of advanced food preservation and storage techniques. Such advanced techniques would also be consistent with a more focal adaptation, for it would eliminate at least some of the pressure for diversification. Surely this or some other competitive advantage must have been a factor if indeed a population replacement or even the submergence of one population by another took place in central New York after 1700 B.C. Once again we have an archaeological problem that demands the attention of a skilled and energetic researcher. Among the lines of evidence that should be investigated are those recently opened by Chomko and Crawford (1978). Their work indicates that domesticated squash from Mesoamerica was present in the Ohio River drainage by 2300 B.C. and that some locally native plants such as sunflower and sumpweed were being domesticated by 1000 B.C. The scene may have been set for these developments as early as the Late Archaic period, for there is evidence that the Canada onion (*Allium canadense*) was spread by hunter–gatherers of that period (Barber 1977). The flowers of the plant do not produce seeds, and it must reproduce exclusively from bulbs. It occurs naturally no farther north than Pennsylvania, but is still found growing on Late Archaic sites in Ontario and perhaps elsewhere in the Northeast. The implication is that Late Archaic people were establishing the plant at traditional camp sites either accidentally or deliberately and then exploiting the beds on subsequent visits. This would have established the plant as a semi-domesticate and provided its users with experience in the manipulation of food plants. Evidence from the Connecticut drainage indicates the use of goosefoot and/or pigweed (*Chenopodium* species) and American lotus (*Nelumbo lutea*). This evidence, which comes from a site dated to the Late Terminal Archaic time boundary, indicates that people were already gathering *and storing* plant resources almost as if they were domesticates (McBride 1978). It would have been a small step from this kind of exploitation of wild resources to the introduction of other wild plants beyond their natural ranges or the adoption of a true domesticate such as squash. We should not be surprised if we find that the people responsible for Frost Island were carrying such nonindigenous plants with them when they arrived in New York.

It is interesting to note that several archaeologists have invoked environmental, particularly climatic, change as a factor in presumed Terminal Archaic population movements. Sanger (1975:73) sees conditions in Maine as favorable for immigration, apparently on the basis of palynological work at Moulton Pond by Davis *et al.* (1975). Turnbaugh (1975) refers to both a general warming trend and the stabilization of sea levels as factors favoring the expansion of a dominant cultural system. However, our understanding of prehistoric climates and the environments they helped produce is poor. Moreover, our understanding of how those natural conditions may have selected for or against cultural systems is even less well developed. We cannot really be sure that a warming trend would enhance cultural development or movement. Recent analysis of records from A.D. 1816, the disastrous "year without a summer," indicates that in some areas crops of maize and buckwheat were wiped out but at the same time wheat and rye were unusually productive (Stommel and Stommel 1979). I doubt that we really know what effect a slight but prolonged change in average temperature or precipitation, or a change in their patterns, would have on plant and animal (including human) populations during the Terminal Archaic. For now we can do little more than establish that there were human population movements on archaeological grounds and assume post hoc that the environmental conditions of the time, which we perceive so dimly, must have been favorable for those movements.

Funk and Rippeteau (1977:55) have noted a sharp increase in the number of components per century for the Terminal Archaic period in the Susquehanna drainage. They discuss this as a Late Archaic phenomenon because they put the period boundary at 1300 B.C. However, by moving it to 1700 B.C. as I have done here, the apparent increase and subsequent decline in the number of sites per century fall around the period boundary. Not only are there more components per century at this time as compared to previous centuries, there are many more when compared to later centuries as well. Funk (1976:312) notes a similar pattern for the Hudson drainage at this time, and Dincauze noted the phenomenon for Massachusetts in an unpublished essay written in 1971 (Dincauze 1971b). Of course, no one claims that the number of components per century is an accurate indicator of relative population sizes. Terminal Archaic sites may well be better preserved and more visible than those of earlier periods, and band consolidation in later centuries could have reduced the number of components per century even while the population continued to grow. There are still other possible explanations, some having to do with the ways in which archaeological strategies might be producing the phenomenon of fewer post-Archaic components per century. There are several diagnostic projectile point types defined for the Terminal Archaic period, and thousands of specimens are known from hundreds of sites. By comparison, there are relatively few diagnostic types from more recent sites and some evidence that aboriginal preferences shifted to points of bone and other perishable materials after 700 B.C. Charles Fisher (1979 personal communication) has investigated the effects of selective bias against sites that do not produce diagnostic projectile point types by submitting samples for radiocarbon dating from such sites. He has discovered that many such sites yield age determinations that postdate the Terminal Archaic, and suggests that archaeologists may have contributed to the apparent scarcity of such sites in the record by simply ignoring them.

Edward Curtin (1979) has examined the problem from a slightly different perspective. He points out, as I have in Chapter 4, that "projectile point types do not unambiguously define populations or phases in a simple way [Curtin 1979]." Thus, identifying components on the basis of diagnostic point types and going on to inferences having to do with phases and prehistoric populations may be a satisfying but nevertheless misleading archaeological exercise. Curtin abandons as I have the notion that point types should occur within narrow time periods and consequently avoids a priori judgments about "good" versus "bad" radiocarbon dates except in those instances where they are so far away from expected ages as to suggest errors in association. Furthermore, Curtin assumes that an increase in the number of components per century could result from an increase in the number of different kinds of special-purpose sites as well as an overall population increase. Operationally, Curtin abandons phase designations, which are too often small time–space compartments defined by single point types and a few "good" radiocarbon dates. Instead he examines time as a continuous scale against which are plotted radiocarbon dates from the Susquehanna drainage in the range 1200–2600 B.C. What the analysis shows is not a sharp increase around the 1700 B.C. boundary between the Late and Terminal Archaic periods but a gradual increase beginning around 2100 B.C. that peaks around 1900 B.C. and declines to a stable level by 1700 B.C. The level after 1700 B.C. is noticeably higher than it was prior to 2100 B.C. even though it is lower than the 1900 B.C. peak. Analysis of site function shows that 1900 B.C. was also a time of diversification in site-specific activities, further reducing the probable influence of overall population growth on the master curve. Indeed, the analysis suggests that 2100–1700 B.C. was a time of considerable instability in the economic subsystem of the region. Curtin sees centuries following 1700 B.C. as more stable and indicative of the emergence of a new equilibrium in the economic subsystem. The first four centuries of the Terminal Archaic period are also a time in which there was important long-distance movement of chert, steatite, and other lithic material in the Susquehanna Valley and central New York generally. Both of these factors are consistent with a hypothesis identifying the Frost Island sites of central New York with an immigrant population from the south, a population that brought a new stability to the region after an episode of disruption and change at the end of the Late Archaic.

Similar analyses of the evidence for increases in the number of components per century in the Hudson drainage and elsewhere in New England might produce similar results. However, we must accept the possibility that there were fluctuations in population sizes throughout prehistory. More than that, we must be aware of the kinds and magnitudes of fluctuations that might have occurred so that we can deal realistically with that possibility when specific opportunities for archaeological testing present themselves.

We have seen that the Paleo-Indian population of aboriginal New England prior to about 10,000 years ago was probably not more than 25,000. The native population at A.D. 1600 was probably between 158,000 and 191,000. To find the rate of growth over 9600 years we can apply the equation

$$p_2 = p_1(1 + r)^t,$$

where p_1 is the initial population, p_2 is the final population, r is the average annual rate of increase, and t is time in years (Cook 1972:25). If we solve for r using the lower final population figure, we discover that $r = .0002$. A solution using the higher final population figure yields almost exactly the same rate. Either way the rate is shown to be exceedingly low. The world rate of population increase has recently been as high as .018, and Carneiro and Hilse (1966) see .005 as a low rate of increase. Using that low rate and solving for t shows that the aboriginal population could have gone from 25,000 to its A.D. 1600 level in a few centuries. An initial population of 25,000 would reach the 191,000 level in only 408 years at a growth rate of .005 and would reach 158,000 in only 370 years. A growth rate of .01, twice .005 but still modest by modern standards, would cut those times in half. Carneiro and Hilse (1966:179) conclude that the Neolithic population growth rate in the Near East was between .0008 and .0012. Taking the middle figure of .001 and applying it to our data leads to 2034 and 1845 years for the periods necessary for an increase from 25,000 to 191,000 and 158,000, respectively. The point is that the Late Archaic period lasted for 2800 years, more than enough time for the Indian population to increase from Paleo-Indian to historic levels, even assuming a very low growth rate. While we cannot be sure (and can even doubt) that the apparent surge in the Late and Terminal Archaic periods is evidence of population increase, simple demographic models suggest that it could have been a factor. Put in broader context, the figures show that at any time during 9600 years of prehistory the rate of population increase could have jumped from the very shallow slope projected by the apparent overall rate of .0002 to the steeper slope projected by the still modest rate of .001. This observation complements the point made in Chapters 3 and 4 regarding the potential for catastrophic drops in population. The overall picture is one of an *average* growth rate of .0002 for the 9600-year period, with occasional episodes of rapid growth and sharp decline. The straight slope implied by the .0002 growth rate in fact probably had waves in it, with some of the downslopes nearly vertical, and the increase of components during the Late and Terminal Archaic periods could be evidence of a major wave of this sort. Finally, it is clear that sharp increases and precipitous decreases in local population do not require migration for explanation. Thus, we need more analyses like Curtin's to test for changes in population levels and stricter application of Rouse's criteria as a test for population movement.

The issue has even broader implications. Anthropologists continue to debate the relationships between population growth and technological changes in food gathering and food production. The debate is often carried on in a limbo of imaginary carrying capacities (Cowgill 1975). Grayson (1974:36) has published figures that show that the most popular game animals alone would have supported 120 people for 100 km^2 in western New York, a higher density than the one I have proposed for the historic Mohawk. Given an abundance of other resources and relatively simple storage techniques, it seems clear that catastrophic discontinuities like those discussed in Chapter 4 and a variety of factors not related directly to nutrition must have contributed to the maintenance of stable populations far below the supposed maximum carrying capacity of the land. The debate has sometimes continued as if these complications did not exist. Moreover, there has been a curious polarization of opinion between those who see technological advances as causing population growth and those who see population growth as forcing technological change. The conflicting arguments between the Malthusians on one hand and the Boserupians on the other are curious because each side considers that one of the two factors is necessarily an independent variable, the heart of the disagreement being a simple but profound difference in opinion as to which one it is. Discussion of the debate is often framed in terms of this dichotomy and the need to choose between polar views (see, for example, Cohen 1975), an example of what Fischer (1970:9–12) would call the fallacy of false dichotomy. Such forced choices between extreme views do little to illuminate prehistory. In the case of population growth and technological change we see that there are waves in the general trend that suggest that at some points in time and space population pressure could have encouraged technological change, while at other times the relationship was reversed. Dumond (1972), taking a systems perspective, has argued convincingly for this broad and realistic view. This position is not a compromise but a recognition that there are no simple answers, a principle that underlies much of what is said in this volume.

END OF THE TERMINAL ARCHAIC

For as long as the Transitional has been used as a chronological unit in the Northeast it has been defined primarily on the basis of the presence of steatite vessels. This definition, with all of its evolutionary implications, has made the Transitional almost impossible to use as a period. Local groups adopted and then abandoned steatite vessels at different times such that no single pair of dates for the beginning and the end of the unit is satisfactory everywhere in the region. The Orient sites of the Hudson drainage and Long Island have long been assigned to the Transitional, which when used as a period is usually dated 1300–1000 B.C. Yet, of 11 radiocarbon dates from these sites, fewer than half fall before 1000 B.C. The mean of the 11 dates (themselves means) is 985 B.C., and the range is 1230–720 B.C. Meanwhile, the Meadowood phase, successor to Frost Island in central New York, has been dated at least eight times, including one date of 1230 ± 95 B.C. (I-6740) that is the oldest Meadowood date yet obtained (Funk 1976:278). The mean of this and seven other reported dates is 772 B.C., and the range is 1230–285 B.C. Yet Meadowood does not exhibit diagnostic steatite vessels and therefore is not classified as a Transitional phase. Therefore, as long as phases are regarded as normative and the Transitional is used as if it were a stage unit, no generally applicable ending date can be given it. Any ending date late enough to include most Orient age determinations will also include most of those attributed to Meadowood, and any end date that excludes most Meadowood determinations will also exclude many of those attributed to Orient. The problem is acute even though there are possibly still other older Meadowood dates and younger Orient dates that have not been reported because they were judged to be "bad."

Once again we must recast the evidence in terms of the realities of human behavior. I have chosen 700 B.C. as a convenient but not entirely arbitrary end date for the Terminal Archaic. Orient components in our region date from before that time, and what follows 700 B.C. is new to aboriginal New England. In central New York, however, Meadowood components begin appearing around 1250 B.C. as Frost Island components dwindle, and the Meadowood development continued there until at least 500 B.C. and to perhaps as late as 300 B.C. Steatite bowls were dropped from the inventory relatively early in central New York and replaced by Vinette I pottery, ceramics alone being found in Meadowood components. Ceramics replaced steatite in Orient components as well, but the transition was apparently more gradual and the disappearance of steatite bowls was later in New England than to the west. Meadowood culture therefore bridges from the Terminal Archaic to the subsequent period, the mean of a sample of eight dates attributed to it falling nearly on the period boundary. This development anticipated what would happen in aboriginal New England in the subsequent period, and in that sense, Ritchie, Funk, and others have been correct in discussing Meadowood apart from their discussion of Orient and the other developments of the Terminal Archaic. I follow them in this and discuss the Meadowood cultural system in the next chapter, where its religious subsystem is in better context. Orient, however, is entirely a creature of the Terminal Archaic.

LINGUISTIC PREHISTORY

I noted at the end of Chapter 5 that linguistic evidence would not support the hypothesis that Northern Iroquoian speakers entered the Northeast before or during the Late Archaic. Yet there is general agreement among linguists that they must have done so sometime after that period. Lounsbury (1978:336) sees the evidence "as favoring a long occupation of the area of central New York State and north-central Pennsylvania, extending back in time for perhaps as much as four millennia, with expansions or migrations first to the south and then to the north and immediate west." This is supported by Buell's (1979) hypothetical mapping of the proto-Iroquoian homeland based on key plant and animal species. Goddard (1978c:586) says that "the linguistic break between the last-named [Central Algonquian languages] and the other languages is abrupt enough to suggest that Eastern Algonquian has been separated from the rest of the family by intervening Iroquoian languages since the very earliest period of its development; the distinctness and internal cohesion of the Eastern Algonquian languages as a group rule out any possibility that the continuum of Central and Eastern languages could have been split by a northward movement of Iroquoian speakers after the Eastern languages had become differentiated." In another place he estimates that "they must have been diverging from each other for something on the order of 2000 years [Goddard 1978a:70]." In other words, the Eastern Algonquian languages were cut off suddenly from the other Algonquian speech communities at least 2000 and perhaps as much as 4000 years ago by intervening Iroquoians moving south to north.

Archaeologically, we shall see that there is continuity from the Meadowood system that succeeds Frost Island to the historic Iroquois, continuity that would have ensured the insulation of Eastern Algonquians from at least

1200 B.C. on. Thus, linguistics in prehistory is not necessarily the sheer speculation that some prehistorians insist it must be (Snow 1977b:109). In this case linguistic and archaeological evidence when considered together make a very strong case for the hypothesis that Iroquoians entered New York (if only from central Pennsylvania) during the Terminal Archaic period. When considered in light of my previous arguments regarding evidence for population movements during this period, it is clear that Frost Island sites contain the most likely archaeological evidence for that intrusion. As we shall see, its successor phase, Meadowood, has a wider distribution that includes western New York and the Mohawk tributary drainage of the Hudson, much the same distribution as the late prehistoric Iroquois. From this point on, the Mohawk drainage became archaeologically a thing apart from the bulk of the Hudson drainage, and the boundary between them became a cultural frontier that lasted 2000 years.

EARLY HORTICULTURAL PERIOD

The 1700-year period we now enter breaks with archaeological tradition, for it stands in place of two period names that have been used by archaeologists for many years. The replaced periods are the Early and Middle Woodland, and the reason for their replacement again has to do with an unfortunate confusion of periods with stages and culture types. The Woodland was first defined by McKern (1939) as a pattern, a culture type, marked by evidence of horticulture and ceramics. In the later centuries of its existence, the Woodland was paralleled by the Mississippian pattern, a separate culture type that never directly influenced the Northeast and so did not impede the conversion of the Woodland into a series of stages or periods here. Griffin (1967) uses Woodland explicitly as a series of periods, placing Early Woodland at 1000–200 B.C. and Middle Woodland at 200 B.C. to A.D. 400. Griffin uses the florescence of the Adena and Hopewell cultures of the Ohio drainage as respective determinants of Early and Middle Woodland as periods, thereby avoiding the complications that arise when the terms are used as culture types or stages of development. Willey (1966) attempts to do the same thing by defining Burial Mound I (1000–300 B.C.) and Burial Mound II (300 B.C. to A.D. 700) periods for the Eastern Woodlands. However, none of this wisdom has prevented others from confusing the issue by using these terms as if they were stage or culture type definitions. Thus, Early Woodland has sometimes been defined not as a period but as a stage of development represented by sites producing early ceramics and evidence of early horticulture. Though they might date to the Early Woodland as defined by Griffin, sites lacking evidence of one or both of these characteristics have often been defined as not Early Woodland. It has even sometimes been concluded that independent radiocarbon dating of such sites must be in error simply because the criteria for membership in the Early Woodland are lacking.

The knowledge that some local cultures adopted ceramics much earlier than others and that some without horticulture lived for centuries cheek by jowl with others having it has not prevented the confusion. One frustrated prehistorian has complained that "the definition of Early Woodland cultures in the Northeast has been one of the most perplexing, but perhaps least important, questions facing prehistorians for several decades. . . . The distinctions between Early and Middle Woodland are somewhat more numerous but unhappily no less confusing [Tuck 1978a:39]." Thus, Griffin's definitions have not worked in the Northeast because too many others have refused to abandon old concepts and use them as periods. Willey's period definitions do not work because they were developed for the Eastern Woodlands as a whole and do not apply well in aboriginal New England, where burial mounds were never as important as they were elsewhere. Finally, even Stoltman's (1978) recent revisions are unsatisfactory because, while they meet the needs of the Eastern Woodlands generally, they too fail to fit events in the Northeast.

So we have the Early Horticultural period, defined by the dates of 700 B.C. and A.D. 1000 (Figure 7.1). These dates are convenient because they separate contrasting cultural developments in time, but they imply no universality in those shifts. During this period many local cultures adopted ceramics, although some already had pottery before 700 B.C. and others may have postponed its adoption for centuries. It was also during this period that many northeastern cultures adopted a few cultigens, although we have already seen that a few did not do so until after the arrival of Europeans. I have specified that this activity was horticulture, not agriculture, because these people did not adopt animal husbandry and forestry, both implications of the standard definition of agriculture. Finally, I have called the period Early Horticultural using "early" only as an informative adjective and with the hope that no one will expect me to follow it with "middle" or "late" horticultural periods.

NEW YORK SEQUENCE   The prehistory of central New York is from this time on the prehistory of Iroquoian speakers. It is a necessary part of my discussion here because it provides contrast and background through time for the less well-understood New England sequences, and because it pertains directly to the Mohawk drainage. The first phase of the sequence is the Meadowood (Table 7.1), which derived from Frost Island in the Terminal Archaic period and held over into this period. Meadowood also expanded beyond the limits of Frost Island and became the first in the sequence to be strongly present in the Mohawk drainage. As we shall see, its mortuary subsystem was at first influenced by Glacial Kame practices from the west and later by Adena practices from the central Ohio drainage. The latter influences were so strong by the last cenuries B.C. that they were long regarded as evidence of a separate Adena-related phase in New York that Ritchie (1969a:201–205) named "Mid-

FIGURE 7.1. Sites of the Early Horticultural period.

TABLE 7.1
Phases of the Early Horticultural Period in the Hudson Drainage System[a]

	Mohawk drainage	Upper Hudson drainage	Lower Hudson drainage
A.D. 1000			
900	Hunters Home phase		
800			
700	Kipp Island phase	Fourmile phase	
600			
500			
400		Fox Creek phase	Clearview phase
300			
200	Canoe Point phase		
100			
0			
100			
200			
300			
400			
500	Meadowood phase		North Beach phase
600			
700 B.C.			

[a] Meadowood persisted from the previous period. Others had life spans of about 2 centuries. Each is an archaeological snapshot of a larger evolving cultural continuum.

dlesex." It is now apparent, however, that Middlesex was an Adena mortuary subsystem grafted onto the Meadowood cultural system, not the intrusive culture from Ohio that Ritchie and others initially thought it to be.

The next major development in the New York sequence was the emergence of the Canoe Point phase in the first centuries A.D. This phase appears to have developed out of Meadowood, It, too, has a distinctive mortuary subsystem for at least part of its life, in this case a complex related to the Hopewell developments of the central Ohio drainage. Hopewell developed as Adena waned during the last centuries B.C. Both spread and thrived as long-distance trading networks linked to mortuary ideology by way of the luxury grave goods that moved through the trading system. As with Adena-related developments in the Northeast, Hopewell-influenced sites were long thought of as being in a phase temporally separate from Canoe Point. It is now clear that once again a foreign mortuary subsystem was grafted onto an indigenous cultural system in such a way as to make them appear separate (Snow 1978c:88). Squawkie Hill (Ritchie 1969a:214–228) is therefore not a separate phase in the sequence, but the mortuary subsystem of the larger Canoe Point cultural system. It is less important than earlier Adena influence only because Hopewell never appears full-blown in the Mohawk drainage or eastward into the rest of aboriginal New England.

Canoe Point is followed by the Kipp Island phase in this sequence, which in turn is followed by the Hunters Home phase. The last takes us to the end of the period and to a series of major cultural changes that initiate the Late

Prehistoric Period. Thus, the New York sequence is defined by four phases for the period, the first two showing evidence of participation in a much larger trading network that centered first on Adena and later on Hopewell developments in Ohio. The second two phases of the sequence reflect the increasing isolation of the Northeast from the rest of the Eastern Woodlands as well as the beginnings of trends that eventually emerge as major elements of historic Iroquois culture.

Meadowood sites are found through western and central New York and into the Mohawk drainage. Many are cemetery sites. Sinking Pond and Nahrwold are seasonal camps, whereas Scaccia appears to be a central base camp (Ritchie and Funk 1973:96–116, 346–349). As with the preceding Frost Island phase, Meadowood remains rarely occur in small open sites or rock shelters away from main streams. Habitation sites contain storage pits and direct evidence of the harvesting and storage of *Chenopodium* and other plant foods. A post mold pattern at the Scaccia site indicates a 3.5 × 5-m house with a northeast–southwest orientation and perhaps doors at both ends. While Ritchie and Funk propose that all of this is evidence of a central-based wandering settlement system, I would add that there is a clear evolution in the direction of semipermanent sedentary settlement by this time.

Meadowood Cultural System

Much has been made for many years of the classic Adena house form, which is usually described as a structure that was round in floor plan, but having walls that sloped slightly outward. The outward sloping walls have been projected from slanting post molds, and their presumed aboveground structure has led to the further conjecture that the house roof had a conical shape. The resulting reconstructed house form has been illustrated in many books and articles, but no survival of it has been documented in the ethnohistorical literature. Sturtevant (1975) has recently challenged the reconstruction and has pointed out that the outward sloping post molds are consistent with construction details of the domed wigwam house that was in widespread use around A.D. 1600. It seems unlikely to me that the reconstructed Adena house that has been so widely illustrated was ever used in Ohio or anywhere else.

The Meadowood household unit was probably an extended family. The settlement unit was probably a lineage. Participation in the Adena trade network in the latter part of the phase has some implications for the social subsystem. Tooker (1971:364) has argued very persuasively that clans in North America "did not develop as a device to maintain knowledge of genealogical connections between lineages, but rather were a device to establish and maintain relationships with non-kin through the fiction of kinship. Certain features of these groups further suggest that they originally served to facilitate trade." Archaeological evidence for the kind of trade she predicts on ethnological grounds first arises in this period, and it seems likely that the origins of historic Iroquois clans therefore lie in this period as well. It is noteworthy that Adena and later Hopewell trade extended to the parts of the Northeast where clans were later observed to be well developed, but did not extend to most of aboriginal New England, where clans never developed fully.

The issue of the origin of clans is complex, and the archaeological means by which the hypotheses might be tested have not yet been devised. The debate is fraught with semantic traps, and the protagonists often unknowingly talk past one another. All must struggle to discuss native American customs in European languages (mainly this one) that spring from a very different conceptual tradition. Thus, the argument over whether or not clan members generally regarded themselves as having descended from a totem might seem to be a significant one to people raised in the European intellectual tradition where such distinctions seem clear, but make no sense at all in native American intellectual context. Another problem with the debate has been the tendency for scholars to argue from very different yet unstated premises. One critic suggests that Tooker's hypothesis gives no particular significance to the role of diffusion while another labels the hypothesis as diffusionist. The first appears to think of diffusion as an explanation in itself which needs no particular mechanism to be useful, while the second emphasizes the mechanism of trade as amounting to a kind of diffusion. The latter is nearer the mark, for diffusion per se is no more an explanation than is change per se in archaeology or ethnohistory. Tooker has advanced a hypothesis that proposes a trade network as the mechanism and vehicle for the emergence of clans and has done so on the basis of ethnological evidence alone. The archaeological data to test the proposition would appear to be at hand.

Diagnostic artifacts include the Meadowood point type and the Meadowood cache blade (Figure 7.2). The cache blades were apparently stored blanks, most of which were later converted to Meadowood points. The blanks and points were almost always made of Western Onondaga chert, which occurs only outside our region. Even those specimens found in the Hudson drainage are made of this material, indicating that Meadowood was never established as a resident system in the drainage. Vinette I pottery is also diagnostic of Meadowood, but it was apparently never used as a grave offering. Stone gorgets occur in several shapes, along with birdstones, adzes, and a few gouges. Tubular pipes, which mimic Adena stone pipes, were made of clay having the same paste characteristics as Vinette I. This is the first appearance of smoking pipes in the region, an indication that native tobacco (*Nicotiana rustica*) was being used in the Northeast. The native tobacco is more powerful than the variety sold today (*N. tabacum*) and in later times was linked to both public ritual and shamanistic practices. It seems likely that the pipes and the tobacco that must have accompanied them were ritually very important within both the trading system and the mortuary practices it served.

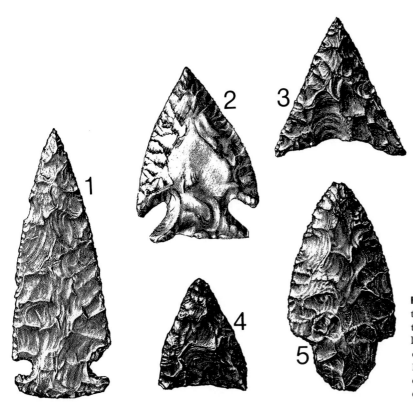

FIGURE 7.2. Central New York point types of the Early Horticultural period that appear sporadically in New England. 1, Meadowood; 2, Jacks Reef corner-notched; 3, Levanna; 4, Jacks Reef pentagonal; 5, Adena. (Courtesy of New York State Museum and Science Service.)

Both finished products and raw materials indicate Meadowood participation in long-distance trade. There are artifacts of purple marine shell, copper beads, tubes, celts and awls, chalcedony from Quebec, chert and steatite from Pennsylvania, banded slate gorgets, birdstones and boatstones from Ohio, points of Indiana and Ohio cherts, and tubular pipes of Ohio pipestone. Grave goods made from Ohio raw materials occur in inverse proportion to their distance from the Adena heartland: the farther removed the site the more frequent the items of local manufacture. Adena style points are sometimes found to be made of local cherts in the Northeast. These, the clay tubular pipes, and other copies of Adena artifacts are indicative of Adena influence that went beyond simple trade and exchange.

Early Meadowood cemeteries are comprised of individual grave pits, usually closely packed. Natural knolls were often chosen, as was the case for Glacial Kame burials. In some instances the graves were dug only on the east sides of knolls, and cemeteries were often relatively close to habitation sites. Cremation predominated as a method of disposal. Some cremations were carried out on recently deceased people, whereas others were carried out on dry bone, indicating that remains of the dead were probably saved for periodic burning and burial. Cremation was sometimes carried out in place, sometimes on stone crematories, in which case the burned remains were redeposited in burial pits. The burial pits were often lined with bark and the remains were often deposited in shrouds and with red ocher. Although pottery was never included, grave goods were quite variable. Nodules of graphite and pyrite were often included, as were points, cache blades, and the luxury items of both imported and local origin I listed earlier. In its later centuries, the Meadowood mortuary subsystem came to be so strongly influenced by Adena that we can consider it to have been transformed into a regional expression of Adena.

Adena Mortuary Subsystem

The heartland of Adena culture is the central Ohio drainage. Although there have been some claims that the Adena development began as early as 1500 B.C., Griffin (1975) has disputed them. Three Adena-related sites in the Northeast have produced 10 radiocarbon dates averaging 116 B.C., the two most reliable averaging 443 B.C. (Thomas 1970:76), and it seems clear that, whatever very early developments might have taken place elsewhere, Adena appears after the 700 B.C. beginning of the period here. It is now generally agreed that Adena sites outside the Ohio drainage heartland were the consequence of an extensive trade network in the Eastern Woodlands, which facilitated the exchange of luxury items used as grave goods as well as the mortuary system that served as an ideological base. The system can be thought of as a cult, and the grave goods the trappings of that cult (Figure 7.3).

An earlier development called Glacial Kame culture presaged Adena. The diagnostic artifact of this is the sandal-sole gorget, usually found with burials in natural glacial kame mounds. Most known sites are in southern Michigan and adjacent portions of Indiana, Ohio, and Ontario. Once again we are dealing with a mortuary subsystem and not a whole culture system; indeed, we have little idea what the rest of the system looked like. The gorgets themselves may have been archer's wrist guards rather than true gorgets (Haviland 1970; Peets 1965). Their discovery with burials in glacial kames originally sparked considerable speculation about the origins of mound building. The burials seemed older than those in artificial Adena and later mounds, and many thought that the natural kames were the inspiration for later artificial mounds. Like the development of pottery out of the stone bowl industry in the Potomac drainage, it seemed like a good idea at the time. However, we now know of many Late Archaic burial sites on similar natural mounds, and of artificial mounds dating back perhaps 7000 years (see Chapters 4 and 5), so things cannot have been that simple. Glacial Kame sites remain undated, although some archaeologists regarded it as older than 1000 B.C. on grounds that the burials contain no associated pottery. The problem with this is that it assumed that the people responsible for the burials did not have pottery, for if they did they would have used it for grave offerings. This is a dangerous assumption, for we have seen that the burials of this period often contain associated goods that were used for that (and

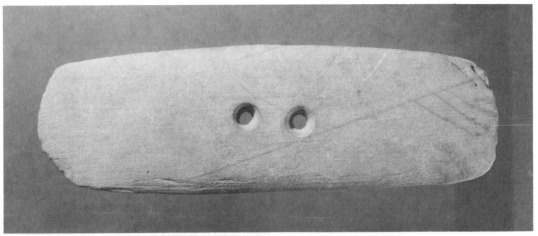

FIGURE 7.3. Gorgets. Top, 170 mm long (Bronson Museum collection). Bottom, 72 mm long (Rogers collection, American Indian Archaeological Institute).

only that) purpose, and everyday Vinette I pottery was kept strictly out of burial contexts. For the moment we can risk saying only that Glacial Kame burials are probably older than Adena burials in the Northeast and that they may well turn out to date to after 700 B.C. Indeed, Glacial Kame, existing as it did on the periphery of Adena, may have been contemporary with it.

The only Glacial Kame site reported for New England is Isle La Motte, near the northern end of Lake Champlain in Vermont (Figure 7.4). The site produced individual cremation burials associated with red ocher sandal-sole and other gorgets of shell, discoidal shell beads, copper adzes, and nodules of

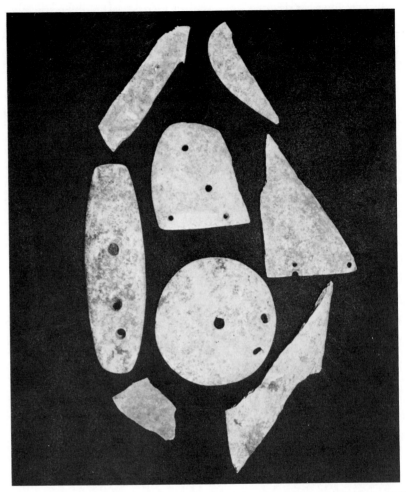

FIGURE 7.4. Marine shell gorgets and amulets from the Glacial Kame site at Isle La Motte, Vermont. Round gorget in center is 8 cm in diameter. Grave goods also included copper adzes, galena nodules, and discoidal shell beads. (Photo courtesy of Louise Basa.)

galena (a lead mineral) (Ritchie 1969a:132–134). Galena can be found in a portion of the northwestern Adirondacks, in the St. Lawrence drainage. Basically, the mortuary system at the site resembles that which came to characterize all of New England during the Terminal Archaic. In all likelihood, the Isle La Motte site was used by people influenced by others farther west. We may look in that direction for the source of the copper adzes and the shell gorgets, but we need not entertain any migration hypotheses. The adzes may derive ultimately from the older Old Copper developments of the upper Great Lakes, but copper implements like these persisted well into the period after 700 B.C. and do not necessarily indicate any greater antiquity. In fact, Ritchie (1955:36) has noted the influence of Glacial Kame burial practices on the Meadowood system, which dates to about 1200–300 B.C. This in turn further suggests that Glacial Kame was contemporary with or only slightly older than Adena.

Adena mortuary practices had a much greater impact in the Northeast than Glacial Kame. Sites, though few, have been found across southern Ontario, New York, and southern and western New England. Even more impressive is a series of sites in the lower Delaware drainage and on the Delmarva Peninsula. All are burial mound sites that contain artifacts diagnostic of Adena, some of which may be made of raw materials from the Ohio heartland. Adena sites have traditionally been defined in terms of a list of diagnostic traits, and a major goal of archaeological research in the Midwest for some time was to add a trait or two to this list. The traits include burial mounds, sometimes surrounded by ditches and earthen rings, log tombs, "reel-shaped" gorgets, tubular pipes, bear canines, discoidal shell beads, birdstones (Figure 7.5), copper bracelets and boatstones (Figure 7.6), and stone adzes. The complete list has risen above 200, but many of the traits are simply variations on a few basic themes, and as a whole the listing does little to illuminate Adena. Indeed, their use has to some degree impeded progress toward an understanding of the cultural system of which they were a part.

Ritchie and Dragoo (1960) analyzed the contents of 19 sites in New England, New York, and New Jersey, along with a number of isolated finds, in their monograph on Adena in the Northeast. They identify 7 diagnostic Adena traits at 9 or more sites. The 7 are blocked end tubular pipes (at 18 sites), leaf-shaped blades (10 sites), rolled copper beads (14 sites), copper pins (9 sites), *Marginella* beads (10 sites), cylindrical shell beads (11 sites), and red ocher (10 sites). Ritchie and Dragoo itemize 27 additional traits that are found at an average of only 4 sites each, 18 even less frequent Adena traits, and 41 traits that occur at Adena-related sites in the Northeast but are absent in Ohio Adena sites. Despite this variability, the authors hypothesize that the Northeast Adena-related sites were the consequence of the expulsion of Adena people from the Ohio valley by invading "Hopewell groups." The evidence, however, does not meet the criteria laid down in Chapter 6. Among other things, there is no evidence for the spread of a whole cultural system. The hypothesis was attacked almost immediately on the ground that "there is no appreciation [by Ritchie and Dragoo] that Adena is a functioning complex of some 800 to 1000 years duration, spread over an area 300 miles in diameter, which participated in cultural changes and complexes of many other groups over a much wider area [Griffin 1961b:573]." Ritchie and Dragoo's (1961) comment on Griffin's review of their work reasserts their view of Northeastern Adena as a complete cultural system despite the lack of any evidence beyond burial mounds and isolated artifact finds. They stuck by their interpretation despite the criticism by Griffin and the inadequacy of the evidence when considered in light of Rouse's criteria for migration. By 1970 statistical techniques were being rigorously applied in archaeology, and

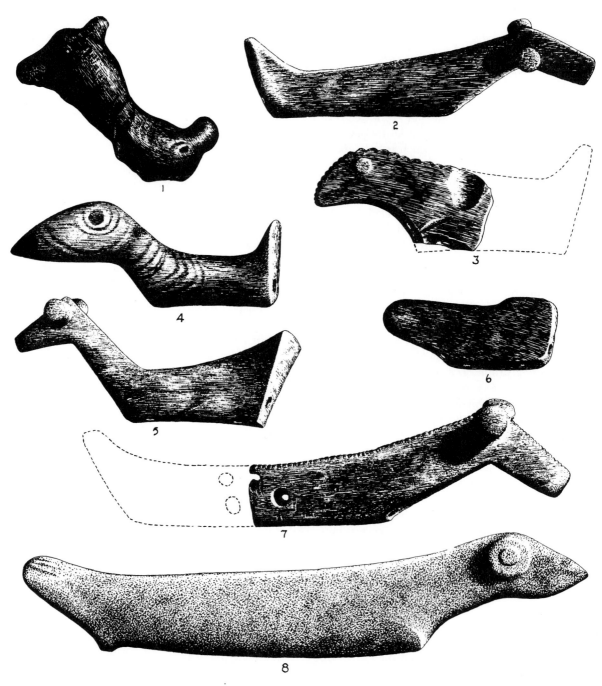

FIGURE 7.5. Birdstones, probably used as spear-thrower weights. 1 and 8 not perforated. 1, Brookfield, Mass.; 2–4, 6, 8, Narragansett Bay drainage; 5, North River site, Mass.; 7, Duxbury, Mass. Shown at three-quarters actual size. (After Fowler 1966:48. Courtesy of Massachusetts Archaeological Society.)

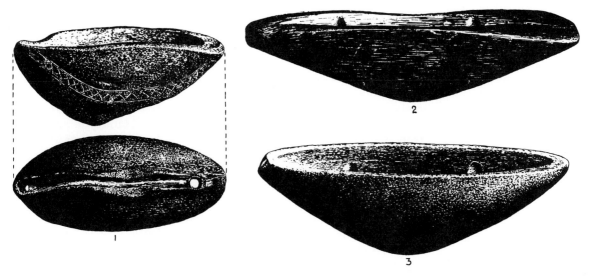

FIGURE 7.6. Boatstones, probably used as spear-thrower weights. 1, 3, Narragansett Bay drainage; 2, central Massachusetts. Shown at three-quarters actual size. (After Fowler 1966:49. Courtesy of Massachusetts Archaeological Society.)

Donald Grayson (1970) took a fresh look at the Adena migration hypothesis. Among its other faults, the master Adena trait list invites statistical manipulation, yet too many Adena traits overlap others in their definitions and sample sizes from Adena sites are uniformly too small for statistical analysis. The controversy is now largely behind us and most archaeologists, including Dragoo (1976), now agree that Adena in the Northeast was a mortuary subsystem grafted onto indigenous Northeastern systems. The vision of "ceremonial leaders who gathered their wealth of prized possessions when they fled the Ohio Valley [Ritchie and Dragoo 1960:64]" may be an exciting one, but it has little to do with either the evidence at hand or our general understanding of human behavior.

A much more reasonable set of mechanisms was suggested by Gary Wright (1972) for the later Hopewell development. As is the case for Adena, the heartland of Hopewell is in the central Ohio drainage. In this case, however, there are many more secondary centers scattered around the Eastern Woodlands. Raw materials appear to have come from several parts of the East, and finished luxury items were deposited with burials both in the heartland and in the secondary centers. Overall the evidence suggests a widespread network of trade, the center of which was in southern Ohio. Luxury grave goods were kept separate from everyday items, grave goods not normally being deposited in village refuse and everyday items not being put in graves. The network was maintained by steady demand, which in turn was sustained by the steady deposition of luxury items as grave goods. Secondary centers developed in areas that supplied raw materials or other unknown goods, and the whole subsystem was undoubtedly sustained by an ideological system that we can now only guess at. The exchange mechanism was probably either individual trading partnerships or transactions between kin group heads. At least some long-distance travel by individuals or small groups was involved, as evidenced by obsidian in Ohio that was apparently all imported from what is now Yellowstone Park, quite possibly as a result of a single expedition.

We can see the outlines of the Hopewell system more clearly, but the general structure probably characterized Adena as well, and may even have been the mechanism underlying the spread of Glacial Kame. It is interesting that, even though it was earlier and more weakly developed in the Eastern Woodlands generally, Adena is more strongly present in New England than the later Hopewell. Ritchie and Dragoo (1961:116) argue that dates from Northeast Adena sites cluster in time and are rather late relative to Ohio Adena. They, and later Tuck (1978a:43), go on to make the dubious assertion that this supports a migration hypothesis over diffusion or trade. Quite apart from the questionable logic of that assertion, eight dates from the West River, Maryland site range from 360 B.C. (2310 ± 200 B.P., M-416A) to A.D. 320 (1630 ± 400 B.P., M-418). This is a range of 680 years, wide despite the broad standard error allowed by the Michigan lab. The mean of the eight dates is 1985 B.P. (35 B.C.), and either this or the dates individually can be compared to a date of 275 B.C. (2225 ± 80 B.P., Y-933) from the St. Jones, Delaware, site and another of 610 B.C. (2560 ± 120 B.P., Y-1384) from the Rosencrans Ferry, New Jersey, site (Thomas 1970:76). These dates seem late when compared to Ohio Adena, but not brief. It seems clear that even in the Northeast Adena persisted as a mortuary subsystem for at least a few centuries. The interpretation of Northeast Adena sites as the remains of some sort of North American version of the Diaspora must be abandoned.

Canoe Point Cultural System

The Canoe Point phase is known primarily from a series of small temporary camps described by Ritchie and Funk (1973:349–352 with references). The use of storage pits continues. Although there are no known house patterns in New York, those found at the Donaldson, Ontario site were probably used in New York as well. The dimensions of the Donaldson houses are 5 × 7 m and 3 × 5 m, only slightly larger than what we presume to have been typical of the previous phase. Each had a single hearth, indicating that the household social unit was a single extended family. Subsistence, seasonality, and the larger settlement unit continued much as previously, although the settlement system was probably more decidedly semipermanent sedentary.

Projectile points are rare in Canoe Point, apart from a few Snyders points, which have clear stylistic similarities with Hopewell types, and a few untyped side-notched and stemmed specimens. Ceramics show technological advances over the previous phase and decorations including pseudo-scallop shell, dentate, complex dentate, and rocker stamping. There are rectangular stone gorgets and hooks, gorges, and beads of copper. There are no known locally made pipes, and all imported pipes occurred with burials. Other grave goods include a range of typical Hopewell materials such as platform pipes, copper ear ornaments, copper axes, pearl beads, and chipped knives of Ohio chert. Cut mica and sheet silver are also known, but Hopewell pottery has not been found in New York. Imported raw materials include Ohio chert and pipestone.

Ritchie (1969a:205–214) did much of his work on Canoe Point sites before the advent of radiocarbon. He excavated mainly small temporary camps which produced the assemblages described earlier (not including the itemized grave goods). He found few data concerning the burial practices at these sites, and it appears that in this phase burials were made some distance away from habitation sites. However, in the same general area he also found artificial burial mounds containing lavish Hopewell-related burials and grave goods. Since there was little or no correspondence between the artifact types found in the burial mounds and those found in Canoe Point habitation sites, he concluded that the mounds belonged to a separate phase, and this he named the Squawkie Hill phase. We now have four radiocarbon dates, two from separate components in each of the two phases, all of which fall within a span of 170 years, and all of which could easily date to about A.D. 200. Once again we have a mortuary subsystem that was so completely set apart from the rest of the cultural system that without radiocarbon dating we would hardly know that they were related. Burial mounds were situated away from habitation sites and the materials deposited in them were luxury items that almost never turn up in village refuse. Grave goods, whether locally made or imported from Hopewell centers, were conserved and used only as grave goods, while everyday items were not used in this context. The Hopewell trade network was much more extensive than the Adena in most parts of the Eastern Woodlands, but not in the Northeast. It never penetrated aboriginal New England to any appreciable degree, even though it reached its western boundary.

Kipp Island and Hunters Home Cultural Systems

The Kipp Island system flourished around A.D. 700, after the breakdown of the Hopewell trade network had been proceeding for about 200 years. The economic and social subsystems appear to have continued as in Canoe Point. Diagnostic projectile point types include Jacks Reef corner-notched and pentagonal types, with a few rare Levanna points. Clay pipes of local manufacture included both straight and elbow forms, and pottery was made in two or more corded types of the Point Peninsula series. Imported items included sharks teeth and pendants of banded Ohio slate. Platform pipes continued to be made, but it is unclear which if any of these were imports. Thus, although there was some lingering participation in long-distance trade, it was much reduced from the heyday of Hopewell. Cemeteries remained some distance from habitation sites, but there was no longer a clear distinction made between items used in everyday life and those deposited as grave goods. Furthermore, there was a shift away from cremation burials although some still occurred. There were now more primary burials, some of them flexed and in sitting positions.

The Hunters Home phase completes the trends of the period. The economic and social subsystems remained much as before, but with some important additions. Storage pits, which turned into refuse pits with use, were very numerous. Mortars and pestles were added to the artifact inventory and maize may have been added to the range of domesticated and semidomesticated plants. Only shark teeth persisted as imported items; Levanna points, corded Point Peninsula ceramics, straight and semi-elbow pipes, and crude maskettes, which make up the bulk of the diagnostic artifact inventory, were all of local manufacture. Burial mounds were no longer built by this time, and graves were once again located in or near settlements. Cremation was rare by now, and most burials were either primary flexed or secondary bundle interments. Grave goods of any kind were rare, and usually consisted only of elbow pipes and/or iron pyrites buried with adult men.

Sites of the Hunters Home phase date from 850 to 1000 B.C. With its end we reach the end of a major period of prehistory in the Northeast. New developments had already been under way in the Mississippi lowlands for 3 centuries, and their effects were about to be felt here as well. Those developments are the subject of Chapter 8.

NEW ENGLAND SEQUENCE

Events of this period in New England can only be understood in the context of the New York background just summarized. This is partly because outside influences on New England came largely by way of New York from this time on. Unfortunately, it is also partly because the archaeology of this period of New England prehistory is as yet only poorly developed. This is perhaps doubly unfortunate because this is the very period of prehistory for which a number of completely unsubstantiated claims for transatlantic contacts have been made. Celts, Phoenicians, and Egyptians are once again riding high in the popular imagination, and sober archaeology has produced less analysis than I would wish about the native American cultures that we know were here at the time. Nonetheless, enough is known to allow me to sketch the prehistory of the period, a sketch that contains no provision for currently popular myths.

In New England, this and the following Late Prehistoric period are sometimes defined together as the "Ceramic" period (Sanger 1979:99–114). Ceramics occur in some later Orient sites of the preceding period, in southern New England at least. Vinette I pottery (Figure 7.7) is clearly part of the Lagoon complex of Martha's Vineyard, which Ritchie (1969b:224–228) dates to 400–500 B.C. Smith's (1950:135) North Beach ceramic complex is probably contemporary with the Lagoon complex and therefore with the Meadowood phase of central New York. The early ceramics are often accompanied by Rossville and Lagoon points (Figure 7.8). The Rossville type is lozenge shaped, whereas the Lagoon type is slightly larger and has a lobate stem. Yet they resemble each other in that each is typically thick and crudely made of quartz, felsite, or (occasionally) chert (Ritchie 1971a:46, 123–124). Both types are found widely scattered in the southern drainages of aboriginal New England, Rossville points extending southward as far as Chesapeake Bay. It is

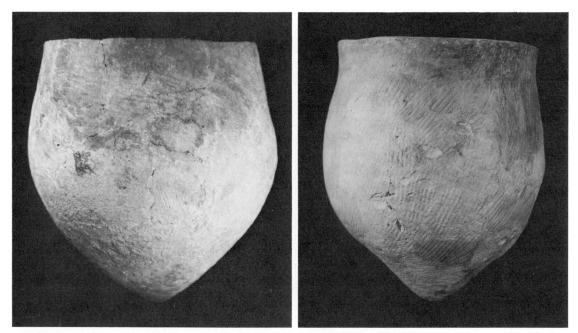

FIGURE 7.7. Vinette I vessels. Left, 30 cm tall, from Wareham, Mass. (Bronson Museum collection). Right, 24 cm tall, from Milford, Conn. (American Indian Archaeological Institute.)

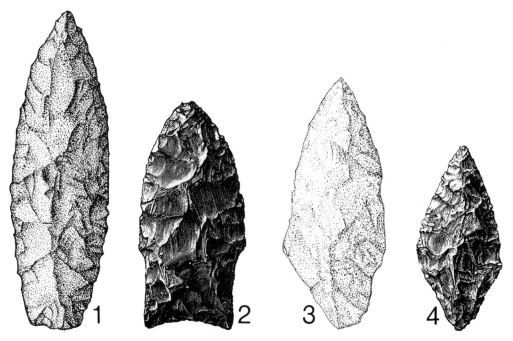

FIGURE 7.8. Early Horticultural period point types from the Hudson drainage. 1, Greene; 2, Fox Creek; 3, Lagoon; 4, Rossville. Shown at actual size. (Courtesy of New York State Museum and Science Service.)

curious that, despite their occurrence in the Hudson drainage, little is really known of the early part of this period there. This may be partly because the early centuries of this period are dominated by Meadowood and its Adena subsystem in central New York, and equivalent remains have been expected but not found in the Hudson drainage apart from the Mohawk tributary drainage. However, if Meadowood was carried by Iroquoians as I suspect it was, then we should not expect to find it in the main Hudson drainage. Neither should we necessarily expect to find a strong Adena presence at this time. Funk (1976:278) has noted the presence of Vinette I pottery at several sites in the Hudson Valley, just as Ritchie has noted the scattered distribution of Lagoon and Rossville points there. Perhaps once the search for Meadowood and Adena remains is set aside and attention is turned to the purely local evidence, the prehistory of the last centuries B.C. will seem clearer.

Southern New England

The cultural distinctions of the Late Archaic were largely wiped away during the Terminal Archaic. Except for the contrasting intrusive Meadowood culture of the Mohawk drainage and the possibility of some remnants of Lake Forest or Maritime Archaic adaptations in the north, aboriginal New England appears to have been dominated by variations on the theme of a single broad cultural system around 700 B.C., a system that descended from the Mast Forest Archaic of the Late Archaic period. After 700 B.C., however, we can begin to see the development of regional variation within this large system. Our knowledge is uneven, but for the moment southern New England apart from the Mohawk appears to be a single cultural unit during the Early Horticultural period.

The initial centuries of the period in the Hudson drainage were dominated by the North Beach cultural system. North Beach was initially defined by Smith (1950:135) as a focus, using the old McKern Midwestern Taxonomic System. Smith followed the practice of defining the focus almost entirely on the basis of ceramic evidence. The advent of radiocarbon dating and the well-known epistemological overhaul of American archaeology by Willey and Phillips (1958) led Ritchie and others to redefine North Beach as a phase.

There appears to be no doubt that North Beach descended from Orient. They have much the same distributions, both turning up frequently in the lower Hudson and Connecticut drainages and on Long Island. Smith (1950:150) saw the connection and, lacking radiocarbon dates and other information, suggested that Orient might be only the mortuary component of North Beach culture. Ritchie (1959) later clarified the relationship by demonstrating that Orient was an older and culturally complete phase. There are several lines of continuity connecting Orient and North Beach over time. The Vinette I pottery of Orient becomes a series of similar derivative types in North Beach. Soapstone pots with lug handles continue to be made, though not as frequently. Finally, there is continuity in the stemmed and side-notched projectile point types, particularly the fishtail form, which clearly derives from the Orient Fishtail type (Smith 1950:150).

It is difficult to sketch the North Beach phase given our present level of understanding. Most or all of the known sites are small coastal camps around Long Island Sound, special-use sites that presumably inform us about only part of the seasonal round. Smith's (1950:135) conclusion that "the principal means of livelihood was apparently the collection of shellfish and deer hunting" implies a focal adaptation that is based on excavations of sites such as North Beach, Matinecock Point, and Pelham Boulder. These are all sites of a single type that probably do not represent the total seasonal round, and generalization on subsistence based on data from them probably misrepresents a more diffuse overall adaptation. Certainly the presence of charred corn at the Matinecock Point site indicates that these people were in the stream of horticultural development at some time in the period. Charred beans were also found here, and it may well be that there has been some mixture from later levels. Cultigens may have been incorporated into the subsistence economy on a gradual basis through the period.

We know little of the full range of North Beach site types, house types, and their distributions. Consequently we know almost nothing about the settlement pattern and the social units it might imply. The technological subsystem is better known because the work of Smith and others has tended to concentrate on artifacts and typology. Smith (1950:135) lists the pottery types as Vinette interior cord marked, North Beach brushed, North Beach net marked, Matinecock Point stamped, Matinecock Point incised, and North Beach incised, none of them unexpected in the last centuries B.C. One unusual flat-bottomed vessel from the Throgs Neck site may have been the result of a rare attempt to mimic soapstone vessels. The Rossville point type dominates the projectile point artifact class, although point derivatives from the Orient Fishtail persist as a minority (Ritchie 1971a:46). There is the usual range of rough stone implements, to which soapstone vessels, cylindrical pestles, and crude hoes are informative additions. The first represent a survival from the previous period, while the latter two are further evidence of the new importance of horticulture. There are only a few tools of bone or antler, and Smith concludes that industries in these materials were only weakly developed.

What little information we have on mortuary practices suggests that these people favored secondary bundle burial of disarticulated bones (Smith 1950:135). Unless Smith was right about the possible temporal overlap between North Beach habitation sites and some Orient cemeteries, this indicates a shift away from the more elaborate practices of the Late and Terminal Archaic. Since the Adena–Hopewell pattern never became fully established in southern New England, it is no surprise that the North Beach practices presaged the simplified secondary burial rituals that came to be widely practiced by the end of the period. One of a few exceptions to this general observation may be the flexed primary burial found with Adena traits at East Windsor Hill, Connecticut (Cooke and Jordan 1972). The burial was associated with shell columella beads, *Olivella* shell beads, rolled copper beads, and a 22-cm knife made of what appears to be Flint Ridge (Ohio) chert. Thus, the Adena cult, which is solidly present around the same time in New Jersey and Delaware, and which has also turned up at the Boucher site in the Champlain drainage (discussed later in this chapter), makes a brief appearance in the Connecticut drainage as well.

North Beach is followed in time by Clearview. Smith (1950), using the old McKern system, calls them each a "focus" and combines them into the Windsor "aspect." Ritchie and others have adopted newer terms and refer to North Beach and Clearview as phases of a Windsor tradition, North Beach being assigned to the Early Woodland period and Clearview to the Middle Woodland period. As I have defined it here, the Early Horticultural period contains all of the old Middle Woodland and most of the old Early Woodland. Consequently, I see the North Beach and Clearview phases as parts of a single system that changed over the course of a long period. Like Ritchie (1969a:269), I see Clearview as still too poorly known to allow much description. Like North Beach, Smith (1950:134–135) defines Clearview almost entirely on the basis of ceramic evidence. The three pottery types Windsor brushed, Clearview stamped, and Throgs Neck simple-stamped make up almost the entire range of known types. While earlier North Beach types were all grit tempered, these are tempered by either grit or shell, with no clear preference for one over the other. Although much has been made of the grit–shell distinction in typological analysis, little attention has been paid to the possibility that the rise in shell tempering might be related to shifts in seasonality. The use of shell tempering might be related to where the potter was residing when the pots were made, but so far no one has devised an adequate test for this hypothesis.

The Clearview phase probably dates to the first few centuries A.D. To the north away from Long Island Sound, Funk (1976:287–293) has found evidence of a contemporaneous phase he calls "Fox Creek." The phase is named for the Fox Creek point type, which was previously suspected of dating to the latter part of the Paleo-Indian period. However, Funk's work has produced two radiocarbon dates for the phase, 450 ± 80 (Y-2349) and 410 ± 80 (Y-2350). Unfortunately, Funk has found relatively little ceramic evidence and has defined the phase primarily on the basis of lithic evidence. This has made it difficult to relate the phase to Clearview, which Smith defined almost entirely on the basis of ceramic evidence. Moreover, Smith reports no Fox Creek points in association with either North Beach or Clearview ceramics. Fortunately, Edward Kaeser's (1963, 1968) work has helped to bridge the gap. He has found Fox Creek points, which he calls "Cony" points, in association with Clearview Stamped, North Beach Net-Marked, and Abbott Zoned Net-Impressed pottery types. This shows that not only were the Fox Creek, Clearview, and North Beach phases linked within a single evolving system, but also that the system has connections with some of the remains found at the Abbott Farm site in New Jersey. The evidence from the present period at Abbott Farm is somewhat confused with remains from other periods, but there is evidence to indicate that styles there and elsewhere in the Delaware drainage were different enough from those to the east to indicate that there was a separate cultural system operating there. As we shall see, that system grew and expanded into the lower Hudson drainage after A.D. 1000.

The Fox Creek phase is defined on the basis of evidence from three type sites, Fredenburg, Westheimer, and Ford, which lie in the Susquehanna, Mohawk, and Hudson drainages, respectively. The fit with the riverine model is therefore not a good one. Nevertheless, the phase is basically a Hudson drainage manifestation, traces of which can be found in several other parts of the Northeast. Traces of the phases of central New York can similarly be found sporadically in Hudson drainage sites. These interpretations are useful for cross dating, but should not be allowed to blur our perceptions of intraregional variation. The Fredenburg site in the Susquehanna drainage is a small site only 10 m in diameter that Funk (1976:288) infers to have been a winter hunting camp. The Westheimer site in the Mohawk drainage is about four times larger, but apparently was used for only a few years as a fall–winter camp. Central bases like the Ford site appear to be consistently located adjacent to the Hudson River.

The technological subsystem in the Hudson drainage shows clear contrasts with its comtemporary in the Mohawk drainage. Pottery generally carries net-, fabric-, or cord-impressed decoration, and the resulting types are not a simple extension of the Point Peninsula series out of central New York (Figure 7.9). Perhaps because of intraperiod time differences, cord-marking is more frequent at the Ford and Westheimer sites than at coastal sites around Long Island Sound (Funk 1976:292–293). The Jacks Reef corner-notched and Jacks Reef pentagonal point types, along with the Levanna point type, are frequent in central New York sites around this time, but are minority types in the Hudson drainage. Instead, the period here is characterized by stemmed Fox Creek points, lanceolate Greene points, and the large Petalas blade. They seem to make their first appearances around A.D. 350, which may explain why they do not appear in the possibly earlier coastal sites investigated by Smith (1950). On the other hand, Funk (1976:292) has noticed a tendency for Fox Creek points to occur mainly on high bluff sites overlooking the middle Hudson, so there may be some functional connection between the points (which look like knives) and special-purpose sites. Their absence from low coastal shellfish-gathering sites may simply mean that they were used elsewhere for specific purposes. Similarly, Funk (1976:295) has noted the association between Petalas blades (Figure 7.10) and sea sturgeon remains and has suggested that they were specialized butchering tools. These huge fish were still being taken in the middle Hudson in the last century. Special equipment for dealing with this important resource would be no surprise, and its absence from both interior hunting camps and coastal sites is predictable. Further testing of Funk's hypothesis will be necessary, but for the present it appears to fit the evidence well.

Near the end of the period, the Fox Creek phase is replaced by the Fourmile

FIGURE 7.9. A rare zoned-incised vessel fragment from the Westheimer site, associated with a radiocarbon date of A.D. 450 ± 80 (Y-2349) (Ritchie and Funk 1973:133–148). Shown at three-quarters actual size. (Courtesy of New York State Museum and Science Service.)

phase in the middle and upper Hudson drainage. The phase dates to about A.D. 700. Once again we have a phase that is analogous but not equivalent to developments in central New York. Levanna and Greene points predominate, with the Jacks Reef types still no more than minorities. The Petalas blade is still present in this phase, still carrying with it its implication of an important sturgeon fishing industry. Storage pits, which appear sporadically in Fox Creek sites, were numerous, large, and sometimes deep by A.D. 700. At the Tufano site they ranged up to 2 m in diameter and 1 m deep. Funk (1976:295) suggests that they were used to store acorns, hickory nuts, and perhaps fish along with other gathered foods. However, the apparent cultivation of corn and beans at least at more coastal locations by this time suggests that the use of storage pits had an even broader application and that the ways in which they were used may have depended on season and site location.

Overall the archaeological evidence for the period in the Hudson drainage is unusually spotty and uneven. The situation is made worse by the publica-

FIGURE 7.10. Petalas blades from the Joy site, adjacent to the Dennis site, N.Y. All Normanskill chert. Shown at one-half actual size. (Courtesy of New York State Museum and Science Service.)

tion of that evidence in a variety of noncomplementary formats. Evidence from the Connecticut drainage is so thin that we can do little more than assume that it was substantially similar to that from the Hudson for the time being. While it is possible to use changing styles in lithic and ceramic artifacts to make finer temporal divisions for the period, such an exercise would scatter other lines of evidence even more by relegating them to separate compartments in time. Furthermore, it would obscure the essential unity of the period. Perhaps in a few years it will be possible to say much more about North Beach, Clearview, Fox Creek, and Fourmile as separate phases (if indeed they all are), but for now much more is to be gained by treating them all as distinctive nodes in time and space within a single evolving cultural system.

Southeastern New England lacks rivers the size of the Hudson and Connecticut, so the settlement trends of the period are more clearly toward the coastal fringe. There was probably the same gradual addition of cultigens to the system as we saw for the Hudson drainage, but attention to shellfish resources intensified as well. Ceramics, which were present here too by the end of the previous period, went through an analogous but not identical series of permutations during the course of this one. Unfortunately, the only attempts to classify and describe the pottery of this part of our region have emphasized their division into four broad classes called "stages," two of which apply to the present period (Fowler 1966:51–61). The only advantage of this imprecise system is that it prevents us from placing undue emphasis on pottery, something that has plagued New York archaeology.

Dincauze (1974:50–53) regards this as "a period of population decline and cultural fragmentation." It may be, however, that this is another instance in which we have been fooled by the number and variety of Terminal Archaic projectile point types and the sites producing them. We do not yet have unequivocal evidence that there was an absolute population decline, although we can be quite sure that there were some important adaptive shifts. The historic shorelines of southeastern New England had still not been reached in the last centuries B.C., but it is nonetheless clear that the human population was exploiting shellfish beds more than in previous centuries. Ritchie's (1969b:224–228) Lagoon phase on Martha's Vineyard dates to around 500 B.C., at which time oyster (*Crassostrea virginica*), quahog (*Venus mercenaria*), and scallop (*Pecten irradians*) shells frequently found their way into shell middens. With time, these species all but disappeared from the aboriginal diet relative to the increasing importance of the common clam (*Mya arenaria*). Both Ritchie (1969b:216) and I (Snow 1972:220) have suggested that the shift was the result of an evolution within the technological subsystem. However, Braun (1974) has since found evidence to suggest that rising sea level and falling seawater temperature through the period governed the relative availability of the shellfish species and therefore their frequencies as midden refuse.

Dincauze (1973) has examined several sites from this time level in the Charles River drainage of eastern Massachusetts. Here there is a strong association between sites and intertidal conditions on the estuary. Shellfish were gathered and their shells discarded in sites along the estuary, and, because the sea level was slowly but steadily rising through time, site locations were steadily displaced westward along with the shellfish beds. Few earlier sites associated with the intertidal zone have survived the rising water. However, sites dating to the present period and later show a clear association with shellfish beds, and both show a clear tendency to shift westward with rising sea levels. Braun (1974) has expanded on these observations by examining the prehistory of changes in average seawater temperature and their effects on the relative abundance of shellfish species. Braun applied an analysis of marine paleotemperatures by Andrews (1972) to the archaeological prehistory of Boston Harbor. Andrews' work indicates that marine conditions were colder than at present during the Paleo-Indian and Early Archaic periods, after which they began to warm steadily. They gradually became warmer than they are today and remained that way until the end of the Terminal Archaic, at which time they began to lower once again. The cooling continued through the Early Horticultural period and reached a low point around A.D. 1000, after which it rose once again to its present level. Thus, the period we are examining now witnessed a steady decline in seawater temperature from a higher than present to a lower than present level. This produced a general drop in the abundance of shellfish species that are sensitive to cold water conditions, namely, bay scallops, oysters, and quahogs. There was, however, a relative and perhaps absolute increase in the abundance of soft clams (*Mya arenaria*) over the same period. These changes in natural abundance are reflected in changing frequencies of their relative abundance in coastal archaeological sites. Ritchie (1969b:217) notes a sharp decline in the utilization of quahogs on Martha's Vineyard after the Late Archaic, but a slow increase during the Early Horticultural period. Utilization of oysters increased while quahogs decreased, but then apparently decreased as quahogs increased once again. While Braun's relationship of species abundance to seawater temperature appears to be valid, the data from Martha's Vineyard suggest that there are additional complications that we do not yet fully understand.

As in the Hudson drainage, Rossville and Fox Creek points predominate in period assemblages here. In addition to the small number of sites indicating sporadic contact with the Adena trade network, there is some evidence that the Meadowood culture of central New York acted as a kind of secondary center for southern New England. Meadowood points made of Onondaga chert from central New York are not uncommon here. A bit later in the period, Hopewell-related platform pipes (Figure 7.11) also made their way into the area (Dincauze 1974:51). There were also clumsy attempts to copy New York's Jacks Reef point types in local cherts (Figure 7.12), the results of which are found together with local untyped side-notched points in some sites. Ritchie's (1969b:245) Lagoon point type bears some superficial similarities to Adena points, but its technological links are clearly with the indigenous Rossville point. Taken together, it all suggests that in this period aboriginal New England was marginal to the mainstream of prehistory in the East.

The Early Horticultural system of southeastern New England was, so far as we can tell, not much different from that of the Hudson drainage. What differences there were probably derived from subtly different stylistic preferences, differences in local resources, and a greater remoteness from Adena–Hopewell developments. There is little to convince me that I should not describe all of southern New England at this time, from the Hudson drainage eastward, as a single cultural system. There were local differences to be sure, particularly stylistic differences, but we know too little to gauge their significance. Furthermore, it is unlikely that people on Cape Cod interacted regularly with people living on the Hudson, but they appeared to have shared a generalized system nonetheless. Goddard's (1978a:75) linguistic data show considerable unity within southern New England, and it seems likely to me that cultural fragmentation did not begin here until the Late Prehistoric period. In contrast, the cultures of the Delaware drainage and those of northern New England were already diverging from those of southern New England.

Within the economic subsysten, there appear to have been several site types. There were winter hunting camps on small streams and ponds in

FIGURE 7.11. Platform pipes showing Hopewell influences, all from Essex County, Mass. Smallest is 5 cm long. Shown at actual size. (Courtesy of Peabody Museum of Salem.)

back-country locations. In the Hudson drainage the Westheimer site appears to have been a fall–winter camp at which hunting and nut collecting were important. There were summer coastal camps at which shellfishing was an important activity, and there is evidence to indicate that corn was cultivated near these sites. There were central base camps along main river estuaries, the Ford and Tufano sites being prime examples (Funk 1976:70–89, 124–132). Nucleated semipermanent sedentary communities did not emerge here as they did in central New York through the same period, and the settlement system remained closer to central-based wandering.

We know almost nothing of the house forms or their distributions. A partial post-mold pattern at the Tufano site has led Funk (1976:78) to guess that an oblong wigwam was the rule, probably a safe bet. Food resources and seasonality point to a diffuse subsistence economy into which domesticates such as corn and later beans were gradually introduced. It seems likely that cultigens were tended around summer camps near the coast. Storage techniques improved through the period as indicated by the rising importance of storage pits, and it is likely that both domesticated and wild plant foods were stored. This is another point of contrast with central New York, where a more focal adaptation to horticulture was developing.

The Social subsystem probably had the nuclear or small extended family at its core. There is little to indicate anything more than sporadic contacts with the Adena and later Hopewell trade networks and consequently no reason to presume the emergence of clans through this period. Lineages probably existed, however, and these took on some matrilineal characteristics by historic times. The Mahican, who appear to have descended from this system, had some matrilineal tendencies, including clans, which they may have borrowed as social institutions from the neighboring Mohawk (Brasser 1978b:200). But most of these shifts probably did not occur until the Late Prehistoric period. Moreover, the other cultures of southern New England who also descended from this system were not so heavily influenced by the Iroquois.

The technological subsystem shows much less influence from Adena and Hopewell near the beginning of the period than was the case for central New York. The pottery types I have described carry many of the same decorative elements found farther to the west, but the vessels are not simple copies of New York prototypes (Figure 7.13). Instead, we have a series of indigenous New England types that have thus far been only superficially described. Point types include Jacks Reef corner-notched and pentagonal points, Fox Creek, Greene, and later Levanna points. The Petalas blade, with its possible specialized use for butchering sturgeon, is an important period marker. Storage pits also carry technological implications.

There are only a few scattered indications of participation in the Adena and Hopewell trade networks. There are a few known Adena-related burial sites and scattered finds of Adena points, blocked-end tubular pipes, and slate gorgets (Figures 7.14, 7.15, 7.16, and 7.17). Isolated finds of Hopewell-

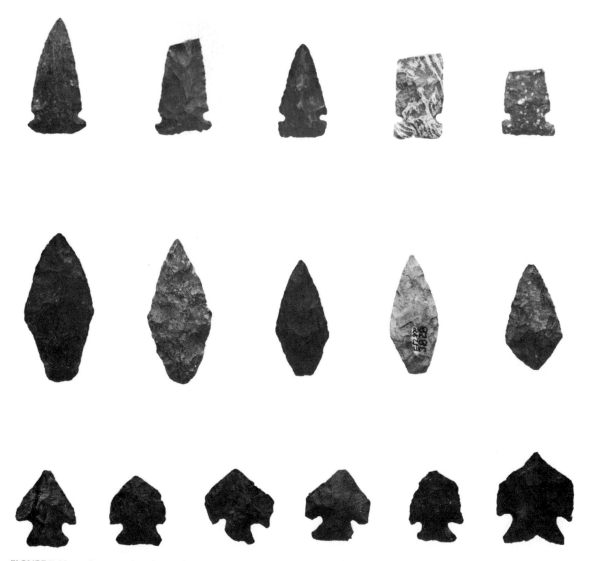

FIGURE 7.12. Early Horticultural period points from New England. Upper left point is 46.5 mm in length. Top, Meadowood points often made from Onondaga or other New York cherts. Middle, Rossville points. Bottom, Jacks Reef corner-notched points. Shown at two-thirds actual size. (Courtesy of Peabody Museum of Salem.)

FIGURE 7.13. Ceramic vessels from the latter centuries of the Early Horticultural period. Left, 21 cm tall, from E. Providence, R.I. Right, 21 cm tall, from Duxbury, Mass. (Both from Bronson Museum collection.)

derived platform pipes indicate a remote connection with that later network, but there are no outstanding Hopewell cemetery sites known.

Trade goods are not frequent, and artifacts appear to be made mostly of local materials. There are few items of either bone or antler even in shell heaps (Figure 7.18), where artifacts of these materials would have been preserved if present. This lack of bone or antler implements is another point of contrast with central New York, where they were preferred materials. A few clay pipes indicate that the smoking complex was present in this period, and tubular pipes have been found in the rare Adena burials to the north and east. But the practice seems not to have been as well established here as it was to the west at this time. Meadowood points made from Onondaga chert and Hopewell-related platform pipes provide some further evidence of trade contacts with central New York.

The ideological subsystem shows little or no sporadic participation in the Adena–Hopewell developments. The Tufano site yielded 24 burials, most of them flexed primary burials in shallow individual graves. There were some double burials and apparently a bundle burial. Grave goods were infrequent and limited to a few points, a pipe, and pendant. There was some use of red

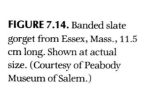

FIGURE 7.14. Banded slate gorget from Essex, Mass., 11.5 cm long. Shown at actual size. (Courtesy of Peabody Museum of Salem.)

ocher, but apparently no attempt to orient the burials in any particular direction. It is interesting to note that Funk (1976:77) regards the condition of the teeth to have been "abnormally good for an Indian population," further evidence that they still maintained a diverse diet.

Northern New England

At least for the present, it is unclear whether or not there was a lag in the spread of ceramics to northern New England. We can say only that they were introduced there sometime before 2000 years ago (Sanger 1979:99). Vinette I pottery was found by Byers (1959:244) at Ellsworth Falls, but it is rare elsewhere in Maine and northern New England generally, and Bourque (1971:252) concludes that it spread there late in its life, probably not more than a few centuries B.C. That puts the introduction of ceramics well after the beginning of the period in the north. By the time it became widely used in Maine, decorative techniques such as incising, dentate rocker stamping, and pseudo-scallop shell impression were part of the manufacturing process. Vessels of this period were generally smaller and more thinly walled than vessels of the Late Prehistoric period, and there was a preference for grit temper that was replaced by shell later on. Pipes are rare, but overall the ceramics of the period are technologically superior to those made after A.D. 1000. The significance of the contrast in ceramics between periods is not yet fully known, but it may be that a developing birchbark industry and changing seasonal movements played a role in the decline of ceramics. As I have suggested for southern New England, it may also be the case that the increase in shell tempering was a secondary consequence of a shift in seasonal settlement patterns. If coastal residence and pottery manufacture came to fall together in the seasonal round, shell tempering could have been one quite unintentional result. In addition, the smaller sizes of vessels made in this period when compared to those of the Late Prehistoric period suggest a change in the customary use(s) of pottery over time.

FIGURE 7.15. Unusual double-grooved axe from Wenham, Mass., 14 cm long. Shown at actual size. (Courtesy of Peabody Museum of Salem.)

Like Glacial Kame, the Adena network never fully penetrated northern New England. The Mason site in Maine, which Ritchie and Dragoo (1960) identify as Adena, is surely a Late Archaic cemetery. There are scattered finds of Adena artifacts, such as the tubular pipe from Weirs Beach, New Hampshire, and points and tablets from a number of other places, but almost no major sites. A very important exception is the Boucher site in the Champlain drainage of Vermont (Figures 7.19, 7.20, 7.21, and 7.22). The site is not far from the Glacial Kame Isle La Motte site mentioned earlier. The site was excavated by Louise Basa and others from the University of Vermont in 1973. Basa (1980 personal communication) reports that there were 92 features in

FIGURE 7.16. Finely polished birdstone from Wenham, Mass., 11 cm long. Shown at actual size. (Courtesy of Peabody Museum of Salem.)

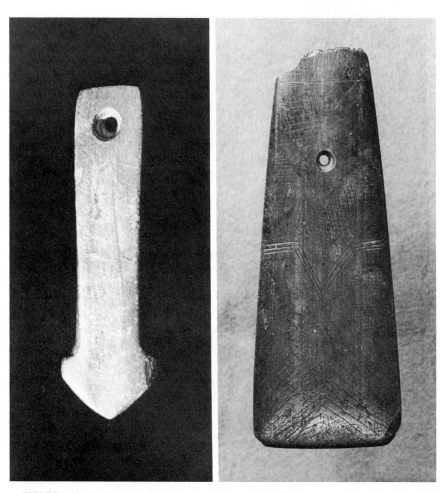

FIGURE 7.17. Holed pendants from early in the period. Left, 99-mm specimen from Southold, L. I. (Messenger collection, Garvies Point Museum.) Right, 131-mm specimen (Rogers collection, American Indian Archaeological Institute).

FIGURE 7.18. Elbow pipe made of antler spike, found in the Squantum Woods shell heap, R.I., 79 mm long. Shown at twice actual size. (Bronson Museum collection.)

the site, of which 69 were graves. Of these, 44 contained primary burials and 23 contained cremation burials. Two, therefore, contained both burial types. Of the remaining features, 4 were hearths and 18 were pits containing artifacts only. The site produced over 3000 beads of copper and shell. All or parts of over a dozen tubular pipes were uncovered, many of them made of Ohio claystone. Similarly, many of the chipped stone artifacts were made from New York or Ohio cherts. In contrast with mortuary practices of the Terminal Archaic, none of the artifacts, even those associated with cremations, was burned. Burials and grave goods were often deposited with red (hematite) and/or black (graphite) pigments. There were also occasional remains of cloth made from vegetable fiber, leather bags, cordage, beaver incisors, bear teeth and jaw fragments, dog bones, and even whole snakes and fish. Finally, the site has also yielded pottery, much of which fits the type definition of Vinette I. To our amusement, however, some of it is also incised with triangular decorations that many archaeologists presumed to have been a later development. Once again, types and the attributes that define them have lives of their own and do not necessarily conform well to the horizon style concept of mid-twentieth-century archaeology.

It is significant that Adena remains are so strongly present in the Champlain drainage while being scarce elsewhere in northern New England (Figure 7.23). There are other Adena sites near the shores of Lake Champlain (though none other as large is known), and the Glacial Kame site at Isle La Motte combines with these to suggest that people in this drainage were participating in an exchange network through perhaps most of the first 7 centuries of the period. Native copper artifacts probably came from the upper Great Lakes, and *Olivella* and *Marginella* shells probably came from

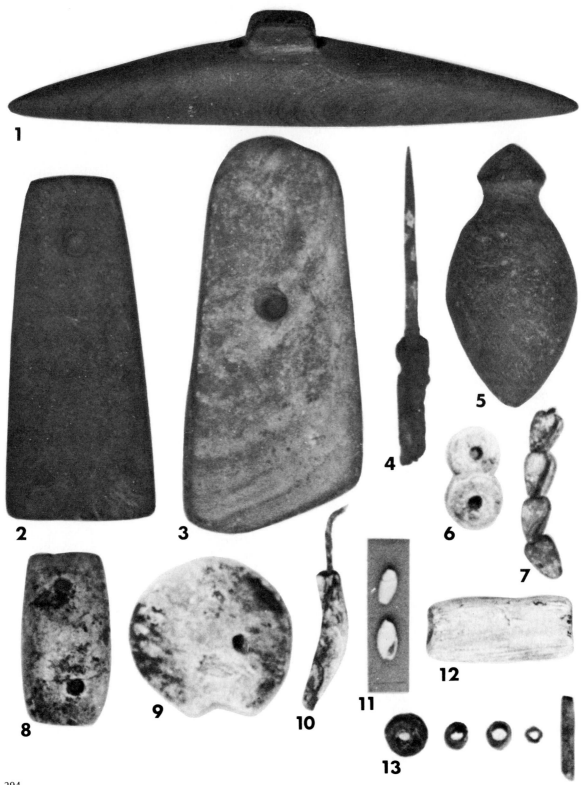

1

2 3 4 5

6

7

8 9 10 11 12

13

294

FIGURE 7.19. Adena artifacts from the Boucher site. 1, banded slate boatstone; 2, 3, holed pendants; 5, plummet; 8, prismatic gorget; 4, copper awl with handle; 9, shell pendant; 6, two discoidal shell beads; 11, two *Olivella* shells; 7, four *Marginella* shells on cord; 10, whelk (*Buccinum*) column bead on cord; 12, large whelk column bead; 13, five copper beads. Shown at actual size. (Photo courtesy of Louise Basa.)

FIGURE 7.20. Whole and fragmentary tubular pipes from the Boucher site. Stone or clay pills internally blocked the constricted ends of the tubes to prevent the inhaling of burning tobacco. Shown at one-half actual size. (Photo courtesy of Louise Basa.)

FIGURE 7.21. Selected points from Adena burials at the Boucher site. Side-notched and lobate-stemmed forms may link this development with the much older Maritime Archaic. Shown at one-half actual size. (Photo courtesy of Louise Basa.)

FIGURE 7.22. Vinette I rim sherds from the Boucher site. Filled triangle incising anticipates later ceramic motifs. Shown at one-half actual size. (Photo courtesy of Louise Basa.)

the Carolina coast. On the surface, Vermont seems a strange out-of-the-way place for these exotic materials to have come together, but it may not be so strange after all. Presuming that canoes were the primary means by which these and other exotic artifacts were moved through the Adena trading network, the Great Lakes, Lake Champlain, and the Hudson, St. Lawrence, and Ohio river systems were probably important routes of commerce. In addition, the Champlain drainage may have been the source of some desirable item such as graphite or bear canines. Unfortunately, the entire Adena network, within which the Vermont, New York, and New Jersey sites were all important nodes, still awaits the kind of locational analysis that could answer our questions about the system and its operation.

Ground stone implements are much less frequent in northern New England during both the Early Horticultural and Late Prehistoric periods than previously. Most late sites have a few celts and adzes, but they are smaller and less numerous than previously. This suggests that the construction of birchbark canoes grew in importance through the later centuries of prehistory here. By A.D. 1600, travel in bark canoes on fast northern streams contrasted sharply with the use of dugouts and overland trails in southern New England.

Artifacts of bone and antler are common in coastal sites where shell matrices afford good preservation (Figure 7.24). There is a wide variety of harpoon heads, bodkins, simple bone points, needles, awls, and fragments that were apparently parts of sophisticated composite tools. Beaver incisors were modified into cutting tools—sometimes hafted onto handles, sometimes left in the natural haft of a split mandible.

As in the previous period, the distinctive Kineo felsite of Maine was a preferred raw material. Although the primary quarry sites for this material are in the vicinity of Moosehead Lake, nodules of it can be found in gravels in many other parts of Maine. Various cherts were also used where they were available, and they predominate in those parts of northern New England where the tough green Kineo felsite was not easily available. "During the last 2,000 years two basic forms emerged; side-notching and corner-notching produced expanding stems, while other points were triangular with straight to slightly concave bases [Sanger 1979:110]." Bourque (1971:170–176) has attempted a preliminary typology of points from coastal Maine, but as with ceramics, most contemporary archaeologists in northern New England do not regard lithic typology as a panacea. While we are likely to see both ceramic and lithic analyses progress well beyond current levels, that analysis is not apt to follow the typological model established earlier by New York archaeologists.

FIGURE 7.23. Blocked end tubular pipe from Weirs Beach, N.H., 24 cm long. Shown at three-quarters actual size. (Courtesy of Peabody Museum of Salem.)

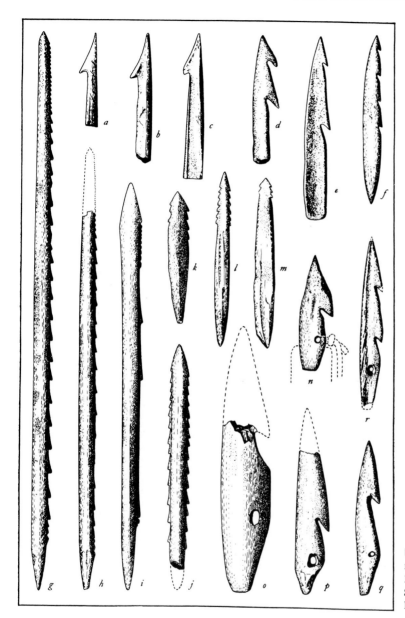

FIGURE 7.24. Spear and harpoon points made of bone and antler, all from coastal Maine sites. Specimen g is 30 cm long. Shown at one-half actual size. (After Willoughby 1935:215.)

The adaptation to shellfish exploitation is even more confusing in northern than in southern New England. The rise in sea level from Boston northward has been the result of progressive crustal downwarping in that direction. The farther northeastward one travels the more rapid this geological process has been and therefore the greater has been the total amount of submergence over the past 4200 years. At least 10.7 m of submergence has occurred in southwestern Maine during that time, yet archaeological evidence on the Damariscotta estuary indicates that only 1.2 m of it could have occurred during the past 2000 years (Snow 1972:215). The characteristics of the estuary are such that if the sea level were lower than 1.2 m below present mean level oysters could not have existed in its upper reaches, yet Indians were gathering oysters from this portion of the estuary at least as early as A.D. 340 and probably earlier. Farther to the east sea level rise has been more dramatic, many sites have been destroyed, and those sites containing evidence of shellfishing have much later beginning dates. The Grindle site on Salt Pond, for example, dates to the Late Prehistoric period because the clam beds that the people who lived there exploited did not develop until sea level approached its present level shortly before A.D. 1150 (Snow 1972:217).

Thus, in addition to changing seawater temperature, archaeologists studying this period must deal with sea level rise that was greater in some places than in others and faster at some times than at others. These forces caused changes in shellfish bed locations and changes in relative abundance of the various shellfish species. Indian populations responded to these changes, but during the period they were responding to other changes as well, and any adequate explanation of change in the system over time must account for all of them.

Domesticated plants were probably being adopted in southern New England during the period, but not in the north. Yet everywhere in New England this shift must have had at least indirect effects on the cultural systems. The northern communities adopted ceramics even though they did not adopt horticulture, and the ceramics of this period were superior to those made in the north during the Late Prehistoric period. Furthermore, this was the period during which relatively substantial pit houses were built on coastal sites in Maine and New Brunswick (Sanger 1971b). The houses, which appear to have been used during A.D. 0–1200, were first discovered almost a century ago, but were ignored by archaeologists until recently. They were apparently used along much of the Maine and New Brunswick coasts, but those of Passamaquoddy Bay are best known. They are semi-subterranean, ranging 10–60 cm in depth below ground level. They are always oval in outline, and range 3.5–4.0 m in length and a bit less in width. The best-preserved examples have sunken hearths near their entrance ends. There were apparently slightly elevated benches around the walls, and these probably served as sleeping areas. Post hole remains around the pits suggest that the houses were either wigwams or conical tipis that were made warmer and more permanent by excavation (Sanger 1979:107).

There was a major change in climate around A.D. 1000 (Wendland and Bryson 1974), and evidence that average temperatures up until that time were warmer than at present, an interesting contrast with the declining seawater temperatures through this same period. The improved climate for agriculture affected the St. Lawrence valley, for this was the period during which horticultural Iroquoian groups moved into that region. It may be that the previous inhabitants, whom we must presume to have been Algonquian-speaking non-horticulturalists, were adversely affected by the resource changes brought on by declining seawater temperatures.

In the Champlain drainage, the end of the period is marked by the Burnt Hill phase, similar but not identical to the contemporaneous Fourmile phase of the middle Hudson drainage. Funk notes that, while there was relatively little regional variation within the Hudson drainage at this time, the Burnt Hill and other ceramics from the Champlain drainage are quite different. "There are remarkably low frequencies of trailed, net-marked, plain, and Jack's Reef Corded types. On the other hand, scallop shell-like and dragged stamp decorative modes have the highest incidence [Funk 1976:297]." The latter techniques link the ceramics of the Champlain drainage to the Laurel tradition of Ontario as well as the Point Peninsula types of the lower Great Lakes. Laurel ceramics were almost certainly made by Algonquian-speaking potters, while Point Peninsula types are clearly associated with northern Iroquoians. There are some large village sites, mostly on the Vermont side of the lake, and many small lakeshore and streambank sites that were apparently fishing camps. Current work by the University of Vermont will clarify the settlement system. For the moment, it appears that there were nucleated semipermanent sedentary villages in the Champlain drainage by this time. Again, however, these Algonquian-speaking communities probably did not reach the level of nucleation we have seen for the contemporaneous Iroquois populations of central New York. The change in conditions around this time also facilitated the expansion of Norse immigrants to Iceland and Greenland, where their agriculture did rather well for a while. The Norse probably touched North America, so that both they and the expanding Iroquoians affected the people of northern New England at least indirectly. Indeed, analyses of seasonal animal species in coastal sites by Bonnichsen and Sanger (1977) and by Bourque (1973) suggest that during this period people were spending fall, winter, and spring in pit houses on coastal sites. They presumably spent the summer months taking salmon, alewife, shad, and eel at fishing stations on interior streams. Although smaller than Late Prehistoric settlements, the coastal sites were probably occupied for a longer period during the year and may have been more permanent than later coastal camps.

The evidence for this unexpected settlement pattern has turned up in the course of the excavation of coastal sites containing large amounts of shell refuse. The bones of fish, mammals, and birds are well preserved by the shell matrix, and many fragments allow species identification. Furthermore, many of the species are available on the Maine coast for only part of the year. Table 7.2 shows species frequently found in period deposits and the months in which they are most apt to be available. The data in Table 7.2 would be

TABLE 7.2
Seasonality of Various Species Found in Coastal Maine Sites[a]

Wildlife	Jan.	Feb.	Mar.	Apr.	May	June	July	Aug.	Sept.	Oct.	Nov.	Dec.
Mammals												
Deer (no antlers)		×	×	×	×							
Moose	×	×	×	×	×	×	×	×	×	×	×	×
Beaver	×	×	×	×	×	×	×	×	×	×	×	×
Raccoon	×	×	×	×	×	×	×	×	×	×	×	×
Black bear	×	×	×	×							×	×
Red fox	×	×	×	×	×	×	×	×	×	×	×	×
Harbor seal		×	×	×	×	×	×					
Sea mink (extinct)	×	×	×	×	×	×	×	×	×	×	×	×
Mink	×	×	×	×	×	×	×	×	×	×	×	×
Birds												
Greak auk (extinct)			×	×								
Goose			×	×	×							
Scaup	×	×	×	×								
Loon									×	×		
Black duck				×	×	×	×	×				
Black backed gull			×	×	×	×	×	×				
Great yellow legs					×	×						
Fish												
Sturgeon					×	×						
Alewife			×	×	×							
Bass					×	×						

[a] After Bourque (1973).

equivocal were it not for the repeated occurrence of deer without antlers and the fact that no very young animals (less than 6 months old) have been found. Thus, with the possible exception of the loon, which is known from a single fragment in one site, we do not find the kinds of animals we would expect to find had the sites been occupied during the summer. Had the sites been occupied from July into the fall, we should expect to find at least a few antlered deer remains and the remains of relatively young animals. A skeptic can argue that deer are harder to take during the summer and find other reasons to make a case for summer residence, or at least weaken the case against it. Nevertheless, January to June residence seems the most economical explanation of the data at least for the present.

The data further suggest that the Indians of northern New England spent the months of July through December along interior waterways. Sanger (1979:109) would restrict this generalization to the summer only, given his interpretation of Passamaquoddy Bay data suggesting coastal residence for all but the summer months. Interior sites are known, and they appear to have been chosen for their proximity of good fishing and without regard to protection from prevailing winds. Thus, the interior sites must have been occupied during warm months when breezes were, if anything, sought after. By comparison, the coastal sites almost always face eastward or southward with the land and the prevailing winds to their backs. Thus, Sanger is probably correct in seeing coastal residence in pit dwellings as predominating through all but the warmest months. Black flies probably kept people out of the interior until the end of June, extending coastal residence even more. Unfortunately, neither argument satisfactorily accounts for where the Indians would have been during the heavy spring fish runs. March is usually the month when the leanest part of the year ends, and the first green plants and migrating fish would have appeared around interior camp sites. We can hypothesize that between the spring breakup of ice and the onset of the black fly season families traveled briefly to interior locations from their coastal base camps to take advantage of spring food resources, but that extended use of interior camps did not begin until July.

An additional factor that archaeologists are only beginning to try to understand is the possibility that there were local systems of food redistribution. Harold McGee (1979 personal communication) suggests that there could have been such systems operating in the small coastal drainages of the Maritime Provinces and is designing research efforts to test the hypothesis. It is possible that families living at coastal locations exchanged goods with families living at interior sites and that their system of redistribution operated in place of scheduled seasonal movements by individual families. If not disproven, the hypothesis could help explain the emergence of near permanent coastal residence in this period, but it would also require an extensive rethinking of our assumptions surrounding seasonal scheduling.

Figure 7.25 can be compared with Figure 2.2 in Chapter 2. The latter figure

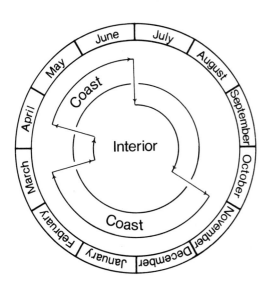

FIGURE 7.25. Hypothetical seasonal movements of a family in the Penobscot drainage near the end of the Early Horticultural period. The settlement pattern would be dual central-based wandering.

shows the hypothetical seasonal movements of a Maliseet family. Figure 7.25 on the other hand shows the hypothetical seasonal movements of a family in the same drainage during the Early Horticultural period. Both allow for easy trips to the interior by canoe when ice was not on the rivers, possibly a greater portion of the year in A.D. 1000 than now. Winter travel to the interior was on snowshoes in historic times, a technology that may not have been well developed before A.D. 1000. Moreover, there may have been less game, particularly moose and caribou in the interior during the warmer years prior to A.D. 1000 than after that time, and therefore less reason to penetrate the interior during the winter. Certainly the intensive exploitation of fur-bearing animals that began around A.D. 1600 was not yet encouraging people to spend their winters in the more remote interior portions of their drainages.

Leaving aside the poorly understood and perhaps unique case of the Champlain drainage, it is possible to piece the evidence from northern New England together as a single cultural system. We have seen that there were coastal and interior sites between which small communities appear to have alternated seasonally. Coastal sites were occupied in the winter months and tend to be located in places sheltered from the northern and western winds. Exceptions are those sites located near special resources such as rock outcrops. Interior sites were occupied in warmer months and tended not to be placed in especially protected locations. Relatively substantial pithouses were constructed at the coastal sites, whereas houses at interior sites were probably little more than temporary shelters. There was probably a relatively diffuse adaptation to food resources at both coastal and interior sites, although shellfish and waterfowl may have been particularly important on the coast and migratory fish particularly important in the interior. Despite its importance to the south, horticulture was not part of the subsistence of northern New England Indians. Although there is evidence that the birchbark canoe was being used by this time, the exceptional mobility of the Late Prehistoric period was not yet necessary. The settlement pattern appears to have called for only seasonal travel between coastal and interior camps, and daily movement in the food catchment areas around either of them would not have necessarily stressed speed or distance. Thus, the settlement pattern was dual central-based wandering in which the central bases were nearly sedentary communities.

The household unit probably continued to be the nuclear family. The settlement unit was probably a collection of such families in a cognatic tribal organization in which membership was based on family connections through either the father's or the mother's side, or perhaps even through one's spouse. There is little or nothing on which to base further inference.

The technological subsystem has already been described piecemeal. Its elements have a distinctly utilitarian flavor. Typology has been left deliberately underdeveloped by archaeologists here, and neither distinctive trade goods nor exotic raw materials played much of a role in the subsystem. The ideological subsystem was similarly unexceptional in this period. Adena practices reached the Champlain drainage but no farther, and cremation and secondary burial gave way to simpler primary interments early in the period.

LATE PREHISTORIC PERIOD

The six centuries that followed A.D. 1000 stand apart from previous centuries. The Late Prehistoric period was initiated by profound changes in the cultural systems of New England, which we are only beginning to understand. Warmer conditions around A.D. 1000 opened up some northern areas to plant cultivation. This was the attraction that drew the Norse westward to Iceland, Greenland, and beyond. Closer to New England, Iroquoian-speaking communities split off from Pickering culture just north to Lake Ontario and moved northeastward to sites along the St. Lawrence estuary. There they became the Laurentian Iroquois that were encountered by Cartier and other early explorers. Parallel movements took place in southern New England.

While warmer conditions and the resulting longer growing season may have provided an attractive "carrot" early in this period, there was also the "stick" of population pressure and conflict to the southwest. The combination of attractive and repulsive forces produced a general northeastward slippage of populations through the last six centuries of prehistory. Dispersed settlement became nucleated into few but larger villages in areas where conflict was substantial. Village sites in these areas shifted to defensible locations. While canoe travel remained important in northern New England, it was gradually replaced by the use of overland trails in the horticultural south. The decreased importance of streams as avenues of travel in southern New England facilitated the northeastward shift of populations and led to the blurring of what had been a much closer correspondence of cultural and drainage boundaries. Some of the prehistoric Munsee shifted eastward out of the upper Delaware drainage, into the lower Hudson drainage and onto the western end of Long Island. Some of the prehistoric Massachusett moved northeastward into the lower Merrimack drainage and beyond as far as southwestern Maine, where horticulture was viable. The previous inhabitants of these areas appear to have contracted into smaller though still large portions of their previous territories. The potential for further shifts of this sort can be seen in the population figures for A.D. 1600 discussed in Chapter 2. Even after expanding northeastward, the Massachusett still had a population density almost nine times that of the Western Abenaki they had displaced. Similarly, the Munsee in A.D. 1600 had a population three to six times as dense as that of the Mahican, from whom they had apparently taken the southern Hudson drainage. Thus, the potential expansion of these southern New England horticulturalists may have been limited only by the environmental constraints on cultigens before Europeans and their diseases turned the world upside down.

The movement of Iroquoians into the lower St. Lawrence valley during this period cut the Champlain valley inhabitants off from their northern connections. There is little evidence from the Champlain drainage that can be indisputably assigned to this period, and it may well be that it became a backwater. The role of the Hudson–Champlain corridor as a link between the mid-Atlantic and the St. Lawrence valley appears to have grown at the expense of earlier cultural distinctions between the Hudson and Champlain drainages. Many inhabitants of the Champlain drainage may have been absorbed by the Hudson or other neighboring drainage areas as the Champlain itself became a buffer zone, a status it apparently had by around A.D. 1600. This hypothetical depopulation of the Champlain drainage is clearly a regional problem that cannot be addressed through the examination of Lake Champlain sites alone. However, continued investigation into the prehistory of this period in the lower St. Lawrence, Hudson, and Connecticut drainages will, when analyzed together, afford us some understanding of late prehistoric demographic shifts. Archaeology has always had difficulty dealing with negative evidence, it being easier to talk about the distributions of communities than the empty spaces between them. The riverine model for aboriginal New England has helped us to break loose from that difficulty by designating highlands as both boundary and buffer zones. With the end of the Late Prehistoric period we see the expansion of a buffer zone and the distortion of the model such that the entire Champlain drainage appears to have been occupied by no one but traveled by everyone. Continued representation of the Champlain drainage at this time as a blank space on chronological charts implies that we simply have yet to find evidence we presume is there, an implication that we should explicitly abandon.

NEW YORK SEQUENCE   As in the previous period, the forces of change tended to radiate from the west and south. Because of this, and because so much is known of New York prehistory, it is appropriate to discuss this sequence first as a backdrop for the Late Prehistoric period in aboriginal New England. In the Mohawk drainage and the adjacent Finger Lakes drainages there is a shared sequence of six phases for this period. The first three of these, Carpenter Brook,

Canandaigua, and Castle Creek, are usually classed together as phases of the Owasco tradition (Table 8.1). These phases, and the tradition they define, are separated from the final three phases of the sequence by a transition around A.D. 1300. The final three phases are Oak Hill, Chance, and Garoga, and together they make up the Iroquois tradition. The sequence of three Owasco and three Iroquois phases stems from the earlier Point Peninsula series of phases, and there can be no doubt that Northern Iroquoians were responsible for the entire developmental sequence. The Chance phase was the penultimate prehistoric base from which all five Iroquois nations originated. The Garoga phase is found only in the Mohawk drainage and is ancestral to the historic Mohawk only, but analogous phases could be defined for the latest prehistoric phases of the other four Iroquois nations as well.

It should be noted that, even though we still cannot distinguish clearly among the Five Nations at this time on the basis of archaeological evidence, linguistic evidence indicates that there was already some divergence. But this this needs to be qualified. While the model of historical linguistics infers the descent of the languages of the Five Iroquois Nations from a single protolanguage, the archaeological evidence once again suggests a somewhat different process. Prior to this final period of prehistory, small loosely related communities of Iroquoian people were scattered across much of New York. Village nucleation after A.D. 1000 drew them into five village clusters that we eventually came to know as the Mohawk and the other four Iroquois nations. Within each such cluster, the dialectical variation among the earlier smaller communities must have been standardized into a single language. Thus, it was not so much that the languages of the Five Nations derived from a common protolanguage so much as they emerged from a common pool of Iroquois dialects, much as the modern Romance languages arose through

TABLE 8.1
Late Prehistoric Period Traditions and Phases of the Mohawk Drainage[a]

A.D. 1600	Mohawk
1500	Garoga
	Chance
1400	IROQUOIS TRADITION
	Oak Hill
1300 ———————————
	Castle Creek
1200	
	Canandaigua
1100	OWASCO TRADITION
	Carpenter Brook
A.D. 1000	

[a] All but the Garoga phase and historic Mohawk apply generally to central New York as well.

independent standardization from the dialectical pool left behind by the Roman Empire.

Iroquois origins have not always been seen with such clarity. MacNeish's (1952, 1976) work on the ceramics of this period was designed to demonstrate the validity of the in situ hypothesis of Iroquois origins, the notion that Iroquois culture had evolved in place. The Owasco tradition was once thought by Parker, Ritchie, and others to have been attributable to "Algonkians" (Ritchie 1969a:300). MacNeish's assertion that the Owasco ceramic tradition was carried by Iroquoians and led directly into the later Iroquois tradition, though controversial at first, is now generally accepted, and the discussion over Iroquois origins has largely dissipated. As we have seen, there is still an issue surrounding the arrival of Iroquoian speakers in the Northeast, but it has been pushed to a much earlier level and is not germane to a discussion of the Late Prehistoric period.

There is another related issue that is germane, however, and that is the practice of couching discussion of Late Prehistoric phases solely in terms of ceramic evidence. Like the Point Peninsula tradition, the Owasco and Iroquois traditions are customarily (albeit implicitly) discussed as ceramic traditions, and evidence pertaining to other cultural subsystems does not often contribute much to their definitions. As a consequence, the Owasco tradition in particular has often been extended to embrace components outside the Mohawk drainage and the other home areas of the historic Iroquois. Thus, components in the Hudson and Delaware valleys have not infrequently been classed as Owasco on grounds that pottery found in them can be classified as Owasco types. This extension of Owasco ignores striking contrasts in house types, settlement types, and other criteria that I have argued should contribute equally to any definition of a cultural system. Consequently, I use Owasco and Iroquois here to refer only to those components and phases that are clearly in the stream of evolving cultural systems that lead to the historic five Iroquois nations. There are no Owasco or Iroquois sites in the Hudson or Delaware drainages.

This position does not ignore, deny, or otherwise obscure Owasco or Iroquois influences. On the contrary, it has the advantage of highlighting the presence of Owasco ceramics in drainages where other features of the Owasco system are generally not found. Now that we are no longer obscuring this phenomenon by classifying as equivalent components that clearly are not, we can turn to formulating hypotheses to explain it. However, that will first require some discussion of the nature of ceramic evidence. Many older and some recent discussions of archaeological ceramics are couched largely as art history. Such discussions center on pottery types and specific motifs, and the evidence tends to be presented in an anecdotal way. There are frequent but vague references to "influences" with (usually) no explicit discussion of the specific mechanisms that might have operated to effect them. Unless we have some notion of the possible mechanisms by which ceramic attributes made their way from the work of one potter to another, we cannot adequately devise or test hypotheses relating ceramic evidence to phenomena in other cultural subsystems. For example, Engelbrecht's (1972, 1974) unsuccessful attempts to find evidence of the emergence of the League of the Iroquois through ceramic analysis may well have foundered because we have all failed to pay enough attention to the nature of links between the technological and social subsystems of culture.

Whallon has noted a general trend toward increasing stylistic homogeneity in Iroquois ceramics through the Late Prehistoric period. This trend is of only the most general sort as seen through analysis of decorative techniques, vessel shape, decorative motifs, collar shapes, and lip profiles. He makes no attempt to move from the general observation to specific attributes and makes only general inferences regarding the supposed association between this trend and the evolution of Iroquois society. This is commendable caution given the level of our understanding of ceramic evidence in the context of evolving cultural systems. He concludes that there was a trend over time for more homogeneity within villages, and less homogeneity within the whole set of Iroquois villages over time. "The general trend towards a slight increase in stylistic homogeneity from early Owasco to Iroquois is interpreted as a reflection of a gradually decreasing rate of social contact between villages [Whallon 1968:236]." And this is seen as possible evidence for intensifying matrilocal residence over time.

Engelbrecht (1972:10–11) suggests that what we have traditionally (and vaguely) referred to as "influences" when assessing similarities between ceramic types can be ascribed to three distinct processes. Specifically, he notes an increase in ceramic similarity between Five Nations Iroquois sites from A.D. 1500 to 1640. He attributes this to (1) voluntary residential shifts of women between tribal areas, (2) capture of women between tribal areas, or (3) female trading activity. Note that the first of these processes presumes peaceful coexistence, the second presumes warfare, and the third could thrive in either context. Unless we can identify which of these possible mechanisms was operative or at least assess the relative importance of each, we cannot formulate a hypothesis predicting the effect of League formation on ceramics. Engelbrecht (1972:10) concludes that "no evidence of the formation of the League . . . was found ceramically" and suggests that the League formed after the period he studied (i.e., after A.D. 1640). However, it seems certain on the basis of ethnohistorical evidence that the League was founded before the 1630s (Tooker 1978:418) and virtually all conjectures as to the precise date of its founding have fallen within the 140-year period Engelbrecht studied. I conclude that our inability to see that event reflected in ceramic evidence is the consequence of our inability to sort out the mechanisms just listed. We should probably be looking instead for significant shifts in relative settlement locations through locational techniques such as nearest-neighbor analysis. At least for now it appears we cannot go beyond Whallon's (1968) level of generalization on the basis of ceramic evidence alone.

Another problem in ceramic analysis has to do with the disjunction between how we have thought types should be defined and how we have actually been defining them. MacNeish (1952) discusses Iroquois pottery types as polythetic sets of attributes, an approach that has been explicit among archaeologists for three decades. Thus conceived, types are defined as sets of attributes, no one of which is more significant than any other. However, Whallon (1972) has shown that we have in fact been defining types as sets of attributes arranged hierarchically. Similar types are in fact distinguished by the presence or absence of a single attribute and are in that sense monothetic types. This explains why cluster analysis of attributes so often fails to work, since this form of analysis presumes equivalent significance of all attributes. It also explains why a system of key attributes for type definition does work. Thus, ceramic types are in fact analogous to biological species in the sense that one can type a vessel by means of a hierarchical sequence of key attributes. This is due to the contingent nature of the choices made during the process of manufacturing a vessel. Decisions made by the potter early in the process limit later choices. For example, a decision early on to make a collared vessel opens possibilities in the area of collar decoration that would not be there if the potter decided to make an uncollared vessel. Evolution of types over time involves the addition and subtraction of attributes within this hierarchical manufacturing process, and the possibilities for new types depend to a large degree on the contingencies inherent in older types. Again the analogy with biological species is instructive, for it helps us conceptualize the ways in which ceramic types evolve over time.

Future analysis of Late Prehistoric ceramic types should concentrate on the reconstruction of manufacturing sequences and the isolation of key attributes. The notion of types as polythetic sets should be explicitly abandoned in the course of this refinement so that attention can focus on the means by which key attributes (and therefore new types) become established. To Engelbrecht's three proposed mechanisms, we can add such things as the founder principle, wherein a single innovator sets a standard for pottery manufacture that is followed by others until another innovator comes along. Another factor might be that of cultural dominance, a principle that might explain why Iroquois ceramic types came to be established in the Hudson and Delaware valleys. Once types are understood in terms of key attributes and the mechanisms by which change can occur are understood in principle, analyses such as that attempted by Engelbrecht will be less likely to fail and words like "influence" and "interaction" will come to be replaced by more precise language.

All of this has struck some archaeologists as a reversion to a pre-Linnean version of science, but it is quite the opposite. The history of archaeology in the Northeast is punctuated by vain attempts to settle problems once and for all, dead-end efforts that often delay scientific progress. It is the recognition of this failing that led James Wright into his long campaign to shift the focus of attention on ceramic attributes and away from ossified ceramic types. It is the recognition of this failing that eventually dawns on us when we set out to define standard inventories of all possible attributes for a given artifact class, but too often not until after we have spent months laboring on what we vainly hope will be a finite list. The sections that follow may suggest ways in which the new principles of ceramic analysis might be frutiful and the old pitfalls might be avoided.

This evolving system began about A.D. 1000 with the Carpenter Brook phase, passed through the Canandaigua phase between A.D. 1100 and 1200, and passed through the Castle Creek phase by A.D. 1300. Sites of essentially two types are known for the Carpenter Brook phase. There are spring–summer fishing camps and village sites, the largest of which is the 1 hectare Maxon–Derby site near Syracuse. The villages are larger than those of the preceding Hunters Home phase, and they are typically located on the second terraces of large streams. Smaller seasonal camps are located along river rifts or on the margins of marshes and lake shallows. None of the villages is palisaded, but all look down on fields on the river flood plains (Ritchie and Funk 1973:165–225).

Owasco Cultural System

Seven houses were found at the Maxon–Derby site, and these show that the well-known Iroquois longhouse was developing with the emerging nucleated settlements. The smallest example was a 6 × 7-m squarish house with partitions and four hearths. There was also a 7 × 10-m oblong house with one or two doors and a single line of hearths. Finally, there was an 8 × 18-m oblong house with doors at the ends and hearth rows along the sides. These and the 27-m-long house at the Roundtop site in the Susquehanna drainage clearly show that house form was evolving toward the very long standard form of later times, although standardization was still some way off.

This semipermanent sedentary settlement system strengthened during the Canandaigua phase, and village earthworks and palisades appear at this time as well. The Sackett site near Canandaigua is a site of well over 1 hectare, within a ditch and palisade wall having a 62 × 74-m elliptical shape. While ever-longer longhouses appear to have been built at sites such as the Bates site in the Susquehanna drainage, Ritchie and Funk (1973:213–252) show circular houses with 4-m diameters at the Sackett site. However, I find their circular plots on the confusion of post molds to be less than entirely convincing, for there are linear arrangements as well (Ritchie and Funk 1973:215). It seems likely to me that at least some of the round structures may be imaginary and that there were longhouses on the site as well. The Sackett site may not be all that out of step with the times.

By Castle Creek times most main villages were palisaded, although undefended seasonal camps along rivers, marshes, and lakes continued to be used as well. The Chamberlain site near Elbridge had an earth ring that was still visible in the nineteenth century and is presumed therefore to have had a palisade wall as well. Tuck (1971b) excavated two houses at the site, both about 7 m wide. One was 15 m long while the other was 26 m long, lengths that approach the very long structures of the historic Iroquois.

Only one storage pit was found at the Maxon–Derby site. These are much more frequent by the Castle Creek phase, but only in sites in the Mohawk and Susquehanna drainages. They are rare or absent at Chamberlain and other sites in the Lake Ontario lowlands, suggesting that there were different storage techniques in use there.

Subsistence had clearly taken a quantum leap forward by A.D. 1000. Maize, beans, and squash were in heavy use at the Roundtop site in the Susquehanna drainage, and we can infer their use in the Mohawk drainage as well. Deer hunting and the gathering of wild plant foods continued as before, but the primary emphasis in subsistence was clearly on horticulture by this time. Many archaeologists have noted the sudden jump in the incidence of serious tooth decay in skeletal populations about this time, further evidence of the new emphasis on foods high in carbohydrates. Small task groups continued to use small specialized sites for hunting and fishing, but through the period intervillage warfare probably constrained this activity. The development of palisaded villages and networks of overland trails is consistent with these changes.

The Owasco social subsystem appears to have been close to that of the descendant Iroquois. Houses were already large enough to contain several nuclear families each, and we can infer that the household unit was the lineage. I have inferred the emergence of clans in the previous period, so these too were part of the Owasco system. Given the ways in which clans functioned in later times, there were probably two or more in each village (Fenton and Tooker 1978:466). The emergence of warfare as a social institution is hinted at by skeletal evidence. Adult males riddled with arrows are frequently found in cemetery sites. Furthermore, the presence of scattered human bones in village refuse indicates that early historic cannibalism has its origins in the Owasco system (Ritchie 1969a:272–300; Ritchie and Funk 1973:360–366). Careful examination of the ethnohistorical record also indicates that both warfare in general and scalping in particular were already part of native American cultures and were not among the benefits brought by European civilization as some historians have insisted. Ritchie (1947) has also inferred bear ceremonialism from remains found in a ceramic dump at the Carpenter Brook site. The dump contained the sherds of 200 vessels, an anatomically perfect clay phallus, and mammal bones that were primarily those of black bear. Stone phalli have also been found at other Owasco sites, but their use and their possible connections with the hypothetical bear ceremonialism can only be guessed at. Indeed, the historic practice of keeping and fattening bear cubs for food seems to point to a more practical explanation than Ritchie infers, notwithstanding that the bears were usually killed and their bones disposed of in a prescribed way (Ritchie 1950).

Furthermore, phalli often decorated the upper ends of otherwise mundane pestles.

The dominant stone artifacts in the Owasco technological subsystem are triangular Levanna points. Jacks Reef corner-notched points appear to survive from the preceding period, but are very rare (Ritchie 1971a:28–32). The smaller triangular Madison points that characterize the later Iroquois system begin to appear in the Canandaigua phase, but do not dominate until after A.D. 1300. Recent analysis has shown that these two types can probably be viewed as a single type that evolved from generally larger to generally smaller size through the course of this 600-year period.

The Carpenter Brook phase is characterized by a series of Levanna and Owasco pottery types. Most types are decorated with cord impressions around their necks. Earlier Point Peninsula types tend to be more conical at their bases and flare near their rims like inverted bells. Later Iroquois types have constricted necks, pronounced collars, and globular bases. The Owasco and Levanna types are intermediate between these earlier and later forms, having definite necks, flaring rims, and bases that are parabolic in vertical cross section, neither as conical as earlier forms nor as globular as later forms. In addition to the Owasco and Levanna types there are phase-specific types such as Carpenter Brook Cord-on-Cord, Wickham Corded Punctate, and Canandaigua Plain.

While types in the earlier Point Peninsula series appear to have been constructed of clay coils, Owasco vessels show no evidence of coil construction and may have been made by more advanced modeling techniques. The paste consistently contains grit tempering, but the grit is finer in later vessels. The vessels are also large, some of them able to contain up to 45 liters (12 gallons). Collars began to appear above constricted necks on vessels of the Castle Creek phase, a trend that reaches a peak in the Iroquois types made after A.D. 1300. Ritchie (1969a:239) has emphasized that these vessel collars were integral parts of the Owasco and Iroquois vessels they adorned and were technologically different from the appliqued collars sometimes found attached to Point Peninsula pottery from the preceding period. The cord impressions that dominate in the decoration of Owasco and Levanna types are confined to the rims, necks, and shoulders of the vessels. The decorative designs, which allow the subdivision of these wares into types, usually consist of simple lines, plats, and herringbone patterns in horizontal, vertical, and oblique arrangements. Earlier types have their decorations laid over cord-wrapped paddle surface treatments. Later types had their decorated areas smoothed before the application of decorative designs. By the Castle Creek phase, appliqued human effigies and other supplementary decorations such as incising were beginning to appear on collared vessels. Detailed descriptions of the types and attribute trends through time can be acquired from Ritchie and MacNeish (1949), Ritchie (1969a:290–292), and the sources they cite.

The Owasco technological subsystem is also characterized by a rich array of elbow pipes. Most are made of clay, but there are early examples in stone as well. Their decoration was usually by incising or punctation, but human effigies begin to appear as early as the Carpenter Brook phase. These plus the human effigies that appear on later Owasco vessels may signal the beginnings of behavior that culminates in the Iroquois False Faces of historic times. Stone pipes disappear by A.D. 1100, but bowl forms and decorations become increasingly elaborate in clay pipes. The complex and artistically rich sequence of Owasco pipe forms is touched on by Ritchie (1969a:294–296) but treated in much greater detail by Weber (1970, 1971).

Elsewhere in the Owasco technological subsystem, there appears to be a decrease in fishing equipment over time except in the case of net sinkers. This might indicate a decrease in the importance of fishing. However, the apparent decrease could also have resulted from differential preservation of bone implements or a shift to the use of material that preserved less well, hawthorn spines for example. Fishing had never been important on the Mohawk, due largely to the lack of migratory fish in that tributary of the Hudson, and the rise of horticulture and warfare may have reduced its importance even more. However, additional well-controlled investigations will have to be carried out before we can test the hypothesis that fishing actually declined in this period.

A few Owasco cemeteries have been investigated, and there are occasional burials in abandoned storage pits. The burials are nearly always primary flexed interments, and there is no evidence of the storage of the dead for periodic mass burial. Thus, the occasional burials in storage pits are probably the consequence of deaths during the winter months, when burial in cemetery plots would have been impossible. There is no evidence of any consistent orientation of the burials, and grave goods are rare. There is an occasional pot with a child burial or a pipe with an adult, but most items buried with the dead appear to have been parts of their clothing. This observation is significant because it indicates that the dead were buried clothed and not in burial shrouds. Mounds were by now completely things of the past. The mortuary subsystem therefore contrasted strikingly with that of the previous period in terms of site types and burial programs. However, there is no sharp break and nothing to suggest that the Owasco practices did not evolve out of earlier ones. Indeed, the trends away from special grave goods, the decrease in the overall frequency of grave goods, and the trend toward immediate burial all marked the Kipp Island and Hunters Home phases of the preceding period. The Owasco ideological subsystem was the logical outgrowth of those trends.

Iroquois Cultural System

The system described here is that which thrived from A.D. 1300 to 1600 in the Mohawk drainage and westward across central New York. It grew out of the Owasco system and from it derived the Mohawk system described in Chapter 2. The systems of the other four Iroquois nations derived from this one as well, but these lie beyond the scope of this volume. The Oak Hill and later Chance phases are found throughout Iroquoia, but the final Garoga phase has been defined for the Mohawk drainage alone. Each lasted for about a century as was the case for the three Owasco phases. Once again it is useful to treat them as a single evolving cultural system rather than as three separate systems. Readers looking for greater detail can refer to Ritchie's (1969a:300–324) major synthesis, Ritchie and Funk (1973:165–332, 359–368), Lenig's (1965) description of the Oak Hill phase, and Tuck (1978b).

Some sites of the Oak Hill phase are small, less than 1000 m^2, but others approach a hectare in size. By the end of prehistory, village sizes range up to 3 or 4 hectares (8–10 acres), although the average remained around a hectare. The preference for defensible hilltop sites continues from the previous phase, but palisades are now more elaborate. There are double and sometimes triple palisades, and the walls in some places were at least 4 m high as indicated by the angle of slanted wall braces. Village size increases with time, and the very late Garoga site contains a full hectare (10,000 m^2, or 2.5 acres). Many late sites were fully palisaded, while others such as Garoga took advantage of steep hill slopes and needed palisades only at points of level access. None of the sites of these three phases lies outside historic Iroquoia. Ritchie (1952) originally included the Kingston site of the Hudson valley in the Chance phase, but that inclusion is based on ceramic evidence alone and cannot be retained (Figure 8.1).

The Kelso site of the Oak Hill phase had both longhouses and smaller houses ranging from 5 × 6 m to 8 × 10 m in size. Kelso longhouses measured 39 m long (Ritchie and Funk 1973:253–262). The longhouses were round-ended during the Oak Hill phase, but tended to be square-ended by the Chance phase. The Garoga site produced nine such longhouses, the longest of which measured 64 m, but none of the smaller houses still seen in the Oak Hill phase 200 years earlier. Subsistence and seasonal movements cannot be distinguished from those of either Owasco or historic Mohawk.

The household social unit was clearly the lineage. At the Oak Hill level, the smaller houses such as those found at the Kelso site indicate that some lineages were relatively small. However, by the time of the Garoga phase near the end of the period, all houses were large longhouses. Lineages must have been correspondingly large and stable by this time. Villages in the Mohawk drainage would have had two or three clans each. This would be a clear case of lineal tribal organization as defined in Chapter 2. There is as yet no unequivocal archaeological evidence of the formation of the League of the Iroquois, an event that almost certainly occurred during this period. I have already discussed Engelbrecht's attempt to discover traces of it in ceramic evidence and suggested that the search might better be conducted through the application of locational analysis to Iroquois sites of the period. While the League probably formed after A.D. 1500, one curiously precise tradition places the data at which the Seneca joined as coinciding with a total eclipse of the sun. The only one that qualifies took place on June 28, 1451 (Julian

FIGURE 8.1. Sites of the Late Prehistoric period.

date, see Tooker 1978:420). Perhaps we will have to abandon the search in the face of evidence that is either too vague or too precise and conclude that the formation was a long process, not a single event.

Emergence of the distinctive globular and collared Iroquois pottery types characterizes the last 300 years of prehistory. Oak Hill Corded derives from the earlier Owasco Corded Collar type, and there are other examples of the derivation of Oak Hill ceramics from Castle Creek. However, overall the Oak Hill types seem stylistically restricted to those who worked with it, an impression that is supported by Whallon's (1968) statistical analysis. The gradual replacement of impressed by incised designs accompanies the emergence of collared and castellated vessels within a narrow developmental track. In contrast, variability and experimentation characterize clay pipe manufacture, and most archaeologists conclude that this contrast reflects the difference between a conservative female pottery-making tradition and a liberal male pipe-making tradition. Pipe decoration is innovative to the end, with human effigies growing in frequency over time, and animal effigies being added as well near the end.

Stone artifacts are limited in number and variety. Madison points come to replace Levanna entirely with time. Apart from these, stone implements are restricted to hoes, mortars, pestles, celts, and adzes, none very distinctive. Whallon's (1968) analysis shows steadily increasing stylistic similarities in ceramic remains from a range of late prehistoric villages, but there is no unequivocal evidence of substantial intervillage trade. There are no exotic raw materials or finished goods until the appearance of European trade goods. Indeed, even through the period in which the League probably emerged, each village gives the appearance of being self-contained and completely self-sufficient.

Little is known of the ideological subsystem. The false face complex may have emerged in Owasco times and evolved through the last half of the period, but the evidence is indirect, as we have seen. Flexed primary burials without grave goods continued to be the rule. This changes at the end of prehistory with the arrival of European trade goods. Trade items such as beads, brass kettles, items made from them, and axes appear as grave goods, sometimes in large amounts. Both adults and children were treated this way, and the practice peaked simultaneously with the height of the fur trade. Primary extended burials in wooden coffins, the European pattern, replaced these practices in the seventeenth century.

SOUTHERN NEW ENGLAND SEQUENCE

The problems inherent in the way archaeologists have traditionally treated ceramics are even more serious in New England than in New York. The model usually followed by the Massachusetts Archaeological Society uses broad temporal categories called "stages," into which pottery is usually classified without any attempt at finer type classification. When types are used, they are usually borrowed from the New York sequence even though most ceramics at any particular site are clearly of local manufacture and do not conform to New York type descriptions in anything more than a general way (Dincauze 1974:84). The problem persists in large part because there have been relatively few large-scale analyses of New England ceramic assemblages. The analysis of ceramics from the Guida Farm site (Byers and Rouse 1960) and Rouse's (1945, 1947) work in the coastal Connecticut area are notable exceptions, but these and a few other studies are not in themselves sufficient to counteract the intellectual domination of New York archaeology. Moreover, as Dincauze (1975b:5) has pointed out, ceramic analysis remains more art than science in New England. Thus, if it is to break out of its stultifying tradition, pottery analysis in New England must adopt the same new principles I have proposed for New York, but at the same time cut itself loose from continued domination by the New York sequence. Kenyon's (1979) recent contribution is a small but important step in that direction.

In many ways, the developments of the Late Prehistoric period in New England continue trends started in the previous period. There are no major breaks or disjunctions in the record except in a few places where population shifts caused some disruptions. Thus, while we may not be able to trust the apparent evidence for a population decline between the Terminal Archaic and Early Horticultural periods, we can probably trust the evidence for overall growth from the Early Horticultural to the Late Prehistoric period. Dincauze (1974:53) has noted increases in artifact frequencies and site sizes beginning even before A.D. 1000. Levanna and Madison points (Figure 8.2) are found with largely shell tempered pottery in sites that are distributed about as they had been previously. The settlement differences were not so much that locational preferences had changed as that sites were now larger, particularly those located at the heads of estuaries. For the last few centuries of prehistory, the settlement system was heading toward the A.D. 1600 pattern in which major nucleated villages were located on main streams, often at the heads of estuaries, while smaller satellite sites such as shell middens served as special-purpose camps. The most unfortunate aspect of the Late Prehistoric settlement plattern is that the large central village sites were virtually all located at the very places most favored by European settlers. Few if any of these important sites have survived well enough to yield much information through excavation.

Ritchie and Funk have also complained about the dearth of Late Prehistoric sites in the Hudson valley specifically, but here as elsewhere most of the sites lie under modern construction. It is worth noting that, in contrast, most Mohawk sites lie atop river bluffs and thereby away from historic population centers. What little has been found in the Hudson valley includes pottery and chert implements that generally echo those of the Mohawk. Levanna and Madison points and pottery types similar to Owasco and Iroquois types predominate. The connections of artifact style are so strong that Ritchie (1952) was led to include the Kingston site in his definition of the Chance phase—this despite the fact that three of the pottery types found at Kingston

FIGURE 8.2. Late Prehistoric points from New England. Top, Jacks Reef pentagonal; middle, Levanna; bottom, Madison. Shown at one-half actual size. (Courtesy of Peabody Museum of Salem.)

(Kingston Incised, Hudson Incised, and Hudson Crescent Incised) were not found at the Mohawk drainage sites assigned to the phase. Brumbach (1975) attempted to distinguish the ceramic assemblages of three Mohawk and seven Hudson sites on the basis of attribute analysis, but was unable to show their division into two distinct classes along presumed ethnic lines. Brumbach concludes "that using ceramics alone to locate tribal boundaries is a chancy procedure despite the accepted belief that ceramics are the most sensitive indicators of time and space differences [1975:28]." This strikes me as a pungent comment on the nature of contemporary archeological belief but does not dispute the existence of ethnic differences between the Late Prehistoric Mohawk and Mahican. The two do contrast if they are viewed as whole systems. Funk (1976:301) has noted important points of contrast by merely expanding the comparative base from ceramics to the whole technological assemblage. While Madison points predominate almost to the exclusion of anything else on Late Prehistoric Mohawk sites, they are rare on sites occupied at the same time in the Hudson drainage. Levanna points predominate on these Mahican sites into the seventeenth century. Similarly, smoking pipes are frequent in the Mohawk but relatively rare in the Hudson drainage. If we had data on house types, settlement types, and their distributions, we would undoubtedly see even stronger contrasts. The available evidence suggests that Late Prehistoric sites on the Hudson were located near the river floodplain rather than on bluffs and that they were relatively small compared to Iroquois villages. This contrast persisted past A.D. 1600, as described in Chapter 2.

Both Goddard (1978a) and Warne (1979) note fundamental linguistic connections between Mahican and Delaware, which in the Mahican case appear to be overridden by more superficial similarities with other northern New England languages. The linguistic evidence suggests a divergence of Delaware and Mahican, which on archaeological grounds we could assign to the Early Horticultural period, followed by substantial interaction between Mahican speakers and speakers of other northern languages. This is consistent with the known events of the Late Prehistoric period, when the Mahican came to be denied access to the lower Hudson drainage and may have absorbed some Algonquian speakers out of the Champlain drainage.

Kraft (1975a) divides the pottery types of the Late Prehistoric upper Delaware drainage into early and late categories separated by an intermediate transitional set of types. The earlier set is called Pahaquarra and the later Minisink, a name that Kraft prefers to Munsee for historical reasons. It was this sequence of Late Prehistoric types, analogous in many ways to the Owasco–Iroquois continuum in central New York, that gave rise to the intrusive East River tradition described by Carlyle Smith. Phases of the East River tradition appear in the lower Hudson drainage and on western Long Island early in this last period of prehistory. They appear to displace the Windsor tradition, which, however, continued to thrive until A.D. 1600 on central and eastern Long Island and in Connecticut. In more modern terms, this amounts to the incursion of a dominant Munsee cultural system into the Hudson drainage from the upper Delaware and a consequent displacement of the previous inhabitants eastward and northward. Smith's North Beach and Clearview phases (see Chapter 7) are succeeded in turn by the Sebonac and Niantic phases (Table 8.2), but the evolving system and therefore the last two phases of it were pushed out of the lower Hudson. The intrusive system, called East River by Smith, is defined archaeologically by an earlier Bowmans

TABLE 8.2
Phases of the Lower Hudson Drainage
(Smith 1950)[a]

	East River	Windsor
A.D. 1600		
1500	Clasons Point	Niantic
1400		
1300		
1200		
1100	Bowmans Brook	Sebonac
A.D. 1000		

[a] The East River tradition displaced the indigenous Windsor tradition eastward.

Brook phase and a later Clasons Point phase. As always in Smith's analysis, the phases are defined almost entirely on the basis of ceramic evidence, but this narrow perspective is nonetheless sufficient to show the contrast between the two systems and the origins of the dominant intruder.

It is noteworthy that the proto-Munsee of the upper Delaware and lower Hudson drainages shared many pottery styles with the Iroquois, but few with their linguistic relatives in the lower Delaware drainage (Figures 8.3 and 8.4). The pottery of the southern part of the Delaware drainage area seems to share most of its features with the pottery of the Delmarva peninsula. Similarly, the proto-Munsee buried their dead with heads to the west or southwest, while the burials of the southern Delaware drainage tend to be

FIGURE 8.3. Late Prehistoric collared and incised vessel from the Tiorati rock shelter site, 23 cm tall. Human face, small castellations, and other features reflect the influence of the Iroquois tradition (A.D. 1300–1600). (Courtesy of New York State Museum and Science Service.)

FIGURE 8.4. Clay masquette (45 mm high) from a pit on the Miller Field site. This very late prehistoric specimen may represent a miniature corn husk mask analogous to historic Iroquois masks. Originally perforated near the bottom for inverted suspension. Shown at actual size. (Photo by Herbert C. Kraft.)

oriented toward the east. This difference in mortuary practices, with its implications for contrasting ideological systems, is still observed by Oklahoma (Unami) Delaware Indians, who derive from the southern area, and Canadian Munsee Delaware Indians, who derive largely from the north (Kraft 1975b:90).

Smith (1950:133–134) defined the indigenous Sebonac phase on the basis of evidence from several sites on Long Island and coastal Connecticut. Several others have added to that list in more recent years (Ritchie 1969a:266). Salwen and Ottesen (1972) have challenged Smith's definition of Sebonac by four diagnostic pottery types, asserting that one of them is actually a later type. The type, Sebonac Stamped, appears to be later than the other Sebonac diagnostics, Windsor Brushed, Windsor Fabric-marked, and Windsor Cord-marked, at the Shantok Cove and Muskeeta Cove 2 sites. A radiocarbon date from the latter site dates the type to A.D. 1300 ± 200 (L-1178A).

Except for inland Connecticut drainage sites, the Sebonac components are generally situated on well-drained locations on bays and estuaries, always close to shellfish beds. The people lived in circular wigwams up to 6 m in diameter and in communities that Ritchie estimates to have contained 100 or more inhabitants. There is typically good preservation on these sites due to the large amount of shell debris. The food remains point to a diffuse subsistence economy that included several species of shellfish, deer and smaller mammals, turkey and other fowl, sturgeon, whale, and corn. Thus, while horticulture was part of the system, it did not dominate it to the degree seen in the Mohawk drainage. Sebonac sites are dotted by pits of two types: shallow pits that were used as baking ovens for shellfish and deeper pits that were used for either cooking or storage.

Sebonac fishermen apparently fished from dugout canoes, often with angling equipment that would have effect in deep or shallow water. The dugouts were built using ground stone axes, celts, and adzes. The chipped stone industry was dominated by the Levanna point. Sebonac pottery includes types having conical to globular bases and collarless rims that are either straight or slightly constricted, flaring rims being less frequent. "Decoration usually extends from the lip to the shoulder area and consists of various combinations of stamping, brushing, and punctating. True incising is rare or totally absent [Smith 1950:133]." All such vessels fall into the Stage 3 category in the system used by the Massachusetts Archaeological Society. Straight or elbow smoking pipes of clay or more rarely soapstone were also made (Figure 8.5).

Sebonac burials are usually flexed primary interments in old storage pits. Grave goods are rare. It therefore appears that these people, like the Iroquois to the west, played down the importance of mortuary activities in this last period of prehistory.

The Niantic phase, lineal successor to Sebonac in Smith's Windsor tradition, is still not well known. The evidence uncovered by Salwen and Ottesen (1972) suggests that it probably did not exist except as a set of late Iroquois-derived pottery types within the local technological subsystem. From the brief description just provided, it can be seen that the Sebonac system was not much different from that described in Chapter 2 for the historic culture of the same area. Given its intermediate position between them in time, we should expect Niantic, if it existed, to conform to the same general description. The primary difference setting Niantic off from Sebonac is in the appearance at this time of globular-based, collared pottery types. These vessels are often shell tempered, thinner than previous types, and often decorated with cord and shell stamp impressions. The forms, with their round bases and frequently castellated collars, reflect the strength of Iroquois influence in southern New England, at least in this part of the technological subsystem. Shell beads are present, but the long tubular wampum beads for which these people would later become famous were a historic period phenomenon that could only be made using metal tools of European origin.

The initial intrusion of people from the Delaware drainage into the lower Hudson is marked by the appearance of the Bowmans Brook phase. This later becomes the Clasons Point phase (Figures 8.6 and 8.7), which in turn leads to the historic Munsee. This intrusive sequence is called the East River tradition by Smith (1950:190–193). As described by Smith and later by Ritchie (1969a:268–270), Bowmans Brook appears to contrast with Sebonac in terms of pottery types used, but little else. While it is the case that types such as Bowmans Brook Incised (Figure 8.8) and Bowmans Brook Stamped contrast with Sebonac types, the level of that contrast is superficial in the sense that it hardly implies any major contrast between the two cultural systems. Indeed, Bowmans Brook can scarcely be distinguished from Sebonac except on these stylistic grounds, and it is difficult to perceive in the technological subsystem the nature of the dominance of Bowmans Brook. Looking beyond ceramics one sees much the same inventory of artifacts and implied subsistence activities here as in the Sebonac and Niantic phases. Yet there must have been cultural dominance of some sort, given the displacement of the indigenous system by this intruder from the Delaware drainage.

A clue to the dominance of the East River system over the Windsor system comes from contrasts in house types and their distributions. While the

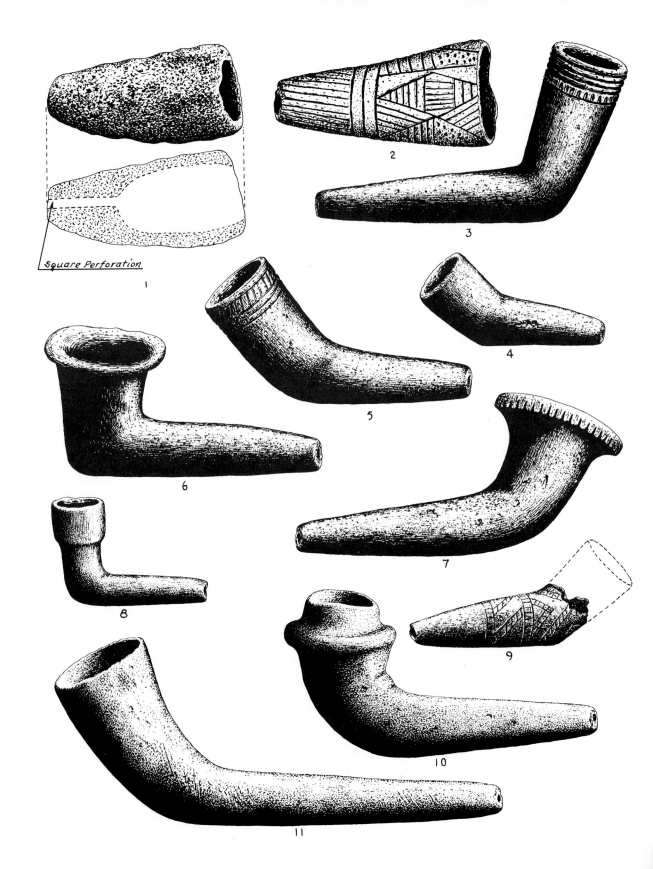

Square Perforation

1

2

3

4

5

6

7

8

9

10

11

FIGURE 8.6. Restored Van Cortland stamped vessel from the Denniston site. Clasons Point phase, 15 cm tall. (Courtesy of New York State Museum and Science Service.)

Windsor phases show the use of wigwams, the Late Prehistoric people of the upper Delaware lived in longhouses 6 m wide and up to 18 m long. The longhouses differed both in size and in form from Iroquois longhouses in that they were shorter in average length and had hearths arranged along one wall rather than down a center aisle (Kraft 1970b, 1975b:83). Nonetheless, they imply that the residential unit was either a lineage or a rather large extended family, something nearer the Iroquois case than the nuclear or

FIGURE 8.5. Ceramic pipes of the Early Horticultural and Late Prehistoric periods. 1, Plymouth, Mass.; 2, Conn.; 3,6,7, central Mass.; 4, Greenwich, R.I.; 5, S. Windsor, Conn.; 8, Norton, Mass.; 9, E. Providence, R.I.; 10,11, Scituate, Mass. Shown at three-quarters actual size. (Courtesy of Massachusetts Archaeological Society.)

FIGURE 8.7. Restored East River cord-marked vessel from the Sheep Shelter rock shelter. Clasons Point phase, 32 cm tall. (Courtesy of New York State Museum and Science Service.)

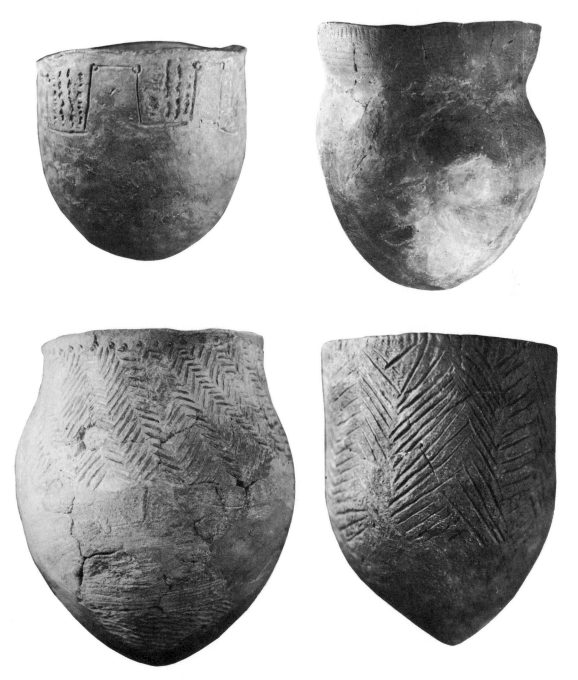

FIGURE 8.8. Late Prehistoric vessels dating to around A.D. 1400. Upper left, 13 cm tall, Apponaug, R.I.; upper right, 30 cm tall, Wareham, Mass.; lower right, 20 cm tall; and lower left, 29 cm tall, Bowmans Brook incised from Indian Wells rock shelter, Shelton, Conn. (Last specimen at the American Indian Archaeological Institute; others at Bronson Museum.)

small extended family implied by Windsor wigwams. The historic Munsee were organized matrilineally and had three major clans to which lineages belonged, while the population they replaced in the lower Hudson was probably organized patrilineally. It can be further inferred that the Munsee were somewhat more focally adapted to horticulture than were the people they displaced. Thus, in social organization, settlement pattern, and subsistence we can see the adaptive advantage enjoyed by the Late Prehistoric Munsee that cannot be seen in any analysis of their pottery alone.

Salwen (1968) has commented on the lack of clear evidence to indicate a dramatic population replacement in the lower Hudson. Smith (1950:156) talks in terms of invasion and physical displacement, but Salwen's evidence from Muskeeta Cove 2 suggests a more subtle process. Salwen has found the attributes of East River, Windsor, and Owasco pottery types blended, often on the same vessels. He suggests that "diffusion, rather than invasion, is seen as the central process, though some population movement . . . may well have been a contributing factor [Salwen 1968:334]." Unfortunately, diffusion is a traditional term in anthropology that is sublimely vague, implies no specific mechanism, and is therefore useless as explanation. Still, Salwen is apparently on the right track. Dispersed settlement and the lack of stockades indicate peaceful interaction. The penetration of the lower Hudson drainage by prehistoric Munsee could have been a slow process in which much of the indigenous population was absorbed rather than displaced by the dominant immigrant communities, with the resultant stylistic blends described by Salwen. Under these circumstances, Munsee would have emerged as the dominant language in much the same way as dominant languages have submerged others at other times and other places. The specifics of this gradual nonviolent replacement of one system by another have yet to be modeled in any detail. It could be modeled, however, and the results would be useful not only for the resolution of the current problem but for the analysis of similar displacements through the whole length and breadth of prehistory.

The late prehistory of the Connecticut drainage apart from its coastal sections is still rather poorly known. Most generalizations made available to date add little to what we might infer from our previous understandings of adjacent drainages (Powell 1971). The lower Connecticut drainage was part of the Long Island system. The historic people of this area all spoke a language Goddard (1978a:75) has called Quiripi–Unquachog. The middle Connecticut drainage, however, contained a separate system that contrasted with the other much as Mahican contrasted with Munsee in the Hudson drainage. The best-known site in the middle part of the drainage is Guida Farm. Byers and Rouse (1960) see coastal influences during the Early Horticultural period in the form of some Clearview phase ceramics. However, influences from the upper Hudson appear to be stronger both here and at the Hunter site in the northern Connecticut drainage. In the Late Prehistoric period there are influences on Guida Farm pottery styles from three directions. Windsor, East River, and Owasco styles all show up here. But they are dominated by styles of apparently local origin, and the result is a distinctive middle Connecticut variation on the Late Prehistoric theme. All of this is consistent with the scraps of ethnohistoric and linguistic evidence from the region that I outlined in Chapter 2. These people would have been the "Horikans" of Johan de Laet, the Pocumtuck of Chapter 2, and probably speakers of Goddard's "Loup A" language, who lived between the coastal culture and the prehistoric Western Abenaki of the upper Connecticut.

The late prehistory of the Thames drainage is well within the general pattern for southern New England. It is the historic importance of the Mohegan–Pequot and the confusion regarding their origin that led to their separate treatment in Chapter 2. The superficial similarity of the name "Mohegan" to "Mahican" has led to the widespread belief that the historic Mohegan–Pequot moved to the Thames drainage in a Late Prehistoric migration from the upper Hudson. There are neither archaeological nor linguistic data to support this idea. The Mohegan–Pequot emerged in place as part of the southern New England cultural continuum, and their linguistic connections with the Mahican are more distant than connections with Massachusett and other southern New England languages. There is, in short, nothing to challenge the hypothesis that the southern New England peoples developed in place from a common origin (Salwen 1969). The Shantok Cove site, which was first occupied around A.D. 770, has produced both Windsor and East River pottery. The nearby historic site of Fort Shantok has produced a distinctive Shantok ware, which Salwen (1969) interprets as indicating some Late Prehistoric individuality on the part of the Mohegan–Pequot. Similar pottery types are known from Guida Farm and various sites in Rhode Island and southeastern Massachusetts, but there are significant differences in detail. Thus, both archaeological and linguistic evidence indicate that, even while overall population density was increasing during this period, southern New England was breaking up into a series of independent cultural systems.

Shantok pottery is also found at the Fort Corchaug site on eastern Long Island. This site was occupied by the Montauk, who are known to have spoken the Mohegan–Pequot language. The occupation of the eastern end of Long Island by people from the Thames drainage apparently occurred prior to the end of the period (Solecki 1950). Because of this and the Munsee presence on the western end of the island, Long Island was occupied by parts of three separate cultural systems, carried by speakers of three separate languages by A.D. 1600. Unfortunately, ethnic identities have been obscured in much of the literature by the application of "Montauk," "Metoac," and other inappropriate names to all the Indians of Long Island.

The prehistory of the period is much the same for the small drainages that make up southeastern New England. Sites of the period produce Stage 3 and late Stage 4 ceramics as classified in the system of the Massachusetts Archaeological Society (Figures 8.9 and 8.10). Main villages at the heads of estuaries grew through the period and satellite farmsteads proliferated until

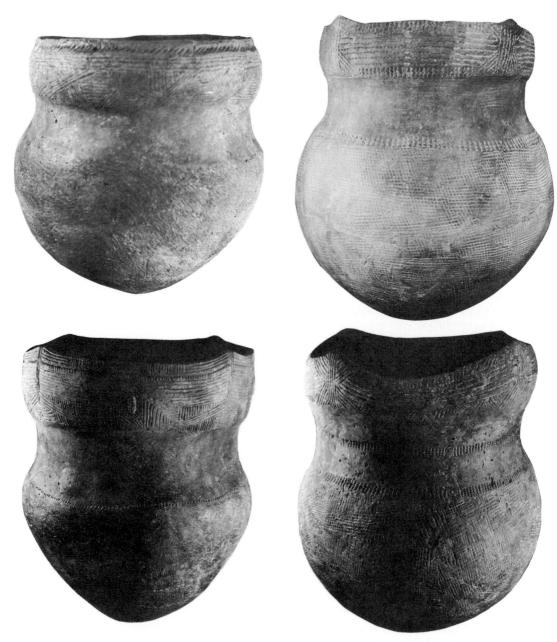

FIGURE 8.9. Late Prehistoric vessels dating to around A.D. 1600. Upper left, 30 cm tall, Indian Hill site, Middleboro, Mass.; upper right, 29 cm tall, Niantic stamped from Tubbs shell heap, Niantic, Conn.; lower right, 34 cm tall, Wapanucket site, Middleboro, Mass.; lower left, 32 cm tall, Titicut site, Bridgewater, Mass. (Niantic stamped vessel at American Indian Archaeological Institute; others at Bronson Museum.)

FIGURE 8.10. Late Prehistoric vessel from Hyannis, Mass. Note shell temper, exterior cord markings, globular base, parallel incised lines on collar, and diagonal punctate lines on shoulder. (Photograph by F. P. Orchard. Courtesy of Peabody Museum, Harvard University.)

the end of the period, when the pattern and density described in Chapter 2 were reached. Northern Massachusett villages grew and expanded into the lower Merrimack drainage much as the Munsee expanded into the lower Hudson and perhaps by means of the same mechanism. Once again there is no clear evidence of invasion and displacement, although this time we do see some evidence of hostility along the new cultural boundary. The earliest known Western Abenaki villages of the upper Merrimack drainage were all palisaded and located on defensible bluffs, suggesting that the Late Prehistoric northeastward expansion of the Massachusett was contained not only by the limits of the growing season, but by the objections of nonhorticulturalists as well.

There is no question about the importance of horticulture in the Late Prehistoric period of southern New England. Ritchie (1969b:32) found carbonized corn on Martha's Vinyard associated with a radiocarbon date of A.D. 1160 ± 80 (Y-1653), and there is no reason to believe that this represents the first appearance of corn in southeastern New England. Along with beans, squash, and various semi-domesticates of the sort described in previous chapters, corn fueled the increases in population density and absolute size through the period. This is not to say that I accept the Malthusian notion that the population exploded as a consequence of a quantum leap in horticultural productivity. I do not. Neither do I hold to the Boserupian position that population pressure drove the advances in the subsistence system. I doubt that either of these polarized views has much to offer archaeology, particularly since both of them imply cause–effect relations that are simplistic at best and misleading at worst in the examination of cultural systems. The development of horticulture and the growth of population accompany each other and many other factors known and unknown in the evolution of Late Prehistoric systems in New England.

Table 8.3 is derived from Bennett's (1955) excellent analysis of the aboriginal food economy of southern New England. It shows the contrast between the aboriginal diet and modern United States diet in 11 food groups. One can see the relative importance of horticulture in the aboriginal diet and the effect removal of cultivated plants from that diet would have. Even more important was the storage potential of cultigens as compared to wild or semi-domesticated food sources. The Indians of northern New England not only lacked the domesticates that made up well over half the diet of southern New England Indians, but thereby also lacked the foods that would store best

TABLE 8.3
Approximate Food Intake in the United States (1952) and in Southern New England (1605–1675)[a]

	Percentage consumption	
Food	United States 1952	Southern New England 1605–1675
1. Grain products	22.8	65 −
2. Animal and bird carcasses	21.6	10 +
3. Milk and milk products	15.8	0
4. Sugars and syrups	15.4	0
5. Visible vegetable fats	8.5	1 −
6. Vegetables and fruits[b]	6.5	4 ±
7. Grain alternatives[b]	2.9	2 −
8. Nuts and leguminous seeds	2.9	8 +
9. Eggs	2.8	1 −
10. Fish and shellfish	.4	9 ±
11. Chocolate	.4	0
	100.0	100

[a] After Bennett (1955).

[b] Potatoes included as grain alternative but excluded from vegetables and fruits.

for use during lean months. Little wonder the population densities of the two parts of the region contrasted so much in A.D. 1600.

The Late Prehistoric cultural system of southern New England need not be reviewed. The principal elements of the system have been discussed in the preceding pages (Figure 8.11). Moreover, this was the period in which the baseline system of A.D. 1600 emerged, and that system has already been described in Chapter 2. Although linguistic and other ethnic differences arose in the drainages of southern New England during this period, and those differences were exacerbated by the colonial warfare that followed A.D. 1600, the cultures of the area before that date were variations on a single theme. The Munsee, with their Iroquois-like settlement pattern, were exceptions to this generalization, but it holds for the rest of the area. For all of the participants in this system, the last six centuries of prehistory appear to have been a period of generally peaceful growth and prosperity. There could have been no hint of the catastrophe that would be visited upon them from beyond the eastern horizon.

Northern New England by this time is defined as those drainages or major portions of drainages that lie primarily north of the line of 150 frost-free days. Horticulture was not viable north of this line, at least not until there was some fallback option to get communities through years of crop failure. The Champlain drainage could support horticulture at least at shoreline locations, but it was a buffer zone for part of the period for other reasons. The upper Connecticut and Merrimack drainages were unsuitable for horticulture and the communities there found themselves linked by that circumstance to the nonhorticultural communities of the Maine drainages. Consequently, the contrasting population densities between southern and northern New England seen in Table 2.1 (Chapter 2) were a subsistence-based dichot-

NORTHERN NEW ENGLAND SEQUENCE

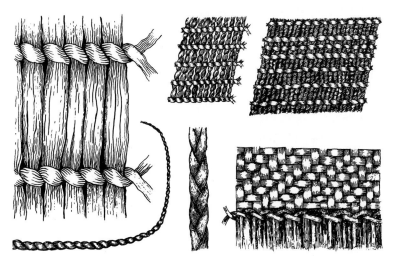

FIGURE 8.11. Bast textiles from a grave at Manchester, Mass. Shown at actual size. (After Willoughby 1935:247.)

omy that became more and more pronounced through the Late Prehistoric period.

Yet despite the unreliability of horticulture in northern New England, the Indians there were able to coalesce into a rather small number of large villages in this period. As we saw in Chapter 2, they adjusted to their nonhorticultural circumstances by spending relatively more time at summer camps on the coast and winter camps in the interior, an adjustment that made them less sedentary than southern New England communities. On the other hand, main villages in the north were more permanent because there was less need to relocate them every few years. The locations the Northerners chose for their main villages tended to be at estuary heads, falls, and other key points on main rivers. We have seen that the Eastern Abenaki had about 22 such main villages, most of which are now under modern towns and cities. The pattern of living at dual central places, coastal and interior, was replaced by a pattern of living at single intermediate central places on lower stream courses. Interior and coastal camps were by now not themselves central places, but temporary camps, and the criteria for their specific locations changed.

The contrast between Figures 7.25 and 2.2 reflects the dramatic change in settlement pattern that Bourque dates to around A.D. 1100 in Maine and Sanger dates to around A.D. 1200 in the St. John drainage. When compared with the A.D. 1000 threshold for major readjustments in New York, the shifts seem to reflect a general episode of change that was of a different character and somewhat delayed in the drainages of northeastern New England. Here the dominant forces appear to have been changes in average air and seawater temperatures. Air temperatures reached a high point around this time and began their descent to modern levels. Conversely, seawater temperatures reached their nadir and began rising once again. We have yet to carry out the research that will tell us whether or not these environmental changes were prime movers in the shift of settlement and subsistence from the system shown in Figure 7.25 toward that which was observed historically in the area.

The rise of large central villages in northern New England after A.D. 1000 was accompanied by a decline in the importance of coastal camps. Coastal pit houses, and presumably winter residence on the coast, disappear after A.D. 1200 in the St. Croix and St. John drainages. None of Bourque's (1971:166–216) sites on the Maine coast show evidence of occupation after A.D. 1100. Indeed, Bourque had trouble finding any sites postdating A.D. 1100 along the coast, but that may have been because he was looking in microenvironments that had produced sites dating to the previous period. The more temporary coastal camps of the Late Prehistoric period may well have been chosen with other priorities in mind and used so briefly that they can be easily missed by archaeologists. The Grindle site (Figures 8.12 and 8.13), which is located on a shore of a tidal pond rather than on the seacoast, was occupied both before and after A.D. 1100, suggesting just such a shift.

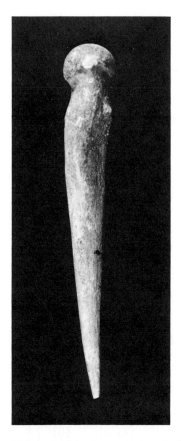

FIGURE 8.12. Styliform bone awl from the Grindle site, 94 mm long. Shown at actual size. (University of Maine collection.)

Although this site contains shell fragments, it is not an obvious midden, and could easily have been overlooked. The Goddard site on Naskeag Point is an even more important Late Prehistoric period site that lacks an obvious shell midden or evidence of winter residence. This site has produced a Norse coin (Seaby 1978) (Figure 8.14), one of the few believable traces of a Norse presence in North America. The coin need not be evidence of direct contact, of course, but even this scrap of evidence of indirect contact is an improvement over the wild speculation that has characterized debate on the subject for over a century. The circumstances of its discovery leave little doubt about the coin's authenticity. But having said that I must add that, while a single spark of contact may be a significant event in the eyes of Norse historians, it probably indicates little or no impact on the aboriginal cultures of New England. Once again, a systems approach puts isolated finds like this one in perspective and keeps our enthusiasm for the unique in check.

I tested one of the primary Eastern Abenaki villages in 1970 in an effort to verify its occupation around A.D. 1600. The Old Town Indian Island site has been the main village of the Penobscot Indians for most of the time since then as well, so part of our effort was directed at uncovering traces of an

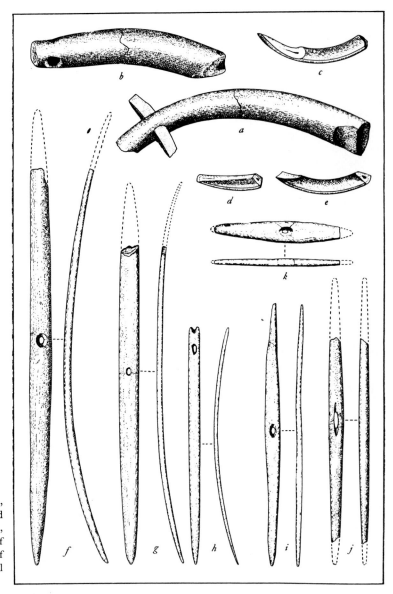

FIGURE 8.13. Artifacts of bone, tooth, and antler: a–e, beaver incisor blades and antler handles; f–j, mat sewing needles; k, snowshoe weaving shuttle. All typical of the Grindle site and other coastal sites of the same age. Shown at one-half actual size. (After Willoughby 1935:223.)

eighteenth-century stockade and other later features. As is the case with most of the villages listed by Purchas, later activities have nearly destroyed all traces of the earlier occupation. Some Late Prehistoric remains were found, however. There were fragments of stone pipes, conical tinklers of rolled copper, native pottery, and what appears to have been a shaman's medicine bundle secreted under a hearthstone. The bundle consisted of a wrapping of birch bark that contained 35 shark teeth, 6 rolled copper beads, the de-

FIGURE 8.14. Norse coin from the Goddard site, Maine. Left is obverse, right is reverse. Shown at four and one-half times actual size. Longest diameter is 16.5 mm. (Courtesy of Maine State Museum.)

ciduous dentition of a human child, and a small amount of red ocher (hematite). Clearly the native towns and villages of A.D. 1600 have some archaeological potential even in those cases where there has been nearly continuous occupation for 400 years. While it is true that all over aboriginal New England the late native communities lie buried under modern towns, the Old Town case shows that not all of the evidence has been lost. Indeed, these are the very sites that are most apt to receive funding for archaeological survey, testing, and salvage in connection with public construction. We are likely to learn a great deal more about Late Prehistoric archaeology throughout the region over the next few decades.

The pottery made in Maine during this period shows some of the trends described for New York ceramics, but reverses some others (Bourque 1971:166–216) (Figure 8.15). Shell tempering replaces grit tempering after A.D. 1200, a shift we have already observed in southern New England. Decorative techniques such as incising and punctation survive from the previous period, while others such as rocker and other kinds of stamping do not. Cord-wrapped paddle surface treatment was popular after A.D. 1000. While the tendency for pots to fracture along coil lines disappeared in New York ceramics at this time, the same tendency appears around A.D. 500 in Maine and persists through the Late Prehistoric period. Once again, we have to conclude that while ceramics might provide a convenient means to establish periods of prehistory, by themselves they tell us little about the evolution of specific cultural systems and can even interfere with our undersanding of regional variation and change over time.

FIGURE 8.15. Fragmentary vessel from the Grindle site, Maine, A.D. 1150. Rim diameter 16 cm. (University of Maine.)

Sanger (1979:113) notes that in the last centuries of prehistory there appears to have been a spread of thinner pottery along the coast from a southern New England source (Figure 8.16). This change partially reversed the general trend toward thicker, coarser pottery in this period, but did not stem the decline of the craft. By A.D. 1600 pottery had been replaced by birchbark and European copper kettles. Thus, while village nucleation was going on, ceramics were in decline and being replaced by birchbark. It may be that this reversal of ceramic trends elsewhere in aboriginal New England was one consequence of the new settlement pattern, which may have required more travel to and from temporary camps than had been the case in the previous period. Indeed, the permanent nonhorticultural villages of the period could not have been maintained without swift travel by canoe (Figure 8.17) and frequent trips to temporary camps. The settlement system, which stressed both permanent villages and mobility, made ceramics maladaptive after A.D. 1000.

Changes in projectile point attributes in the same period do not appear to

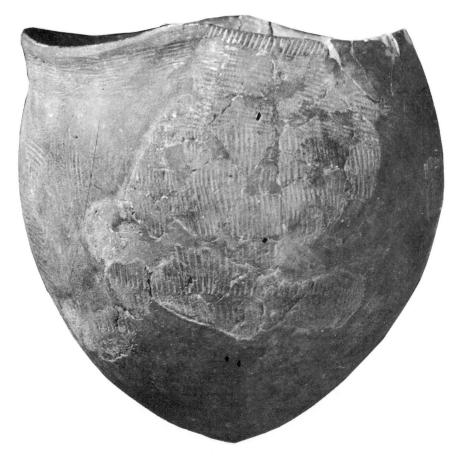

FIGURE 8.16. Restored vessel from the Nevin site. (Collection of the R. S. Peabody Foundation.)

reflect any broader changes in the system. "By historic times two main forms were in use. In eastern Maine prevalent forms were well made with narrow side or corner notches, while in central and western Maine triangular points were more common [Sanger 1979:113–114]." This stylistic contrast appears to have no functional significance, and we can infer that it reflects the Late Prehistoric divergence of Maliseet–Passamaquoddy from Eastern Abenaki culture.

Artifacts like those just described are occasionally found with burials (Figure 8.18), but, as in southern New England, burial ceremonialism was no longer as important as it had once been. Burials tend to be flexed primary interments as elsewhere in the Northeast at this time.

As in the case of southern New England, the cultures of northern New England in this last period of prehistory present us with variations on a single cultural system. That system emerged in a few centuries prior to A.D. 1600 and culminated in the form described for the northern drainages in Chapter

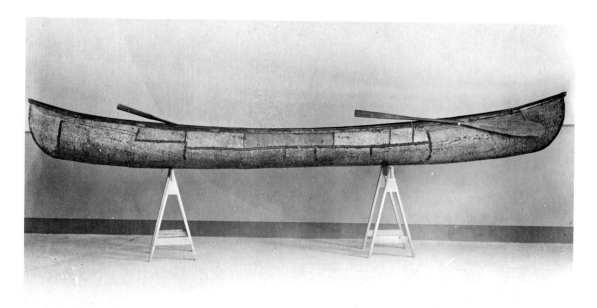

FIGURE 8.17. Passamaquoddy birchbark canoe with paddles. (Courtesy of Peabody Museum, Harvard University.)

2. The avoidance of horticulture until after A.D. 1600, the decline in ceramics before that date, and other trends that ran contrary to those of southern New England and New York have been seen to make sense in terms of the evolving cultural system of the north. Northern population densities, governed as they were by the midwinter carrying capacity of the land, could not rise to the levels of southern New England under aboriginal conditions. But it should be clear by now that the northern communities were not the squalid backwaters many have presumed them to have been. The reader might well return to Chapter 2 and see all the historic Indians of New England in a new light.

The riverine model was an implicit organizer of aboriginal New Englanders for thousands of years and has been an important organizing principle in this synthesis of their prehistory as well. But at the end of prehistory we see that the model was distorted, breaking down under the weight of new principles that better fitted the circumstances accompanying horticulture and warfare. The lower Champlain drainage was occupied by St. Lawrence Iroquois. The older Algonquian-speaking inhabitants of that drainage were probably partly absorbed by the Mahican of the Hudson drainage, while others may have joined communities in the upper Connecticut and Merrimack drainages to form the broad Western Abenaki culture of northern New England. For their part, the Mahican found themselves hemmed in by the Mohawk to the west and by intrusive Munsee in the south. Just as the Munsee moved eastward into the lower Hudson drainage and onto Long Island, so

FIGURE 8.18. Sheet copper gorget from Amoskeag Falls, Manchester, N.H., about 25 cm tall. Probably made from a piece of copper kettle. (Photo by Hillel Burger. Courtesy of Peabody Museum, Harvard University.)

too the Massachusett expanded into the lower Merrimack drainage. In the end, the trajectory of 12,500 years of prehistory brings us back to the target set up in Chapter 2, and the task is finished for now. But there is much more. There will be expansions, revisions, new problems, and probably whole new visions of the nature of prehistory and archaeology. It is inevitable that the best of the past is yet to come.

REFERENCES

Andrews, J. T.
  1972 Recent and fossil growth rates of marine bivalves, Canadian arctic, and Late-Quaternary arctic marine environments. *Paleogeography, Paleoclimatology, Paleoecology* 11:157–176.

Antevs, E.
  1955 Geologic-climatic dating in the West. *American Antiquity* 20(4):317–335.

Arber, E., and A. G. Bradley
  1910 *Travels and works of John Smith* (2 vol.). J. Grant, Edinburgh.

Archer, G.
  1843 The relation of Captain Gosnold's voyage. *Massachusetts Historical Society Collections, Third Series* 8:72–81.

Asher, G. M. (editor)
  1860 *Henry Hudson the navigator*. Burt Franklin, New York.

Banfield, A. W. F.
  1974 *The mammals of Canada*. University of Toronto Press, Toronto.

Barber, R. J.
  1977 Disjunct plant distributions and archaeological interpretation. *Man in the Northeast* 13:103–107.

Bates, O., and H. E. Winlock
  1912 *Archaeological material from the Maine littoral with especial reference to the Bates collection*. Unpublished thesis for Anthropology 20, Harvard University.

Beardsley, R. K., P. Holder, A. D. Krieger, B. J. Meggers, J. B. Rinaldo, and P. Kutsche
  1956 Functional and evolutionary implications of community patterning. Seminars in archaeology: 1955. *Society for American Archaeology, Memoir* 11:129–155.

Bell, R. E.
  1960 Guide to the identification of certain American Indian projectile points. *Oklahoma Anthropological Society Special Bulletin No. 2.*

Bennett, M. K.
  1955 The food economy of the New England Indians, 1605–75. *The Journal of Political Economy* 63(5):369–397.

Bock, P. K.
  1978 Micmac. In *Handbook of North American Indians*, edited by Bruce G. Trigger, Vol. 15, pp. 109–122. Smithsonian Institution, Washington, D.C.

345

Bolian, C. E.
   1977   *Evidence for the presence of Early and Middle Archaic cultures in the Lakes Region of New Hampshire.* Paper read at the 17th annual meeting of the Northeast Anthropological Association, Providence, R.I.
Bonnichsen, R., and D. Sanger
   1977   Integrating faunal analysis. *Canadian Journal of Archaeology* 1:109–133.
Bormann, F. H., and G. E. Likens
   1979   Catastrophic disturbance and the steady state in northern hardwood forests. *American Scientist* 67(6):660–669.
Borns, H. W., Jr.
   1971   Possible Paleo-Indian migration routes in northeast North America. *Maine Archaeological Society Bulletin* 11(1):1–3.
Bourque, B. J.
   1971   Possible Paleo-Indian migration routes in northeast North America. *Maine Archaeological Society Bulletin* 11(1):1–3.
   1973   Aboriginal settlement and subsistence on the Maine coast. *Man in the Northeast* 6:3–20.
   1975   Comments on the Late Archaic populations of central Maine: The view from the Turner Farm. *Arctic Anthropology* 12(2):35–45.
   1976   The Turner Farm site: A preliminary report. *Man in the Northeast* 11:21–30.
Bourque, B. J., K. Morris, and A. Spiess
   1978   Determining the season of death of mammal teeth from archaeological sites: A new sectioning technique. *Science* 199(4328):530–531.
Bradford, W.
   1908   *Bradford's history of Plymouth Plantation*, edited by William T. Davis, Scribner's Sons, New York.
Brasser, T. J.
   1974   Riding on the frontier's crest: Mahican Indian culture and culture change. *National Museum of Man Ethnology Division Mercury Series* 13 (Ottawa).
   1978a Early Indian European contacts. In *Handbook of North American Indians*, edited by Bruce G. Trigger, Vol. 15, pp. 78–88. Smithsonian Institution, Washington, D.C.
   1978b Mahican. In *Handbook of North American Indians*, edited by Bruce G. Trigger, Vol. 15, pp. 198–212. Smithsonian Institution, Washington, D.C.
Braun, D. P.
   1974   Explanatory models for the evolution of coastal adaptation in prehistoric eastern New England. *American Antiquity* 39(4):582–596.
Brennan, L. A.
   1967   The Taconic tradition and the Coe axiom. *New York State Archeological Association Bulletin* 39:1–14.
   1974   The lower Hudson: A decade of shell middens. *Archaeology of Eastern North America* 2(1):81–93.
   1975   *Artifacts of prehistoric America.* Stackpole, Harrisburg, Penn.
   1976   Coastal adaptation in prehistoric New England. *American Antiquity* 41(1):112–113.
   1977a The lower Hudson: The Archaic. In Amerinds and their paleoenvironments in northeastern North America. *Annals of the New York Academy of Sciences* 288:411–430.
   1977b The midden is the message. *Archaeology of Eastern North America* 5:122–137.
Broyles, B. J.
   1966   Preliminary report: The St. Albans site. *West Virginia Archaeologist* 19:1–43.
Brumbach, H. J.
   1975   "Iroquoian" ceramics in "Algonquian" territory. *Man in the Northeast* 10:17–28.
   1978   *Middle Woodland fishing economics: The upper Hudson River drainage.* Unpublished Ph.D. dissertation, Dept. of Anthropology, State University of New York at Albany.
Buell, N.
   1979   *The Proto-Iroquoian homeland.* Unpublished M.A. thesis Dept. of Anthropology, State University of New York at Albany.

Bushnell, D. I., Jr.
  1913 The "Red-Paint People." *American Anthropologist* 15:707–710.
  1915 The "Red-Paint People" II. *American Anthropologist* 17:207–209.
Butzer, K. W.
  1971 *Environment and archeology: An ecological approach to prehistory.* Aldine, Chicago,
Byers, D. S.
  1953 "Red Paint Tombs" in Maine. *Massachusetts Archaeological Society Bulletin* 15(1):1–8.
  1954 Bull Brook—A fluted point site in Ipswich, Massachusetts. *American Antiquity* 19(4):343–351.
  1956 Additional information on the Bull Brook site, Massachusetts. *American Antiquity* 20(3):274–276.
  1959 The Eastern Archaic: Some problems and hypotheses. *American Antiquity* 24(3):233–256.
  1961 Second comment on William Ritchie's "Iroquois archaeology and settlement patterns." In Symposium on Cherokee and Iroquois culture, edited by William Fenton and John Gulick. *Smithsonian Institution, Bureau of American Ethnology, Bulletin* 180:47–50.
  1979 The Nevin shellheap: Burials and observations. *Papers of the R. S. Peabody Foundation for Archaeology, Vol. 9.*
Byers, D. S., and Irving Rouse
  1960 A re-examination of the Guida Farm. *Archaeological Society of Connecticut Bulletin* 30:5–39.
Carneiro, R. L., and D. F. Hilse
  1966 On determining the probable rate of population growth during the Neolithic. *American Anthropologist* 68(1):177–181.
Ceci, L.
  1975 Fish fertilizer: A native North American practice? *Science* 188(4183):26–30.
Chapman, J.
  1976 The Archaic period in the lower Little Tennessee River valley: The radiocarbon dates. *Tennessee Anthropologist* 1(1):1–12.
Chomko, S. A., and G. W. Crawford
  1978 Plant husbandry in prehistoric eastern North America: New evidence for its development. *American Antiquity* 43(3):405–408.
Clarke, D. L.
  1968 *Analytical archaeology.* Methuen, London.
Cleland, C. E.
  1976 The focal–diffuse model: An evolutionary perspective on the prehistoric cultural adaptations of the eastern United States. *Mid-Continental Journal of Archaeology* 1(1):59–76.
Coe, J. L.
  1964 The formative cultures of the Carolina Piedmont. *Transactions of the American Philosophical Society* 54(5).
Cohen, M. N.
  1975 Archaeological evidence for population pressure in preagricultural societies. *American Antiquity* 40(4):471–475.
Conkey, L. E., E. Boissevain, and I. Goddard
  1978 Indians of southern New England and Long Island: Late period. In *Handbook of North American Indians*, edited by Bruce G. Trigger, Vol. 15, pp. 177–189. Smithsonian Institution, Washington, D.C.
Connally, G. G., and L. A. Sirkin
  1971 Luzerne readvance near Glens Falls, New York. *Geological Society of America Bulletin* 81:989–1008.
Cook, S. F.
  1972 Prehistoric demography. *McCaleb Module in Anthropology*, 16 (Addison-Wesley, Reading, Massachusetts).

1973a   The significance of disease in the extinction of the New England Indians. *Human Biology* 45(3):485–508.

1973b   Interracial warfare and population decline among the New England Indians. *Ethnohistory* 20(1):1–24.

1976   The Indian population of New England in the seventeenth century. *University of California (Berkeley) Publications in Anthropology*, 12.

Cook, T. G.
1976   Broadpoint: Culture, phase, horizon, tradition, or knife? *Journal of Anthropological Research* 32(4):337–357.

Cooke, D., and B. Jordan
1972   An Adena-like burial at East Windsor Hill. *Archaeological Society of Connecticut Bulletin* 37:47–51.

Cowgill, G. L.
1975   Population pressure as a non-explanation. In Population studies in archaeology and biological anthropology: A symposium, edited by Alan C. Swedlund. *Society for American Archaeology Memoir* 30:127–131.

Cox, S. L.
1972   A Re-analysis of the Shoop site. Unpublished report, Smithsonian Institution.

Crane, H. R., and J. B. Griffin
1959   University of Michigan radiocarbon dates IV. *American Journal of Science Radiocarbon Supplement* 1:173–198.

Curran, M. L., and D. F. Dincauze
1977   Paleoindians and paleo-lakes: New data from the Connecticut drainage. In Amerinds and their paleoenvironments in northeastern North America. *Annals of the New York Academy of Sciences* 288:333–348.

Curtin, E.
1979   *Demographic and economic changes in the upper Susquehanna Late Archaic.* Paper read at the 19th annual meeting of the Northeast Anthropological Association, Henniker, New Hampshire.

Davis, M. B.
1965   Phytogeography and palynology of northeastern United States. In *The quaternary of the United States*, edited by H. E. Wright, Jr. and David G. Frey, pp. 377–401. Princeton University Press, Princeton.

1967   Late-glacial climate in northern United States: A comparison of New England and the Great Lakes region. In *Quaternary paleoecology*, edited by E. J. Cushing and H. E. Wright, Jr., pp. 11–43. Yale University Press, New Haven.

1969   Palynological and environmental history during the Quaternary period. *American Scientist* 57(3):317–322.

Davis, R. B., T. E. Bradstreet, R. Stuckenrath, Jr., and H. W. Borns, Jr.
1975   Vegetation and associated environments during the past 14,000 years near Moulton Pond, Maine. *Quaternary Research* 5(3):435–466.

Day, G. M.
1962   English–Indian contacts in New England. *Ethnohistory* 9(1):24–40.

1971   The eastern boundary of Iroquoia: Abenaki evidence. *Man in the Northeast* 1:7–13.

1978   Western Abenaki. In *Handbook of North American Indians*, edited by Bruce G. Trigger, Vol. 15, pp. 148–159. Smithsonian Institution, Washington, D.C.

Dincauze, D. F.
1968   *Cremation cemeteries in eastern Massachusetts.* Peabody Museum, Cambridge, Massachusetts.

1971a   An Archaic sequence for southern New England. *American Antiquity* 36(2):194–198.

1971b   Population dynamics in southeastern New England: An essay in prehistory. Manuscript in Dincauze's possession.

1972   The Atlantic phase: A Late Archaic culture in Massachusetts. *Man in the Northeast* 4:40–61.

1973 Prehistoric occupation of the Charles River Estuary. *Archaeological Society of Connecticut Bulletin* 38:25–39.

1974 An introduction to archaeology in the greater Boston area. *Archaeology of Eastern North America* 2:39–66.

1975a The Late Archaic period in southern New England. *Arctic Anthropology* 12(2):23–24.

1975b Ceramic sherds from the Charles River Valley. *Archaeological Society of Connecticut Bulletin* 39:5–17.

1976 The Neville site: 8000 years at Amoskeag. *Peabody Museum Monographs* No. 4.

Dincauze, D. F., and M. T. Mulholland

1977 Early and Middle Archaic site distributions and habitats in southern New England. In Amerinds and their paleoenvironments in northeastern North America. *Annals of the New York Academy of Sciences* 288:439–456.

Dobyns, H. F.

1966 Estimating aboriginal American population, 1: An appraisal of techniques with a new hemispheric estimate. *Current Anthropology* 7(4):395–416.

Dragoo, D. W.

1976 Adena and the eastern burial cult. *Archaeology of Eastern North America* 4:1–9.

Driver, H. E., and W. C. Massey

1957 Comparative studies of North American Indians. *Transactions of the American Philosophical Society* 47(2):165–456.

Dumond, D. E.

1972 Population growth and political centralization. In *Population growth: Anthropological implications*, edited by Brian Spooner, pp. 286–310. MIT Press, Cambridge.

Dumont, E.

1974 *Rockelein I: The Archaic component.* Paper presented at the annual meeting of the New York State Archaeological Association.

Eckstorm, F. H.

1941 *Indian place-names of the Penobscot valley and the Maine coast.* University of Maine Press, Orono.

Edwards, R. L., and K. O. Emery

1977 Man on the continental shelf. In Amerinds and their paleoenvironments in northeastern North America. *Annals of the New York Academy of Sciences* 288:245–256.

Edwards, R. L., and A. S. Merrill

1977 A reconstruction of the continental shelf areas of eastern North America for the times 9,500 B.P and 12,500 B.P. *Archaeology of Eastern North America* 5:1–43.

Eisenberg, L.

1978 Paleo-Indian settlement pattern in the Hudson and Delaware river drainages. *Man in the Northeast, Occasional Publications in Northeastern Anthropology* No. 4.

Ellis, G. W., and J. E. Morris

1906 *King Philip's War: Based on the Archives and Records of Massachusetts, Plymouth, Rhode Island and Connecticut, and Contemporary Letters and Accounts, with Biographical and Topographical Notes.* Grafton, New York.

Emery, K. O., and R. L. Edwards

1966 Archaeological potential of the Atlantic continental shelf. *American Antiquity* 31(5):733–737.

Engelbrecht, W.

1972 The reflection of patterned behavior in Iroquois pottery. *Pennsylvania Archaeologist* 42(3):1–15.

1974 Cluster analysis: A method for studying Iroquois prehistory. *Man in the Northeast* 7:57–70.

Erikson, V. O.

1978 Maliseet–Passamaquoddy. In *Handbook of North American Indians*, edited by Bruce G. Trigger, Vol. 15, pp. 123–136. Smithsonian Institution, Washington, D.C.

Feest, C. F.

1978a Nanticoke and neighboring tribes. In *Handbook of North American Indians*, edited by Bruce G. Trigger, Vol. 15, pp. 240–252. Smithsonian Institution, Washington, D.C.

1978b Virginia Algonquians. In *Handbook of North American Indians*, edited by Bruce G. Trigger, Vol. 15, pp. 253–270. Smithsonian Institution, Washington, D.C.

Fenton, W. N.

1940 Problems arising from the historic northeastern position of the Iroquois. *Smithsonian Miscellaneous Collections* 100:159–252.

1978 Northern Iroquoian culture patterns. In *Handbook of North American Indians*, edited by Bruce G. Trigger, Vol. 15, pp. 296–321. Smithsonian Institution, Washington, D.C.

Fenton, W. N., and E. Tooker

1978 Mohawk. In *Handbook of North American Indians*, edited by Bruce G. Trigger, Vol. 15, pp. 466–480. Smithsonian Institution, Washington, D.C.

Fischer, David H.

1970 *Historians' fallacies.* Harper & Row, New York.

Fisher, D. W.

1955 Prehistoric mammals of New York. *New York State Conservationist* Feb.–March:18–22.

Fitting, J. E.

1968 Environmental potential and the postglacial readaptation in eastern North America. *American Antiquity* 33(4):441–445.

Fitting, J. E., J. DeVisscher, and E. J. Wahla

1966 The Paleo-Indian occupation of the Holcombe Beach. *University of Michigan Museum of Anthropology Paper* 27.

Fitzhugh, W.

1972 The eastern Archaic: Commentary and northern perspective. *Pennsylvania Archaeologist* 42(4):1–19.

Flannery, K.

1973 Archaeology with a capital S. In *Research and theory in current archaeology*, edited by Charles L. Redman, pp. 47–53. Wiley, New York.

Flint, R. F.

1971 *Glacial and quaternary geology.* Wiley, New York.

Fowler, M. L.

1959 Summary report of Modoc Rock shelter: 1952, 1953, 1955, 1956. *Illinois State Museum Report of Investigations* No. 8.

Fowler, W. S.

1966 Ceremonial and domestic products of aboriginal New England. *Massachusetts Archaeological Society Bulletin* 27(3&4).

Funk, R. E.

1972 Early man in the Northeast and the late-glacial environment. *Man in the Northeast* 4:7–39.

1976 Recent contributions to Hudson valley prehistory. *New York State Museum and Science Service Memoir* 22.

1977a Early cultures in the Hudson drainage basin. In Amerinds and their paleoenvironments in Northeastern North America. *Annals of the New York Academy of Sciences* 288:316–332.

1977b Early to Middle Archaic occupations in upstate New York. In Current perspectives in northeastern archeology. *New York State Archeological Association Researches and Transactions* 17(1):21–29.

1978 Post-Pleistocene adaptations. In *Handbook of North American Indians*, edited by Bruce G. Trigger, Vol. 15, pp. 16–27. Smithsonian Institution, Washington, D.C.

Funk, R. E., D. W. Fisher, and E. M. Reilly, Jr.

1970 Caribou and Paleo-Indian in New York State: A presumed association. *American Journal of Science* 268:181–186.

Funk, R. E., and B. E. Rippeteau
  1977 Adaptation, continuity and change in Upper Susquehanna prehistory. *Man in the Northeast, Occasional Publications in Northeastern Anthropology* No. 3.

Funk, R. E., G. R. Walters, and W. F. Ehlers, Jr.
  1969 A radiocarbon date for early man from the Dutchess Quarry Cave. *New York State Archeological Association Bulletin* 46:19–21.

Funk, R. E., T. P. Weinman, and P. L. Weinman
  1969 The Kings Road site: A recently discovered Paleo-Indian manifestation in Greene County, New York. *New York State Archeological Association Bulletin* 45:1–23.

Goddard, I.
  1971 The ethnohistorical implications of early Delaware linguistic materials. *Man in the Northeast* 1:14–26.

  1978a Eastern Algonquian languages. In *Handbook of North American Indians*, edited by Bruce G. Trigger, Vol. 15, pp. 70–77. Smithsonian Institution, Washington, D.C.

  1978b Delaware. In *Handbook of North American Indians*, edited by Bruce G. Trigger, Vol. 15, pp. 213–239. Smithsonian Institution, Washington, D.C.

  1978c Central Algonquian languages. In *Handbook of North American Indians*, edited by Bruce G. Trigger, Vol. 15, pp. 583–587. Smithsonian Institution, Washington, D.C.

Goldthwaite, R. P.
  1935 The Damariscotta shell heaps and coastal stability. *American Journal of Science* 30(175):1–13.

Goodwin, W. B.
  1946 *The ruins of Great Ireland in New England*. Meador, Boston.

Gookin, D.
  1970 *Historical collections of the Indians in New England*. Towtaid, Boston.

Gorges, F.
  1890 Sir Ferdinando Gorges and his province of Maine. In *Publications of the Prince Society*, edited by James P. Baxter, Vol. 2, No. 19. Burt Franklin, New York.

Grant, W. L. (editor)
  1907 *Voyages of Samuel de Champlain*. Scribner's Sons, New York.

Grayson, D. K.
  1970 Statistical inference and northeastern Adena. *American Antiquity* 35(1):102–104.

  1974 The Riverhaven No. 2 vertebrate fauna: Comments on methods in faunal analysis and on aspects of the subsistence potential of prehistoric New York. *Man in the Northeast* 8:23–39.

Griffin, J. B.
  1961a Some correlations of climatic and cultural change in eastern North American prehistory. *Annals of the New York Academy of Science* 95:710–717.

  1961b Review of the eastern dispersal of Adena by William A. Ritchie and Don W. Dragoo. *American Antiquity* 26(4):572–573.

  1967 Eastern North American archaeology: A summary. *Science* 156(3772):175–191.

  1975 Review of "Adena: The seeking of an identity" by B. K. Swartz, Jr., ed. *American Antiquity* 40(3):377–378.

Gruber, J. W.
  1978 Archaeological strata and cultural process. *Archaeology of Eastern North America* 6:91–94.

Guilday, J. E.
  1968 Archaeological evidence of caribou from New York and Massachusetts. *Journal of Mammalogy* 49(2):344–345.

  1969 A possible caribou–Paleo-Indian association from Dutchess Quarry Cave, Orange County, New York. *New York State Archeological Association Bulletin* 45:24–29.

Gyles, J.
  1853 John Gyles's statement of the number of Indians. *Maine Historical Society Collections, First Series* 3:355–358.

Haas, M. R.
1958   A new linguistic relationship in North America: Algonkian and the Gulf languages. *Southwestern Journal of Anthropology* 14(3):231–264.

Hadlock, W. S.
1941   Observations concerning the "Red Paint Culture." *American Antiquity* 7:156–161.

Hadlock, W. S., and T. Stern
1948   Passadumkeag, a Red Paint cemetery, thirty-five years after Moorehead. *American Antiquity* 14:98–103.

Hakluyt, R.
1965   *The principall navigations, voiages, and discoveries of the English Nation 1589* (2 vols.). The University Press, Cambridge.

Hall, J., and E. Woodman
1973   Beehive-shaped stone structures: Ancient or recent origin. *Man in the Northeast* 5:60–62.

Hammer, J., L. Fagan, and D. R. Snow
n.d.   Report on excavations at the Harrisena site. Manuscript on file, Dept. of Anthropology, State University of New York at Albany.

Haugen, E.
1972   The rune stones of Spirit Pond, Maine. *Man in the Northeast* 4:62–80.
1973   Comment on O. G. Landsverk's "The spirit pond cryptography." *Man in the Northeast* 6:75–76.

Haviland, W. A.
1970   Gorgets: Ornamental or utilitarian? *Massachusetts Archaeological Society Bulletin* 31(3-4):30–32.

Haynes, C. V.
1964   Fluted projectile points: Their age and dispersion. *Science* 145:1408–1413.
1969   The earliest Americans. *Science* 166:709–715.
1977   When and from where did man arrive in Northeastern North America: A discussion. In Amerinds and their paleoenvironments in northeastern North America. *Annals of the New York Academy of Sciences* 288:165–166.

Hencken, H. O.
1939   The "Irish Monastery" at North Salem, New Hampshire. *The New England Quarterly* 12:429–442.
1940   What are Patee's Caves? *Scientific American* 165(5):258–259.

Hester, J. J.
1960   Late Pleistocene extinction and radiocarbon dating. *American Antiquity* 26(1):58–77.

Hockett, C. F.
1958   *A course in modern linguistics.* Macmillan, New York.

Hoffman, B. G.
1955   *The historical ethnography of the Micmac of the sixteenth and seventeenth centuries.* Unpublished Ph.D. dissertation, Dept. of Anthropology, University of California, Berkeley.

Hough, J. L.
1963   The prehistoric Great Lakes of North America. *American Scientist* 51:84–109.

Howley, J. P.
1915   *The Beothucks or Red Indians.* Cambridge University Press, Cambridge.

Hunt, C. B.
1967   *Physiography of the United States.* Freeman, San Francisco.

Ingstad, A. S.
1977   *The discovery of a Norse settlement in America.* Columbia University Press, New York.

Irving, W. N., and C. R. Harington
1973   Upper Pleistocene radiocarbon-dated artefacts from the northern Yukon. *Science* 179:335–340.

Jameson, J. F. (editor)

1909 *Narratives of New Netherland.* Scribner's Sons, New York.

Johnson, F. (editor)

1942 The Boylston Street fishweir. *Papers of the Robert S. Peabody Foundation for Archaeology*, Vol. 2.

Jordan, D. F.

1960 *The Bull Brook site in relation to "fluted point" manifestation in eastern North America.* Unpublished Ph.D. dissertation, Dept. of Anthropology, Harvard University.

Kaeser, E. J.

1963 The Morris Club site. *New York State Archeological Association Bulletin* 27:13–21.

1968 The Middle Woodland placement of Steubenville-like projectile points in coastal New York's Abbott complex. *New York State Archeological Association Bulletin* 44:8–26.

Kehoe, A. B.

1962 A hypothesis on the origin of northeastern American pottery. *Southwestern Journal of Anthropology* 18(1):20–29.

Kenyon, V. B.

1979 A new approach to the analysis of New England prehistoric pottery. *Man in the Northeast* 18:81–84.

Kinsey, W. F., III

1968 A Pennsylvania transitional period radiocarbon date. *American Antiquity* 33(2):245–247.

1971 The Middle Atlantic culture province: A point of view. *Pennsylvania Archaeologist* 41(1–2):1–8.

Kirkland, J. T., and D. R. Coates

1977 The Champlain Sea and Quaternary deposits in the St. Lawrence lowland, New York. In Amerinds and their paleoenvironments in northeastern North America. *Annals of the New York Academy of Sciences* 288:498–507.

Kraft, H. C.

1970a *The Miller Field site, Part 1.* Seton Hall University Press, South Orange, New Jersey.

1970b Prehistoric Indian housepatterns in New Jersey. *Archaeological Society of New Jersey Bulletin* 26.

1973 The Plenge site: A Paleo-Indian occupation site in New Jersey. *Archaeology of Eastern North America* 1(1):56–117.

1975a The Late Woodland pottery of the upper Delaware Valley: A survey and reevaluation. *Archaeology of Eastern North America* 3:101–104.

1975b *The archaeology of the Tocks Island area.* Seton Hall University Museum, South Orange, New Jersey.

1977a Paleoindians in New Jersey. In Amerinds and their paleoenvironments in northeastern North America. *Annals of the New York Academy of Sciences* 288:264–281.

1977b The Paleo-Indian sites at Port Mobil, Staten Island. In Current perspectives in northeastern archeology. *New York State Archeological Association Researches and Transactions* 17(1):1–19.

Kraft, J. C.

1977 Late Quaternary paleogeographic changes in the coastal environments of Delaware, Middle Atlantic Bight, related to archaeological settings. In Amerinds and their paleoenvironments in northeastern North America. *Annals of the New York Academy of Sciences* 288:35–69.

Krieger, A. D.

1964 Early man in the New World. In *Prehistoric man in the New World*, edited by Jesse D. Jennings and Edward Norbeck, pp. 23–81. University of Chicago Press, Chicago.

Kroeber, A. L.

1939 Cultural and natural areas of native North America. *University of California Publications in American Archaeology and Ethnology* 38.

LaFleur, R. G.

1976 Glacial Lake Albany. In *Pine Bush: Albany's last frontier*, edited by Don Rittner, pp. 1–10. Pine Bush Historic Preservation Project, Albany.

Landsverk, O. G.

1973 The Spirit Pond cryptography. *Man in the Northeast* 6:67–75.

Lenig, D.

1965 The Oak Hill horizon and its relation to the development of Five Nations Iroquois culture. *Researches and Transactions of the New York State Archeological Association* 15(1).

Lenik, E. J.

1975 Excavations at Spirit Pond. *Man in the Northeast* 9:54–60.

1977 The Spirit Pond shellheap. *Archaeology of Eastern North America* 5:94–107.

Levett, C.

1905 My discovery of diverse rivers and harbours. In *Sailors' narratives of voyages along the New England coast*, edited by G. P. Winship, pp. 259–292. Burt Franklin, New York.

Lounsbury, F.

1961 Iroquois–Cherokee linguistic relations. In Symposium on Cherokee and Iroquois culture, edited by W. N. Fenton and J. Gulick. *Bureau of American Ethnology Bulletin* 180.

1978 Iroquoian languages. In *Handbook of North American Indians*, edited by Bruce G. Trigger, Vol. 15, pp. 334–343. Smithsonian Institution, Washington, D.C.

Lull, H. W.

1968 *A forest atlas of the Northeast.* Northeastern Forest Experiment Station, Upper Darby, Pennsylvania.

MacDonald, G. F.

1968 Debert: A Paleo-Indian site in central Nova Scotia. *National Museum of Canada Anthropological Paper* 16 (Ottawa).

MacNeish, R. S.

1952 Iroquois pottery types. *National Museum of Canada Bulletin* 124 (Ottawa).

1976 The in situ Iroquois revisited and rethought. In *Cultural change and continuity*, edited by Charles Cleland, pp. 79–98. Academic Press, New York.

MacNeish, R. S., A. Nelken-Terner, and A. Garcia-Cook

1970 *Second annual report of the Ayacucho archaeological-botanical project.* R. S. Peabody Foundation for Archaeology: Andover, Mass.

Martin, P. S.

1967 Pleistocene overkill. In *Pleistocene extinctions: The search for a cause*, edited by Paul S. Martin and Herbert E. Wright, Jr., pp. 75–120. Yale University Press, New Haven.

1973 The discovery of America. *Science* 179:969–974.

Martin, P. S., and J. E. Guilday

1967 A bestiary for Pleistocene biologists. In *Pleistocene extinctions: The search for a cause*, edited by Paul S. Martin and Herbert E. Wright, Jr., pp. 1–62. Yale University Press, New Haven.

McBride, K. A.

1978 Archaic subsistence in the lower Connecticut River valley: Evidence from Woodchuck Knoll. *Man in the Northeast* 15-16:124–132.

McGhee, R. J., and J. A. Tuck

1975 An Archaic sequence from the Strait of Belle Isle, Labrador. *National Museum of Man Mercury Series* 34 (Ottawa).

McKern, W. C.

1937 A hypothesis for the Asiatic origin of the Woodland culture pattern. *American Antiquity* 3(2):138–143.

1939 The midwestern taxonomic method as an aid to archaeological culture study. *American Antiquity* 16(3):310–313.

McNett, C. W., Jr., J. Evans, and R. J. Dent

1977 Report on third and fourth seasons of the Upper Delaware Valley Early Man Project. Manuscript on file, Dept. of Anthropology, American University.

Michels, J., and I. F. Smith
    1967 *Archaeological investigations of Sheep Rock shelter, Huntingdon County, Pennsylvania*,
          Vols. 1 and 2. State College, Department of Anthropology, Pennsylvania State Univer-
          sity.
Michlovic, M. G.
    1975 Social interaction and point types in the eastern U. S. *Pennsylvania Archaeologist*
          46(1–2):13–16.
Miller, V. P.
    1976 Aboriginal Micmac population: A review of the evidence. *Ethnohistory* 23(2):117–
          127.
Moeller, R. W.
    1980 6LF21: A Paleo-Indian site in western Connecticut. *American Indian Archaeological
          Institute Occasional Paper* No. 2.
Mooney, J.
    1928 The aboriginal population of America north of Mexico. *Smithsonian Miscellaneous
          Collections* 80(7):1–40.
Moore, C. B.
    1914 The Red Paint people of Maine. *American Anthropologist* 16:137–139.
    1915 The "Red Paint People" II. *American Anthropologist* 17:209.
Moorehead, W. K.
    1913 The Red Paint people of Maine. *American Anthropologist* 15:33–47.
    1914 "The Red Paint People"—A reply. *American Anthropologist* 16:358–361.
    1922 *A report on the archaeology of Maine.* Department of Anthropology, Phillips Academy,
          Andover.
Morison, Samuel E.
    1971 *The European discovery of America: The northern voyages A.D. 500–1600.* Oxford
          University Press, New York.
Newman, W. S.
    1974 A comment on Snow's "Rising sea level and prehistoric cultural ecology in northern
          New England." *American Antiquity* 39(1):135–136.
Ogden, J. G., III
    1977a The late Quaternary paleoenvironmental record of northeastern North America. In
           Amerinds and their paleoenvironments in northeastern North America. *Annals of the
           New York Academy of Sciences* 288:16–34.
    1977b The use and abuse of radiocarbon dating. In Amerinds and their paleoenvironments
           in northeastern North America. *Annals of the New York Academy of Sciences* 288:167–
           173.
Oswalt, W. H.
    1966 *This land was theirs: A study of the North American Indian.* Wiley, New York.
Palter, J. L.
    1976 A new approach to the significance of the "weighted" spear thrower. *American
          Antiquity* 41(4):500–510.
Peets, Orville H.
    1965 What, really, were gorgets? *American Antiquity* 31(1):113–116.
Perino, Gregory
    1968 Guide to the identification of certain American Indian projectile points. *Oklahoma
          Anthropological Society Special Bulletin* No. 3.
Potter, S. R., and G. A. Waselkov
    1976 Eastern archaeology: Directions for a reorientation. *Archaeology of Eastern North
          America* 4:122–128.
Powell, B. W.
    1971 First site synthesis and proposed chronology for the aborigines of southwestern Con-
          necticut. *Pennsylvania Archaeologist* 41(1–2):30–37.
    1977 Observations on "The lower Hudson: A decade of shell middens." *Man in the Northeast*
          13:99–103.

Purchas, S.

1625   The description of the countrey of Mawooshen, discovered by the English in the Yeere 1602.3.5.6.7.8. and 9. In *Hakluytus Posthumus or Purchas his pilgrims*, Vol. 4, pp. 1873–1875. Henry Fetherston, London.

Quinn, D. V., and T. Dunbabin

1966   Ingram, David, English mariner, who claimed to have walked from Mexico to Acadia, 1568–69. *Dictionary of Canadian Biography* 1:380–381.

Rafn, C. C.

1837   *Antiquitates Americanae sive scriptores septentrionales rerum ante-Columbianarum in America.* Copenhagen.

Renfrew, C.

1978   Trajectory discontinuity and morphogenesis: The implications of catastrophe theory for archaeology. *American Antiquity* 43(2):203–222.

Ritchie, W. A.

1947   Archaeological evidence for ceremonialism in Owasco culture. *Researches and Transactions of the New York State Archeological Association* 11(2).

1950   Another probable case of prehistoric bear ceremonialism in New York. *American Antiquity* 15(3):247–249.

1951   A current synthesis of New York prehistory. *American Antiquity* 17(2):130–136.

1952   The chance horizon. *New York State Museum and Science Service Circular* 29.

1953   A probable Paleo-Indian site in Vermont. *American Antiquity* 18(3):249–258.

1955   Recent discoveries suggesting an Early Woodland burial cult in the Northeast. *New York State Museum and Science Service Circular* 40.

1957   Traces of early man in the Northeast. *New York State Museum and Science Service Bulletin* 358.

1958   An introduction to Hudson valley prehistory. *New York State Museum and Science Service Bulletin* 367.

1959   The Stony Brook site and its relation to Archaic and Transitional cultures on Long Island. *New York State Museum and Science Service Bulletin* 372.

1969a   *The archaeology of New York State* (2nd ed.). Natural History Press, Garden City, New York.

1969b   *The archaeology of Martha's Vineyard.* Natural History Press, Garden City, New York.

1971a   A typology and nomenclature for New York projectile points. *New York State Museum and Science Service Bulletin* 384.

1971b   The Archaic in New York. *New York State Archeological Association Bulletin* 52:2–12.

Ritchie, W. A., and D. W. Dragoo

1960   The Eastern Dispersal of Adena. *New York State Museum and Science Service Bulletin* 379.

1961   Comments on Griffin's review of the Eastern Dispersal of Adena. *American Antiquity* 27(1):115–117.

Ritchie, W. A., and R. E. Funk

1971   Evidence for Early Archaic occupations on Staten Island. *Pennsylvania Archaeologist* 41(3):45–59.

1973   Aboriginal settlement patterns in the Northeast. *New York State Museum and Science Service Memoir* 20.

Ritchie, W. A., and R. S. MacNeish

1949   The pre-Iroquoian pottery of New York State. *American Antiquity* 15(2):97–124.

Robbins, M.

1968   *An Archaic ceremonial complex at Assawompsett.* Massachusetts Archaeological Society, Attleboro.

Robbins, M., and G. A. Agogino

1964   The Wapanucket No. 8 site: A Clovis–Archaic site in Massachusetts. *American Antiquity* 29(4):509–513.

Rodin, M., K. Michaelson, and G. M. Britan
  1978 Systems theory in anthropology. *Current Anthropology* 19(4):747–762.
Rosier, J.
  1905 A true relation of Captaine George Waymouth his voyage, made this present yeere
        1605; in the discouerie of the north part of Virginia. In *Sailors' narratives of voyages
        along the New England coast 1524–1624*, edited by G. P. Winship, pp. 101–151. Burt
        Franklin, New York.
Rouse, I.
  1945 Styles of pottery in Connecticut. *Massachusetts Archaeological Society Bulletin* 7(1):1–
        8.
  1947 Ceramic traditions and sequences in Connecticut. *Archaeological Society of Connecticut
        Bulletin* 21:10–25.
  1958 The inference of migrations from anthropological evidence. In Migration in New World
        culture history, edited by Raymond H. Thompson. *University of Arizona Social Science
        Bulletin* 27:63–68.
Sahlins, M. D.
  1968 *Tribesmen.* Prentice-Hall, Englewood Cliffs.
Salmon, M. H.
  1978 What can systems theory do for archaeology? *American Antiquity* 43(2):174–183.
Salwen, B.
  1962 Sea levels and archaeology in the Long Island Sound area. *American Antiquity*
        28(1):46–55.
  1965 *Sea levels and the Archaic archaeology of the northeast coast of the United States.* Ph.D.
        dissertation, Dept. of Anthropology, Columbia University. University Microfilms No.
        65-13,990, Ann Arbor.
  1968 Muskeeta Cove 2: A stratified woodland site on Long Island. *American Antiquity*
        33(3):322–340.
  1969 A tentative "in situ" solution to the Mohegan–Pequot problem. In *An introduction to
        the archaeology and history of the Connecticut valley Indian*, edited by William R.
        Young, pp. 81–88. Springfield Museum of Science, Illinois.
  1970 Cultural inferences from faunal remains: Examples from three Northeast coastal sites.
        Pennsylvania Archaeologist 40(1–2):1–8.
  1975 Post-glacial environments and cultural change in the Hudson river basin. *Man in the
        Northeast* 10:43–70.
  1978 Indians of southern New England and Long Island: Early period. In *Handbook of
        North American Indians*, edited by Bruce G. Trigger, Vol. 15, pp. 160–176. Smithsonian
        Institution, Washington, D.C.
Salwen, B., and A. Ottesen
  1972 Radiocarbon dates for a Windsor occupation at the Shantok Cove site, New London
        County, Connecticut. *Man in the Northeast* 3:8–19.
Sanger, D.
  1971a Deadman's pool—A Tobique complex site in northern New Brunswick. *Man in the
        Northeast* 2:5–22.
  1971b Passamaquoddy Bay prehistory: A summary. *Maine Archaeological Society Bulletin*
        11(2):14–19.
  1973 Cow Point: An Archaic cemetery in New Brunswick. *National Museum of Man Mercury
        Series* 12 (Ottawa).
  1975 Culture change as an adaptive process in the Maine–Maritimes region. *Arctic Anthro-
        pology* 12(2):60–75.
  1979 *Discovering Maine's archaeological heritage.* Maine Historic Preservation Commission,
        Augusta.
Sanger, D., R. B. Davis, R. G. MacKay, and H. W. Borns, Jr.
  1977 The Hirundo archaeological project—An interdisciplinary approach to central Maine
        prehistory. In Amerinds and their paleoenvironments in northeastern North America.
        Annals of the New York Academy of Sciences 288:457–471.

Seaby, P.

1978 The first datable Norse find from North America? *Seaby Coin and Medal Bulletin* Dec. 1978.

Service, E. R.

1962 *Primitive social organization.* Random House, New York.

Severin, T.

1977 The voyage of "Brendan." *National Geographic* 152(6):770–797.

Siebert, F. T., Jr.

1967 The original home of the proto-Algonquian people. *National Museum of Canada, Contributions to Anthropology: Linguistics I, Bulletin* 214:13–47.

Silverberg, R.

1968 *Mound Builders of Ancient America: The archaeology of a myth.* New York Graphic Society, Greenwich, Conn.

Simmons, W. S.

1970 *Cautantowwit's house.* Brown University Press, Providence.

1978 Narragansett. In *Handbook of North American Indians,* edited by Bruce G. Trigger, Vol. 15, pp. 190–197. Smithsonian Institution, Washington, D.C.

Skelton, R. A., T. E. Marston, and G. D. Painter

1965 *The Vineland map and the Tartar relation.* Yale University Press: New Haven.

Smith, B. L.

1948 An analysis of the Maine cemetery complex. *Massachusetts Archaeological Society Bulletin* 9:17–72.

Smith, C. S.

1950 The archeology of coastal New York. *Anthropological Papers of the American Museum of Natural History* 43(2).

Smith, W. B.

1929 *The lost Red Paint People of Maine.* Lafayette National Park Museum, Bar Harbor, Maine.

Snow, D. R.

1968a Wabanaki "family hunting territories." *American Anthropologist* 70(6):1143–1151.

1968b A century of Maine archaeology. *Maine Archaeological Society Bulletin* 8:8–25.

1969 A summary of excavations at the Hathaway site in Passadumkeag, Maine, 1912, 1947, and 1968. Department of Anthropology, University of Maine, Orono.

1972 Rising sea level and prehistoric cultural ecology in northern New England. *American Antiquity* 37(2):211–221.

1973 A model for the reconstruction of late eastern Algonquian prehistory. *Studies in Linguistics* 23:77–85.

1974 Reply to Newman. *American Antiquity* 39(1):136–137.

1975 The Passadumkeag sequence. *Arctic Anthropology* 12(2):46–59.

1976a The archaeological implications of the proto-Algonquian urheimat. In *Papers of the Seventh Algonquian Conference,* edited by William Cowan, pp. 339–346. Carleton University, Ottawa.

1976b The Solon petroglyphs and eastern Abenaki shamanism. In *Papers of the Seventh Algonquian Conference,* edited by William Cowan, pp. 281–288. Carleton University, Ottawa.

1976c Abenaki fur trade in the sixteenth century. *Western Canadian Journal of Anthropology* 6(1):3–11.

1976d The ethnohistoric baseline of the eastern Abenaki. *Ethnohistory* 23(3):291–306.

1976e *Archaeology of North America.* Viking, New York.

1977a The Archaic of the Lake George region. In Amerinds and their paleoenvironments in northeastern North America. *Annals of the New York Academy of Sciences* 288:431–438.

1977b Archeology and ethnohistory in eastern New York. In Current perspectives in northeastern archeology. *New York State Archeological Association Researches and Transactions* 17(1):107–112.

1978a   Late prehistory of the East Coast. In *Handbook of North American Indians*, edited by Bruce G. Trigger, Vol. 15, pp. 58–69. Smithsonian Institution, Washington, D.C.

1978b   Eastern Abenaki. In *Handbook of North American Indians*, edited by Bruce G. Trigger, Vol. 15, pp. 137–147. Smithsonian Institution, Washington, D.C.

1978c   Shaking down the new paradigm. *Archaeology of Eastern North America* 6:87–91.

Solecki, R. S.

1950   The archeological position of historic Fort Cochaug, L. I., and its relation to contemporary forts. *Archaeological Society of Connecticut Bulletin* 24:3–40.

Spaulding, A. C.

1966   Archeology of New York State. *Science* 151(3711):677–678.

1973   Archeology in the active voice: The new anthropology. In *Research and theory in current archeology*, edited by Charles L. Redman, pp. 337–354. Wiley, New York.

Speck, F. G.

1935   Mammoth or stiff-legged bear. *American Anthropologist* 37(1):159–163.

Staples, A. C., and R. C. Athearn

1969   The Bear Swamp site: A preliminary report. *Massachusetts Archaeological Society Bulletin* 30(3–4):1–8.

Starbuck, D. R.

1977   Post-glacial environments and cultural change in the Hudson River basin. *Man in the Northeast* 13:96–99.

Starna, W. A.

1979   *Mohawk Iroquois populations: A revision.* Paper read at the annual meeting of the American Society for Ethnohistory, Albany.

Steward, J. H.

1955   *Theory of culture change: The methodology of multilinear evolution.* University of Illinois Press: Urbana.

Stoltman, J. B.

1978   Temporal models in prehistory: An example from eastern North America. *Current Anthropology* 19(4):703–746.

Stommel, H., and E. Stommel

1979   The year without a summer. *Scientific American* 240(6):176–186.

Stuckenrath, R., Jr.

1966   The Debert archaeological project, Nova Scotia radiocarbon dating. *Quaternaria* 8:75–80.

1977   Radiocarbon: Some notes from Merlin's diary. In Amerinds and their paleoenvironments in northeastern North America. *Annals of the New York Academy of Sciences* 288:181–188.

Stuiver, M., and H. W. Borns, Jr.

1975   Late Quaternary marine invasion in Maine: Its chronology and associated crustal movement. *Geological Society of America Bulletin* 86:99–104.

Sturtevant, W.

1975   Two 1761 wigwams at Niantic, Connecticut. *American Antiquity* 40(4):437–444.

Swigart, E. K.

1974   *The prehistory of the Indians of western Connecticut.* American Indian Archaeological Institute, Washington, Conn.

Taylor, W. B.

1976   A bifurcated-point concentration. *Massachusetts Archaeological Society Bulletin* 37(3–4):36–41.

Terasmae, J., and R. J. Mott

1965   Modern pollen deposition in the Nichicun Lake area, Quebec. *Canadian Journal of Botany* 43:393–404.

Thom, R.

1975   *Structural stability and morphogenesis.* W. A. Benjamin: Reading, Mass.

Thomas, P. A.

1976   Contrastive subsistence strategies and land use as factors for understanding Indian–White relations in New England. *Ethnohistory* 23(1):1–18.

1977   Review of "The Indian population of New England in the seventeenth century" by S. F. Cook. *American Anthropologist* 79(4):932.

1979   *In the maelstrom of change: The Indian trade and cultural process in the middle Connecticut River Valley: 1635–1665.* Unpublished Ph.D. dissertation, Dept. of Anthropology, University of Massachusetts.

Thomas, R. A.

1970   Adena influence in the middle Atlantic coast. In *Adena: The seeking of an identity*, edited by B. K. Swartz, Jr., pp. 56–87. Ball State University, Indiana.

Thompson, C. W.

1975   "Crooning his own quaint runes": The professional runologist and the enthusiastic amateur. *Man in the Northeast* 9:2–8.

Thwaites, R. G., ed.

1959   *The Jesuit relations and allied documents 1610–1791* (73 vols.). Pageant, New York.

Tooker, E.

1971   Clans and moieties in North America. *Current Anthropology* 12(3):357–376.

1978   The League of the Iroquois: Its history, politics, and ritual. In *Handbook of North American Indians*, edited by Bruce G. Trigger, Vol. 15, pp. 418–441. Smithsonian Institution, Washington, D.C.

Trigger, B. G.

1966   Comment on estimating aboriginal American population. *Current Anthropology* 7(4):439–440.

Tuck, J. A.

1971a   An Archaic cemetery at Port au Choix, Newfoundland. *American Antiquity* 36(3):343–358.

1971b   *Onondaga Iroquois prehistory: A study in settlement archaeology.* Syracuse University Press, New York.

1974   Early Archaic horizons in eastern North America. *Archaeology of Eastern North America* 2(1):72–80.

1977   A look at Laurentian. In Current perspectives in northeastern archeology. *New York State Archeological Association Researches and Transactions* 17(1):31–40.

1978a   Regional and cultural development, 3000 to 300 B.C. In *Handbook of North American Indians*, edited by Bruce G. Trigger, Vol. 15, pp. 28–43. Smithsonian Institution, Washington, D.C.

1978b   Northern Iroquoian prehistory. In *Handbook of North American Indians*, edited by Bruce G. Trigger, Vol. 15, pp. 322–333. Smithsonian Institution, Washington, D.C.

Tuck, J. A., and R. J. McGhee

1976   An Archaic Indian burial mound in Labrador. *Scientific American* 235(5):122–129.

Turnbaugh, W. A.

1975   Toward an explanation of the broadpoint dispersal in eastern North American prehistory. *Journal of Anthropological Research* 31(1):51–68.

1976   The survival of a native craft in Colonial Rhode Island. *Man in the Northeast* 11:74–79.

1977   An archaeological prospect of the ulu or semi-lunar knife in northeastern North America. *Archaeology of Eastern North America* 5:86–94.

Ubelaker, D.

1976   Prehistoric New World population size: Historical review and current appraisal of North American estimates. *American Journal of Physical Anthropology* 45(3):661–665.

Vastokas, J. M., and R. K. Vastokas

1973   *Sacred Art of the Algonquians.* Mansard Press, Peterborough, Ontario.

Vescelius, G. S.

n.d.   The antiquity of Pattee's caves. Unpublished report in the files of the Early Sites Foundation, Hanover, New Hampshire.

Warne, J. L.

1979 *Time depth in Mahican diachronic phonology: Evidence from the Schmick manuscript.* Paper read at the 11th Algonquian Conference, Ottawa.

Weber, J. C.

1970 *Types and attributes in the study of Iroquois pipes.* Unpublished Ph.D. dissertation, Dept. of Anthropology, Harvard University.

1971 Types and attributes in Iroquois pipes. *Man in the Northeast* 2:51–65.

Weeks, J. M.

1971 Steatite tempered pottery in New England. *Man in the Northeast* 2:103–104.

Weinman, P. L., T. P. Weinman, and R. E. Funk

1967 The Pickle Hill site, Warren County, New York. *New York State Archeological Association Bulletin* 39:18–22.

Wellman, B.

1975 Prehistoric site survey and salvage in the upper Schoharie valley, New York. *Eastern States Archeological Federation Bulletin* 34:15.

Wendland, W. M., and R. A. Bryson

1974 Dating climatic episodes of the Holocene. *Quaternary Research* 4:9–24.

Werner, D. J.

1964 Vestiges of Paleo-Indian occupation near Port Jervis, N.Y. *New World Antiquity* 11:30–52.

Whallon, R., Jr.

1968 Investigations of late prehistoric social organization in New York State. In *New perspectives in archeology*, edited by Sally R. Binford and Lewis R. Binford, pp. 223–244. Aldine, Chicago.

1972 A new approach to pottery typology. *American Antiquity* 37(1):13–33.

White, R. S., Jr.

1974 Notes on some archaeological faunas from the northeastern United States. *Archaeology of Eastern North America* 2(1):67–72.

Willey, G. R.

1958 Archaeological perspective on Algonkian–Gulf linguistic relationships. *Southwestern Journal of Anthropology* 14:265–272.

1966 *An introduction to American archaeology.* Vol. 1: *North and Middle America.* Prentice Hall, Englewood Cliffs.

Willey, G. R., and P. Phillips

1958 *Method and theory in American archaeology.* University of Chicago Press, Chicago.

Williams, B. J.

1974 A model of band society. *Society for American Archaeology Memoir* 29.

Willoughby, C. C.

1898 Prehistoric burial places in Maine. *Archaeological and Ethnological Papers of the Peabody Museum* 1(6) (Cambridge).

1915 The "Red Paint People" of Maine. *American Anthropologist* 17:406–409.

1935 *Antiquities of the New England Indians.* Peabody Museum of Harvard University, Cambridge.

Witthoft, J.

1949 An outline of Pennsylvania Indian history. *Pennsylvania History* 16(3):3–15.

1952 A Paleo-Indian site in eastern Pennsylvania: An early hunting culture. *American Philosophical Society Proceedings* 96(4):464–495.

1953 Broad spearpoints and the transitional period cultures. *Pennsylvania Archaeologist* 23(1):4–31.

1954 A note on fluted point relationships. *American Antiquity* 19(3):271–273.

Woodcock, A., and M. Davis

1978 *Catastrophe theory.* Dutton, New York.

Wright, G. A.

1972 Ohio Hopewell trade. *The Explorer* 14(4):4–11.

Wright, H. E., Jr.
  1971   Late Quaternary vegetational history of North America. In *Late Cenozoic glacial ages*, edited by Karl K. Turekian, pp. 425–464. Yale University Press, New Haven.
Wright, J. V.
  1972a   The Shield Archaic. *National Museums of Canada Publications in Archaeology* No. 3 (Ottawa).
  1972b   *Ontario prehistory*. National Museum of Man, Ottawa.
  1978   The implications of probable Early and Middle Archaic projectile points from southern Ontario. *Canadian Journal of Archaeology* 2:59–78.
Wroth, L. C. (editor)
  1970   *The voyages of Giovanni da Verrazzano: 1524–1528*. Yale University Press, New Haven.
Wyatt, R. J.
  1977   The Archaic on Long Island. In Amerinds and their paleoenvironments in northeastern North America. *Annals of the New York Academy of Sciences* 288:400–410.

GLOSSARY

API (absolute pollen influx) measurement of number of pollen grains of
each genus falling on a square cm of pond surface in a particular year.
Used as a means to reconstruct extinct forests.

absolute dating the independent dating of remains in years before present,
usually radiocarbon dating in the Northeast.

adaptation specifically human adaptation to the physical environment
through the application of technology and information.

advanced nuclear centered a settlement pattern having a clear administrative center and satellites. Not found in prehistoric New England.

agriculture the combined practice of horticulture, animal husbandry, and
forestry, usually implying relatively complex tools and techniques.

assemblage the collection of artifacts recovered from a single site, a component of a site, or some other subunit of a site.

band a set of nuclear families that regularly live and travel together.

carrying capacity the capacity of a region to support a human population
continuously, as measured by population density. As used here, it includes provision for community spacing and other cultural factors.

catastrophe in archaeological context, a sharp discontinuity in a record of
otherwise gradual change over time.

central-based wandering the seasonal dispersal of a community from a
relatively large central base to smaller sites and back again.

chalcedony a translucent, high-quality form of chert.

channel flake the waste flake resulting from the creation of the flute on the
side of a fluted point.

chert a dense glassy stone usually found in limestone outcrops that was the
most popular material for chipped-stone tools in New England. Sometimes called flint, jasper, or chalcedony.

chiefdom a super-tribal organization having a system of chieftainship, with a hierarchy of authorities and subdivisions, and a chain of command linking levels of leadership.

cognatic tribe a tribe in which membership is based on family connections through either the father's or the mother's side, sometimes alternatively by marriage.

complex a set of traits or artifact types that typically occur together in archaeological context, and as a set are diagnostic of a period, region, or cultural subsystem.

component the archaeological expression of the occupation of a site by a culture. Sequential occupation of a site by two or more cultures produces an equivalent number of components.

connubium an abstract set of bands including a reference band and those other bands with which it regularly interacts. Each band has a separately defined connubium.

continuity in archaeological context, the observation of steady and gradual cultural development over time.

cross dating the relative dating of components through the use of key artifact types that are assumed to have been used widely for brief periods of one to a few centuries each.

dendrochronology an absolute dating technique that uses tree ring sequences, not generally applicable in the Northeast.

diffuse adaptation human adaptation that maximizes the exploitation of a wide range of food resources.

drift any deposit of glacial origin.

drumlin a hill of drift with a bedrock core deposited under moving glacial ice and having a characteristic teardrop shape.

edaphic due to soil or topography rather than climate.

ethnography the description of living cultures.

ethnology the study of living cultures.

fire rotation the natural cycle of growth to maturity, burning, and regrowth of forests.

flint a term that should be used to refer only to cherts occurring in chalk deposits, such as those in France and England, but which is often used interchangeably with chert.

fluted point any of several Paleo-Indian period point types having long thinning flakes struck from their sides.

focal adaptation human adaptation that in its most extreme form focuses on one or a few specific food resources.

free wandering the frequent and unrestricted movement of a band, direction and distance conditioned by the availability of game and other food resources.

guide flakes small flakes taken from the bases of fluted points prior to the removal of the channel flakes, intended to guide the direction and width of the flute.

history   used here to mean recorded human history, defined as beginning around A.D. 1600 in New England.

horizon   a widespread time marker, often used in cross dating in the past, but now mostly abandoned in favor of absolute dating techniques.

horticulture   the cultivation of domesticated plants, usually implying relatively simple tools and techniques.

isopoll   a line connecting all points in a region at which there was equivalent deposition of a particular pollen type in a particular year.

jasper   red chert.

kame   a distinctive hillock of drift deposited by stagnating glacial ice.

knapping   the manufacture of tools from chert or other similar rock by chipping techniques.

law-and-order archaeology   a nomothetic approach to the study of cultural processes, which stresses the search for general laws and cause-effect relationships.

leister   a fish spear having three or more prongs, usually barbed.

lineal tribe   a tribe having basic rules of unilocal residence in which individuals reckon descent through lineal groups such as lineages.

matrilocal residence   the practice of postmarital residence in which the married couple resides with the family of the female.

moraine   a thick, topographically distinct deposit of drift, conveyed and deposited along the margin of moving glacial ice.

NAP (nonarboreal pollen)   the pollen from plants other than trees, most of which are low pollen producers.

palynology   the study of pollen grains.

patrilocal residence   the practice of postmarital residence in which the married couple resides with the family of the male.

petroglyph   a symbol pecked or incised into rock.

phase   the archeological evidence of a prehistoric culture, usually defined by artifact assemblages from two or more related components.

prehistory   the entire time period preceding the advent of written history in a particular region. Prior to A.D. 1600 in New England.

protolanguage   the linguistically reconstructed parent language from which a set of related historic languages descend.

radiocarbon dating   an absolute dating technique that uses the decay of a radioactive isotope of carbon at a known rate to determine age in years before A.D. 1950, widely used in the Northeast.

relative dating   the dating of artifacts or components relative to each other rather than to an absolute time scale, often by analysis of stratigraphy.

reservoir, disease   the set of carriers harboring a disease, which may or may not be ill themselves.

restricted wandering   movement of a band within a defined territory, either erratic or following a seasonal round.

rune stone   a stone bearing runic inscription, no authenticated example of which has ever been found in the New World.

runology   a pseudoscience involving the creation of alleged translations of inscriptions, themselves usually of fraudulent, accidental, or nonhuman origin.

sachem   the word used for a local leader in New York and southward. Cognate with the New England *sagamore.*

sagamore   the local New England name for an Indian leader. Becomes *sachem* to the south and west.

sedentism   the practice of living all or much of the year in settled communities.

semipermanent sedentary   a stable and sedentary community that moves its settlement to successive locations occupying each for a period of years.

Serutan archaeology   a systemic approach to the study of cultural processes, which stresses the search for systemic regularities.

shaman   a person possessing magical powers, most particularly the power to transform into an animal form.

shell middens   sites made up primarily of shell refuse, typically found at seashore locations.

sherd   a broken fragment of pottery.

simple nuclear centered   a settlement pattern having a permanent center, with or without satellites.

stratigraphy   the superposition of younger deposits over older ones.

supranuclear integrated   a settlement pattern having administrative centers integrated within a single system. Not found in prehistoric New England.

systems theory   a method of explanation through the modeling of multiple relationships, which remains more a perspective than a formal theory in anthropology.

till   a glacial deposit that is unsorted according to grain size.

tool kit   the reconstructed set of tools carried by a prehistoric man or woman.

tradition   a continuous record of a prehistoric culture, complex, or artifact type as evidenced by a sequence of phases, components, or individual specimens.

tribe   a set of extended families or lineages that regularly reside together for at least part of the year.

uniformitarianism   the principle that prehistoric processes of change were not substantially different from those than can be observed today.

unilocal residence   in New England, either patrilineal or matrilineal residence.

SUBJECT INDEX